Torsten Caeners

Poetry as Therapy

Contemporary Literary Theory as a Foundation of Poetry Therapy

Heinz Kosok, Heinz Rölleke, Michael Scheffel (Hg.)

SCHRIFTENREIHE
LITERATURWISSENSCHAFT

Bd. 84

Torsten Caeners

Poetry as Therapy

Contemporary Literary Theory as a Foundation of Poetry Therapy

wvt Wissenschaftlicher Verlag Trier

Caeners, Torsten: Poetry as Therapy: Contemporary Literary Theory as a Foundation of Poetry Therapy / Torsten Caeners. - Trier: WVT Wissenschaftlicher Verlag Trier, 2011
 (Schriftenreihe Literaturwissenschaft; Bd. 84)
 ISBN 978-3-86821-276-1

Cover illustration: Stefanie Albers

Cover design: Brigitta Disseldorf

© WVT Wissenschaftlicher Verlag Trier, 2011
ISBN 978-3-86821-276-1

No part of this book, covered by the copyright hereon, may be reproduced or used in any form or by any means without prior permission of the publisher.

WVT Wissenschaftlicher Verlag Trier
Bergstraße 27, 54295 Trier
Postfach 4005, 54230 Trier
Tel.: (0651) 41503 / 9943344, Fax: 41504
Internet: http://www.wvttrier.de
E-mail: wvt@wvttrier.de

Acknowledgements

As with most books, this one began as a promising but vague idea, a train of thoughts revolving around poetry and therapy, and the question of their mutual interrelation and interaction. Looking more deeply into the matter, I discovered the interdisciplinary approach of poetry therapy as an already existing therapeutic method and practice. My next step was to do more research into poetry therapy as an institutionalised discipline, especially in the USA. It became clear that the poetic aspect was underdeveloped and, sometimes, even underappreciated in Poetry Therapy circles. With the agenda to remedy this and approach Poetry Therapy from a literary perspective, I began in earnest to write this study, the completion of which would not have been possible without the assistance, support and goodwill of a lot of people. I want to thank all of them. Those not mentioned by name know how much I appreciate their support and help.

First and foremost, I would like to thank Prof. Jens Martin Gurr for the time spent discussing my ideas, for his support and invaluable advice. Many thanks are also due to Prof. Frank Erik Pointner for his input and commentary during the writing of this study. Furthermore, I am very much indebted to Prof. Michael Gassenmeier, who suggested the above field of research to me in the first place and whose support during the early phases of research is immensely appreciated. Cordial thanks go to Gordon Meade, poet and poetry therapy facilitator, who welcomed me warmly to Scotland and gave me my first fascinating insight into the practicalities of poetry as therapy in a primary school environment. I owe special, heartfelt thanks to Stefanie Albers for having endured my often erratic ups and downs while working to complete this study.

Table of Contents

Introduction   1

1. The Current State of Poetry Therapy   15
   1.1 Poetry Therapy, Bibliotherapy, Writing Therapies: Overlapping Principles and theoretical Uncertainty   18
   1.2 Freud and the Importance of Literary Theory in writing-based Therapies   31
   1.3 The Pervasiveness of the Romantic Tradition in contemporary Psychotherapy and its Influence on Poetry Therapy   38

2. Poetry Therapy in the Context of Art Therapy   51
   2.1 Art Therapy vs. Art *as* Therapy   55
   2.2 Humanistic Art *as* Therapy as an alternative to Clinical Models predominant today   60

3. The Unconscious, Poetic Writing and Poetry   72
   3.1 From the Freudian Unconscious to Lacan's 'Unconscious as Language'   76
   3.2 The (post-)structural Unconscious and its Implications for the poetic Aspect of Poetry Therapy   81
   3.3 From 'Being' to 'Meaning': The Real, the Imaginary and the Symbolic   86
   3.4 Crossing the Bar: The Sliding of the Signifier, *Points de Capiton*, and the Production of Meaning   95
   3.5 The dipartite Unconscious: Signification and the *Chora*   100

4. Textual Manifestations of the Unconscious: Figurative Language as the *Via Regia*   112
   4.1 Creativity, Dreaming and the Writing of Poetry   114
   4.2 Poetry and Dreams: Semiotic Infusion – Symbolic Crystallisation   124

5. Revision and Reception: Negotiating the Interplay between Creation and Interpretation within Foucauldian Discourse   141
   5.1 Communication vs. Understanding: The Process of Revision in Poetry Therapy   143
   5.2 Negotiating the Interplay of Creation and Interpretation in Poetry Therapy on the Basis of Narrative Therapeutic Concepts and within a Foucauldian Context   151

	5.3	The Appropriation of Foucauldian Discourse for Poetry Therapy	159
	5.4	Breaking Discursive Normalisations: Externalisation and 'Unique Outcomes'	169
6.	Re-negotiating Textual *Author*ity in Poetry Therapy: The Function of the Author, 'Writing', and the Palimpsest		185
	6.1	The Need for Resurrection: The Death of the Author and Poetry Therapy	188
	6.2	The Extension of the Concept of 'Writing' in Poetry Therapy	196
	6.3	Poetry Therapy as Palimpsest	212
7.	Poetry Therapy and the Question of Form: Free Verse and/or Formal Verse		227
	7.1	Free Verse: The Modernist Legacy and its Implications for Poetry Therapy	230
	7.2	Formal Verse: Misconceptions and Advantages for Poetry Therapy	240

Conclusion   252

Works Cited   256

Introduction

> Poetry is a natural medicine; it's like a homeopathic tincture derived from the stuff of life itself – *your experience*. Poems distill experience into the essentials. Our personal experiences touch the common ground we share with others. The exciting part of this process is that poetry used in this healing way helps people integrate the disparate, even fragmented parts of their life. Poetic essences of sound, metaphor, image, feeling and rhythm act as remedies that can elegantly strengthen our whole system – physical, mental and spiritual. (Fox 3; emphasis original)

Fox's above statements about poetry, its therapeutic value and applicability contain all the fundamental aspects of what poetry therapy is and, also, what remains unfulfilled in the promise of the concept. Indeed, poetry is "natural medicine" in the sense that the activity of writing poetry is conducive to stress release, self-reflexivity and contemplation. One need only consider the activity of writing a diary to understand that writing down one's own experiences in life is a means of organising and coming to terms with them. Poetry can increase this inherently therapeutic potential of writing as it "distill[s] experience into the essentials" – it is condensed language which holds valuable therapeutic potential to be released. Poetry has been used therapeutically and has been recognised as a means of healing throughout history. These roots extend as far back as pre-historical, shamanistic practices. In antiquity, the therapeutic potential of poetry was common knowledge: "[i]n ancient times, Greek libraries were designated as healing places of the soul, and Greek tragic theatre was viewed as cathartic for the entire community. King David sang psalms to comfort Saul and the ancient poets were recognized as shamans and healers in various cultures" (Chavis/Weisberger 1). There is thus a long tradition that links poetry to therapeutic effects. This potential for healing inherent in poetry can be utilised more effectively if combined with psychotherapeutic techniques. This is the fundamental idea behind the concept of poetry therapy. Simple as this may appear at first glance, there are certain aspects that need to be kept in mind when thinking of poetry and therapy in a modern, psychotherapeutic sense.

Firstly, there has to be serious doubt as to whether poetry therapy currently exists at all as a discernible discipline. Although art therapies have gained ground in recent decades and have become an accepted form of therapy, they do remain ancillary in many cases. Considering that poetry therapy constitutes a minor and relatively underrepresented discipline within the art therapies themselves, it becomes obvious that it is the more difficult to establish it as an independent and accepted discipline among other forms of psychotherapy.[1] Secondly, there is the inherent interdisciplinarity of

---

[1] I will use the term psychotherapy generically to include all forms and schools of mental health therapy. Although I will implicitly concentrate on psychoanalysis of the Freudian

poetry therapy. Poetry therapy consists of 'poetry' and 'therapy', and in order to function smoothly and effectively, it has to be aware of and take into consideration its dual character. Poetry therapy has to recognise its interdisciplinary nature and take it seriously. It is true that poetry as such is already therapeutical, but it needs a sound psychotherapeutical framework to be truly effective.[2] On the other hand, an intimate knowledge of poetry is indispensable to its application in psychotherapy. Without an in-depth understanding of its diverse forms and mechanisms, poetry cannot become an integral part of the therapeutic process. Being an interdisciplinary endeavour, poetry therapy requires disciplinary competences in order to be effective; this is required not only to achieve a maximum of therapeutic effectiveness, but also to safeguard the practice against dilettantism and amateurishness. Poetry therapy does have a sound and functioning psychotherapeutic framework and basis; this, however, has resulted in denigration or even subjugation of the poetry aspect. Consequently, only the latter is in need of a theoretical foundation. As a literary scholar, it is precisely this foundation that I intend to provide with this study. At the same time, since I am a literary scholar rather than a trained psychotherapist, I do not presume to evaluate the psychotherapeutic aspects of poetry therapy. As already noted: there is nothing wrong or theoretically unfounded with the psychotherapeutic side of poetry therapy, and the problem clearly lies in the discipline's lack of knowledge of poetry. Still, I cannot enter into a discussion of poetry therapy without commenting upon and dealing with these psychotherapeutic aspects. Therefore, in those cases that deal critically with aspects, methods and theories from psychotherapy, I do so only with reference to and within the context of poetry therapy. More precisely, my comments on psychotherapeutic methods and theories are directed towards the implications these notions have within and on the relationship between therapy and poetry, and within the agenda of establishing a balanced interdisciplinarity in poetry therapy. Since poetry therapists are well-trained in the therapeutic side, but frequently lack a sound understanding of poetry, this study will provide the necessary theoretical foundation by appropriating post-structuralist literary (theoretical) concepts for poetry therapy. That this cannot be done without recourse to psychotherapeutic notions and theories goes without saying. However, my focus will be on the literary side, and the concepts discussed in the following chapters (and this includes psychotherapeutic concepts) are evaluated from a literary perspective alone. When I thus speak of 'effects', 'therapeutic effectiveness' and the like, I do so with regard to the possibilities of enhancing the effectiveness by the application of literary and poetic theories. I do not wish to insinuate that psychotherapeutic methods and practices lack effectiveness or efficiency, but that a joint and well-founded application of literary and psychotherapeutic methods and theories can increase the effectiveness of poetry therapy as an interdisciplinary approach.

---

      school via Lacan, the arguments are taken to be valid for all psychotherapeutic approaches.

[2]   Additionally, this is a prerequisite for being integrated into and taken seriously by the institutionalised forms of psychotherapy.

As was already hinted at before, the current problem of the discipline lies in the failure to recognize and realise poetry therapy's interdisciplinarity in theory and practice: the interdisciplinary nature of poetry therapy, while widely acknowledged in theory, has for the most part remained unrealised in practice. Also, in those cases in which this has indeed been recognised, it is being given little more than lip service. Poetry therapists, more often than not, are therapists with a superficial knowledge of poetry or literature: "few [art therapists] accentuate their greatest strength, the thing that makes them different, their expertise in their art form. It is little wonder that despite many protestations to the contrary, creative therapy remains firmly under the grip of the medical community" (Warren 5). There is nothing fundamentally wrong with conducting and organising poetry therapy under the auspices of the medical community. In fact, it is hardly possible to do otherwise given the institutional structures in contemporary society. It is, however, a mistake not to balance medical and artistic procedures and practices. Unfortunately, it is precisely this balance that is lacking in contemporary poetry therapy. Poetry therapy as it presents itself today largely leaves untapped the one resource that "makes [it] different" from the rest of the therapeutic community, namely the poem and the creative process. Poetry therapy either employs poetry purely receptively or the poem is taken as a facilitating tool only, utilised to open and guide the therapeutic discussion along more or less predetermined lines. In order to assert its independence from other therapeutic approaches and to take its own interdisciplinary nature seriously, poetry therapy has to take poetry seriously; its practitioners have to be as well 'versed' in poetry as in traditional therapeutic theory and practice.[3] This is not only a matter of untapped potential and reduced effectiveness, but may also be downright counterproductive to therapy. Hands-on "experience in [poetry therapy] situations has consistently suggested that enthusiasm and even love for poetry without the literary training needed to exploit this tool fully can be frustrating and sometimes counterproductive. I see the need for a systematic, organic

---

[3] The lack of knowledge or disinterest of poetry therapists in poetry and literary studies can be glimpsed from the following quotation: "Herein lies the significant difference between the English class and the poetry therapy session: the first objective of the English class is to determine the poem's meaning, of the poetry therapy session to seek the meaning that the poem has for the various members. There may be as many meanings as there are persons, and each meaning is valid in the context of the individual's peculiar experiences" (Crootof 44). Crootof's comment – albeit somewhat dated – suggests that literary studies are concerned with explicating some form of universal meaning from the poem. Nothing could be further from the truth. While literary studies strive towards interpretations that can be validated, this does not imply that there can be a reading of a work of literature which is true once and for all (for this dated view, cf., for instance, Hirsch's "Objective Interpretation," a source roughly contemporary with Crootof). Crootof's understanding of the fundamental distinction between literary studies and poetry therapy is hence based on a misconception. This is only one case of many – Crootof's understanding of literary studies being still predominant in the literature on poetry therapy today – and one can easily see how misconceptions of this kind can be disadvantageous to a discipline such as poetry therapy.

course of study in poetry for the therapeutic practitioner" (Jaskoski 77). Jaskoski's point here is as simple as it is essential: poetry therapists need as solid a training in poetry as in psychotherapy. This insight is invaluable for poetry therapy and it is incomprehensible that it has fallen on such deaf ears. Jaskoski's insight and its failed reception in the field of poetry therapy is the *raison d'être* for this study. It is precisely the lack of literary knowledge and training in poetry therapy that I seek to alleviate. Without this, poetry therapy's two disciplines cannot come into balance and the therapeutic potential cannot be fully exploited. Moreover, any method or practice that is not fully understood inevitably produces effects which cannot be foreseen by its practitioners; more often than not, these effects have negative implications, or are at least disruptive to the activity in question. When it comes to psychotherapy, this is untenable as one is here concerned with the (mental) health of human beings. It is thus essential that research in poetry therapy is steered towards investigating contact areas of the two disciplines of literary studies, more specifically the study of poetry, and psychotherapy. Identifying such contact areas can make possible new and effective therapeutical approaches, approaches which duly consider the creative, poetic aspects of poetry therapy. By redirecting the focus of poetry therapy onto the poem and the process of poetic creation within the therapeutic context, poetry therapy can achieve a balance between its two fundamental disciplines.

Returning to Fox's statement, one can isolate two essential features of poetry that pertain to its application in therapy. As Fox rightly states, the potential for healing in poetry is a "natural medicine" (3) that pertains to the "physical, mental and spirtual" (ibid.) realms (where "spiritual" is to denote the emotional world of the client[4] and not some esoteric sphere or ghostly realm). In simultaneously addressing these areas, poetry concerns the human being as a whole. Consequently, the understanding and treatment of human beings in the context of poetry therapy has to be a holistic endeavour. Both clients and their problems have to be perceived in the entire complexity of their socio-cultural embeddedness, in "the common ground we share with others" (Fox 3). These two fundamental aspects of poetry – its natural healing properties and its holistic effects – also constitute the greatest obstacles to a satisfactory realisation of poetry therapy in the therapeutic practice.

I will begin by surveying some of the implications of the first aspect isolated above, namely poetry as a "natural medicine." Poetry's natural healing properties are generously evoked in books and articles on poetry therapy; what is seldom mentioned, however, is that it is difficult to tap into these qualities within the constraints of a modern health care system. Generally, the institutionalisation and systematisation of and within the health care system of any modern, industrialised nation is counterproductive to art therapies and inevitably robs poetry therapy of much of its spontaneity: there are time constraints when it comes to the therapeutic sessions, for example, which hamper the flow of creativity necessary for poetry therapy to be effective. It is

---

[4] In this study, the persons seeking psychotherapeutic help will not be designated as 'patients', but as 'clients' in order to underline their free choice of therapeutic participation.

difficult – and actually goes against the fundamental nature of the activity – to force or press creativity into an artificial framework of weekly or daily appointments. Likewise, hospitalised clients often react negatively to the clinical environment of (mental) institutions. This, too, is hardly conducive to artistic/poetic expression. As a consequence, the "natural medicine" of poetry is difficult to realise within contemporary health care environments.

The implications from the second fundamental aspect of poetry therapy – its holistic approach – are closely connected to the above arguments. Refocusing on the poem inevitably refocuses the attention on the human being who is seeking help in therapy. This is why it is vital that the poems under discussion are created by clients themselves. Discussing client-created poems – poems which are individual and idiosyncratic tokens of creation – inevitably humanises the client in the context of the therapeutic situation and precludes negative effects of labelling which continue to exist in the modern health care system. Along the same lines, a careful and exhaustive discussion of poems in therapy should not see the activity as a static one-way process. A poem is not a frozen object which can provide information about its creator. Rather, it continues actively to influence and change its readers:

> For most of the twentieth century, [...] psychology has focused largely on what the art object says about the person who made it. When attempting to reveal hidden states of consciousnesses according to a particular psychological construct, we not only project our views into the artwork but also overlook what it presents and how its expression influences us. (McNiff, *Art Heals* 21)

This reciprocal function of the poem in poetry therapy can only be tapped into when the poem is at the centre of the therapeutic encounter. In addition to this, the poem represents a cultural artefact which embodies the client's socio-cultural embeddedness; it is a storehouse of virtually all of the client's diachronic and synchronic cultural experiences. Arguing from the point of view of a semiotic understanding of culture,[5] the poem not only constitutes a means and form of communication, but also a vault of knowledge ready to be decoded and used by the client and the therapist in therapy:

> But common artistic experience also teaches us that art not only elicits feelings but also *produces further knowledge*. The moment that the game of intertwined interpretations gets under way, the text compels one to reconsider the usual codes and their possibilities. Every text threatens the codes but at the same time gives them strength; it reveals unexpected possibilities in them, and thus changes the attitude of the user towards them. Through the close dialectical interrelationship between message and code, whereby each nourishes the other, the addressee becomes aware of new semiotic possibilities and is thereby compelled to rethink the whole language, the entire inheritance of what has been said, can be said, and could or should be said. By increasing one's knowledge of codes, the aesthetic message changes one's view of their history and thereby *trains* semiosis. (Eco, *A Theory of Semiotics* 274; emphasis original)

---

[5] Cf., for instance, Eco, *A Theory of Semiotics*; Geertz, *The Interpretation of Cultures*; Lotman, *Universe of the Mind. A Semiotic Theory of Culture*; Posner, "Kultur als Zeichensystem;" Silverman, *Cultural Semiosis*.

Literary interpretation as described by Eco here *"trains* semiosis," that is, it trains the ability to make or deduce information from a heterogeneous realm of semiotic traces, organising these in a manner so that they produce meaning, i.e. knowledge. This is what one of poetry therapy's main aims must be: to train semiosis in the client so as to allow for an active resituating of the individual in its socio-cultural environment, an environment which is also conceived of as a semiotic space. Such an approach obviously entails fundamental notions of post-structuralism, which have to be applied not only to the textual tissues of the poem, but to the entire field of poetry therapy. If culture is text, the client and the client's life, naturally, may also be perceived as text(s) that can and need to be read in therapy by the client and the therapist. In this context, the reading of poetry and psychotherapeutic analysis as processes and methods are closely related and can interface relatively easily. Both poetry and therapy can be conceptualised as forms of communication or as textual tissues. "[The] analogy [of culture as text] [makes] it possible to conceive of the evolution of lives and relationships in terms of reading and writing of texts, insofar as every new reading of a text is a new interpretation of it, and thus a different writing of it" (White/Epston 9). Dealing with poetry, and dealing with poetry in therapy, is thus a thoroughly semiotic process that pertains to the entire sphere of human existence, capable of activating, challenging and changing psychological, cultural, social and emotional faculties of the client. Since the client is embedded in his or her culture and since culture is perceived as an endlessly complex system of negotiating semiotic signs and traces, poetry trains cultural and social behaviour and helps the client to (re-)organise and (re-)structure his or her position in and relationship to society. This is a holistic process taking the client's entire personality as well as the client's life world into account. Thus, the poetry dealt with in poetry therapy has to reflect as closely as possible the idiosyncratic semiotic embeddedness of the individual client. This is achieved best (and may indeed be the only way of achieving it) by dealing therapeutically with poems created by clients themselves:

> Inviting persons to be the audience of their own performance [...] enhances the survival of stories and the sense of personal agency. This can be facilitated by encouraging persons to identify those expressions of aspects of lived experience that would have previously gone unstoried and to review the real effects of these expressions in their lives and relationships.[6] (White/Epston 17)

In becoming "the audience of their own performance," clients also become critics of their own performance. The poem externalises problems and conflicts, thus generating the distance necessary to enable clients to engage with their problems and conflicts in a more objective and conscious manner. This, in turn, leads to a rational evaluation of past performances.

---

[6] Cf. also McNiff: "Nothing creative exists in complete isolation. Artists, like Shamans, draw their medicine and inspiration from highly individuated relationships to familiars – themes, figures, methods, styles, and materials – that interact with the artist throughout the creative process" (*Art Heals* 84).

While the process of reading poetry is essential, dealing with poetry only receptively in therapy denies poetry therapy one of its main therapeutic assets, namely the experience of creativity. It is thus equally essential to concentrate on the actual creative process as such. A combination of creativity and critical reflection ensures the centrality of the poem in therapy. The poem at the centre of therapy also places the client at the centre of therapy, the individual as a human being both in its multifarious complexity as well as its inevitable fragmentation and alienation. It links these two areas and can thus become a means of psychological re-balancing. The semiotic concept of culture as text – and thus implicitly also of poetry, the client and therapy as a whole as text – guarantees that the client is treated and perceived as a complex human being. This approach is most closely represented by the psychotherapeutic concept of humanistic therapy, which has close ties to the art therapies. Humanistic art therapy – the central concepts of which, I contend, are shared by poetry therapy –

> is known as the third force of psychology and emerged as an alternative to psychoanalytic and behavioral approaches. [...] The humanistic approaches to art therapy developed in reaction to psychoanalytic approaches to art therapy and as a result of the human potential movement of the 1960s and 1970s. [...] According to Garai, the goal of a humanistic approach to art therapy is not so much to eliminate anxiety, unhappiness or other emotions but to assist the individual in transforming them into authentic expression through art modalities. His observation is consistent with the values of humanistic psychology and, in particular, reinforces the centrality of creativity as a means of experiencing and actualizing the human potential as a healing agent. (Malchiodi 58)

With their focus on creativity and a holistic approach that is specifically geared towards the client as a unique individual in the world, humanistic art therapy principles are congruent with those of poetry therapy based on semiotic principles. The field of application of humanistic art therapy and poetry therapy is thus the same.

The principles of humanistic art therapy delineated above give an indication as to the range and limits of the applicability of poetry therapy in the treatment of mental conditions.[7] Poetry therapy's primary field of application, the area in which it is an effective method of treatment, is in transforming "anxiety, unhappiness" and similar states of emotional imbalance. The field of application for poetry therapy is thus not to be found in severe cases of mental disorders. In this sense, poetry therapy

> has a broad range of applications with people of all ages and is used for health and maintenance, as well as with individuals requiring treatment for various illnesses and conditions. Examples of these are veterans, substance abusers, adolescents, the learning

---

[7] Little to nothing is said about the limits and the scope of the applicability of poetry therapy to specific mental disorders in the literature on the subject. This is understandable on the one hand as every case requires individual and client-specific evaluation, but, on the other hand, a rough classification of poetry therapy's applicability with regard to common mental disorders would have been desirable. For lack of such information, the following argument is therefore based on art therapy's range of applicability. Poetry therapy's scope of applicability, being itself an art therapy, is congruent with that of art therapy in general.

disabled, families with problems, prisoners in rehabilitation, the frail elderly, the physically challenged, and survivors of violence, abuse and incest. (http://www.nccata.org/poetry_therapy.html)

It is apparent from this list that poetry therapy is most effective when it comes to mental imbalances that can be traced back to a change in the client's life; cases where clients are suffering from mental imbalances originating in life crises of various kinds. This presupposes that clients are conscious of their situation and of their own position in life and society and that they are aware of some form of fragmentation and disruption with regard to a former state of relative – for lack of a better word – 'happiness' in life. This is not to say that clients must have an understanding of post-structuralist theories and/or must consciously apply during therapy any of the notions introduced in the following chapters. This is the therapist's duty and it is with the aim to supply a thorough theoretical foundation to this endeavour that this study has been written. The theories of Lacan, Derrida, Foucault, Kristeva and others, which form the backbone of this study and which all serve to interlink the two disciplines of psychotherapy and poetry, will lead poetry therapists to a different and enriched understanding of their practice, allowing them to apply poetry as therapy more effectively and more universally. The therapist is required to have a firm grasp of these theories in order to integrate poetry fully into the therapeutic process; for the client this is neither necessary nor desired. What is essential for the client are self-recognition, self-reflexivity and awareness of his or her own socio-cultural position. Only in this way can clients become aware of their fragmented state. This awareness, as explained above, need not be theoretically informed. It is more the conscious acknowledgement that something in life is 'out of joint' and needs fixing. The task of poetry therapy, then, is to isolate exactly what is 'out of joint' and to find a way of repairing it.

Language is the medium in and through which self-recognition, self-reflexivity and social awareness are expressed and mediated. More than for other forms of therapy, the client's command of language – while it need not be out of the ordinary – is essential for poetry therapy; the client's ability to use language is thus an essential prerequisite. Crootof states:

> In the creative process, the magnet of unconscious interest scans the storehouse of memories and their associated affects, attracting the image experiences related to the conscious theme. The organizing ego so moulds and shapes these into a communicable form that other egos that perceive reality in a somewhat similar fashion can sense the poet's ideation and affective messages. Thus it is the world of reality that provides the standard datum that serves as the common medium enabling the patient's unconscious to receive stimuli from the poet's unconscious. (46-47)

Crootof delineates the interaction between the poet-persona active in the creative process and the "patient"-persona, both of which are united in the client. In order to ensure and facilitate this interaction, which is essentially a form of communication, "the world of reality [...] provides the standard datum." Thus, reality constitutes the *conditio sine qua non* for poetry therapy and is indispensible for poetry therapy to function properly. Consequently, the loss or distortion of reality which is characteristic of, for instance, schizophrenia cannot be cured or treated with poetry therapy as the client has lost the connection to reality and, in many cases, also linguistic abilities. The same goes for the diverse forms of psychoses in which the contact to reality is shattered. In general it can be said that poetry therapy can be used in the treatment of all forms of anxiety disorders (social phobia, posttraumatic stress, etc.), forms of mood disorders such as depression, personality disorders (borderline, OCD, or pathologies like Dependent-Personality Disorder), cognitive disorders such as light or beginning dementia and light forms of autism, plus virtually all forms of substance-related disorders.

For the model of poetry therapy expounded in the following chapters, its application, usefulness or effectiveness as a therapeutic approach, I take for granted that the therapy is conducted within the area of applicability outlined above. Furthermore, I presuppose that the client is a willing participant in the therapeutic encounter and that he or she has a regular command of language which is not affected by the psychopathology in question. I will further assume that the client's medical and psychiatric history and immediate anamnesis has ruled out any physical causes of the mental disorder and has established an indication for poetry therapy. In order to identify clients that can profit from a treatment via poetry therapy, traditional methods of diagnosis are employed. Another point is that my model of poetry therapy is based primarily on a setting of individual therapy, making no further distinction between private practice or mental institution. I do not wish to suggest that the methods and principles proposed in the following chapters are not applicable to group therapy settings; in fact, I believe them to be transferable to group settings with little to no change. The reason for choosing the setting of personal therapy is primarily methodological since this makes it possible to outline the concepts, functions and processes of my model of poetry therapy more understandably and clearly.

As a whole, the present study strives to alleviate the blind spots that exist in contemporary poetry therapy when it comes to poetry. In doing so, I will attempt to reestablish, or rather: to create disciplinary balance between the poetic and the therapeutic side of poetry therapy. The interdisciplinary nature of poetry therapy creates interfaces with a large number of therapeutic approaches beyond those of the writing therapies. This widening of the field of poetry therapy is counterproductive to a formulation of a practical definition. The uncertainty of the boundaries of the discipline of poetry therapy – the lack of a clear delineation of borders separating poetry therapy from its sister therapies – is at the heart of the methodological confusion that can be traced in the field. It is therefore the aim of this study to replace this confusion with a theoretical foundation. This study will thus tackle the current state of poetry therapy as it is and evaluate it critically. The critical examination will predominantly proceed from a literary studies point of view, analysing the usage and understanding of the poetic aspect of poetry therapy. I will explore the poetic side in depth – for the first time in the critical writing on poetry therapy – by applying theoretical insights from literary studies to the field of poetry therapy. By putting the poetic aspect of poetry therapy on firm foundations in contemporary literary theory, it becomes possible to exploit the full interdisciplinary potential of poetry therapy as well as to demarcate the borders of the discipline more precisely. As already briefly mentioned, the semiotic approach delineated above calls for a post-structuralist approach to poetry therapy which is to be harmonised with the classical humanistic approach of art therapy. The following chapter-by-chapter overview specifies the methods, theories and assumptions that will be used in this study. The outcome of my study will be a two-phase model of poetry therapy, based on post-structuralist principles (both literary and psychotherapeutical), which will describe the therapeutic possibilities of poetry when employed fully and will be based on giving equal weight to the poetic and therapeutic sides.

Chapter 1 describes the current state of poetry therapy. It delineates the theoretical principles and the practices on which poetry therapy is based, and situates these within contemporary psychotherapeutic discourse. A central point of discussion in this chapter is the lack of a proper definition of poetry therapy. Based on an analysis of the writings of poetry therapy pioneers such as Leedy and Lerner, I criticise the more or less arbitrary application of the name 'poetry therapy' to therapeutic approaches which are only peripherally concerned with poetry or even with writing. What is problematic in this respect is the frequent conflation of poetry therapy with bibliotherapy, which has implications on the theory and practice of poetry therapy and also on the training of poetry therapists. A discussion of the term 'poetry' and the problems in defining this term makes obvious the problems faced in attempting to define poetry therapy. In order to arrive at a manageable concept of poetry therapy, it is essential to take 'poetry' in its narrow sense. The second part of the first chapter deals with the Freudian roots of psychoanalysis in the context of poetry therapy and emphasises that poetry therapy demands a good command and knowledge of literary theory on the part of the poetry therapist. In the last part of the first chapter, I discuss the current understanding of literary theory and 'poetry' within poetry therapy circles. This understanding is based on Romantic principles of poetic creation, principles which are (a) some 200 years old and (b) often misunderstood by poetry therapists.

Chapter 2 deals with poetry therapy in the context of art therapy. Due to the broad range of applicability of poetry therapy delineated above, Chapter 2 does not try to assign poetry therapy to one specific school or approach of psychotherapy. Rather, poetry therapy is situated within the art therapies in general and, more specifically, is shown to have close ties to humanistic art therapy on the basis of shared therapeutic principles. Art therapy is compatible with the entire range of psychotherapeutic approaches, meaning that it can be practiced on the basis of psychological principles or psychotherapeutic ones. It can be used by, for instance, Freudian or Jungian analysts, by behavioural psychologists or cognitive therapists. Having situated poetry therapy in this manner, the second part of the chapter differentiates between 'art in therapy' and 'art *as* therapy'. 'Art in therapy' denotes the ancillary application of art in psychotherapy. It follows that art is used in therapy as a supplementary tool in order to either create therapeutic entrance points or elaborate aspects dealt with in therapy in a more tangible manner. 'Art *as* therapy', on the other hand, places art at the centre of therapy. This approach centrally makes use of the therapeutic potential inherent in art and takes the creative expression of the client as the core of therapy. Poetry therapy is currently employed mostly as 'art in therapy' while its true place is in 'art *as* therapy'; only when taken as central to therapy can the process of poetic creation develop its full potential. The last part of the chapter construes poetry therapy understood as 'art *as* therapy' as a form of therapy in its own right and defines poetry therapy as an artefactual expressive art therapy.

Having surveyed and discussed the contemporary situation of poetry therapy in the first two chapters, the next chapter entitled "The Unconscious, Poetic Writing and Poetry" delineates the first phase of my model of poetry therapy, the creative phase. Taking the concept of sublimation as a starting point, the third chapter delves into Freudian and Lacanian theory. The chapter takes recourse to Freudian and Lacanian theories for two main reasons: firstly, both these psychoanalysts have had a profound impact on literary studies and, secondly, Freud, and to an even greater extent Lacan, base their theories on principles of language. My discussion of Lacanian theories is particularly extensive. This is necessary, because his notions form the basis of and underpin the entire structure of my model of poetry therapy. Lacan postulates a re-reading of Freud, which is why those Freudian principles necessary for an understanding of Lacan are recapitulated at the beginning of the chapter. In a second step, the unconscious as 'structured like language' is posited on the basis of Lacanian theories. By means of a discussion of Saussure's concepts and Lacan's reinterpretation of Freudian principles along Saussurean lines, it becomes obvious that language is the main interface between psychotherapy and poetry, and consequently the area where both disciplines overlap and can proceed in a productive, interdisciplinary manner. The semiotic principle of unlimited signification is incorporated by means of Derrida's (non-)concept of structure, which is also used to reconceptualise the psychic places of the Id, Ego and Superego as (linguistic) functions. In a further step, Lacan's post-structuralist re-reading of the Freudian Oedipus Complex is delineated. In the context of the three developmental phases Lacan identifies (the Real, the Imaginary, and the Symbolic), the chapter sets up the social realm – the Symbolic – as a potentially oppressive and yet necessary realm for human beings, effectively constructing the symptom as a socio-linguistic entity. The final part of the chapter further deals with the structure of the unconscious. Julia Kristeva's concept of the unconscious as what she terms 'the Semiotic', which originates from the so-called *chora*, sets up the dichotomy of the Semiotic vs. the Symbolic which is essential for my model of poetry therapy and will be the fundamental bipolarity within which poetry therapy will be conceptualised.

The fourth chapter constitutes an 'interchapter' that links the first part of my study – the creative part of my model of poetry therapy – with the second part, which mainly deals with the receptive phase. The key concept that connects these two phases of poetry therapy – and also the unconscious with consciousness – is that of the symbol. Symbols are essential in both poetry and psychotherapy and constitute the object of interpretation in both disciplines. This connection is explained by means of Freud's principles of the interpretation of dreams, which can be shown to be essentially the same as those of the interpretation of poetic symbols. Also, the emergence of symbols from the unconscious during dreaming is linked to the emergence of symbols during creativity and both processes are put into the context of the Symbolic and the Semiotic by means of Kristeva's concepts of the 'genotext' and 'phenotext'. On the basis of New Historicist ideas, 'Semiotic energy' is put forth as a crucial notion to conceptualise the indefinite nature of the symbol in the poetic text. Symbols are thus defined as linguistic entities within the Symbolic which are charged with Semiotic energy (i.e. unconscious content) and thus constitute a Semiotic incursion into the Symbolic. Having thus identified symbols as the key entity for an interdisciplinary poetry therapy, the chapter continues to deal with 'symbols' from a literary point of view. Symbols are figurative linguistic elements of the poetic text, and metaphor is taken as a generic example of figurative language. The discussion of metaphor which closes this chapter is thus exemplary for the range and possibilities of figurative language as such, as well as for the possibilities of applying this knowledge about figurative language to poetry therapy.

The fifth chapter studies in detail the second, receptive phase of my model of poetry therapy. This phase deals with the interpretation of client-written poems, particularly their figurative content, in the context of the client's life and the therapeutic situation. At the beginning, the chapter discusses the tendency of the Symbolic towards normalisation. Due to this tendency, those unconscious influences that have come to the fore during the creative phase of poetry therapy are immediately marginalised or, even worse, completely repressed when they become manifest in language. Hence, the best place to discover unconscious traces in language is in indeterminate figurative elements. These require interpretation to be translated into therapeutically relevant meanings. Therefore, the interpretative processes of the second phase oscillate between communication and understanding; together these two processes constitute a method of revision. Concepts of narratology and *différance* are integrated and made useful for poetry therapy, turning the receptive phase into a communicative space that is inhabited by three main entities: the client – the poem – the therapists. This guarantees the centrality of both the poem and the client in therapy. In the next step it is argued that the act of interpretation is in fact another creative act producing meaning that is contingent and heavily influenced by the client's and the therapist's socio-cultural situation. Foucauldian theories of discourse are applied in this context in order to account for the marginalising tendencies of discourse. The function of discourse on the social level is thus equal to that of the Symbolic on the individual, linguistic level. Therefore, Foucault's theories are discussed in the same detailed manner as Lacan's in the third chapter. They have the same importance for the second phase as Lacan's have for the first. Having delineated the nature and challenges of interpretation in general and of interpreting texts in particular, and having thus, via Foucault, constituted poetry therapy as such as a discursive space, these insights are integrated into the practice of poetry therapy proper by means of the therapeutic approach of narrative therapy. Narrative therapy puts the client's life-story at the centre of its approach and conceptualises this by means of Foucault. Foucault thus serves as a link between the client's social embeddedness and the client's inner or psychical being, between the Semiotic and discourse. The narrative therapeutic principles of externalisation and 'unique outcomes' become central to the second phase of poetry therapy: poetry as such is a form of externalisation and its figurative elements are so-called 'unique outcomes', which narrative therapy constitutes as plot devices for the re-authoring of an oppressive life-story. In Foucauldian terms, 'unique outcomes' represent marginalised discourses that have become manifest in figurative language.

The methodological unification of the concepts and principles expounded in the previous chapters is achieved in the following chapter entitled "Re-negotiating Textual *Author*ity in Poetry Therapy: The Function of the Author, 'Writing', and the Palimpsest." The emphasis on authority in the title reflects the main aim of the chapter to unify the essentially post-structuralist approaches used in the main part of the study with its humanistic base. The figure of the author is crucial in this: in order to be useful in therapy, the client, as the empirical author of the poems used in therapy, has to be at the same time the psychological origin of the poem and a non-entity according to post-structural theory. This paradox is overcome by reconfiguring the author as a function rather than a physical entity. The traditional figure of the author is divided into three manifestations, each of which is endowed with a different function. These are (1) the author as an empirical being, (2) the poet-persona in the poem, and (3) the speaker of the poem as constructed by the client-as-reader. Having dealt with poetry therapy in the context of Foucauldian discourse in the last chapter, this chapter refashions another central concept of poetry therapy, namely that of 'writing'. Chapter 6 extends the notion of writing via concepts taken from Derrida so as to encompass the entire practice of poetry therapy. Poetry therapy with all its individual constituents such as the client, the poem, the therapist, the life stories, etc., thus becomes a palimpsestuous textual space. The poem as an empirical text – a palimtext[8] – is only one manifestation of the many layers of the whole palimpsest that is poetry therapy. By conceptualising poetry therapy as a palimpsest it becomes possible to grasp theoretically the divergent influences and processes that partake in poetry therapy, thus establishing an interdisciplinary space that can be charted and theoretically delineated.

The final chapter "Poetry Therapy and the Question of Form: Free Verse and/or Formal Verse" addresses the question of poetic form, its role and its usefulness in poetry therapy. Starting from a brief overview of the beginnings of free verse in the Modernist era, the question of free vs. formal verse in poetry therapy is further analysed by scrutinising the fundamental principles of free verse. The contemporary – frequently negative – notions about formal verse are thus questioned and a number of

---

[8] I take the term from Davidson's essay "Palimtexts." Cf. Chapter 6 for more detailed information.

problematic notions and possible fallacies in using free verse in poetry therapy are delineated. In the end, formal verse is constituted as having a close connection to the Semiotic *chora*, and the features and structures of metre are conceptualised as another effective layer of the palimpsest of poetry therapy.

The "Conclusion" will briefly recapitulate the central arguments and concepts of the study and provide a summary evaluation of the results.

1. The Current State of Poetry Therapy

> Our commonwealth is the intersection of the humanities with healing, a locale for the integration of empathy and intuition with organised scientific knowledge. We seek an arena for the taming and transformation of raw, primitive emotions through the discipline and structure of psychotherapy. If poetry therapy is such a fertile amalgam of science and art, then the selection of poems to be used is itself one of the most critical points in the practice of poetry therapy. (Adams/ Rojcewics, "Mindfulness on the Road Ahead" in Chavis and Weisberger, *The Healing Fountain* 7)

This first chapter will give a summary of the modern history and the current state of poetry therapy. In the course of doing so, the chapter will adumbrate areas of (theoretical) uncertainty in the field of poetry therapy which contribute to a wide-spread confusion regarding poetry therapy's range of applicability and, most importantly, the lack of a narrow definition. The chapter will outline reasons why no satisfying definition of poetry therapy has been formulated so far and it will demonstrate the flaws of those definitions of poetry therapy that do exist. It is doubtful whether there can be a concise definition of poetry therapy at all, given the interdisciplinarity of the subject matter and the need for dynamic applicability to a broad range of psychotherapeutical approaches and individual clients.[9] The aim should be the formulation of a practical definition that narrows down the field of poetry therapy. Such a definition will provide a minimum level of guidance and structure to the discipline of poetry therapy and mark the discipline off from neighbouring therapeutic approaches.

Psychoanalysis started out as what Bertha Pappenheim termed a *talking cure*[10] and the discourse between analyst and client has remained at the heart of the psychoanalytic and psychotherapeutic experience ever since. The close interaction between the analyst and the client via dialogue constitutes the therapeutical discourse which establishes a unique and intimate relationship that serves as the basis of therapy. The client's contributions to the therapeutic discourse are the primary means of gaining access to the client's conflicts and problems for the analyst. In addition to the fundamental importance of the therapeutic dialogue, there is a significant number of further aspects the psychotherapist has to take into consideration during the therapy session such as indications for and changes in behavioural pattern, the dialectic of transference and counter-transference, cross-references in the client narrative and so forth. In spite

---

[9] The use of the term 'client' in contrast to 'patient' was already briefly touched upon in the introduction. In line with the understanding of the human being in art therapy (and especially humanistic art therapy), the persons seeking psychoanalytic help will be denoted as 'clients'. This is to underline their free choice of therapeutic participation and also to express their active role in the therapeutic process.

[10] Cf. "The Case of Anna O. (Breuer)" in Freud's *Studies on Hysteria* (21-47).

of all the complexities of the interpersonal therapeutic encounter, made more complex even by the continuous advances in psychotherapy research and method, the statements of the client remain at the heart of therapy.[11] Without the words of the client, without the stories told during therapy sessions, without a disclosure of the client's problems through discourse with the analyst, there cannot be a successful treatment. Psychotherapy has always been and remains a *talking cure*. The basis of psychotherapy in dialogue/discourse anchors the whole endeavour firmly in the client's speech and language. Through the medium of speech, psychotherapy, in whatever shape or form, is intricately bound to language. Thus, linguistic expression, language understanding and interpretation are at the very heart of all psychological and psychoanalytical practice.

The above notwithstanding, the importance accorded to language in the therapeutic process varies widely depending on the form of therapy. While dialogue between the client and the therapist is present in virtually every form of psychotherapy, there are forms of analyses that are concerned more closely with language than others. These forms of therapy use verbal expressions other than solely the client-analyst dialogue to augment their practices. In this sense, singing or story-telling are employed therapeutically, as are writing diaries, stories and, of course, poetry. These latter forms of therapy use written language in addition to the classical techniques of the *talking cure*. Clients have to engage with written texts either receptively, i.e. through reading, or productively, by creating texts themselves. Therapeutic approaches that are purely receptive with regard to language can be classified as literature-based therapies or writing-based therapies; they present works of literature (short stories, novels, poetry) to clients in an effort to encourage them to respond emotionally to the texts. The basic idea is that the texts presented to clients serve to make them more consciously aware of their own feelings. At the same time, the works offered serve to initiate the therapeutic discourse. Productive approaches with regard to written language encourage clients to write a diary, or keep records of their anxieties so that in therapy these instances can be more clearly recounted and discussed. Some therapies even encourage a creative use of language and stimulate their clients to write short stories or fiction thus to confront and overcome their conflicts and fears.

In the productive writing therapies mentioned above, clients do engage with language creatively, but it is the language of prose. This is the fundamental difference that sets poetry therapy, as it is defined in this study, apart from all other forms of

---

[11] There have been far-reaching developments during the past 100 years in psychotherapeutic theory and practice. Despite state of the art scanning and recording devices employed in psychological research nowadays and despite the fascinating possibility for neurologists and researchers to watch the brain during the process of thinking clients still have to *talk* about their experiences. All experimental data has little relevance without feedback from the subjects under scrutiny. This is certainly true for psychological experiments, but it is even more relevant in the daily practice of psychotherapy, which consists primarily of the discourse between client and therapist.

therapy, literature-based and otherwise. The very fact that poetic language is bound or versified language serves to differentiate poetry therapy from other therapies using the written word. In spite of this fundamental distinction between prose and verse, formulating a definition of poetry therapy or, at the very least, demarcating poetry therapy from other forms of (writing-based) therapy is a methodological problem. As will be shown shortly, even the differentiation via the prose-verse dichotomy is difficult to uphold in the face of the available literature on the subject.

In poetry therapy, the client deals with a form of language that is different from everyday use, namely a language cast in verse, and this is a language particularly well suited to the expression and treatment of psychological symptoms:

> Writing poetry seemed to have deeper consequences. As a verbal and imaginative art form, poetry appeared to be uniquely suited to serve the psychotherapeutic goal. Regardless of the diagnosis, the patient hospitalized for mental illness has often slipped along the continuum from well to sick. In crucial areas of this development, ego functions are impaired. In all cases, the goal of psychotherapy is to bring about a more mature integration of personality. Poetry seems to be geared to this integrative purpose. (Robinson/Mowbray 191-192)

Robinson and Mowbray base the effectiveness of poetry therapy on the imaginative and verbal properties of poetic writing. Prose texts, however, also exhibit imaginative and specific verbal properties. Writing fiction is no less a "verbal and imaginative art form" than poetry is. Whenever a person engages with language in a creative manner, this involves a consideration of the properties and possibilities of language on the linguistic, or, in terms of narratology, the discourse level, on the one hand, and an imaginative, or story level, on the other. Robinson and Mowbray are, however, not wrong in what they suggest. Poetry, by employing verse, is concerned with the linguistic properties and possibilities of language more intimately. The verbal shaping proper of the poem is more intimately concerned with the structure of language as such. In a therapeutic context this leads to an additional focus on language and the client's language in particular thus amplifying the fundamental concern of psychotherapy with language. Consequently, it can be argued that poetry therapy is more specifically "geared" to improving mental health than other writing-based therapies. Poetry therapy that employs client-created poetry, i.e. personal expressions in versified language, in a therapeutic capacity has at its disposal a highly effective means of mental treatment, because it places the creative process of the client at the therapeutic centre. Suffice it to say for now that in utilising the inherent human faculty of creativity, poetry therapy taps into a potential source for healing and facilitates therapeutic encounters that are beyond forms of poetry therapy that only apply prefabricated poems to therapy. It is precisely the creative activity of poetry writing, however, which is not part of the discipline of poetry therapy as it presents itself today.

1.1 Poetry Therapy, Bibliotherapy, Writing Therapies: Overlapping Principles and theoretical Uncertainty

The understanding of poetry therapy as focused on client-created poems serves as the basis for a demarcation of the discipline's boundaries, namely by implicitly excluding poetry therapy approaches that are purely receptive. Currently, poetry therapy that is practiced on the basis of the client's creative achievements is the exception rather than the rule. In fact, poetry therapy is in most cases understood as purely receptive. The application of the name poetry therapy to both creative and receptive practices poses a fundamental problem for the definition of poetry therapy. To this must be added the broad range of therapeutic approaches to which the label poetry therapy is applied. As a result, vague and heterogeneous definitions of poetry therapy proliferate.

The literature on poetry therapy, comparatively sparse as it is in the first place,[12] uses the term poetry therapy in such a wide sense that it can and often does include such diverse fields as narrative therapy, bibliotherapy and creative forms of therapy in general. Such a comprehensive definition leads to a neglect of the linguistic-literary aspect that is the basis of poetry therapy's effectiveness as a therapeutic approach. The following pages will provide an overview of the confusion that exists in the contemporary understanding of poetry therapy and the difficulties arising from it.

The pervading uncertainty about the disciplinary boundaries of poetry therapy and its definition are due to the interdisciplinary nature of poetry therapy as well as the vague theoretical status of many of the literature-based therapies. Franklin Berry comments on the wide-ranging uncertainties regarding the position of poetry therapy within the theoretical and practical realm of psychotherapy. He states:

---

[12] With regard to relevant secondary literature on poetry therapy, the official organisation for poetry therapy in America (The National Association for Poetry Therapy [NAPT]), lists only two books on its homepage: Leedy's *Poetry as Healer: Mending the Troubled Mind* (1985) and *The Healing Fountain (2003)* by Geri Chavis and Lila Weisberger. The quarterly *Journal of Poetry Therapy* completes the list of relevant scholarly sources on poetry therapy on the homepage. Further research in library databases only returns a handful of books, the most relevant of which are: Greifer, *Principles of Poetry Therapy* (1963); Leedy, *Poetry Therapy: The Use of Poetry in the Treatment of Emotional Disorders* (1969); Harrower, *The Therapy of Poetry* (1972); Lerner, *Poetry in the Therapeutic Experience* (1978); Petzold, *Poesie und Therapie* (1985); McCarty Hynes/Hynes-Berry, *Bibliotherapy – The Interactive Process: A Handbook* (1986) Mazza, *Poetry Therapy. Theory and Practice.* (2003). Journal articles are more numerous, appearing, naturally, in the *Journal of Poetry Therapy*, but also in a broad range of interdisciplinary psychological journals. Generally it can be observed that there is a large number of books available that are concerned with the subject of poetry and well-being as well as anthologies of poems from poetic therapy groups or for the use in such settings. On the subject of poetry therapy in a narrow, or a theoretical sense, however, the literature is extremely limited.

> Poetry therapy is also in a state of uncertainty with particular reference to other currently practiced therapies. One source of this uncertainty concerns poetry therapy's relation to nonliterary therapies; another concerns its relation to other currently practiced literature-based therapies, using books, short-stories and one-act plays. With respect to the view involving nonliterary therapies, one finds poetry therapy conceptualized by some [...] as an "adjunctive therapy" analogous to art, dance, and music therapy, and by others [...] as a full or complete method of psychotherapy in its own right. With respect to the other literature-based therapies, one finds writers holding widely divergent views of how poetry therapy is related to bibliotherapy or literatherapy. Some writers treat poetry [sic] as identical to bibliotherapy [...]. (127-128)

Berry mentions two problematic areas concerning the theoretical basis of poetry therapy. Firstly, poetry therapy and bibliotherapy (and other forms of literature-based therapies) are used interchangeably by a large number of practitioners. This is due to the fact that poetry therapy is predominantly identified by its receptive use of poetic texts, which, indeed, makes it nearly synonymous with bibliotherapy. Bibliotherapy, to define the concept, is based on the idea of carefully selecting literature that corresponds to the client's problems. This allows the client to (a) see that s/he is not alone in having the respective problem and (b) draw solace and inspiration from a positive message that the story or poem conveys. The range of literature employed in bibliotherapy is wide and includes the use of poetry in therapeutic sessions; in fact, poems are frequently used as a means to introduce a session and to motivate clients to come to terms with their internal conflicts. As long as poetry therapy is understood as merely receptive, it can indeed be considered part of bibliotherapy. Poetry therapy is, however, not purely receptive; it also involves the active creation of poems by clients. Such an understanding of poetry therapy cannot be subsumed under bibliotherapy and has to be regarded as a therapeutic approach in its own right, one closely related to other forms of therapies involving the creation of written texts, but distinct from these in that both language and the client's use of it differ fundamentally.

The second problematic area posed by Berry is whether or not poetry therapy is an "adjunctive therapy." Not surprisingly, there is no straight answer to this question. Leedy has the following to say about this: "Poetry therapists act as cotherapists in a poetry therapy group. They work with the psychotherapist in selecting the poems for the patients, in teaching them to read aloud and to cultivate their ability to listen to poetry, and in discussing in the group both the lives of the poets, where helpful, and the poetry itself" ("The Principles of Poetry Therapy" 69). For Leedy, poetry therapy is thus purely adjunctive.[13] The poetry therapist works "with the psychotherapist," a

---

[13] Leedy's book *Poetry Therapy* (1969) constitutes a first serious venture into the realm of poetry therapy. It is therefore only natural that the book is predominantly descriptive of the state of poetry therapy rather than dealing with it on a theoretical meta-level. As the first standard work on poetry therapy, Leedy's book has exerted significant influence on all later publications. Since it is one of the first books to take seriously the approach of poetry therapy, however, the concepts and ideas included have had the more weight in influencing the development of poetry therapy as a discipline. This makes the book's

statement which not only subordinates the role of the poetry therapist with regard to the psychotherapist, but actually insinuates that poetry therapists are in fact no psychotherapists at all. Leedy's statement is interesting for two other reasons. Firstly, it states that poetry therapists are to be "cotherapists" in their own therapy groups. One should imagine that in poetry therapy groups the poetry therapist would be the therapist in charge. Secondly, the poetry therapy group Leedy has in mind is apparently purely receptive (and may therefore equally well be called bibliotherapy). The productive or creative aspect of poetry therapy does not appear to enter into the argument at all. The latter two aspects in particular, presented in a book entitled *Poetry Therapy*, are blatant evidence for the theoretical confusion and lack of a proper definition of poetry therapy, as well as for the uncertain position of poetry therapy in the vast spectrum of therapeutic approaches resulting from this. Leedy even talks of poetry therapy as an experiment (35) rather than a full-fledged psychotherapeutical approach. A similar view is held by Schloss and Grundy who state that

> [p]oetry therapy is such a new field that most of the literature at present can best be described as primarily anecdotal and testimonial. There is still much more enthusiasm than information. Some theoretical issues have been raised […] and the beginnings of research have been undertaken […]. Little, however, has been written about poetry therapy techniques. This is not surprising, since poetry therapy is essentially an ancillary therapy approach. (81)

Although Schloss and Grundy, too, do not concede to poetry therapy the status as an independent therapy, they, in contrast to Leedy, hint at the possible reasons for this, namely the lack of theoretical works and the status as a "new field." Leedy's *Poetry Therapy* appeared in 1969; roughly ten years later, in 1978, Schloss and Grundy still speak of poetry therapy as "new" and, although conceding that research has started regarding a theoretical foundation, they criticise the theoretical literature that is available as "primarily anecdotal and testimonial," which is to say that there are case studies available and that practitioners offer descriptions of their practical approaches, but that in-depth research into the theoretical and methodological possibilities and suppositions has not occurred. Indeed, Leedy's book *Poetry Therapy* presents exactly the mix of anecdotal and descriptive essays regarding the application of poetry in therapy Schloss and Grundy hint at. The essays assembled in the book represent approaches which are, in Leedy's own words, "eclectic" ("Introduction" 12). Contributors include "a group of practicing psychiatrists, clinical psychologists, psychiatric social workers, a literary critic and philosopher of note, a semanticist and university professors" (ibid.). From this list alone, one cannot help but become aware of the experimental status of poetry therapy in the late 1960s. This also becomes evident in the essays themselves, which generally do not go beyond giving a "historical note" on the therapeutic use of poetry, extensive descriptions of the procedures used to select poetry for therapy sessions and, where production of poetry is part of the approach,

> presentation of poetry therapy as purely adjunctive and the peripheral position accorded to poetry in the therapy session particularly problematic.

pages of sample poems. These sample poems are presented in the context of their creation and their effects on – primarily – the members of group therapy sessions.

Leedy's book shows that poetry therapy is a dynamic form of therapy that can be made to fit virtually every form of therapeutic approach in an adjunctive fashion. As for providing a theoretical basis or opening up roads to develop poetry therapy into an independent form of therapy, the book provides little guidance and information. Ten years later, the situation was unchanged. In the introduction to his book *Poetry in the Therapeutic Experience*, Lerner describes the state of poetry therapy in the late 1970s as follows:

> *Poetry in the Therapeutic Experience* assumes that the field known as "poetry therapy" is presently composed of a wide variety of experiences and interests groping for a central theory or rationale. [...] Beyond doubt, poetry therapy is currently in a state of flux. At first glance, one might even say that it is in a state of confusion. There are as many different "theories" as there are practitioners in the field. There are some who believe there is no such phenomenon as poetry therapy. (XV)

The essays collected in Lerner's book are essentially no less eclectic than in Leedy's. Still, case studies abound,[14] although there are essays that try to bring the use of poetry into the theoretical framework of their respective therapeutic approaches.[15] The understanding of poetry therapy by most of the book's contributors is still as an adjunctive, purely receptive method which is helpful, because it functions well as a means to establish a (verbal) connection between client and therapist; it is perceived (solely) as a useful tool employed to facilitate classical psychotherapeutical methods. Poetry is merely used as a facilitating device for the core techniques of the respective psychotherapeutical approach rather than put at the centre of the therapeutic endeavour. For poetry therapy to be(come) an independent therapeutical approach, however, and for the practice to be able to formulate a valid theoretical framework that sets it apart from other writing-based therapies, it is essential to reduce the level of theoretical and methodological confusion to a manageable proportion.

On the large scale, there has been considerable progress in the field of poetry therapy since the time of Leedy and Lerner. With the general recognition of the art therapies by the psychotherapeutical community during the thirty years since the publication of Lerner's book in 1978, fundamental research has been done, yet the uncertainty surrounding the position of poetry therapy within the contemporary theoretical framework of psychology and psychoanalysis still exists. Bolton, writing from a British perspective, has the following comment regarding the situation of writing therapy on the British Isles: "there is art therapy, music therapy, drama therapy, dance

---

[14] Of course, case studies are a fundamental tool in the exchange of knowledge and new techniques within the psychotherapies. With regard to poetry therapy as understood in this study, however, case studies are of limited use as the creative output of clients is highly idiosyncratic and can only be understood properly in this context.

[15] Cf. especially Charles Ansell, "Psychoanalysis and Poetry;" Robert N. Ross, "Parsing Concepts: A Discovery Technique for Poetry Therapy."

therapy, even smelling therapy (aromatherapy), but where is writing therapy? The potential of writing within mainstream medical care has never been seriously trialled in Britain, or instituted like these other arts" (26). There is indeed no central organisation that is concerned with writing therapy, much less poetry therapy, in Britain. The situation in the USA is somewhat different. Poetry therapy in the United States is institutionalised in the National Association for Poetry Therapy (NAPT), which organises an annual conference on poetry therapy, publishes the quarterly *Journal of Poetry Therapy* as well as books on the subject, and provides a training curriculum for poetry therapists. Bolton makes the following observation regarding the status and achievement of the NAPT:[16]

> Therapists in the USA have been at the forefront of examining the potential of therapeutic writing (often called scriptotherapy), so far. The (American) National Association for Poetry Therapy, which offers post-graduate training in developmental (or clinical) interactive bibliotherapy, only has fewer than 370 members (17 in other countries), however. Much of their emphasis is on reading and listening to poetry. On the process of therapeutic writing, they state: 'Finding one's own voice is a self-affirming process often followed by cathartic release, greater self-awareness and new insight'. (204)

Bolton's statement, which dates from 1999, is evidence of the minor role still played by poetry therapy in the USA. Although the small number of members must not necessarily reflect on the importance of poetry therapy research undertaken, much less the quality of it, it does account for the slow progress of theoretical research since the late 1970s. In spite of the existence of the Association for Poetry Therapy (since 1969), which "became formally incorporated as the National Association for Poetry Therapy (NAPT)" (Mazza 7) in 1981, the *Journal of Poetry Therapy* and a growing awareness of the potential of art therapies in the analytic community in the USA, poetry therapy remains a peripheral approach both in psychotherapy in general and the art therapies in particular. It is a field in search of a true theoretical foundation.

Although poetry therapists now work independently (or, at least, on equal footing with traditional psychotherapists), the precise demarcation of poetry therapy remains controversial. At its core, definitions of poetry therapy that are proposed vary between narrower and wider delimitations of the term. This is mainly due to the continuing oscillation between the understanding of poetry therapy as receptive and as productive. In this context it is interesting to note that Bolton ascribes to the NAPT an emphasis on "reading and listening to poetry," which suggests that the NAPT is primarily interested in the receptive use of poetry therapy. This (once again) brings the concept of poetry therapy precariously close to that of bibliotherapy. Indeed, in the

---

[16] The homepage of the NAPT (http://www.poetrytherapy.org/index.html) not only provides a concise overview of the history of poetry therapy in the USA, but also news on conferences, the *Journal of Poetry Therapy* and new publications in the field. In addition to this, there is a link to the National Federation of Biblio/Poetry Therapy (http://www.nfbpt.com/) which provides information on the training and education of poetry therapists.

above quotation, Bolton's statements can be seen as another expression of the disciplinary blending of poetry therapy and bibliotherapy. Bolton explains without any reservations that the NAPT "offers post-graduate training in developmental (or clinical) interactive biblio-therapy." It is not that the NAPT *also* offers training in bibliotherapy. The quote leaves no doubt that training in bibliotherapy is the *only* form of training offered. This effectively makes the terms 'bibliotherapy' and 'poetry therapy' synonyms of the same practice, thus eliminating any difference between them. The conflation of poetry therapy with bibliotherapy and, on a lesser level, a variety of other forms of therapy can also be observed in the submission guidelines for the *Journal of Poetry Therapy* which state:

> The purview of the *Journal of Poetry Therapy* includes the use of bibliotherapy, journal therapy, creative writing, narrative, lyrics, storytelling, and metaphor in human service settings. Research (qualitative and quantitative), practice (clinical and education), theoretical, and literary studies are emphasized. The intended audience for *JPT* includes those in the allied helping professions; as well as those in literary/artistic fields with a concern for the healing/therapeutic aspects of the language arts. (http://www.poetrytherapy.org/publications.html#books. Visited: 09.01.2010)

To begin with, the *Journal of Poetry Therapy* includes in its purview not only bibliotherapy, but journal therapy, storytelling and the area that is, somewhat enigmatically, termed "metaphor in human service settings." Since the journal is interdisciplinary it strives to include "the allied helping professions," which makes perfect sense. What is less clear is why "literary/artistic fields with a concern for the healing/therapeutic aspects of the language arts" are specifically mentioned. The connecting phrase 'as well as' suggests that these "literary/artistic fields" are of a more peripheral concern for poetry therapy. Now, poetry therapy is an interdisciplinary field combining psychotherapy and poetry. The relegation of "literary/artistic fields" (especially since these are further limited to only those "with a concern for the healing/therapeutic aspects") to such a peripheral position basically negates poetry therapy's interdisciplinary nature, because the artistic aspects of poetry are apparently only tertiary when they should be recognised for their due importance and impact in the therapeutic process. This is not a question of whether or not poetry works as a therapeutical tool in the actual practice of analysis. Rather, it is a question of maximising its effectiveness as a therapy.

One has to keep in mind, of course, that, in practice, poetry therapy is not without a methodological framework. The fact that there is no unified theory/definition of poetry therapy does not mean there is no theory at all. Practitioners naturally take recourse to the fundamental concepts of psychology/psychoanalysis and tailor them to fit the needs of their individual clients. This inevitably favours and gives prevalence to the psychotherapeutical. The aim of this study, it has to be noted once more, is to engage with poetry therapy theoretically and from a predominantly literary point of view, a perspective that is currently missing. Since the poem contains and mirrors psychic and mental processes, the literary/artistic aspect of poetry therapy has to be considered as more than simply an additional, ancillary notion in therapy. For poetry therapy to unfold its maximum potential as a therapeutic approach, the artistic aspects of poetry therapy should be taken into account within the framework of a reciprocal relationship between the poetic and the psychological aspects of poetry therapy. In contrast to this, the current state of poetry therapy is dominated by the psychological, which, for reasons we will explore shortly, neglects the poetic aspect. It is in no small part due to this negligence of the poetic in poetry therapy that the conflation of the practice with bibliotherapy and other therapies is so pervading.

The first question to address is, simply put: how is it possible to define and differentiate between what constitutes poetry therapy and what, in contrast, defines writing therapy? The differentiation between these two fields of therapy is one major aspect that needs clarification. The other aspect, which is connected to the first, is how the understanding of poetry therapy as being primarily receptive works against a formulation of a concise theory. The latter will be the focus of the following argument which will lead to a consideration of the former aspect later on. The primacy of the receptive element in the general understanding of poetry therapy today stems from a loose application of the term 'poetry.' In its broad sense, poetry is understood as virtually synonymous with creativity. This becomes obvious in the following statement taken from the NAPT homepage:

> For the past 27 years, NAPT members have forged a community of healers and lovers of words and language. We are psychotherapists, counselors, psychologists, social workers, and psychiatrists. We are poets, journal keepers, storytellers, and songwriters. We are teachers, librarians, adult educators, and university professors. We are doctors, nurses, occupational/recreational therapists; ministers, pastoral counselors, and spiritual directors. We are artists, dancers, dramatists, musicians, and writers. We work in many settings where people deal with personal and communal pain and the search for growth. As poetry therapists, we use all forms of literature and the language arts, and we are united by our love of words, and our passion for enhancing the lives of others and ourselves. (Visited: 02.01.2010)

The NAPT has opted to include in the term poetry therapy every artistic and creative practice remotely concerned with language and words. Poetry therapists thus use "all forms of literature and language arts." While such a definition is forthcoming to the inclusion of a diverse field of practices and approaches, the downside is that it precludes the delineation of a clear-cut definition of poetry therapy. Furthermore, it creates a misunderstanding about poetry therapy as a discipline, confusing it with other literature-based therapies such as bibliotherapy. It is understandable that the NAPT, as an organisation, propagates poetry therapy as encompassing a wide range of writing-based therapies, but this does, in fact, little to add profile to both the NATP and poetry therapy as a field of research.

The most striking evidence of the lack of a definition of poetry therapy can again be found on the homepage of the NAPT. The official organisation for poetry therapy in the USA states that poetry therapy "encompasses bibliotherapy (the interactive use of literature) and journal therapy (the use of life-based reflective writing) as well as therapeutic storytelling, the use of film in therapy, and other language-based healing modalities" (http://www.poetrytherapy.org/about.html. Visited: 23.01.2010). The NAPT thus subsumes bibliotherapy under poetry therapy. This is a complete reversal of the situation found in the theoretical works of Lerner and Leedy, where bibliotherapy serves as the umbrella term for poetry therapy. Indeed, in the section about the historical development of poetry therapy on the same website, there is a headline that reads "Poetry Therapy – A Form of Bibliotherapy." In the text that follows, poetry therapy is defined as "a specific and powerful form of bibliotherapy, unique in its use of metaphor, imagery, rhythm, and other poetic devices" (http://www.poetrytherapy.org/history.html. Visited: 23.01.2010). On the same home-page of the official organisation for poetry therapy in the USA, poetry therapy is defined in one text as inclusive of bibliotherapy and in another as a subcategory of the same. To find two mutually exclusive definitions of the term poetry therapy on one (the official) homepage most certainly results from a lack of proper theoretical foundations and delimitation.

When one inspects the existing definitions of poetry therapy further, the underlying confusion becomes even more apparent. The NAPT's definition of poetry therapy includes such approaches as "journal writing," "therapeutic storytelling" and film. Both "journal writing" and "therapeutic storytelling" have the potential to be creative and therefore 'poetic' in the broad sense of the word, but they are not concerned with poetry. To include the above therapeutic approaches in the term 'poetry therapy' unnecessarily widens the field and calls for a closer investigation into the underlying causes and reasons for this. One reason for this is the following: in the pervading definitions of poetry therapy, the term 'poetry' is not taken specifically to denote versified language, but rather follows the root meaning of 'poetic'.[17] In many such instances, poetry therapy becomes synonymous with creative therapy. This devaluates the one feature of poetry therapy which is the differentiating one with regard to other writing therapies, namely the use of versified language. As a consequence, the healing properties unique to poetic[18] language are only superficially understood and employed by practitioners and theorists of poetry therapy, and, as long as the poetic aspect is regarded as peripheral, it will consequently only feature peripherally both in theoretical discussions and with regard to practical considerations.

---

[17] Cf. the official training manual for poetry therapists, the *NFBPT.TrainingGuide* (2007), which states that "the terms poetry therapy, applied poetry facilitation, journal therapy, bibliotherapy, biblio/poetry therapy, and poetry/journal therapy are all intended to reflect the interactive use of literature and/or writing to promote growth and healing. When the umbrella term 'poetry therapy' is used herein, it is intended to encompass all of the modalities above" (9). The term 'poetry therapy' is used here as an extremely loose umbrella term encompassing practices which are 'poetic' in the root meaning of the word denoting a creative or productive activity from the ancient Greek ποητικός, ποιητικός (cf. *OED*).

[18] When I use the term 'poetic' I will always do so in a narrow sense as pertaining to poetry and versified language.

The fact that other unspecified "language-based healing modalities" are also included in the official definition further complicates and confuses an already problematic matter. One might even assume that the definitions presented on the NAPT homepage are sloppily formulated and the phrase "language-based healing modalities" is actually supposed to denote writing-based therapies. The presence of film therapy in the above list, however, discounts this possibility. Film is used similarly to bibliotherapy in that the client watches a film that has been chosen to reflect the client's feelings. In this sense, the use of film in therapy simply widens the classical – receptive – approach of bibliotherapy transmedially. It thus represents another instance of the confusion between the terms poetry therapy and bibliotherapy. The interrelatedness of these two terms and the respective lack of delimitation between the two forms of therapy are clearly at the heart of the problem at hand. In the FAQ section of the homepage of the National Federation on Biblio/Poetry Therapy this becomes once more strikingly obvious.[19] The answer to the question "Is poetry therapy only about poetry?" reads as follows:

> Credentialed practitioners of poetry therapy use the poetic in all literature. The poetic is the evocative, imaginal language that invites personal and individual response. Journal writing, story telling, creative and reflective writing and poetry are some of the many tools we use to enhance the creative and healing process. Poetry therapy, applied poetry, biblio/poetry therapy, journal therapy, poetry/journal therapy and bibliotherapy are synonymous; all focus on the written, spoken, and auditory aspects of interactive literature. (http://www.nfbpt.com/faq.html. Visited: 02.01.2010)

In one word, the answer to the question of whether or not poetry therapy is "only about poetry" is no. Poetry therapy is apparently about everything that involves writing and/or some form of narrative or story. The diverse forms of therapy listed in the above quote alone are evidence of the theoretical no-man's-land in which poetry therapy is still lost today. The reason for this is the broad range of applicability of poetry within the mental health profession which inevitably leads to a highly pluralistic discipline, a narrow demarcation of which is difficult to achieve.

The most recent book to attempt such a demarcation of poetry therapy from its sister therapies is Nicholas Mazza's *Poetry Therapy: Theory and Practice* (2003). In his book, Mazza endeavours to "ground the practitioner and/or researcher in the fundamental principles and techniques of poetry therapy" (1). This is an aim that the book certainly achieves. Mazza provides a concise history of the theoretical foundations and developments of poetry therapy, describes the current scientific status and attempts to situate poetry therapy within psychology. Without a doubt, Mazza succeeds in providing "a multidimensional model of poetry therapy that can be used with

---

[19] The name of the organisation alone is evidence of both the near synonymy of the terms in the heads of practitioners and the proximity of the two practices. The NFBPT organises, implements and performs the training of poetry therapists for the NAPT, which may be one reason for the near synonymy of both approaches that abounds in the field and especially for the dominance of the receptive approach of poetry therapy.

a wide range of populations and applied in numerous settings" (ibid.). This is also the drawback of the book, however. Once again, as Leedy and Lerner before him, Mazza is faced with a broad spectrum of therapeutic approaches in which poetry therapy plays a part, which eventually keeps Mazza from succeeding in bringing poetry therapy into a more manageable methodological framework. Mazza's failure to do so, some twenty-five years after Lerner, confirms my contention that the continuing plurality that characterises poetry therapy is due to a negligence sufficiently to consider the poetic aspect of poetry therapy.

Instead of using poetry therapy as an umbrella term for creative therapies, or even somewhat more narrowly, writing therapies, a limitation to the application of the term 'poetry therapy' to therapies that use poetry in the narrow sense, i.e. language cast in some form of verse, rather than to healing techniques that are in the broad sense 'poetic,' can, if not provide a concise and inclusive definition, then at least circumscribe its own field of application in a more precise way. Ultimately, poetry therapy research cannot hope to progress any further without a definition of its subject matter that is precise enough to narrow down the scope of applicability, thus clearly demarcating it from other literature-based forms of therapy. Mazza is well aware of this problem. He believes that the indeterminate status of poetry therapy stems from its interdisciplinary nature. He states that "[t]here is still not a uniform definition of poetry therapy, and the lack of a rigorous definition of the term 'poetry' poses some obstacles in conducting research" (107). Mazza thus locates the problem in the literary/poetic domain of poetry therapy. The lack of a proper definition of poetry is set up as the reason for a lack of a proper definition of poetry therapy.

It is true that a rigorous definition of poetry has never materialised in literary studies. The reason for this is the diverse nature of the genre of poetry. There are so many different forms of poetry, so many individual styles and such an extensive body of sub-genres that every definition must inevitably fail to encompass all of them. As a result, definitions of poetry remain very general. Two definitions shall serve as examples here. Cuddon's *Dictionary of Literary Terms and Literary Theory* defines poetry as

> a comprehensive term which can be taken to cover any kind of metrical composition. However, it is usually employed with reservations, and often in contradistinction to verse. For example, we should describe Shakespeare's sonnets as poetry, and the wittily ingenious creations of Ogden Nash as verse; though both are *in* verse. The implications are that poetry is a superior form of creation; not necessarily, therefore, more serious. Aristophanes, Chaucer, Ben Jonson, Donne, Marvell, Pope, Byron and Auden, to name a few, have all written witty and humorous poems. (726)

Apart from the acknowledgement that poetry is a comprehensive term, the examples given in the above quote are (necessarily) eclectic and the classification of Nash's works as 'verse' rather than poetry is debatable to say the least. It is not difficult to detect the underlying lack of a universally accepted definition of poetry in the above explication. The same is true of the next definition, taken from the *Oxford English*

Dictionary. In the context of the present discussion, the *OED* lists the following relevant definitions for the term poetry:

1. Imaginative or creative literature in general; fable, fiction.
2. The art or work of a poet.
   a. Composition in verse or some comparable patterned arrangement of language in which the expression of feelings and ideas is given intensity by the use of distinctive style and rhythm; the art of such a composition. Traditionally associated with explicit formal departure from the patterns of ordinary speech or prose, e.g. in the use of elevated diction, figurative language, and syntactical reordering.
   b. The product of this art as a form of literature; the writings of a poet or poets; poems collectively or generally.
   d. The expression or embodiment of thought or feeling in a manner regarded as characteristic of a poem; (also) the products of this expression. Freq. opposed to *verse*, *prose*, etc. Traditionally referring to metrical form (as in sense 2a), but sometimes extended to include comparable expression in non-metrical language;
   e. In extended use: creative or imaginative art in general.
6. *a. fig.* Something comparable to poetry in its beauty or emotional impact; a poetic quality of beauty and intensity of emotion; the poetic quality *of* something.

The dyad of poetry and verse reappears here and proves no less problematic than in the definition taken from Cuddon. The *OED*'s definition(s) underscore the tendencies made obvious in Cuddon, namely that poetry is a term that can be used loosely within literary studies. This accounts for the tendency in poetry therapy to do the same. There is more, however. The *OED* demonstrates that the term 'poetry' extends beyond the literary and is applied to the arts in general and, on a still wider scale, to creative endeavours as a whole. In this context, the *New Princeton Encyclopedia of Poetry and Poetics* provides one of the most extensive definition of poetry and theories of poetry. Here, the definition of poetry begins by stating that a "poem is an instance of *verbal art*, a text set in verse, bound speech. More generally, a poem conveys heightened forms of perception, experience, meaning, or consciousness in heightened lang., i.e. a heightened mode of discourse" (938). Reading the above excerpt shows that there are a number of aspect which contradict the definitions presented by Cuddon and the *OED*. The *Princeton Encyclopedia* also comments on the ambiguity of the term 'poetic', stating:

If either of the criteria indicated by the two words italicized in the first sentence of this entry [*verbal art*] is removed, texts become 'poetic' only in a looser, more general, and metaphorical senses. (1) *Verbal* but not *artful*: any verbal text or piece of verbal discourse, even if not meant as 'art,' can be called 'poetic' if it seems to exhibit intensified speech – an impassioned plea, a stirring speech, a moving letter. Often these texts partake in the resources offered by traditional rhet. [...] and so take the term 'poetic' as a metonym, since verse characteristically deploys these features. (2) *Artful* but not *verbal*: any object skillfully made or intended as art though not a verbal text can be called 'poetic' in the metaphorical sense – an intensive moment in a play or movie, a romantic gesture, a painting, a piece of music. (939)

The fundamental indeterminacy of the term 'poetic' that even the *Princeton Encyclopedia*'s definition recognises is further evidence for the uncertainty surrounding the term 'poetry' in general. The application in the above quote of the label 'poetic' to such areas as music, film and theatre can account for the open definition of poetry therapy found on the homepage of the NAPT.

Faced with such an extensive breadth of meaning, it becomes clear why poetry has never been successfully narrowed down to a universally accepted definition. The multiplicity of meaning of the terms 'poetry' or 'poetic' has not kept literary scholars from appropriating the term to their individual agendas, however. Rather, literary scholars make use of that definition which is most useful for the project in question. Poetry therapy should do the same. Practically, thus, poetry therapist should concentrate on poetry in the narrow sense rather than as synonymous with creativity. Doing so would be beneficial, because a relatively concise definition of poetry automatically narrows down the field of poetry therapy, streamlining its methodological possibilities and making it more manageable theoretically. Instead, however, poetry therapists have chosen the most general definition of poetry in their application of the term to poetry therapy. This has given them the benefit of not having to engage with questions of modern poetics and modern literary studies, but at the expense of utilising the practical advantages of inter-disciplinarity. The sixth meaning of the *OED* is thus the most problematic in connection to poetry therapy. If something comparable to poetry can be termed poetry, basically every creative activity can be subsumed under the heading and can, in turn, be included as a therapeutic device in poetry therapy. Indeed, this is what has happened and, naturally, this adds to the difficulties caused by the already wide applicability of poetry in psychotherapy.

Mazza, who is careful to put emphasis on the interdisciplinary nature of poetry therapy, ventures the following definition, stating that "poetry therapy is defined as the use of the language arts in therapeutic capacities" (105). This is at best a general description of the therapeutic practice of poetry therapy, but far removed from a precise definition that one could use in academic discourse. Mazza faces similar obstacles in his attempt at defining the aims of poetry therapy. He claims that "[u]sing poetic expressions, images, or symbols derived from the client's language and experience can also be helpful in promoting change" (113). Using images and symbols from the client's language in the therapeutic process is not unique to poetry therapy; this has always been the basic principle of psychotherapy since the time of Freud.[20] In addition

---

[20] In the light of this, Mazza's claim that images and symbols "can *also* be helpful in promoting change" (emphasis mine) is astonishing. Which aspect if not the symbols and images in a poem should be central to the process of poetry therapy? The dream-work produces images and symbolically charged sequences in our sleep through which the unconscious manifests its content. Along the same lines, verbal slips of the tongue produce incongruous messages in which the incongruity serves as a symbol of the deeper

to this, Mazza's use of the phrase "poetic expressions" does not make his statement any more precise. After all, there can be an abundance of "poetic expressions" in any given prose text, but these do not turn that text into poetry. Of course, Mazza is not unaware of the problems inherent in his 'definitions', but the current state of theory in his field simply does not allow for anything more specific.[21]

Most attempts at classification and most definitions of poetry therapy proposed have, as was shown, almost exclusively tried to put forth a definition that was informed by the *OED*'s sixth meaning of 'poetry'. By making 'poetry' synonymous with creativity, poetry therapists essentially circumvent the need to define poetry in their area of research. Instead, they are able to define the discipline by its psychotherapeutical approach alone. In this manner, there is no need to inquire deeply about, for instance, the nature of poetry or poetic language. The techniques used in the actual application of poetry therapy are determined solely by the psychotherapeutic approach of the therapist and not influenced by poetic considerations at all. In practice, poetry has remained secondary to the psychotherapeutical side; poetry is relegated to the function of a mere tool. The current denial in poetry therapy circles to acknowledge the inherently therapeutic value of poetry and poetic creation further denigrates the poetic aspect within the discipline. As a consequence, the literature on poetry therapy almost exclusively draws on the practical applications of its approach (case studies, anecdotal reports, etc.) and its relation to other forms of therapy (adjunctive, integrative, independent). The 'poetry' aspect of poetry therapy has received no in-depth treatment equivalent to the psychotherapeutical. It is therefore questionable to say, as Mazza does, that a definition of poetry therapy fails because there is no "rigorous definition of the term 'poetry'" (107). Rather, a definition has not materialised because 'poetry' has not been sufficiently considered in the first place. Thus, it seems, poetry therapists have taken the easy way out and chosen to base their discipline on a definition of poetry that is all-encompassing. Such a definition is harmless in the sense that it does not necessitate a revaluation and adaptation of existing methods and techniques. Hence, the poetic/literary side has never experienced sufficient critical and theoretical attention in poetry therapy. This is particularly surprising considering the importance accorded to literature and poetry in particular by the founding fathers of modern psychotherapy. Jung, Adler, Rank and Freud all placed vital importance on literary

---

meanings. Poetic symbols are artefacts of unconscious participation in the creative process and are of paramount importance when dealing with poetry therapeutically (cf. Chapter 3 and Chapter 4 of this study for a more detailed discussion of this subject matter).

[21] In addition to this, it is not the purpose of Mazza's book to develop new theoretical concepts, but rather to give an overview of the current state of poetry therapy in theory and practice. The title of the first edition, *Poetry Therapy: Interface of the Arts and Psychology,* clearly shows that "it provides a foundation for poetry therapy theory, practice, and research" (1).

examples and artistic expression in the context of mental health and the treatment of psychic disorders.

1.2 Freud and the Importance of Literary Theory in writing-based Therapies

Considering the apparent difficulties in situating poetry therapy in today's therapeutic environment, the best course of action is to return to the source of psychotherapy for the time being rather than to get lost in contemporary theoretical nitpicking. This chapter, therefore, sets out to map the historical roots of poetry therapy as well as the points of contact between psychotherapy and literary studies that are important in the present context. In the beginning there was, of course, Freud. Although a trained physician, he was steeped in the Western humanistic tradition which forms as much a basis of his school of psychoanalysis as does his medical training. Freud always proclaimed a close connection between psychoanalysis and literature:

> It is well known that Freud was steeped in German literature, which, by virtue of an incomparable translation, can be said to include Shakespeare's plays. Every one of his works bears witness to this, and to the continual recourse he had to it, no less in his technique than in his discovery. Not to mention his broad background in the classics, his familiarity with modern folklore, and his keeping abreast of contemporary humanism's conquest in the areas of ethnography. Analytic practitioners should be asked not to consider it futile to follow Freud along this path. (Lacan, "The Function and Field of Speech and Language in Psychoanalysis" 244)

Lacan's appreciation of the humanistic tradition in the evolution of Freudian psychoanalysis could not be more telling in the present context. Throughout his extensive work, Freud pointed out parallels to the great poets and writers of the humanistic tradition. In Freud one can thus observe the reciprocal influences of poetry and therapy and the impressive results of such an interaction. For Lacan, this recourse to literature and poetry is vitally important for another reason: Lacan advocates a reorientation of psychoanalysis and his main agenda is a return to the fundamental principles of psychoanalysis established by Freud. This was imperative in Lacan's view, because he had detected a drifting away of psychoanalytic practice from its Freudian foundations towards, on the one hand, a streamlining of treatment along economic concerns and, on the other hand, a simplification of treatment practices allowing for a more time-efficient, but, in his eyes, less effective treatment. Lacan ascribes these tendencies – not exclusively, yet predominantly – to the developments of psychotherapy in the USA and its pervading influence. He considers these tendencies extremely dangerous and consequently propagates a 'return to Freud'. Lacan's call for a 'return to Freud' originates in a problematic similar to that of poetry therapy today. To Lacan's mind, psychoanalysis is concerned predominantly with the individual and requires a basically idiosyncratic approach for every client. Psychoanalytical concepts serve as a basis for a therapeutic encounter which is always new and singular. The tendencies in psychoanalysis towards a more 'scientific' approach at the expense of the individual aspect mirror the marginalisation of the 'poetry' aspect in contemporary poetry therapy. The latter is not only similar to, but partly originates in the tendencies delineated by Lacan.

Lacan reads Freud in a post-structuralist fashion[22] and in doing so uncovers the linguistic basis of psychoanalysis.[23] Consequently, Freud's use of and interest in literature as the creative use of language takes on new importance. As Lacan argues, analysts should "follow Freud along this path." Freud considered poetry as a particularly useful and potent form of literature when it comes to influencing mental health. "Freud described the poet as a 'professional daydreamer' [who is] aware of his own and others' impulses, dreams and fantasies and has the courage to express them verbally" (Robinson/Mowbray 192).[24] Since dreams are, according to Freud, the *via regia* to the unconscious, it follows that poetry is a path that runs parallel to it. The enormous extent to which language (and literature) enter the psychoanalytic experience and their importance for the success of the whole endeavour is something Freud was acutely aware of. Robinson and Mowbray state:

> To summarize briefly Freud's theories on the qualities necessary for creativity, the artist must have 1. a strong instinctual drive; 2. an extraordinary capacity for sublimation; 3. laxity of repression. The poet, in addition, must be able to verbalize. Poetry, then, of all the arts, comes closest to the therapeutic hour in psychoanalytic terms. [...] In addition to sublimation, the defence mechanisms most frequently used by poets are condensation, symbolization, and displacement, which turn the frightening unconscious into something acceptable. (193)

If poetry alone "comes closest to the therapeutic hour in psychoanalytic terms," poetry therapy, which constitutes a combination of poetry and therapy, promises to be even more effective. It is due to this fact that the practice of poetry therapy can claim particular effectiveness among therapeutic approaches. It is true that the creation of art has been accorded with therapeutical potential by all the founding fathers of psychology and psychoanalysis, but creative writing, and poetry in particular, is, according to Freud, highly therapeutic in itself; a combination of this practice with psychotherapeutic approaches cannot but result in an extraordinarily effective form of therapy.

With this much importance accorded to literature, and especially poetry, by Freud, it becomes clear that for poetry therapy to be most effective, the poetic aspect

---

[22] Lacan sees Freud as a direct precursor to structuralist and post-structuralist thinking who simply did not possess the necessary vocabulary to express his theories accordingly. This is why, for Lacan, a post-structuralist reading of Freud is not a contradiction but an imperative – one that modern psychotherapy has, in his view, neglected.

[23] Cf. in particular Lacan's essays "The Freudian Thing, or the Meaning of the Return to Freud in Psychoanalysis," "Psychoanalysis and Its Teaching," "The Situation of Psychoanalysis and the Teaching of Psychoanalysis in 1956" and "The Instance of the Letter in the Unconscious or Reason since Freud" in *Écrits*.

[24] Cf. also Freud, "Creative Writers and Daydreaming."

has to be accorded the same status as the psychotherapeutical.[25] It has already been shown that definitions of poetry therapy are formulated almost exclusively from the psychological/psychoanalytical point of view. Hence, since "[a] significant portion of the theoretical foundation for the use of poetry in therapy is drawn from the psychoanalytic literature" (Mazza 8), poetics, or the theory of poetry, has little part in the matter. A balance between the two fields involved does not exist. Since interdisciplinary work inevitably presupposes disciplinary competence in order not to slip into dilettantism, practitioners of poetry therapy cannot do without extensive knowledge of both disciplines. For the most part, poetry therapists do acknowledge the interdisciplinary nature of their field (cf., for instance: Mazza, "Introduction;" Harrower 3-7), but in practice the therapists' knowledge about poetry, the process of poetic creation and contemporary poetic theory is often frighteningly limited. Indeed, a lack of proper knowledge of the field of literature and poetry is something that prevails in poetry therapy circles. This has its origins in a number of reasons. For instance, most practitioners who employ poetry therapy have not specifically been trained as poetry therapists, but are psychologist/psychoanalysts who have come to the field indirectly. Along the same lines, the confusion and close connection between biblio- and poetry therapy marginalises poetry as a creative process and strengthens the adjunctive view of poetry therapy. Furthermore, the education of poetry therapists privileges the psychological aspect of poetry therapy at the expense of its literary side (cf. NFBPT homepage [http://www.nfbpt.com/summary.html]).[26] The following is stated in the training requirements for certified poetry therapists: "Unlike an art, music or dance therapy trainee, a poetry therapy trainee is not expected to be proficient in the art form of writing. Basic literacy, grammar, composition, and reading comprehension skills are required and will be assessed as part of the application process" (*Guide to Training Requirements for Certification and Registration in Poetry Therapy* 9, PDF File, Downloaded from http://www.nfbpt.com/trainingguide.html. Visited: 09.01.2010). The "[b]asic literacy, grammar, composition, and reading comprehension skills" required of poetry therapists take the form of courses in "Creative Writing, Poetic Devices,

---

[25] It is important to note at this point that Freud is talking about the effects of creative writing, which does not include the mainly receptive activity of reading or perceiving literature. Consequently, what Freud discusses here excludes such therapies as bibliotherapy or film therapy.

[26] With regard to the aims of a training curriculum for poetry therapists in which the poetry side is given its due, Edgar and Hazley argue that "it is *not* the purpose of [such a] curriculum proposal to train people to the idea that the creative act can be accounted for by psychological analysis. That act, as Jung has said, will forever elude human understanding. It *is* the purpose to provide those interested with the tools by which they may be able to understand more profoundly and communicate more meaningfully to those who are disturbed or who function inadequately the important and permanent truths that are to be found in poetry" (262). Edgar and Hazley contend rightly that knowledge of the poetic aspect of poetry therapy is essential to its proper application and effectiveness, which corroborates the present argument.

Contemporary/Multi-Cultural Poetry, Literature of Various Genres, Memoir/Narrative/ Therapeutic Storytelling" (ibid. 10). This list,[27] which is a list of core competences to be acquired before starting to train as a poetry therapist, contradicts the original statement that no proficiency in the "art form of writing" is necessary. It shows that, indeed, literature and poetry do have a place in the education of poetry therapists (cf. Edgar/Hazley). Lerner's call for "a training program that emphasizes both therapy and poetry" ("Editorial: A Look at Poetry Therapy" I) has thus not gone completely unnoticed. Although inclusion of literary subjects in the curriculum for the training of poetry therapist constitutes an acknowledgement of the necessity of a basic understanding of literature, the fact that these skills are to be acquired prior to the training as a poetry therapist is far from ideal. Teaching of literary knowledge within the training curriculum would be far more efficient as it could be streamlined to the requirements of the job. Also, the content taught could be much more sensibly organised and its quality guaranteed.

Although there is training in literary studies for poetry therapists and notwithstanding the ongoing discussions and still tentative steps towards implementing literary studies in the curriculum, one important aspect of literary studies is completely missing from these deliberations: literary theory. On the following pages I will outline why the knowledge of literary theory is important for a practitioner of poetry therapy and in how far the inclusion of it in the training curriculum and practice will benefit the theoretical foundation of poetry therapy as a whole. One might wonder whether or not it is necessary for a poetry therapist to be proficient in literary theory given that the intricacies of this area of literary studies hardly play a role in the practice of poetry therapy. To begin with, there has long been an exchange of concepts and ideas between literary criticism and psychotherapy. Freud's appropriation of poetic and literary concepts has already been mentioned. In a reciprocal development, literary criticism has taken over psychoanalytical concepts. Psychoanalytical criticism as a literary approach is based on psychotherapeutic concepts which are applied to literature. In the context of this development it seems, at first glance, unnecessary to include literary theory in the training of poetry therapists. After all, the concepts of psychoanalytical criticism, stemming from psychotherapy, are automatically employed in the therapeutic sessions. Since the therapist is expected to be knowledgeable in psychotherapeutic theory and adept at the practical side of it, there is no need for poetry therapists to busy

---

[27] The final two items in the list, "Literature of Various Genres" and "Memoir/Narrative/ Therapeutic Storytelling" obviously go beyond the genre of poetry and are evidence once more of the indeterminate theoretical status of poetry therapy. The same is true about "Creative writing," which is ambiguous. It can mean creative writing in general, which may include short stories, novels, drama etc., or be meant to refer to poetic writing in particular. A course in *poetic* writing would be highly desirable in the education of poetry therapists, whereas creative writing in a general sense can only be deemed of secondary importance.

themselves with literary theory.[28] This line of argumentation is, however, only partly sound. It is true that the therapist, in the therapeutic session, basically engages in a psychotherapeutical reading of the text produced by the statements of the client. Whatever clients utter about their conflicts, fears, and childhood, etc. is received by the therapist through the lens of his/her theoretical approach. This remains the same in the poetry therapy session, but there is an additional text that comes into play, namely the poem. Regardless of whether it is a pre-existing poem that is discussed or a poem produced by the client, the therapist has to be aware of the way the client approaches the poem and the way the poem is constructed in the client's mind via the client-as-reader. This requires knowledge of textual and literary theory.

Christoph Bode tackles the question of the necessity of literary theory in his essay "Why Theory Matters," in the course of which he puts forth arguments that touch upon aspects relevant to poetry therapy. Accordingly, Bode's arguments can illuminate the necessity for literary theory in poetry therapy. Literature as well as psychotherapy deal with texts. While literature in the traditional sense deals with written texts, psychotherapy takes as its subject matter the (ephemeral) text that is produced by the client's statements during the therapy session. Poetry therapy combines both types of texts in the poetic artefact. It is here that Bode's arguments become valid for the topic at hand. According to Bode, a text does not contain one single message, but "a text will, each time, respond to the specific (and inevitably partial) way it has been activated this time, so that each reading is a *necessarily partial* realisation or actualisation of the text's overall signifying potential" (Bode 89; emphasis original). This realisation, commonplace as it is nowadays in the realm of literary studies, has far-reaching consequences for poetry therapy. To begin with, it negates all concepts of poetry therapy that are purely receptive (including, of course, bibliotherapy), which thus become untenable. The basis of receptive poetry therapy/bibliotherapy is to select the poem according to the ISO-principle:

> Leedy believes that the isoprinciple, which Dr. Ira M. Altshuler advocates in music therapy, can be used effectively in poetry therapy as well. The principle of selecting music to correspond with the patient's mood or mental tempo translates, in terms of poetry therapy, into selecting sad or gloomy poems for depressed patients. (Crootof 41)

This may hold true on a general level, but since texts, and especially poems, can be actualised in quite unexpected ways, the therapist can never be sure if a poem fits "the patient's mood," i.e. if the client will realise the poem according to the ISO-principle, or not. A deliberate attempt on the therapist's side to guide the client to a reading according to the ISO-principle inevitably constitutes a poor reading in the sense that the client does not actively volunteer any new information about his condition. It is what Bode terms an "under-reading" (90), a failure to tap into the full potential of the

---

[28] Since 'poetry' is understood in the broad sense – the *OED*'s sixth meaning – there is no need for the poetry therapist to look closely at literary theory for a delineation of the term.

text. Apart from this fundamental drawback, there is another damaging effect resulting from such an approach: by fixing the manner in which a poem is to be understood in therapy (the ISO-principle), the reactions of the client are artificially curtailed. This is to be avoided, because the very way the client reads a poem gives the therapist insight into the client as well. There is

> a certain inevitable element of self-affirmation and self-confirmation in every act of reading and for every imaginable approach. [...] And exactly because this is true for *all* approaches and an inevitable condition of reading, it is so essential to be aware, as a reader, of one's own share in the production of what seems to be "there", in the text. [...] No subjectivity has a greater totalizing and even totalitarian claim than the one that truly believes itself to be objective and miraculously finds confirmation wherever it turns. (Bode 89-90; emphasis original)

The danger resulting from being uncritical of one's (theoretical) approach is the same for both the reader and the poetry therapist, namely "the poverty of [...] readings" (ibid. 90). By following the ISO-principle in poetry therapy one easily closes off the signifying potential of a text. Having chosen a 'sad' poem to work with a client who is suffering from depression, for example, leaves the therapist predisposed towards the reaction of the client. For the client, any response to such a poem can only be a limited form of expression; the client's movement of free association is, in contrast to the process of active poetic creation, curtailed. The result of this is a tendency in poetry therapy towards impoverished readings of the client's responses towards the poetry used. Any predisposition (on both the part of client and therapist) limits the signifying potential of the text. An impoverished reading of the client's text, that is, the client's part of the therapeutic discourse, is fatal to the therapeutic process, because it is simply self-assertive. The (therapeutic) outcome of such is reading is close to zero, because it only produces what is already known in the first place. In contrast to this, it is precisely the openness of the therapist with regard to the client's issues and personality as well as the possibilities for interpretation of what the client discloses in the session and how this is done that ensures therapeutic progress.

Closely connected to this is the well known problem of resistance in therapy. Therapists encounter resistance on the part of the client in almost every therapeutic session. This resistance is an unconscious one which has to be overcome in order for the client to improve. The underlying reason for the resistance of the client is unknown to the therapist and it is his/her job to uncover it. The therapist carefully tunes in on the individual client's moods and fashions the therapeutic method accordingly. In the same way, "every text offers a kind of resistance to my endeavours at understanding it. The resistance varies according to how smoothly my approach is geared to the text. [...] In any case, this resistance of the text is my only chance to escape the always imminent danger of circular self-confirmation and readerly solipsism" (ibid. 91). The above becomes important especially, but by far not exclusively so, when poems are concerned that have been produced by the client. The client, having produced the literary artefact, necessarily has a predisposed attitude towards the text. The client has an idea, a *theory*, about what the text is supposed to say or express and when talking about the text with the therapist, the client will naturally read the text accordingly. It is here that the therapist has to be aware of the "danger of circular self-confirmation." If the therapist is not aware of this, there will be no progress for the client as the poem will yield only that which is already known.[29] There will be no resistance in such a reading as its outcome is basically a foregone conclusion, a poor reading, an "under-reading:"

> It is only in the gap between what I expected and what I actually encountered that I can find room to grow, to become, if ever so slightly, different from what I was before, in short: to change. It is the alterity of the text, its unexpected strangeness, that gives me something I didn't have before, something that in a way enriches me after baffling me. The acknowledgement of this otherness of the text, the respect for its enriching (and disturbing) alterity, presupposes that I am aware of a difference between my own tentative projections and that Other towards which they are directed. (Bode 91)

To become aware of the "unexpected strangeness," or "the otherness of the text" is the function of (literary) theory and it is at the same time the foundation of all psychoanalytical treatment. Only by discovering one's own strangeness within oneself can one gain deeper self-knowledge. The same is true of literary texts. Without discovering the gap in the surface structure of a text, one cannot actualise the hidden or marginalized meanings of that text. The therapist is already proficient in this basic method when it comes to discourse, but what is missing is the skill of applying this to poetry in a manner that goes beyond looking for the use of poetic devices and identifying a poetic genre. The poem basically represents fossilised discourse of the client with his or her other self and it includes all the traces of this discourse. These traces are unknown to both the client and the therapist and can be brought to the surface by a conscious application of principles of literary theory by the therapist. The therapist has to have a range of literary approaches at his disposal. Only from this basis can the therapist arrive at a deeper reading of the client's text, which allows for the discovery of unconscious influences within the text's semiotic system. Thus, the therapist has to guide the client-as-reader, and especially as reader of his/her own poetic artefact, away from the obvious reading – the "under-reading" – towards a reading that generates resistance from the text. This resistance is the manifestation of the "disturbing alterity" the text constitutes for the client. By working with the resistance of the text and eventually overcoming it, clients arrive at a new interpretation which increases their respective self-knowledge and serves to solve unconscious conflicts. This is an approach fundamentally different from the ISO-principle; it is a truly creative approach in that it puts

---

[29] In such a case, the only therapeutic aid from poetry will come from the creative experience of writing the poem. The process of poetic creation has a positive effect on the client. Apart from the short-term relief and pleasure brought about by the creation of the poem as such, a reading according to the client's predispositions will leave much of the therapeutic potential of poetry untapped. This is also a question of transference. Since clients will, at least at the beginning of the therapeutic endeavour, strive to please the therapist, the result of their reading will unconsciously be what they think the therapist wants to hear.

the client in an active position by calling for an innovative interpretation. It leads both participants of the therapeutic encounter into a voyage of discovery.

To sum up, literary theory facilitates a more subtle approach in guiding clients in their own reading(s) of (their own) poetry, opening up possibilities of self-recognition in the individual client. Literary theory and psychotherapy supplement each other congenially since literary theory "is the fascinating instance of a dialectical merger of systematic and methodological thinking on the one hand and free speculation, openness and *imaginative creativity* on the other" (Bode 99; emphasis original).

1.3 The Pervasiveness of the Romantic Tradition in contemporary Psychotherapy and its Influence on Poetry Therapy

Just as psychotherapeutic theory has diversified and evolved in its now over 100 years, incorporating post-structuralist concepts (cf., for instance, Lacan and Kristeva in the case of psychoanalysis), so has literary theory. Any reading and understanding of what a text, and, therefore, what a poem is and how this text or poem relates to the world, is shaped by how a text is approached. Literary theory provides scholarly validation to the manner texts are approached. In order for poetry therapy to be based on a solid theoretical basis it is thus vital to have a certain level of proficiency in literary theory as well. Given this importance, it is surprising not to find it in the official curricula of the NAPT and NFBPT. This is even more astonishing when one considers that there have been curricula proposals as early as the late 1960s which called for an inclusion of literary studies in the training of poetry therapists. Edgar and Hazley proposed a training programme, which

> would require the establishment of a new curriculum that would embrace training in both psychology and literature. While no departure from conventional training in clinical psychology would be necessary insofar as the standard courses are concerned, the courses in literature would need to be specifically designed not only to provide the necessary background but also to make the therapist aware of the symbolism and psychological schemata in poetry. Because the selection of appropriate poems is critical, the therapist must have an extensive knowledge of the literature of poetry and the awareness of psychological schemata that such training should provide.[30] (263)

The above proposal suggests an increase in the literary education of poetry therapists which would go a long way to making the discipline truly interdisciplinary. Edgar and Hazley even state that "at least one course in literary criticism is also suggested" (264) and they include an undergraduate "Introduction to Literary Criticism" course in their proposal for a curriculum for the training of poetry therapists. Their suggestion has apparently not been not taken over. Instead, one can find in the literature on poetry

---

[30] Note the conception of poetry therapy as a purely receptive practice. Edgar and Hazley follow Leedy's ISO-principle and confine poetry therapy to "the selection of appropriate poems."

therapy a pervasive influence of Romantic[31] literary criticism and tradition. One can trace a concept of literary theory at work which dates back more than 200 years. The understanding of the poetic process, the poetic artefact, the process of reading and their interrelatedness to the outside world is charged with notions of the Romantic tradition. To wit, contemporary understanding of the poetic processes in poetry therapy is rooted in Romantic, or, more precisely, Wordsworthian poetics.

I will start by retracing the influence and development of the Romantic tradition on psychotherapy in general, before turning to the repercussions the continued validity of Romantic notions has for poetry therapy today. In this way, the origin and mechanisms of the Romantic influence on poetry therapy will become obvious. The problems specific to poetry therapy which originate from this will be the focus of the final part of this chapter.

Before sketching the historical foundations of poetry therapy (5 passim), Mazza states that "[p]oetry therapy reflects the classic issues in literary analysis and psychological practice: the romantic aspects of empathy and subjectivity vs. reason and observation" (4). Here, Mazza ascribes subjectivity and feeling to the poetic aspect of poetry therapy, while he reserves reason and objectivity for the psychological. In fact, his aim is to make evident the close connection between poetry as an art and psychotherapy as a science. In doing so he takes recourse to Wordsworth, stating that "Wordsworth did not substitute feelings for knowledge, but rather bound them together" (4). This "romantic approach" (ibid.) is prevalent in all the major theoretical works regarding poetry therapy and it is a sub-current in much of the writings on literature-based therapies. Given the pan-European importance of the Romantic Movement and the pervasiveness of its ideas in virtually all forms of discourses, it is not surprising that the psychotherapeutical discourse has not been exempted. Romanticism in psychotherapy has a long history. Indeed, from its earliest beginnings, psychotherapy has always been steeped in Romantic notions (cf. Schneider 277 passim), which is only natural when we remember Freud's familiarity with and inclination toward the Romantic tradition.

Freud's conception of the writer/poet owes much to Romantic thinking. Throughout his correspondence and work, Freud exemplifies his ideas by drawing on Romantic predecessors. In "A Note on the Prehistory of the Technique of Analysis," for instance, Freud mentions Schiller: "Those who are familiar with psycho-analytic literature will recall at this point the interesting passage in Schiller's correspondence with Körner in which (1788) the great poet and thinker recommends anyone who desires to be productive to adopt the method of free association" (264). Another prime example can be found in "Creative Writers and Daydreaming" where Freud describes

---

[31] I will distinguish the term 'romantic' from the term 'Romantic'. The term 'romantic' denotes the common meaning ascribes to it today as in phrases like "a romantic movie" or "He was very romantic, lighting candles and having music played in the background." The term 'Romantic' refers to the Romantic Movement in philosophy, literature and the arts of the late 18th and early 19th centuries.

the creative process as follows: "A strong experience in the present awakens in the creative writer a memory of an earlier experience (usually belonging to his childhood) from which there now proceeds a wish to find its fulfilment in the creative work. The work itself exhibits elements of the recent provoking occasion as well as of the old memory" (151). This statement is reminiscent of Wordsworth's theory of poetic creation (cf. "Preface to Lyrical Ballads"). Wordsworth locates the spark of creation in the poet's world of experience which includes both what is perceived by the senses of the outer world and of past experiences in the form of memories. These two worlds are connected by the poet's thoughts and feelings, "[f]or our continued influxes of feeling are modified and directed by our thoughts, which are indeed the representatives of all our past feelings" (Wordsworth, "Preface" 438-439). Freud, like Wordsworth, conceives of the creative urge as emerging from a nexus of past and present experiences that produce a strong feeling which demands to be expressed. The connection to childhood experiences mentioned by Freud, as well as Freud's concept of sublimation, i.e. wish fulfilment, can easily be traced in Wordsworth's *Prelude*:

> Sometimes it suits me better to invent
> A tale from my own heart, more near akin
> To my own passions and habitual thoughts;
> Some variegated story, in the main
> Lofty, but the unsubstantial structure melts
> Before the very sun that brightens it,
> Mist into air dissolving! Then a wish,
> My last and favourite aspiration, mounts
> With yearning toward some philosophic song
> Of Truth that cherishes our daily life;   230
> With meditations passionate from deep
> Recesses in man's heart, immortal verse
> Thoughtfully fitted to the Orphean lyre;
> (*Prelude* [1850 Version], Book 1, 221-233)

Freud's "wish to find its fulfilment in the creative work" is present almost verbatim in Wordsworth's poem (227-229). The poet talks of an "unsubstantial structure" (225) originating from "passions and habitual thoughts" (223) which can be equated with Freud's "strong experience in the present" connected to childhood experiences. This triggers a "wish" (227) in the poet to cast this feeling/experience in a poem ("philosophic song" 229), which is achieved by "meditations passionate" (231), i.e. a combination of thought and feeling. In the *Prelude,* Wordsworth thus describes a process of wish fulfilment which is very much in line with the theories expounded by Freud.

    Given the close propinquity of Freud's concepts and core notions of Romanticism, the continued presence of Romantic concepts in psychotherapy is no surprise. The Romantic tradition is deeply ingrained in psychotherapy, so deeply, in fact, that Schneider is seriously concerned when he perceives that "American psychology has conspicuously distanced itself from its romantic roots" (277).[32] Although Schneider detects a distancing from the "romantic roots," Schneider's statement proves that, indeed, the Romantic tradition is still at the heart of psychotherapy. The "romantic roots" of psychotherapy Schneider identifies account for the presence of the Romantic discourse in the circles of poetry therapists. There is, however, an important difference between the conception of Romanticism as used by Schneider and Romanticism as it is understood and applied practically by the majority of poetry therapists. The difference is important as it relates directly to the professional application of literary theory in poetry therapy, showing in which way Wordsworthian concepts of (poetic) creativity abound. For Schneider, the term 'Romanticism' has a twofold meaning and legacy within psychotherapeutic practice and discourse. His definition is worth quoting in full here:

> I recognize two basic strains of psychological romanticism. The first strain derives from the literary and artistic legacy of 18th century thinkers such as Lord Byron [sic] and Goethe and stresses individual depth and experience. This lineage was then extended and elaborated on by European and American thinkers, such as Schopenhauer, Kierkegaard, Emerson, and Thoreau, and subsequently by the phenomenological and existential philosophers, such as Husserl, Sartre, and Camus. The individualist lineage culminated, finally, in the humanistic and existential psychology movements of Europe and America. The second strain of romanticism also derives from the 18th century rebellion against 17th century rationalism, but it emphasizes collective depth and experience. This heritage, which originated in the works of Schlegel, Herder, and Schiller in the 18th and 19th centuries and culminated in the philosophical and psychological works of Heidegger, Gadamer, Ricoeur, and others […], focused on the "need for traditional and social order" in self-expression, over and above subjective individualism […]. (280)

Schneider isolates two schools of "psychological romanticism," meaning the adaptation of Romantic concepts within psychological discourses. The first strain of "psychological romanticism" focuses on the individual and its right and capacity for self-actualisation. The second line is interested more in the social dimension of self-expression and the relationship between the individual and society. Having isolated the two traditions, Schneider retraces the lineage of each strain from its origin in classical Romanticism to its modern manifestation. The first tradition culminates in phenomenological and existential philosophy via, predominantly, Husserl, Schopenhauer, and Kierkegaard. Schneider's second strain is carried into the twenty-first century by the

---

[32] These roots have, according to Schneider, been neglected and/or come under assault from postmodernism on the one side and the move of the psychological profession towards "brief, standardized, and so-called cost-effective services" (279) on the other. Schneider is primarily concerned with the contemporary development of psychology as a profession, arguing for a stronger incorporation of "romantic practices" (which can be roughly equated with the humanistic approach to psychology [cf. Chapter 2 of this study]) in the light of "market-driven forces […] to evaluate mental health services" (ibid.). This controversy, while fascinating, lies outside the scope of this study and Schneider's essay is relevant here only in so far as it relates to the current relationship between Romantic theory and contemporary psychotherapeutic practice.

philosophies of "Heidegger, Gadamer, Ricoeur, and others." By retracing the history and the development of the two strains of Romanticism in psychology, Schneider locates and situates Romanticism within contemporary psychological discourse. When he uses the term 'Romanticism' or "romantic approach" he is thus not talking about a 200-year-old concept, but he refers to the contemporary manifestation of the original discursive formation. "The most recent manifestations of the romantic in psychology are seen in the orientations of existential-humanistic, hermeneutical, narrative, semiotic, cultural, relational, transpersonal, and ecological psychologies" (ibid.). This places "psychological romanticism" firmly within the post-structural discourses of our time.[33] The "psychological romanticism" that prevails in the psychotherapies is a form of Romanticism that has naturally evolved with and within the discipline and is therefore a modern and contemporary Romanticism.

Since poetry therapy is a psychotherapeutic approach, it has also taken over this (implicit) Romanticism that exists in psychotherapy in general. The two concepts of Romanticism delineated by Schneider – one primarily concerned with the individual as such and the second with its collective experience – are also widespread in the writings on poetry therapy. Mazza, for instance, states that "[c]entral to a romantic approach to clinical practice is a concern for the human 'lifeworld' featuring: (1) affect, imagination, and intuition; (2) holistic content; and (3) practitioner (investigator) as participant" (4). The theoretical foundations of poetry therapy, insofar as they coincide with those of general psychotherapy, are thus based on Romantic principles as well. Since poetry therapy constitutes an interdisciplinary "interface of the arts and psychology," to quote the subtitle of the first edition of Mazza's book, the Romantic (predominantly in the form of what Schneider calls the first strain) is bound to be more assertive in theoretical works on poetry therapy and this is indeed the case. While the influence of the contemporalised psychological Romanticism is indeed traceable in the literature on poetry therapy, there is also a strain of unaltered literary Romanticism that is taken over for the poetic side of poetry therapy. When it came to constituting its literary side, poetry therapists drew explicit connections to the literary Romantic Movement based on the "psychological romanticism" already partaking in their discipline. When it comes to the creation, use and application of poetry within the therapeutic practice this recourse to the original literary Romanticism becomes problematic, because, in contrast to the psychological, the 'literary' strain of Romanticism in poetry therapy has not been contemporalised. The problem is that poetry therapy failed to bring the Romantic ideas that were appropriated from literary Romanticism into a contemporary theoretical framework. The poetry side of poetry therapy is thus based on concepts that are 200 years old. On the following pages I will delineate the processes, negotiations and effects of the adoption of unaltered Romantic notions for poetry therapy.

---

[33] Schneider addresses the apparent dichotomy of Romanticism and postmodernist thinking in the latter part of his essay (286 passim) and concludes that, indeed, Romanticism as he conceives it has its place in a postmodern context.

In discussing the creative process and its function within poetry therapy, Mazza bases his argument on Wordsworth's "Preface to the Lyrical Ballads" (and to a lesser extent Shelley's *Defense of Poetry*). He does so by citing, among others, Cartwright and Lerner. This is done, first of all, to elucidate the pervasiveness of the Romantic tradition in poetry therapy, but at the same time this means that Mazza's understanding of Romanticism in poetry therapy is gained through the lens of his fellow theorists. Possible misinterpretations and misconceptions are thus perpetuated. Mazza's recourse to Wordsworthian poetics when it comes to literary theory also means that Romantic poetics are applied virtually unchanged in a contemporary, postmodern environment. The fact that Romantic literary theory is employed unchanged pervades theoretical writings on poetry therapy. This manifests itself either by way of direct quotes from Wordsworth and Shelley or through the specific understanding of the creative process and how it is elaborated. The latter is a kind of oblique Romanticism and is evident, for instance, in the connection drawn by Charles Ansell between the poet and perception: "Only the poet knows in a very special way that perception is the artist's principal gift. With perception he can shape and reshape all manner of experience" (14). Ansell's argument echoes Wordsworth's definition of the poet in the "Preface" as "a man endowed with more lively sensibility, more enthusiasm and tenderness, who has a greater knowledge of human nature and a more comprehensive soul" (440). According to Wordsworth, the poet's greater sensibility relates directly to his perception of the world, which poets then "reshape" in their poetry.[34] A similar argument is put forth by Shelley in his *Defense of Poetry*. He states of poets that they are "of the most delicate sensibility and the most enlarged imagination" (527). Furthermore, with regard to perception, Shelley states that "[a]ll things exist as they are perceived; at least in relation to the percipient. [...] But poetry defeats the curse which binds us to be subjected to the accident of surrounding impressions" (ibid.). The parallels to Ansell are obvious.

A similar instance of oblique Romanticism can be found in Leedy. In his essay "The Principles of Poetry Therapy," he observes that "poetry therapy helps patients to become more spontaneous and creative. Poetry is one of Man's deepest expressions, and emotions are thereby released. A poem has been described as the shortest distance between two points, the points representing the writer and the reader" (70). The beginning of Leedy's statement is basically a paraphrase of Wordsworth's famous definition of poetry as "a spontaneous overflow of powerful feelings"[35] ("Preface" 444). The "spontaneous" release of emotions through poetry by clients reflects Leedy's understanding of Wordsworth's poetic theory. The poem as "the shortest distance" between writer and reader suggests the function of poetry as a mediator of knowledge or insight, which, too, can be traced to Romantic poetics. While this idea is definitely

---

[34] Cf., for instance, Wordsworth's poetological poem "I Wandered Lonely as a Cloud."

[35] I am aware that Wordsworth's conception of the poetic process is by far more complicated than this and I will deal with the psychological misinterpretation of it further down. For now it is more important to clarify the pervasiveness of unaltered Romantic poetics in the understanding of poetry therapists.

present in Wordsworth (cf. "Preface," especially 441-443), Shelley's entire *Defense of Poetry* is a means to conceptualise poets as "the institutors of law, and the founders of civil society, and the inventors of the arts of life, and the teachers" (517) of truth and universal knowledge, and poetry as "the center and circumference of knowledge" (526).

The above examples have clearly shown the predominance of Romantic literary theory in the understanding of poetry and poetics in poetry therapy today.[36] The understanding of poetic creativity in poetry therapy thus follows a 200-year-old system which leaves the insights and developments of poetic and literary theory – which include a revaluation of Romantic concepts – unrecognised and untapped. While the unmodified application of Romantic poetics is highly questionable in its own right, there is another problem that affects poetry therapy in particular. The Romantics are often misquoted and/or misunderstood. This inevitably leads to a grave misunderstanding of what Romantic literary theory is in fact about. The most frequently encountered misquotation is Wordsworth's definition of poetry. Crootof, who cites Wordsworth in the following passage in which he links the origin of poetry to that of dreams, will serve as an example here:

> The poem and the dream both originate in the unconscious; both are created by "spontaneous overflow of powerful feelings." Both rely on the "suspension of disbelief." Whether it be the *willing* suspension of disbelief, as in the hearer of the poem, or the *unwilling* suspension, as in the dreamer, in both instances the processes of reality-testing are either completely disregarded or kept waiting in the wings. (45)

---

[36] The list could be continued. In the preface to Leedy's *Poetry Therapy*, Lewis Wolberg cites Keats's "On First Looking into Chapman's Homer" as an example for what he terms "a particular revealing intuitive communication from the poet" (9). Charles Crootof cites Eli Greifer as rejecting the therapeutic use of the modernists such as T.S. Eliot in favour of poems containing "basic verities found in such poetry as Longfellow's" (41). Yet another instance is the list presented by Leedy which consists of Coleridge, Keats, Longfellow, Poe and Byron ("Principles of Poetry Therapy" 70). Allusions to Wordsworth also occur in Robinson and Mowbray's "Why Poetry," who note that "the poet has the sensitivity to be aware of his own and others' impulses, dreams and fantasies and the courage to express them verbally" (192). A Romantic substratum is clearly present in Harrower. In the following example, one of many to be found in the book, taken from Chapter 1 entitled "Poems and Poets Grow," one can spot in the elucidation of the creative process distinct allusions to Romantic poetics. Harrower invokes Wordsworth when speaking about the process of self-understanding: "Early poems, incidentally, reflect a 'child is father to [sic] the man' motif which, if accepted by the poet as expressing certain idiosyncratic needs, may be used as guide lines for self-understanding" (4). Harrower's quote from Wordsworth is faulty. The line is taken from Wordsworth's "My Heart Leaps Up When I Behold" and should read: "The Child is father of the man." Harrower's misquotation is yet another instance of the negligence when it comes to literary/poetic aspects of poetry therapy. Morrison's *Poetry as Therapy*, too, is clearly based on the use of Romantic poetics in psychotherapy (cf. especially Chapter 2: "Poetry Therapy in the Context of Art Therapy").

To which extent and in how far poetry originates in the unconscious is a question that has to be postponed for now.[37] What is relevant at the moment is that poetry, according to Wordsworth, is more than "a spontaneous overflow of powerful feelings" and can only come about by *conscious* thought. Crootof quotes Wordsworth incompletely.[38] The full quotation offers a more subtle and more comprehensive account of the creative process:

> [P]oetry is the spontaneous overflow of powerful feelings; it takes its origin from emotions recollected in tranquillity: the emotion is contemplated till, by a species of reaction, the tranquillity gradually disappears, and an emotion kindred to that which was before the subject of contemplation, is gradually produced, and does itself actually exist in the mind. ("Preface" 444)

Wordsworth states that poetry *is* "a spontaneous overflow of powerful feelings" which is quite different from saying, as Crootof does, that "poetry is created by" it. Wordsworth locates the creation of the poem in "emotions recollected in tranquillity" which is to say, poetry consists of emotions that reappear in moments of mental equilibrium. In contradistinction to what Crootof seems to believe, namely that poetry somehow shapes itself out of a chaotic emotional turmoil, which in itself already constitutes a form of psychic relief, Wordsworth's "spontaneous overflow" is the result of thought processes ("the emotion is contemplated") which brings about a modified emotion ("kindred emotion"). It is this second emotion which will enter the poem. For Wordsworth, poems produced in a state of emotional turmoil cannot but be weak and ineffective as "emanations of reality and truth" ("Preface" 441) since "excitement is an unusual and irregular state of mind; ideas and feelings do not, in that state, succeed each other in accustomed order" (ibid. 444). To state, as Crootof does, in the context of Wordsworthian poetics that in poetry "reality-testing" is non-existent or endlessly deferred is a misconception of Romantic poetic theory on the most fundamental level.

The continued influence and relevance of Romantic ideas in psychotherapy and especially writing-based therapies has led to theoretical misconceptions in the field of poetry therapy. In poetry therapy, the contemporary understanding of the term 'Romanticism' in psychology as elaborated by Schneider became mingled with (the misapprehension of) Romantic literary theory: the oblique Romanticism, which is at the root of most writing-based therapies and art therapies, was taken up by poetry therapist in a literal fashion via Romantic poetics. In poetry therapy, Romantic poetics have been integrated into the discipline unchanged, that is, without adapting it to our postmodern world. Secondly, the original Romantic notions of poetry and creation have been taken over in a highly simplified and often even distorted manner. The theoretical disarray poetry therapy is currently caught in, is entangled with the misconceptions of

---

[37] For an in-depth discussion of this topic cf. Chapter 3 of this study.

[38] The incomplete quotation of Wordsworth's famous definition is a common occurrence not only in psychotherapeutic circles but generally. Mazza is aware of this, noting that "Wordsworth's definition of poetry is often only partially cited as 'the spontaneous overflow of powerful feelings'" (4).

the Romantic and the practice of poetry therapy has in no small part been shaped by this.

In addition to the misapprehensions resulting from partial citations – and consequently partial understandings – of Romantic poetics, a similar tendency can be observed with regard to the discourse pertaining to the difference between prose and verse language. Poetry therapy suffers from a prevalent confusion concerning the Romantic differentiation of prose and poetry/verse. As a result, poetry therapy has not been able to successfully differentiate itself from other writing-based therapies that use prose language. Once again, Mazza provides the first example of the problem. Right at the beginning of his book he states that "the underlying assumption of this book is that, in poetry, form does not supersede content or function" (3). It is not entirely clear what Mazza is aiming at with this statement, but it serves as a point of departure for his discussion of the Romantic approach in poetry therapy. Therefore, it can be safely assumed that the above statement is meant to be understood in the context of psychological Romanticism. If we take Romanticism to denote what Schneider describes as the "first strain," Mazza's statement simply claims a humanistic approach for his book, emphasising that what is important in poetry therapy is the content and function rather than the aesthetic qualities of the poem's formal structure, "that in poetry therapy the focus is on the person, not the poem" (5). This is certainly a valid point and, indeed, should be the basis for all art-based therapies as those involved are, for the most part, amateurs rather than professional artists. Still, within the field of poetry therapy it is problematic to discard form altogether. In order for poetry therapy to be dissociated from other writing-based therapies, it is indispensable to uphold a distinction between the language of prose and of poetry. Unfortunately, this vital distinction is often nullified or even denied in contemporary poetry therapy discourse. Mazza, perhaps to address this question, concedes that "[h]eightened emotions and compressed meaning are central to poetry" (ibid.). This is true as well, but not exclusively so of poetry. "Heightened emotions" appear as much in prose writings (be it fiction, diaries or letters) while one might, somewhat maliciously, argue that "compressed meaning" is a defining characteristic of instruction manuals. The Romantic influence on the theoretical conceptualisation of poetry therapy converges here with a misunderstanding of Romantic concepts and this has led to a misunderstanding of the nature of poetry as such.

When Cartwright quotes Shelley as stating that "every author is necessarily a poet, because language itself is poetry." (Cartwright 390; also qtd. in Mazza 4), he is citing Shelley out of context and only partially. In his *Defense of Poetry*,[39] Shelley

---

[39] Shelley's *Defense of Poetry* was written in answer to Thomas Love Peacock's *The Four Ages of Poetry*. Peacock sympathised with neo-classical critical principles and wrote his *Four Ages* as an attack on Romantic poetics and the state of poetry in the early 19th century. It is in this light that Shelley's arguments have to be evaluated, and the *Defense* is therefore to a certain extent polemical and satirical. Shelley claims enormous powers for the poet with regard to personal insight, philosophical enlightenment, moral virtue and

actually says: "*In the infancy of society*, every author is necessarily a poet, because language itself is poetry" (517; my emphasis). Shelley is in no way arguing that there is no difference between the language of prose and poetry. He is talking about a prehistoric past in which the "copiousness of lexicography and the distinctions of grammar" (ibid.) were not yet developed, which is to say there was no distinction between prose and poetry *yet*. This does not mean that such a distinction has not come into being since. In fact, Shelley concedes that "words [...] become, through time, signs for portions or classes of thought, instead of pictures of integral thought" (ibid.). In its infancy, language, for Shelley, consists of "pictures of integral thought" while in its later stages words are "signs for portions or classes of thought." The latter language is that of prose and Shelley considers it fragmented and cut off from the creative language of verse the poet still has access to. This is made evident by Shelley through the constitution of dialectical opposites. The first dichotomy he sets up is between "pictures" and "signs." Signs are simple representations of concepts and actual things, whereas pictures are a much more engaging way of depicting the world. In contrast to signs, pictures have a mimetic aspect and are thus much more closely related to reality. The second dichotomy Shelley constitutes is related to the first and consists of "integral thought" vs. "portions or classes of thought." The expression of thought in verse is "integral," which means that it is inclusive of all aspects of the experience it describes. In contrast to this, the language of prose is divided into classes which suggest an artificial grouping of thought according to categories. In Shelley's conception there is thus a fundamental difference between verse and prose, which a close reading of the text clearly brings to the surface. It is the function of the poet of modern times to "create afresh the associations which have been thus disorganised" (ibid.). The language of poetry thus revitalises the language of prose. Despite using the term 'poetry' in a very broad sense, Shelley feels it is important "to determine the distinction between measured and unmeasured language," i.e. between poetry and prose. This proves that, indeed, there is a difference between the two types of language for Shelley[40] and Cartwright is wrong to state that "Shelley, in fact, made no distinction between poetry and prose as imaginative literature" (390). In spite of the above examples, the necessity for a clear-cut distinction between prose and poetry as well as the dangers of a recourse to Romantic literary theory have been acknowledged by psychologists and psychoanalysts. Snyder, for instance, writes that

> although poems can be created within a wide range of structures, the poet remains conscious of the structure of each part within the whole as well as of the whole. In a successful poem, as in a successful painting, sculpture, or musical composition, both composer and recipient experience the form as essential to conveying the 'truth' as the subject. (339)

---

incorruptibility, and, finally, the potential to affect changes in society, stating at one point in Platonic fashion that the "poet participates in the eternal, the infinite, and the one" (517).

[40] The same is true for Wordsworth (cf. "Preface" 440 passim).

Snyder argues for a unity between form and function and also conceives of the poetic artefact as a means of communication in which the form is essential for both the "composer" and the "recipient." For Snyder, the "nature of poetic form is that it opens space for whatever 'is', and therefore for experiencing that which is painful, chaotic, contradictory and confusing" (340) and thus it constitutes the very medium through which the conflicts of the client can be approached.

To sum up, the Romantic legacy that proliferates in psychotherapy can also be found in poetry therapy. Given the interdisciplinary nature of poetry therapy this is not surprising. It has been shown, however, that the general neglect of the poetry aspect of poetry therapy has made the appropriation of the Romantic tradition to poetry therapy problematic to say the least. Firstly, theorists and practitioners of poetry therapy, in order to validate their use of poetry theoretically, have taken recourse to Romantic poetics to explicate the process of poetic creation. In doing so, they have not, as Schneider has clearly shown for psychotherapy in general, traced the lineage of Romantic poetics to its contemporary manifestation. Rather, Romantic poetic theories were taken over in their original form. As a consequence, poetry therapy conceptualises the poetic process on the basis of a 200-year-old theory, leaving aside all the developments in literary theory and poetics since then. Secondly, Romantic poetics as taken over by poetry therapy are, in addition to being 200 years old, misapprehended. Misquotations and distorted understandings of Romantic poetics abound, which leads to a disproportional emphasis on spontaneity and the immediate expression of feeling with regard to the client.

Returning to the original question at the beginning of this chapter one can state that the lack of a clear definition and the general uncertainty surrounding the term 'poetry therapy' is based upon and manifests itself in the diverse practices currently associated with poetry therapy. These practices are grouped by Mazza as:

> The receptive/prescriptive component involving the introduction of literature into therapy.
>
> The expressive/creative component involving the use of client writing in therapy.
>
> The symbolic/ceremonial component involving the use of metaphors, rituals, and storytelling.
> (Mazza 17)

Mazza considers these three categories as integrative in the sense that they constitute the parts of a "poetry therapy practice model" (17). Strangely, Mazza continues to explain and elaborate on each category individually and the case studies he presents at the end of his discussions (22-23) do not constitute examples of an integrative model using all of the above approaches. In any case, there are a number of problems with these categories, which arise from the lack of a proper theoretical foundation. The first category could much more sensibly be grouped under bibliotherapy which would at the same time serve to dissociate the two forms of therapy. By including what is essentially the field of bibliotherapy in poetry therapy, the borders of both disciplines are unnecessarily blurred, thus compounding the emergence of what Foucault would call a 'discursive formation' (cf. *The Archaeology of Knowledge*) of poetry therapy.[41] The third, the symbolic/ceremonial component is, firstly, not unique to poetry therapy and, secondly, it can be subsumed under the other two categories. As a result it can be neglected. The second category is closer to the heart of poetry therapy when it is situated within art therapy. In order to be able to narrow down the field I will – for now[42] – restrict the use of the term poetry therapy to the "expressive/creative component involving the use of client writing in therapy." Restricting poetry therapy to the creative aspect helps to close in on a practical definition, which is both reflective and constitutive of a theoretical framework. Such a framework has to be flexible enough to accommodate the diverse practices subsumed under the term 'poetry therapy'. To do so, it must be able to provide answers to the following basic questions:

1) How do poetry therapy methods compare to other methods of therapy using the written word?

2) Is one poetry therapy approach superior to another?

3) How does poetry therapy work, i.e. what happens during the process of poetic writing and what role does creativity play in the outcome of therapy?[43]

The first question is important for the demarcation of poetry therapy from other fields of treatment. It is necessary to ascertain the healing potential and function of poetic language in contrast to prose-based writing therapies in order to establish poetry therapy's right to exist as a therapeutic form in its own right. For the present study, the answer to the second question is of interest only peripherally as it depends to a great extent on the therapist and individual client which approach is to be preferred and deemed most useful. As for the third question, poetry therapy as I understand it involves at its core artistic production by the client. Elucidating the (creative) processes active in poetic writing will provide a better understanding of the way poetry therapy can affect mental health, because

> poetry, created or used during the therapeutic encounter, can often help a patient to reach levels of emotional insight more adequately than conventional dialogue. It enriches the encounter by allowing the patient to identify with other human beings, who have experienced similar conflicts, anxieties, and feelings, and who have been able to state, for all humanity, a universal theme or dilemma. (Berger 75)

---

[41] For the practice of poetry therapy, or bibliotherapy for that matter, it is mostly irrelevant, of course, which label is put on the therapeutic approach. For the task of fundamental research into the theory of poetry therapy – and this is what all research in this field currently belongs to –, however, a careful and sensible demarcation of the field of study is indispensable.

[42] Later on I will introduce a receptive concept into poetry therapy, but one that is not prescriptive and quite different from the one Mazza suggests.

[43] This list is loosely based on the list in Mazza 107.

The only way towards a better understanding of the effectiveness of poetry therapy and, more specifically, poetic processes is by taking seriously the interdisciplinary nature of the approach. Parker notes that "[p]sychoanalytic theory, as well as the introspective reports of creative and re-creative artists, helps [sic] us to understand aesthetic experience and thus to make possible the utilization of poetry as a systematic therapeutic modality" (156), advocating attention to the artistic as much as to the psychotherapeutic aspects. Although Mazza views the interdisciplinary nature of poetry therapy as a hindrance, saying that "[f]or the purpose of research, terminology remains a problem due, in part, to its interdisciplinary base and differential use" (Mazza 105), I believe the interdisciplinary nature of poetry therapy is the key to providing it with a workable theoretical basis. This is even more so since the "professional community of psychology at the moment prefers the rhetoric of research and verbatim case study" (Hillman 3). Consequently, my concern in the following chapters will be predominantly with the creative process in poetic writing, because that aspect has been particularly neglected. Since poetry therapy is interdisciplinary, one must never forget to interface the poetic with the therapeutic for only in unity can both parts be most effective. Questions of applicability and practicality thus always inform the theoretical discussions. In this sense the aim of this study is somewhere between theory and method. "Theories generally provide premises, which lay the foundation for the framework of categories, whereas methods provide the tool for processes of interpretation" (Iser, "Key Concepts" 5). Poetry therapy is in need of both, fundamental premises as well as tools for the interpretation of client poems in a therapeutic setting. If method is basically applied theory, a concrete token of an abstract concept, then the categories of a precisely defined poetry therapy will inevitably lead to a demarcation of the sensible limits of the actual practice of poetry therapy. In the following chapters, I will chart the possibilities of a post-structuralist poetry therapy in a field of constant negotiation between theory and method. I will begin by situating poetry therapy within the art therapies and draw fundamental insight about creativity, the arts and therapy from there. In a second step I will deal with the way unconscious influences seep into writing in general and poetic texts in particular by utilising post-structuralist concepts of Derrida, Lacan and Kristeva. Having done so, I will look into the receptive phase of poetry therapy which involves literary interpretation of the clients' poems and apply reader-response theories to the process as well as concepts drawn from Foucault's writings on discourse.[44] By means of the application of post-structural (literary) theories and concepts, I will bring the 'poetic half' of poetry therapy into the contemporary discourse and neutralise the harmful influence of misconceived Romantic traditions.

---

[44] Cf. also the fact that Mazza lists 19 areas of research in poetry therapy for the 21st century (115-117).

2. Poetry Therapy in the Context of Art Therapy

> My Passions when once they were lighted up, raged like so many devils, till they got vent in rhyme; and then the coming over my verses, like a spell, soothed all into quiet. (Robert Burns, "Letter to Dr. John Moore" 141)

Having established, in the previous chapter, the general validity of poetry therapy concepts for therapeutic purposes, the points of intersection between poetry therapy and psychotherapy, as well as the problems pertaining to the current state of poetry therapy as a discipline, it remains to be determined where exactly poetry therapy can find a home, both with regard to theory and practice, within the wide range of therapies that exist today. In this respect, it is not so much a question of whether or not poetry therapy is particularly useful in ego therapy, behavioural therapy, cognitive psychology, Freudian, Jungian or Kleinian psychoanalysis and so forth. While it is true that some therapeutic practices are more likely to incorporate poetry therapy than others – a Jungian approach as opposed to a classical Freudian one, for instance –, in practice, psychotherapy works with a mixture of approaches, depending on the therapist and the therapeutic institution in question. This basically eclectic procedure is determined by the idiosyncratic needs of the individuals in therapy and also – especially in mental institutions – the variety of therapeutic training represented by the staff members. Therefore, it would be futile to try and assign poetry therapy to one particular 'school' of psychotherapy. Rather, this chapter will situate poetry therapy within the broad field of art therapy. Poetry therapy finds a natural home within art therapy not only because poetry is a form of art, but because art therapy is inherently interdisciplinary and can interface with virtually all forms of classical psychotherapy. The interdisciplinary nature of poetry therapy, which has been considered by Mazza to be among the problematic features regarding the delineation, understanding and theorising of the discipline, is a common feature in art therapy. As a consequence, concepts of art therapy, when applied to poetry therapy, clarify and emphasise the connection not only of the two disciplines within poetry therapy, but also with traditional psychotherapies.

As has already been stated briefly in the previous chapter, poetry therapy belongs to and consequently shares many theoretical foundations with art therapy.[45] A

---

[45] For an introduction to the field of art therapy, cf. Rubin, *Art Therapy: An Introduction*; Warren, *Using the Creative Arts in Therapy: A Practical Introduction*; Moon, *Introduction to Art Therapy: Faith in the Product*; Dalley, *Art as Therapy: An Introduction to the Use of Art as a Therapeutic Technique*. On the question of the theoretical state of art therapy, cf. Rubin, *Approaches to Art Therapy: Theory and Technique*. Of the above books, Rubin's *Art Therapy* is certainly the most comprehensive and informative. While the book discusses virtually all aspects art therapy, Chapter 3 (on the history of art therapy) and Chapter 4 (on the education of art therapists) provide an overview of areas not covered in any of the other introductions. Moon offers the most concise introduction into the principles of art therapy. On a side note, it is interesting to observe that none of

more exact demarcation of these similarities, however, fails to provide any immediately satisfying answer, because of the very nature – the interdisciplinary nature – of art therapy.[46] There are many theories put forth in art therapy today, which reflects the inherently interdisciplinary nature of the field. With so many forms of art employed therapeutically, art therapy has to be and, indeed, is an extremely heterogeneous field practically as well as theoretically. This is the reason why art therapy itself is still in a state of uncertainty as to its theoretical foundations. Judith Rubin acknowledges this situation in her book *Approaches to Art Therapy* by stating that "in many ways, art therapy is still 'a technique in search of a theory'" (343). Like poetry therapy, art therapy in general lacks a coherent theory. This makes the idea of integrating poetry therapy in art therapy for the purpose of anchoring it theoretically seem counterintuitive at first. Nonetheless, poetry therapy's natural home is in the art therapies, if simply for the fact that writing poetry is a creative, artistic act; after all, art therapies do have a common basis, namely the application of the creative process that is central to the emergence of art.

Generally speaking, the importance of creativity, though of considerable significance for the early psychotherapists, has been marginalised in modern psychotherapeutic discourse.[47] Nowadays, therapy is regulated and formalised, not only by its own disciplinary concerns and constrains, but also by the implications of modern health care limitations, whereas "[a]rt adapts to every conceivable problem and lends

---

the above books features a chapter on the therapeutic practice and/or theories of poetry therapy. In those cases where writing-based therapies are dealt with, poetry therapy does not feature at all. This is symptomatic once again of the neglect poetry therapy is suffering from in the therapeutic community. Though this has been established before, the fact that the situation is no different within the area of art therapies, an area which should embrace poetry therapy wholeheartedly as adding to its abundance, truly shows the extent of the neglect of poetry therapy and makes apparent the dire need for the present study.

[46] The effectiveness and status of art therapy has been a subject of discussion in therapeutic circles basically since its inception. With regard to art therapy, Dalley constitutes that "there is no generally agreed consensus, even among its practitioners, about the scope of its applicability, its informing theories, or even its clinical objectives" (IX). The arguments put forward are for the most part congruent with those concerning the therapeutic status of poetry therapy encountered in the previous chapter.

[47] Cf., for instance, Morrison, who states that "creative arts specialists have been challenged on two counts. Their therapeutic activities have been dismissed by some as purely adjunctive. On the other hand, the use of the creative arts for therapeutic purposes has been called a denigration of the artistic purpose. Those who apply the 'adjunctive' label regard the art therapies as busywork – diversionary, and, at best, a means of reducing anxiety. This failure to appreciate the therapeutic potential of creative arts therapies is common among mental health professionals who do not recognize the current achievement in this field" (22). Since Morrison's statement (1987) the art therapies have without doubt gained in acceptance, but especially the question of the 'adjunctive' status of art therapies continues to be discussed.

its transformative, insightful and experience-heightening powers to people in need. [...] The medics of art are not confined within fixed borders" (McNiff, *Art Heals* 5). By taking the artistic aspect of therapy seriously, art therapy as a whole exhibits the adaptive dynamics of art. Despite its own theoretical heterogeneity, art therapy can provide poetry therapy that is conceived as a productive and creative endeavour with a disciplinary home. Consequently, in contrast to the problem of situating and delineating the interrelations of poetry therapy with general psychology and psychoanalysis, the integration of poetry therapy into the theoretical framework of art therapy poses less of a challenge and is facilitated simply by constituting the creative process as poetry therapy's centre. In fact, it is for the most part a foregone conclusion as poetry therapy, by utilising art therapeutically, naturally falls within the confines of art therapy. Although there is and always has been an enormous variety of approaches and practices in use in the art therapies – something which works against the formation of any unified theory – this has from the start been a well-recognised methodological fact, which has in turn led to the formulation of theories on art therapy that are much more broadly conceived and therefore open for the relatively smooth inclusion of poetry therapy. Furthermore, art therapy in general takes seriously its interdisciplinary nature, embedding art intimately in the psychotherapeutic practice. These latter arguments notwithstanding, the question has to be addressed where exactly poetry therapy is best at home within the possibilities of art therapy. This is not only a question of categorisation. An investigation into this matter will contribute further to delineating the borders of poetry therapy and to differentiating it from such sister therapies as bibliotherapy.

There is a consensus among art therapists that the term "art therapy ought to be applicable to any endeavour that generally partakes in both art and therapy" (Ulman, "Art Therapy" 13). This notion of art therapy, namely of a true balance between the two practices involved, is also the basis of poetry therapy as it is conceived in this study. Poetry therapy is most effective when its poetic as well as its therapeutic side are taken seriously. After all, "art alone can be highly therapeutic and therapy alone can be highly artistic, art therapy is the product of the marriage between the two" (Rubin, *Approaches to Art Therapy* 343).[48]

Within art therapy, poetry therapy is not a performance art like drama or dance therapy; it is more akin to such forms of art as sculpturing or painting. Lorenz, taking recourse to Blatner,

> sees poetry as a branch of the expressive arts therapies. They all use a therapeutic process with creative art and share the same goal of healing and growth. The art has a therapeutic meaning when the person and the process are the meaningful ones and not

---

[48] Cf. the central argument of the previous chapter, namely that the mainstream discourse of contemporary psychotherapy reduces poetry therapy to an ancillary form of therapy and, for the most part, ignores the therapeutic potential in the creation of poetic language.

the artistic product as such. Creative poetry therapy uses words as its media like clay or colors used in other art therapies. (79)

Lorenz ascribes to all expressive art therapies the goal of "healing and growth" and singles out the creative process as particularly important. Blatner argues along the same lines. He explains that the "process of personal growth and development involves many aspects of the human experience where the expressive arts serve as channels for integrating intellect and imagination, sensation and emotion, mind and body" (19). Blatner furthermore subsumes divergent forms of art therapies such as psychodrama, "singing, music, art, poetry, movement and dance" (19) under the term expressive art therapy. He argues that by

> [e]mploying a number of unfamiliar metaphors such as can be found in poetry or art, dance or drama, the patient finds ways of expressing nuances of personal feelings. The indirectness of these methods also enables the patient to allow the creative force in his unconscious to contribute more adaptive syntheses of attitudes and behaviours. (ibid.)

For Blatner, the therapeutic benefit of the arts[49] lies in the function of inciting clients to express their feelings. Furthermore, Blatner stresses the function of art as another *via regia* to the unconscious. During artistic production, the creative process involves both the conscious and the unconscious faculties that form a reciprocal causality which effectively constitutes the creative process in the first place.[50] The conscious faculties of the mind are engaged in a decision-making process with regard to the structure and form of the emerging work. Through the involvement in the artistic production, the conscious faculties are dislodged from pondering on internal conflicts. The client is

---

[49] The repeated use by Blatner of the generic term 'art' in his enumerations of expressive art therapies is certainly odd and makes little sense as part of the list above. I assume that art denotes the visual and plastic arts, such as painting and sculpturing here. Painting is certainly the most widely used of the art therapies and it is conspicuous that it is missing from the above list. Cf., for instance, Dalley's *Art as Therapy*, which demonstrates a bias towards painting as the preferred vehicle for art therapy. This becomes obvious in the second chapter by John Henzell entitled "Art, Psychotherapy and Symbol Systems." Henzell exemplifies his concepts by taking recourse to painting and the other visual arts. A similar bias can be observed clearly in the book's third chapter by John Birtchnell, "Art therapy as a form of psychotherapy." Under the heading 'The Scope of Art Therapy' Birtchnell lists eight areas falling within art therapy's scope and in each instance he links these to the art of painting only. Given this bias within the literature on art therapy, painting is conspicuously absent from Blatner's enumerations above. Therefore, I take art to mean painting here.

[50] The creative process itself is of a slightly different nature in every form of art. The presence of the creative process and its healing potential as such is fundamental to all art and all art therapies, but the effects and expressions vary. In dance (therapy) the creative process is at the same time the expressive outcome. The same is true about music. With other forms of art, such as poetry or painting, the creative process and the final outcome are not instantaneous, but consecutive. The cathartic effect in these therapies may not be as strong, but their production of a lasting artistic artefact encourages later conscious scrutiny.

thus, for the time of creation, freed from the constant psychological pressure otherwise exerted by his consciousness. At the same time, the mechanisms of repression are weakened, which makes the expressive art therapies conducive to unconscious influences and discoveries. Insights into the clients' conflicts and state of mind thus come by way of an artistic detour. Hence, the "indirectness of these methods." These are the fundamental principles associated with expressive art therapies, principles that are equally fundamental for poetry therapy. What is said on the following pages for art therapy is, due to the overlapping of principles, thus also true for poetry therapy.

2.1 Art Therapy vs. Art *as* Therapy

The term 'expressive art therapy' used by Lorenz and Blatner is at first glance confusing as it is hard to imagine how there could be an art therapy that is not expressive, given the fact that the very foundation of art is that it expresses something to someone.[51] Just like one cannot not communicate,[52] art cannot not be expressive. The reason for establishing the subcategory of *expressive* art therapy within the art therapies has to be rooted elsewhere.

To begin with, there is the role art is to play within the therapeutic experience. Art can be employed receptively or actively and this determines the level of integration. There can be art therapy, i.e. therapies that use forms of art adjunctively; there can also be art *as* therapy, which denotes, I propose, a full integration of the respective form of art in the therapeutic process.[53] This full integration presupposes an active use of the arts by the client in order to release the full healing potential of the creative

---

[51] This is even more the case when we consider that for psychotherapy, in whatever shape or form, the expressions of the client are the *conditio sine qua non*.

[52] Cf. Watzlawick, Janet Beavin Bavelas and Donald D. Jackson's classic study *Pragmatics of Human Communication*, especially Chapter 2. Watzlawick basically argues against communication as a solely conscious, intentional act. The same is, of course, true for the message contained in the poetic artefact, which contains an unconscious surplus meaning that, once decoded, can be extremely valuable for both client and therapist.

[53] Generally speaking, art therapy is understood as art *as* therapy by those who practice it. It goes without saying that art therapists emphasise the importance of the artistic aspect of art therapy. Accordingly, the difference is not specifically addressed in works on the subject. Dalley's *Art as Therapy*, however, verbalises the difference in the title of her book. Warren comments on the difference, stating: "The recent move towards 'Arts for Health' (which suggests the benefits of participation in creative activity) as distinct from art(s) therapy (which implies the treatment of a condition that produces 'ill-health') is a healthy and honest extension of these developments" (5). Warren uses the expression 'Arts for Health' (which can be considered to be synonymous to art *as* therapy) to distinguish this approach from forms of art therapy that use the arts in a non-creative manner and/or in a merely adjunctive fashion.

process. Bibliotherapy thus falls under the heading of art therapy, but is not to be considered art *as* therapy as it only deals with prefabricated forms of literature. Drama and dance therapy, on the other hand, necessarily constitute art *as* therapy as they cannot do without the active participation of the client.

With regard to poetry therapy, both approaches have been and are practiced today. Discussing the use of poetry in therapy in an interview, Lerner states:

> I use poetry as a vehicle in counseling and therapy sessions to help people help themselves. Please keep in mind that poets have always written about human emotions, love, greed, hate, sex, etc., long before the psychologists or the behavioral scientists came on the scene. In a poetry workshop the accent is on the poem; in poetry therapy, that is poetry *in* therapy, the accent is on the person. We employ all kinds of poetry. The importance of good poetry must be stressed – the better the poem the more honest the feeling. And it's the awareness of a feeling which gets across to people. (Lippin 167)

Lerner speaks of "poetry *in* therapy." He is clearly advocating a shift in importance towards the art, which, he hints, has been around far longer than psychology and has always been a 'therapy' to people. Quite shrewdly, Lerner, in strengthening the poetic aspect of poetry therapy and thereby conceptualising it as poetry *in* therapy (which is to be read as poetry *as* therapy), cautions against a methodological problem inherent in this shift. He emphasises that in the "poetry workshop," which, for him, is a purely literary activity, the focus is on the poem. In poetry *as* therapy, the focus is on the person. Elevating the importance of the form of art in therapy creates the danger of elevating the poem over the client. Doing so would nullify the idea of poetry *as* therapy (or art *as* therapy for that matter) as it would marginalise not only the client, but also the therapeutic aspect of poetry therapy. In essence, this would un-balance poetry therapy to the other extreme.[54]

---

[54] Although Lerner clearly advocates a shift towards what has been defined as art *as* therapy, he does not go the entire way. The contrast he sets up between the nature of the poem in the "poetry workshop" and the therapeutic session constitutes the core of his arguments, namely that in therapy poetry comes second to the client. His phrase "poetry *in* therapy" thus not only denotes a more central concern with the poem in therapy, but at the same time emphasises that poetry is used *in* therapy rather than the workshop. In this sense, Lerner exhibits the bias towards the psychological over the poetic we have encountered in Chapter 1. Also, Lerner is talking of a receptive use of poetry. Along the same line, his use of the term "poetry workshop" is meant to denote a workshop for reading and analysing poetry, not, as has the term has come to signify in recent years, a creative writing workshop. In the light of this, it becomes clear why Lerner can say that "the importance of good poetry must be stressed – the better the poem the more honest the feeling." He is talking about the use of canonical poems in therapy as superior to non-canonical ones (a notion highly questionable in its own right), and not of the artistic or aesthetic value of client poems in therapy. Lerner's comment becomes valuable in the present context precisely because he is a representative (and founder) of the receptive approach of poetry therapy. His gravitation towards integrating poetry more centrally in the therapeutic endeavour rather than as an ancillary tool shows the validity and attractiveness of poetry *as* therapy.

The problem of unduly elevating the form of art in therapy does not present itself at all in most of contemporary psychotherapy. Currently, the clinical and medical model of psychiatric care is predominant in most forms of treatment. This is to say, the psychotherapeutic aspect of poetry therapy supersedes the poetic. Poetry is mostly used in an ancillary fashion and the focus on the client as a multidimensional being is recognized only perfunctorily. While this constitutes a loss of creativity in the therapeutic process, the undue elevation of the artistic aspect would lead to a loss of theory (which as we have seen in Chapter 1 is still in its infancy anyway) and intellectual credibility of poetry therapy, something which is equally counter-productive. The solution, as Lerner rightly points out, lies in centring therapeutic practice and theory – at least in the art therapies – on the human being in question, the client. It is the person of the client who serves as the regulator between the poles of art and therapy. "The primary accent in any experience in which the term therapy is used is focused on the healing experience. Therefore, the object of primary importance is the individual or groups of individuals [...]. [But] the poem is of great importance. It is the materia medica of the moment" (Lerner, "Poetry Therapy Corner" (1997) 119). The poem's importance does not reside in itself, or in its aesthetic qualities, but in its connection to the client, its having originated from the client's mind. It is due to this fact that, in poetry therapy, the importance of the poem as a piece of art is superseded by its importance for the individual. This view of poetry therapy is consistent with what was outlined above as constituting art *as* therapy. Considered therapeutically in relation to the client-author, the function of the poem is automatically elevated above the status of a merely adjunctive tool aiding traditional therapeutic practices. The "interaction with a particular poem, or the performance of it, becomes a rite of passage from one state of awareness of self to another, with the poem as facilitator or guide during the process" (Rice 249). It is here that poetry becomes an integral part of treatment. The client's interaction with the poem is a major aspect of therapy that classical psychoanalysis and psychology lack. This interaction is creative and productive and not limited to a 'reading experience.' Prior to the interactive experience of reading, the client has the experience of interacting with the material – language cast in verse – in a manner that creates something. The poem is thus not something predefined which the client is confronted with to elicit an (emotional) reaction like, perhaps most famously, with the Rorschach inkblot tests. Purely receptive uses of poetry in therapy, i.e. bibliotherapy, leave the better part of poetry therapy's therapeutical potential unused and cannot be part of art *as* therapy.

The poem is the outcome of the client's creative doing; it originates from the client and thus constitutes an externalised representation of his/her emotional state during creation. Rather than to choose poems for reading that fit the client's mood, using poems that are created by clients allows the creative expressions of clients to set the course of therapy and, in doing so, the client is placed firmly at the centre of therapy. This gives vital importance to the client-created poem, but it also draws the focus even more closely to the person of the individual client. Wadeson describes the nature of poetic creation and its particularity in contrast to other forms of writing-based therapies as follows:

> Composing poetry is [...] differentiated from such related activity as journal-keeping and other prose composition. Though such writing may be poetic, poetry is distinguished by its reliance on metaphor, imagery, sound, rhythm, and economy of presentation. Like other art forms, it lends itself well to the expression of primary process and other non-rational material. All these qualities create in the poetry writing experience an opportunity for the integration and synthesis of desperate experience, deepening and broadening understanding; in other words, the stuff of which therapy is made. (225)

According to Wadeson, the synergetic effects resulting from poetry's "reliance on metaphor, imagery, sound, rhythm" and its openness to the expression of unconscious content make the creation of poetry a superior form of writing therapy. In fact, in writing poetry the client quite naturally experiences "the stuff of which therapy is made." Along the same lines, in putting the client-created poems to therapeutic use, therapy automatically centres on the client as an individual. The creative use of poetry *as* therapy thus guarantees a balance between the poles of therapy and poetry, both geared towards the individual conceived of as a multidimensional being. This, in turn, is what accounts for the effectiveness of poetry therapy. The active participation of the individual is thus a prerequisite for employing poetry therapy to its maximum effectiveness.[55] As a result, the client is both the end of therapy and its medium, and since this is so, the client's entire being has to be considered and predominantly so. With this client-centred approach of poetry therapy, which inevitably guarantees that it is art *as* therapy, the fundamental principles of humanistic art therapy have been delineated.

Humanistic art therapy is characterised by taking the life world of the client as its central concern. Generally, it can be said that

> the humanistic approach to art therapy is based on three assumptions. First, people are not seen as "mentally ill," but rather as encountering specific problems in their efforts to cope with life – as a result of intrapsychicially or environmentally caused conflicts. Treatment is directed towards reinforcing the will to live, and developing the ability to find meaning and identity in as fully creative a lifestyle as possible. Second, the inability to cope successfully with life's vicissitudes or to find satisfactory avenues for self-actualization, meaning, and identity is a common phenomenon, affecting most people to a greater or lesser extent. [...] Instead of waiting to "cure" people during periods of tension, a humanistic art therapist helps people to integrate the various "identity crises"

---

[55] Even in Lerner, who has a conception of poetry therapy that is roughly equivalent to bibliotherapy and therefore does not involve the creation of poems by clients, the client is given an active role in the form of selecting the poems used. In this way the client has an influence on the direction of treatment: "When I stress that the accent in poetry therapy is on the person, I do not mean or infer in any way that the poem is of no consequence in the healing experience. Also, I would like to point up that effective healing occurs when the individual in therapy is thought of as a living entity, composed of multidimensional proportions and diverse interests, attitudes, and feelings. This point of view assumes that the individual in poetry therapy participates in the selection of the poetry he or she would like to read" ("Poetry Therapy Corner" (1998) 185).

into creative-expressive lifestyles, and to move towards further experiences of change. Third, *self-actualization* resulting from lifestyles of genuine self-disclosure and honesty remains basically sterile, unless the person can formulate a *self-transcendent* goal that makes life more meaningful by adding a "spiritual" dimension to it. (Garai 149; emphasis original)

There are thus three pillars of humanistic art therapy: (1) The realisation that many a time psychological problems stem from a fundamental inability to successfully cope with life. This is the basic assumption from which all art therapies working with(in) the humanistic approach proceed. The goal is therefore to help the client develop a creative lifestyle s/he can identify with.[56] (2) The acknowledgment of the often troubling realities of existence. This means that, although clients may have no problems coping with life in general, there are events that disrupt the 'normal' course of life, causing "identity crises" which need therapeutic attention. In such cases, humanistic art therapy employs the creative, expressive potential of art to help integrate these crises into a harmonious life-story.[57] (3) The formulation of a *"self-transcendent* goal" in life. This should be regarded as a 'downsized' version of the Faustian premise as conceived by Goethe.[58] Without a goal in life which is, firstly, worth achieving and,

---

[56] In this context, cf. Abrams: "It is good to keep in mind that abnormality is, in essence, a destructively exaggerated state of normality and normal psychological processes. Nearly everyone experiences depressive feelings, paranoid thoughts, and regressive impulses at times. While the use of poetry for therapeutic ends grew out of its popular use, knowledge of the therapeutic techniques of poetry therapy came from the study of abnormality. [...] In the poet's struggle with his psyche he unearths deeper and hidden aspects of himself. The process of successfully creating the poem dealing with these issues leads to relief and resolution" (65). Robert Bjorklund comments on this matter as well, arguing that "[v]alidating the very human feelings of patients who merely want to 'live like everyone else' must become a regular and normalizing role of psychiatric treatment. It is through the use of poetry therapy that this could be more openly fostered" (216-217).

[57] Cf. Payne's statement about his time as a teacher before becoming a counsellor: "When students chose painful experiences as topics, they sometimes not only discovered what they had experienced by putting it into words, but, in the act of shaping and controlling this material, found that they felt better. [...] I am inclined to believe that the act of writing changes meaning for the person retrospectively, by enabling them to recall detail in a more 'experience-near' way. When a person writes, events are recalled, sifted, prioritized, organized into sequence and encapsulated into words on the page. [...] The new associations of past events with the safe present when the account is written can detach the events from their place as a malign presence-from-the-past in the person's life-story" (123).

[58] The character of Faust as depicted in Goethe's play can serve as a highly illustrative example for the importance of a "self-transcendental goal" in life. Faust as we find him at the beginning of the play is indeed a man without any goals. Having probed human knowledge to its farthest limits ("Habe nun, ach! Philosophie,/Juristerei und Medizin, /Und leider auch Theologie/Durchaus studiert, mit heißem/Bemühn" [*Faust I* 354-357]), Faust has truly become a living specimen of the Renaissance *homo universalis*. Faust

secondly, sufficiently ambitious to require the client to become active in its pursuit, life automatically becomes a succession of days of dull routine. This is naturally counterproductive to a full life.

It is obvious that these three areas share common ground and are in many ways interdependent. To cope with reality presupposes a certain stability of character, or in Freudian terms, a strong and functioning Ego that is able to mediate between the individual's desires and the demands of reality. This can be achieved by means of a creative lifestyle. Conflicts, either "intrapsychically or environmentally," can be sublimated via the road of creativity; problems are counterbalanced by creative activities. These creative activities themselves, in the present case the writing of poetry, represent the "self-transcendental goals" required in the third point above.

The task before a therapist in humanistic art therapy is thus not only one of diagnosing the client and working with him towards a verbalisation of his repressed conflicts, but it is also – and specifically – one of providing opportunities of self-actualisation for the client: "[t]he challenge, therefore, is not merely 'solving a problem' by means of 'insight,' but in most cases requires a program of empowerment which develops the patient's abilities in several areas. [...] Another way to regard this general concept is to recognize the essential multidimensionality of human existence" (Morrison 17-18). The concept of client empowerment mentioned by Morrison is at the centre of humanistic art therapy, because it facilitates clients to adopt an active stance in life again. Empowerment is therefore both the prerequisite and the instrument for the formulation of the transcendent goal mentioned above as well as of its actual implementation. Unfortunately, the notion of empowerment goes against the current trends and methods in clinical and, to a lesser extent, private practice.

2.2 Humanistic Art *as* Therapy as an alternative to Clinical Models predominant today

Humanistic art therapy constitutes an alternative form of support for the impaired psyche, one that is less dependent on hard statistical data and the diagnostic labelling of clients. The differences to the more conservative forms of therapy are rooted in the principles of humanistic art therapy. Once again, these are "(1) emphasis on coping

---

> now faces the problem that he has nothing more to live for; he has no more goals in life ("Es möchte kein Hund so länger leben!" [ibid. 376]). He turns to magic to transcend the limits of his human condition. The accord between Faust and Mephistopheles specifically rests on Faust's continual striving for more, i.e. Faust perpetually sets new goals for himself to achieve. It is indeed the lack of such a goal that has Faust pass away in the end ("Zum Augenblicke dürft' ich sagen:/Verweile doch, du bist so schön!/Es kann die Spur von meinen Erdentagen/Nicht in Äonen untergehn. –/Im Vorgefühl von solchem hohen Glück/Genieß' ich jetzt den höchsten Augenblick." [*Faust II*, V, 11581-11586]).

with life's vicissitudes, (2) encouraging of self-actualization through creative expression, and (3) emphasis on relating self-actualization to intimacy and trust in personal relations, and the search for self-transcendent life goals" (Garai 149). These principles reflect the underlying concern of this type of therapeutic approach with the whole person and the healing powers of creativity. Especially the latter is something the mainstream of clinical treatment is concerned with only peripherally.

> Clinical work knows little about how creative sublimation works, because it is mainly concerned with interpreting and translating the contents of unconscious phantasy. Once the unconscious conflicts are resolved, it is left to the automatic action of the ego to sublimate the revealed unconscious drives into useful creative work. This process leaves the creative working of the ego obscure. (Ehrenzweig 5)

Today, creativity and psychotherapy do not often go together;[59] even in art therapy there are constraints originating from the focus on research and statistics. "The professional community of psychology at the moment prefers the rhetoric of research and verbatim case study" (Hillman 3) which, in practice, often has a de-humanising effect on the client treated.

The limitations imposed upon the therapeutic practice by the economic realities of the health care system promote a climate that is characterised by the necessity to diagnose and treat patients[60] in a minimal amount of time. This oftentimes precludes the formation of a true interpersonal relationship between the patient and the therapist and severely limits the number of sessions per patient. Such therapeutic approaches are counter-productive to mental health and constitute a hindrance to mental treatment that aims at curing causes rather than simply treating symptoms. Especially hospitalised patients frequently suffer from the inevitable labelling of their mental status into pre-defined categories and feel alienated from the mental health professionals treating them. The danger on the part of the therapist/clinician is to use the system of diagnosis

---

[59] While it lies beyond the scope of the present study to enquire about the nature of creativity itself, the processes that govern poetic writing are a central concern. The focus lies not so much on creativity, but on understanding the mechanisms of how unconscious traces come to be inscribed into (poetic) texts. Creativity will be considered as a natural part of the human condition. It will not be specified or subdivided according to neurological or psychological criteria. As conceived in this study "regardless of orientation, creativity is synonymous with mental health in that both reflect the capacity to be freely in charge, whether of materials or of the self" (Rubin, *Approaches to Art Therapy* 344).

[60] I specifically use the word 'patients' here in order to highlight the difference between the forms of therapy described here and the holistic understanding predominant in humanistic approaches. 'Patient', therefore, denotes individuals who receive therapeutic treatment that follows certain predetermined structures and does not account for the individual's uniqueness. The word 'client' – used in the bulk of this study – is meant to accentuate (a) the freedom given to the individual within the scope of humanistic art therapy and (b) the efforts of the therapist to always see the client as multidimensional being.

as established by case studies and statistics unreflectedly: "for therapists to concern themselves only with symptom-clusters of behavioral acts, whether conceptualized primarily as thinking or as doing, is to ignore what is crucial in many cases – namely, that the client is demoralized because of the condition of his existence and not necessarily because of acts defined as symptoms" (Stainbrook 3). As in all health professions, there is a danger to confuse symptom and cause. For therapists this danger, Stainbrook implies, becomes greater the more they concentrate on the symptoms without keeping the human being as a whole in focus as well. A one-sided attention on the symptoms and consequently on diagnosis – on labelling – will not only leave the ultimate cause untreated, but will also affect the patient negatively. Bjorklund addresses this problem even more forcefully: "inherent within the medical model of psychiatric care is the overreliance (and potential misuse) of diagnostic labels in treatment. It is up to clinicians to move beyond perpetuating stigma [sic] caused by diagnostic labels and facilitate how patients view their label and, ultimately, their own identity" ("Diagnostic Identity" 211). Bjorklund believes that the "overreliance" on labelling is systemic and is accordingly unavoidable in therapeutic treatment. Scheff, approaching the notion of mental illness from a sociological point of view, ascribes to labelling a key function in the stigmatisation processes at work in the mental health profession today. Scheff basically argues that mental illness is as much a cause of social labelling as it is of psychic predetermination. Social norms, values and accepted patterns of behaviour, like any form of identity, are constituted against an 'Other'. The same is true of the concepts of sanity and normality which exist in contradistinction to madness and abnormality, respectively. Within every society, therefore, certain stereotypical notions of what constitutes 'normal' behaviour and what is labelled 'abnormal' behaviour circulate. Individual members of a society are brought up with these stereotypes, which become firmly internalised. On the grounds of these internalised stereotypes, persons whose behaviour is in violation of the social norm are, when that behaviour is noticed by the public, labelled as 'mentally ill' or 'abnormal'. The problem for clients (especially as patients in mental health institutions) begins with the recognition that their behaviour or mental state is in violation of the social norm. When confronted with the diagnosis of 'mentally ill', individuals are forced to confront, take over and integrate the identity as 'mentally ill' into their existing identities. This is problematic enough as it is, but, within society, the group of the 'mentally ill' constitutes the 'Other' against which society as a whole defines its collective identity.[61] The danger of such labelling is that the newly formed identity of the patient includes the stereotypical stigmata of being "mentally ill."[62] This can, in extreme cases, lead to new symptoms and even

---

[61] For a discussion of this topic (and also the aspect of 'labelling') in the broader context of society, cf. Foucault, *Madness and Civilization*, especially Chapter V: "Aspects of Madness," Chapter VI: "Doctors and Patients," and Chapter IX: "The Birth of the Asylum."

[62] Stuart Hall constitutes the subject's relation to the 'Other' as foundational of identity. Identity is precisely not about unity, but about marking difference. (cf. Hall/du Gay,

aggravate a patient's condition. When they are internalised, these stereotypes become part of the patient's new identity:

> Being labeled "mentally ill" carries with it pejorative connotations and life-long implications in how patients view their identity and how mental health professionals view them. A diagnostic label, as noted earlier, has the potential to lock an individual into abnormal behavior patterns and alter the sense of the self. [...] It is vital for clinicians to explore alternative therapies to create a dynamic and safe environment in which the patient can explore issues relating to their diagnostic identity. (Bjorklund, "Diagnostic Identity" 216)

Far from implicating mental health professionals in consciously stigmatising their patients, Bjorklund emphasises the dangers of this happening unconsciously. Humanistic art therapy helps to guard against a diagnostic labelling of clients that has counterproductive consequences. Two aspects of art *as* therapy are essential with regard to counteracting labelling. Firstly, the holistic concern for clients and the unconditional acceptance of their being in art *as* therapy helps the individual client to feel understood and accepted thus balancing out any feelings of being ostracised. Secondly, by creating art, clients partake in the production of a prestigious cultural artefact, which strengthens their feeling of socio-cultural embeddedness. A positive feedback from the therapist naturally emphasises this feeling.

Diagnosis is naturally a most important aspect of all psychological treatment and undeniably the first step towards healing. Along the same lines it is imperative to share the diagnosis with the patients. This is, indeed, the first step towards enabling patients to take a self-determined stance in life again. Knowing what one suffers from empowers one to deal with it. Thus, it is the first step of turning patients into clients. This, however, can only affect the client positively if the therapist is aware of and ready to counterbalance the negative implications of the diagnosis such as stereotypical notions, stigmatisation and so forth. To achieve this it is often sufficient to consciously and openly acknowledge the client as the complex, multifaceted individual s/he is. This can be facilitated and strengthened via art. Humanistic art therapy thus not only works as a form of therapy in its own right, but can also help guard against the pitfalls of stigmatisation and labelling inherent in all therapeutic treatment. In this respect, the agenda, methods and effects of poetry therapy are fully congruent with those of humanistic art therapy. Indeed,

> [t]here exists a strong desire to work past the stigmatization of psychiatric labels and explore shared experiences not otherwise encouraged on the ward. The value of [the] poetry group lies in its ability to draw out hidden feelings and empower members. The collaborative sharing of feelings provided members with a sense of validation and a safe

---

Questions of Cultural Identity 4). The patient labelled 'mentally ill' is forced to create unity where 'otherness' is needed, which can lead to identity problems. For additional views on the question of identity pertinent to this study cf., for instance, Jacques Derrida's *Positions*, Judith Butler's *Bodies that Matter* (1993) or E. Laclau's *New Reflections on the Revolution of Our Time*.

environment for self-expression. The validation of feelings and synergetic interaction is unique to this group and cannot be duplicated in more traditional therapeutic groups. Such collaboration of feelings shared through a poetry therapy group provides the clinician a unique window into the individual's world within the broader social context. (Bjorklund, "Diagnostic Identity" 216)

We can trace in Bjorklund's arguments his adherence to the fundamental principles of humanistic art therapy. Bjorklund ascribes to the poetry group a therapeutic effect that "cannot be duplicated in more traditional therapeutic groups" because of the "sense of validation" and the opportunities for "self-expression"[63] the poetry group offers. The poetry group Bjorklund talks about has brought forth a number of poems that illustrate quite readily both the dangers of (mis)labelling on patients' identities and the contention that the origins and conditions of psychological problems often have a strong social aspect as well. The following two poems will serve as examples. At the same time, it has to be noted that the individual aspect in these poems, while also addressed by Bjorklund, is treated as secondary to the importance of the poems for the poetry therapy group as a whole.[64] I will augment Bjorklund's analyses of the poems with a brief summary interpretation of my own in order to show in which manner the poems could be applied to an individual therapy session.[65]

The first poem is entitled "Yesterday," and the title captures much of what the speaker is concerned with:

Yesterday

Thinking about yesterday
of how my life used to be
and what could have been.
Those thoughts return to haunt me.

---

[63] Here the term "expression," which as a compound in "expressive art therapy" launched the discussion in this chapter (and to which I will return again at its end), is encountered again. Though obvious, it has to be made clear that "self-expression" here is connected to the poems produced rather than the discussions between clients and therapist. It is this making of art that differentiates the group in question from traditional ones.

[64] On the prevalence of using poetry therapy in a group environment, cf. also Edgar and Hazley, who state of the origins of poetry therapy: "In May of 1963, J.J. Leedy and Eli Greifer read a paper at the meeting of the American Society of Group Psychotherapy and Psychodrama in Washington. It was concerned with the results and the potential of what was then a new approach to group psychotherapy, pioneered by the authors in Cumberland Hospital in Brooklyn. They had conducted an experiment in which they had used poetry as a therapeutic tool. The results obtained, and the enthusiasm of the patients, indicated that their technique, which Dr. Leedy called poetry therapy, could be profitably employed in the group process" (260).

[65] Bjorklund's interpretations of the poems are guided by his diagnosis of the clients which constitutes an implicit narrowing down of the scope of possible textual meanings, effectively blinding the therapist to potentially important actualisations of the clients' texts.

> Straight jacket memories,
> sedative highs.
> So many ghosts to lie inside of me.
> Why must I re-live this tragedy?
> All I want is the same as everyone.
> (printed in: Bjorklund, "Diagnostic Identity" 214)

Bjorklund describes the poem and its effects as follows:

> The [...] poem represents a sense of loss and frustration of a patient misdiagnosed with schizophrenia in early adolescence. This poem was a useful catalyst in assisting other members to express their frustration of what they have lost due to their experiences with mental illness. Feelings of lost innocence was a common theme expressed through the poems. It is evident from poems shared in the group that members felt empowered to articulate their experiences thereby discovering commonalities with each other. (ibid.)

Especially the effects of the poem on the group dynamics are of interest to Bjorklund, and in this respect the poem encouraged the members of the group to open up into a discussion of lost innocence. However, as an artefact of an individual client the poem is a much more potent source. Predominant in the poem is the expression of lost chances; a certain mood of having been betrayed in life. The "yesterday" of the speaker is not so much a place of loss, as Bjorklund argues, but a place of unrealized potential. The speaker, as Bjorklund tells us, has been misdiagnosed as schizophrenic in adolescence, a misdiagnosis which left the potential for "what could have been" (3) unseized. The frustration which is clearly present in the poem is therefore not so much a result of loss, but of unrealised potential. This is an important difference to make and is a valuable insight for therapy.

The speaker has never recovered from the effects of the misdiagnosis. This manifests itself in the recurring references to "thoughts return[ing]" (4), "memories" (5) as well as "ghosts" (7) that still reside inside. Formally, the rhyme scheme underscores this condition as we have the rhyming pairs of "be" - "me" (2, 4) and – even stronger still since a couplet – "me" - "tragedy" (7, 8). Line 8 is ambiguous: the question "Why must I re-live this tragedy?" is both rhetorical and interrogative. It refers to the recurring thoughts of his past under the label 'schizophrenic', but at the same time it has contemporary relevance. Presumably, the identity crisis that is precipitated by the discovery of the misdiagnosis has led to another mental breakdown and hospitalisation. The final line opens the poem to an understanding of the underlying cause of the aforementioned. The "straight jackets" (5) and "sedative[s]" (6) would all have been bearable had it not been for the stigmatisation as a schizophrenic. This has made it impossible to live and be "the same as everyone" (9) and this impossibility must be considered the primary cause of the client's mental instability.

Apart from the relevance for the changing dynamics of the group setting to which Bjorklund primarily applies the poem, it contains valuable insights into the mental state and development of the individual; insights which manifest the individual's multidimensionality thus helping the therapist to conceive the client in his/her whole being.

The next poem under discussion, while thematically different, exhibits traces of underlying social causes for the problems described. Especially prominent here is the aspect of social isolation, which the speaker fashions in numerous ways. The central topic of isolation can be seen as resulting from taking on the identity of being 'mentally ill':

> **Mistress**
> I lie awake in self-imposed solitude,
> afraid to lose my logical lucidity.
> I cautiously greet Mr. Jekyll,
> my chemical aberration once again exposed.
> There I see the shadow of my manic mistress,
> seducing my resurrected aberration.
> Mr. Jekyll's addiction to her grows
> as my resistance weakens with his passion.
> The lines of reality grow blurry as my mind races,
> soon Mr. Jekyll prepares for far away places.
> Once lucid barriers come tumbling down
> in a forbidden world I will not truly find.
> (printed in Bjorklund, "Diagnostic Identity" 214-215)

This is Bjorklund's commentary on the poem:

> The [...] poem romanticizes the mania that this person has experienced through medication noncompliance in the community. Despite the obvious yearning for the manic high, there is a clear sense of realism that the mania comes with a cost. The subtle information yielded in the [...] poem is not readily apparent to the treatment team and without this poetic venue, such information would not have been shared. From a psychoeducational perspective, this is vital in helping the patient understand, better manage, and possibly accept the consequences of their symptomatology. (ibid. 214)

Bjorklund rightly centres the importance of the poem for the therapeutic process in the expression of the speaker's strong desire to continue his medicinal noncompliance. The psychomachia involved in this is expressed by means of reference to *The Strange Case of Dr Jekyll and Mr Hyde*. This offers the therapist a unique vantage point from which to approach the poem. I will only briefly touch upon possible ways of decoding the poem in the light of gaining a starting point for therapy. To begin with, there is the fact that *Dr.* Jekyll is referred to as 'Mr', a difference that may express the speaker's opinion towards doctors and may be connected to the phenomenon of transference and counter-transference.[66] By casting himself in the role of Jekyll the speaker admits to his own weakness with regard to his "chemical aberration" (4). Despite a clear awareness of the problem ("*self-imposed* solitude" [1; my emphasis], "logical lucidity" [1], "cautiously" [3]), desire "grows" (7) while "resistance weakens" (8). This weakening of resistance is clear evidence that the speaker's willpower is not yet sufficiently

---

[66] On transference cf., among others, Freud, "The Dynamics of Transference" and Lacan, "Presentation on Transference."

strong to deal with his problem alone. The speaker of the poem acknowledges within the rendering of his fall into the "forbidden world" (12) that he "will not truly find" (12) that world, i.e. possess it in reality. This constitutes a valuable insight that can be taken up in the therapy session.

Similarly to "Yesterday" above, the poem betrays signs of stigmatisation of mental illness which has taken over the speaker's identity. Firstly, the "solitude" (1) the speaker finds himself in, especially since it is "self-imposed" (1), works as a shield against the reactions of the community, the norms of which the speaker has violated. The "forbidden world" (12) is another such sign as it shows that the speaker does principally adhere to the norms and values he is in violation of. By taking over these norms and values, the speaker inevitably also takes over the stereotypical assumptions about the 'mentally ill,' thus identifying himself in that way.

Such analyses of poems written in the therapeutic environment, both with regard to content and to form,[67] serve a number of purposes that together contribute to the therapeutic endeavour, allowing clients room for expression while giving the therapist a valuable stock of possibilities to actualise in therapy. Since the problem of labelling is, according to Bjorklund, systemic and can therefore not be circumvented without moving outside the discipline of established psychotherapy all together, a way has to be found to work with diagnostic labelling while counteracting the negative implications on clients' identities. This can be done via an individual consideration of the client's poems in the context of theories of humanistic art therapy.

In addition to the advantages in reducing the dangers of diagnostic labelling, humanistic art therapy can also be applied as a means of research and diagnosis thus adding to the traditional forms of data collection and categorisation. McNiff postulates that "[r]esearch is emerging as one of the most promising frontiers for the art therapy profession. Rather than analysing artistic data with conventional behavioural science research methods, I have advocated using the artistic process as a primary mode of inquiry" (*Art Heals* 279). McNiff suggests that wherever art is employed in therapy, the artistic process should be the key factor guiding the therapeutic progress and, especially in humanistic art therapy, this makes perfect sense. Centring therapy on the creative process automatically puts the client – who is the agent of that process – at the centre as well. This, as was already established above, guarantees a balance between

---

[67] For poems written by 'amateur writers' the two poems exhibit aesthetic qualities which are considerable. With regard to form, "Yesterday," while not following a concise metrical structure, plays subtly with the possibilities of rhyme, as has already been hinted at. The rhyming couplet (8-9) is linked through the rhyme with lines two and four. Of these four rhyming words, two are "me" which emphasises the importance of the speaker's own feelings. The word "memories" (5) is linked via assonance to "highs" of the next line, which also connects the two terms. "Mistress" works mainly with alliteration which abound in the first half of the poem ("I lie awake in self-imposed solitude,/ afraid to lose my logical lucidity" [1-2]; "**my** **m**anic **m**istress" [5]). This organising device disappears with the growing emotional agitation and mental disruption that characterises the content of the poem.

the artistic and the therapeutic aspects of art therapy thus constituting art *as* therapy. The creative process determines the pace of the therapy, it determines the depth of the therapist's probing and simultaneously empowers clients and frees them from psychological blockades by means of the free association prevalent during artistic production. Poetry in particular

> can be used as a probing psychodiagnostic to assess illness, personality functioning and behavioral manifestations. Poetry therapy attempts to bring to awareness underlying tension and anxiety, and thus offers the psychological release that hastens healing. By revealing the individuality of the patient, this process also helps the psychologist-therapist to recognize in the patient those attributes that form the personality. (Silverman, "Reflection: Poetry Therapy" 343)

Poetry therapy, like all art therapies, constitutes a device of diagnosis. This is not to say that there is no need for 'traditional' methods of diagnosis. These have proven their reliability and worth in the clinical environment and private practices over and over again. However, diagnosis via artistic means adds another layer of data to the diagnostic whole, a layer which would otherwise be missing. In short, using poetry as a diagnostic tool encourages a holistic diagnosis, a diagnosis which is more synergetic than forms of diagnosis that are concerned primarily with symptom clusters. The additional applicability of poetry therapy as a diagnostic tool is intricately bound to the nature of the poem as a creative artefact. Indeed, "one of the significant advantages of poetry therapy is the opportunity that poetry products provide for review and documentation of a therapeutic and self-evolving process" (Wadeson 225). The poem produced by the client serves as a means of "review and documentation" and thus constitutes a tool of diagnosis. At the same time, it also induces a self-reflective process in the client.[68]

The importance accorded to the client-written poem as both diagnostic tool and therapeutic means effectively excludes all forms of bibliotherapy as defined in the first chapter from the field of poetry therapy as conceptualised in this study. Literature-based poetry therapy – the use of pre-existing poems to facilitate therapeutic reactions in the client – precludes the use of poetry as diagnosis and as a locus for deeper self-reflection on the part of the client.[69] This leads back to the beginning of this chapter where poetry therapy was classed among the *expressive* art therapies. In the course of this chapter, a number of psychological approaches that intersect with the term *expressive* art therapy have been traced. Art therapy in general was described and the concepts of art therapy and art *as* therapy were differentiated. The latter concept is broadly

---

[68] Cf. also Mazza, who states that "[i]f the subjective method of writing can restore choice and one's voice, it seems to be a reasonable practice to use it as both a therapeutic technique and an assessment device. In the instance of creative writing, the intervention is also a measure. It is a special kind of measure that implies respect for the worth and dignity of the individual" (112).

[69] The ISO-principle advocated by Leedy, for instance, presupposes a diagnosis according to which the poems that fit the patient's mood are selected.

synonymous with humanistic art therapy. The principles of humanistic art therapy, in turn, have been shown to constitute a therapeutic formula which guarantees two essential prerequisites: (1) a true balance between the poles of art and therapy in which both areas unfold synergetic potential; (2) that the client is at the centre of therapeutic attention and consequently the recipient of the synergetic outcomes resulting from the first premise. Having thus situated poetry therapy within the art therapies, it is now time to return to the question of how poetry therapy differs from other forms of art therapy. This is not so much a question of poetry therapy vs. other writing-based therapies (cf. Chapter 1), but rather a question of the exact nature of poetry therapy as an 'expressive art therapy'.

For the time being, poetry therapy shall be defined as an expressive art therapy. Included in this term are all the concepts delineated above. Expressive poetry therapy shall thus be considered to be based on the three principles of humanistic art therapy and shall specifically involve the creation of poetry by the client. The creation of poetry constitutes the next step towards a more narrow definition of poetry therapy within what is termed 'expressive art therapies'. The key to such a definition can be found in Lorenz' statement above. Again, Lorenz

> sees poetry as a branch of the expressive arts therapies. [These therapies] all use a therapeutic process with creative art and share the same goal of healing and growth. The art has a therapeutic meaning when the person and the process are the meaningful ones and not the artistic product as such. Creative poetry uses words as its media [sic] like clay or colors used in other art therapies. (79)

Lorenz links poetry only to a specific group within the expressive art therapies as defined by Blatner. According to Lorenz, "[c]reative poetry uses words as its media like clay or colors used in other art therapies" (79). Other than with such forms as dance- and drama therapy, which, though cathartic, do not leave a palpable result, poetry therapy is associated with those expressive art therapies that are involved in the manipulation of raw materials during the creative process and which, secondly, end up with a palpable product – a type of artefact – which is, in essence, the crystallisation of the creative process. Poetry therapy provides the client with a permanent artefact which is the residue of the creative experience. "Once crystallized into words, all-engulfing feelings become manageable, and once challenged into explicitness, the burden of the incommunicable becomes less heavy. The very act of creating is a self-sustaining experience, and in the poetic moment the self becomes both the ministering 'therapist' and the comforted 'patient'" (Harrower 3). Feelings finding expression and embodiment in words during the process of poetic creation serve to lessen the psychological "burden" of the clients. The experience of writing poetry is thus in itself already therapeutic. In addition to this, the poem, that is, the poetic artefact that has come into being, allows the client to re-enter that experience via a reading of the poem. On the one hand, this enables a repetition of that experience and, on the other, puts in train a conscious grappling with the topics ingrained in the poem. Furthermore, the poetic artefact evokes a feeling of pride in the client which, before anything else, serves to strengthen the client's self-confidence and Ego. The production of a creative artefact is therefore central to poetry therapy. In order to differentiate poetry therapy from other expressive art therapies, I will define poetry therapy as an artefactual expressive art therapy. In contrast to music, drama- or dance therapy, artefactual expressive art therapies produce a palpable artefact as a residue of the creative process.

Obviously, the creation of an artefact is not unique to poetry therapy; it is also essential to sculpturing and painting, for example. There is, however, a fundamental difference which demarcates poetry therapy from other forms of artefactual expressive art therapy: poetry therapy deals directly with language and language comes naturally to human beings. As with all forms of art therapy, practice inevitably leads to aesthetically more pleasing results which is true for poetry therapy as well. In contrast to painting and sculpturing, poetry therapy is not a form of therapy that requires any external media to create, i.e. there is no need to learn the specific properties of clay or canvas, the use of perspectives in painting or the rules of colour composition. It can be argued, of course, that, since aesthetic criteria are not of any importance within the therapeutic setting, technique is irrelevant in art therapy. The point here is, however, that poetry uses language and language is the most natural form of expression for human beings. Therefore, clients can approach and perform poetry with a natural proficiency not found in any of the other art therapies.[70] This is a unique feature of poetry therapy. "The language of the poem, the language used to describe the individual's dreams [...] indicate[s] the interplay and synthesis of poem, self, and consciousness" (Rice 250). The performance in poetry therapy is a performance not only with language, but *in* language. Poetry therapy can thus be said to hold a special place within art therapy:

> Writing poetry seemed to have deeper consequences. As a verbal and imaginative art form, poetry appeared to be uniquely suited to serve the psychotherapeutic goal. Regardless of the diagnosis, the patient hospitalized for mental illness has often slipped along the continuum from well to sick. In crucial areas of this development, ego functions are impaired. In all cases, the goal of psychotherapy is to bring about a more mature integration of personality. Poetry seems to be geared to this integrative purpose. (Robinson/Mowbray 191-192)

The reason for poetry to be so uniquely "geared" to therapeutic purposes is that, in contrast to other forms of art therapy, it works with and in language. The Freudian commonplace of psychotherapy as a *talking cure* can be applied here. According to Freud, the (spoken) language in therapy betrays the unconscious conflicts and desires of the client. In art therapy, which naturally includes the traditional discourse between

---

[70] Of course, journal therapy, diary writing and, in fact, writing therapy in general also deal with language first hand. There is, however, generally less of an artistic element present. Journal therapy, for instance, is no art therapy. Poetic language differs from prose and it is here that the client's concern with language is intensified which, in turn, also increases the participation of the unconscious. Cf. the following chapter for greater detail.

therapist and client, this is supported by the creative expression through art. Poetry therapy is a *verbal* form of art which thus offers a twofold access to the unconscious via language: first, by means of the traditional therapist-client discourse and, second, by the creation of a verbal artefact, the poem.

Poetry therapy thus conceived redirects the focus of interest towards language and its relation to the poetic artefact in therapy. How do unconscious influences become part of the poem? Where do they become manifest and why do they apparently do this with more vigour and frequency in poetry than other (prose) forms of writing? More fundamental questions that play a part here are: Why does language serve as a home for the unconscious in the first place? On which roads do the unconscious influences travel in order to lodge themselves in verbal expressions? Why is poetry more inviting to such processes than prose? These questions and more will be addressed in the coming chapters which will lead to a post-structuralist conception of the unconscious. Still working within a Freudian understanding which equals the unconscious with chaos and the consciousness with order, Ehrenzweig feels

> that art, almost perversely, creates tasks that cannot be mastered by our normal faculties. Chaos is precariously near. We arrive back at our central problem, the role which the unconscious plays in controlling the vast substructure of art. Its contribution appears chaotic and altogether accidental, but only as we rely on the gestalt-bound discipline of conscious perception. In spite of the caution built into the foundation of psycho-analytic thinking, which makes it beware of superficial impressions of chaos and accidentality, psycho-analytic aesthetics have so far faltered and succumbed to the chaotic impression which the substructure of art so seductively presents. Once we have overcome the deception the eminently constructive role of the primary process in art can no longer be ignored. (31)

The contention that will be discussed in the following chapter is that the unconscious does in fact not "control the vast substructure of art" but creates this substructure in the first place.

3. The Unconscious, Poetic Writing and Poetry

> And if only GPs who are so quick to prescribe instant tranquilisers to silence distress would suggest the cleansing therapy of putting pen to paper instead. [...] It can clear our heads when we are faced with choice and indecision. It doesn't make us fat, sick, or wreck our liver. And since nobody can possibly know more about us than we know about ourselves, infinitely superior to any psychiatrist. (Potter, L.L., *The Daily Mail,* 17th October 1990, "Write Therapy")

Having outlined the position of poetry therapy within both psychotherapy in general and the art therapies in particular, the last chapter arrived at a definition of poetry therapy as an artefactual expressive art therapy. Having thus outlined the advantages of a creative, productive poetry therapy, I will now continue by concentrating predominantly on the poetic aspect of poetry therapy. I will argue that what makes language poetic is also what makes it therapeutic. It follows as a natural consequence from this that poetry therapy draws a great deal of its healing potential from its poetic language. In this chapter, I will thus delve into and appropriate for poetry therapy a poststructural understanding of language which will uncover the close connections between language and the unconscious, and constitute poetry as the catalyst of these two. Keeping in mind the importance of creativity as a means of healing and the poetic process as an expression of it, this chapter will begin by delineating the closeness that does in fact exists between concepts of psychotherapy and linguistic/literary ones. Secondly, drawing on Lacan, this chapter will constitute the unconscious as based on language and expand on this insight to conceptualise the participation of the unconscious in the production of language and (poetic) texts. In a third step, I will show in how far and in which manner poetry is prone to manifest unconscious influences and will give a first idea of how these influences can be identified. While the main emphasis in this chapter will be on the philological aspects of poetry therapy by drawing on theories of language and text production, the applicability within the field of poetry therapy as defined in Chapter 2 will not be lost sight of. It will, however, take a background position in order to allow for the necessary focus on the philological concepts and ideas.

At the beginning there was, of course, Freud. Since their inception at the beginning of the previous century, Freud's central theories have entered everyday discourse, permeating the fundamental conceptions of psychoanalysis throughout the world. Virtually every person, for example, knows about 'Freudian slips'. More than any other, the sexual aspect of Freudian psychoanalysis "has caught the public imagination, becoming an endless source of everyday amateur psychologizing and embarrassing 'knob jokes.'[71] Even the advertising industry has seized upon these Freudian symbols"

---

[71] This area has indeed been the most controversial aspect of his theories during Freud's lifetime. Modern psychoanalysis has, rightly so, moved away from this.

(de Berg 20).[72] Since there are so many misapprehensions of Freud's concepts, it is indispensable to revisit certain aspects of Freudian psychoanalytic theory first hand. To do so will not only help to avoid falling victim to pervading misunderstandings that make up the dominant public discourse on Freud, but will also pave the way towards Lacan's re-reading of Freud in (post-)structuralist terms, a re-reading that is the basis of Lacan's radically refashioned concept of the unconscious. This concept is central to my model of poetry therapy and will be appropriated to make evident poetry's close connection to the unconscious and thus its unique value for psychotherapy.

Freud sets up a tripartite system of the psyche which consists of the Ego, the Id and the Superego.[73] The Id is Freud's concept for the activities of the unconscious, which is governed only by the animalistic urge to satisfy its needs. In direct opposition to it Freud posits the Superego, representing the moral, ethical and social obligations and rules necessary for human beings to live together in a civilised manner. Between these two Freud places the Ego, which is constantly under pressure from both sides and has to mediate between the desires of the Id and the demands of the Superego. According to Freud, it is when the Ego is not strong enough to perform its mediator function that psychopathologies arise. The Ego is where Freud situates the cogito, the self. Although these three entities are conceptualised individually by Freud as the building blocks of the psyche, it would be wrong to envision them as fixed and separate places, or even as places at all. Rather, they are processes which are always in flux and exercise their influence continuously on the individual. This is how Henk de Berg summarises this with respect to the unconscious:

> Like the conscious, the unconscious is not a place but a process, always active, always in motion, always exerting its influence. Therefore, to think of the unconscious as a kind of cellar where we stack away our unwanted urges and memories is to overlook its most fundamental feature, dynamism. Our unconscious is a force that is always operative, not some Pandora's Box, effective only when its contents are brought to the light of day. At every given moment, the human mind is an interplay of consciousness and unconsciousness. (5)

---

[72] Hollywood can serve as another example of the (ab)use of Freudian concepts in popular culture. To begin with, the very use of these concepts by Hollywood studios attests to this. Directors and film studios would not include Freudian references in their movies if they did not believe them to be readily discernable by the audience. One could produce an endless list of movies containing, more or less implicitly, Freudian theories. Recent examples dealing overtly with Freudian concepts are, among others, *The Cell* (2000) which attempts to visualise the unconscious of a killer. A more comic turn is provided by Harold Ramis' *Analyze This* (1999) and its sequel *Analyze That* (2002), which pitches a stereotypical Freudian therapist (Billy Crystal) against a stereotypical mafia boss (de Niro).

[73] The following summary of Freud's concepts is based on: *The Interpretation of Dreams* (1900), "Formulations on the Two Principles of Mental Functioning" (1913), "Instincts and their Vicissitudes" (1915), "Repression" (1915), "The Unconscious" (1915), "A Metapsychological Supplement to the Theory Of Dreams" (1917), "Beyond the Pleasure Principle" (1920), "The Ego and the Id" (1923).

It is essential to keep in mind that the three 'parts' of the psyche are no stable sites or places, but processes or functions which continually act upon each other. The Superego, while it might seem a rather stable construct, is changing with the social norms and values it represents. For instance, the social conventions that apply at work demand a different set of censorship and control than, for instance, a family reunion, while a birthday is different from a funeral and so forth. The Superego has thus to be envisioned as a function, namely one of censorship and control, the extent and characteristics of which are dynamic and dependent on ever-changing internal as well as external circumstances. The dynamism of the Superego is thus essential to its function. The same is true of the Id. The unconscious is the realm of drives and instincts. These can either be active or dormant. They are activated by outside stimuli (for example, pain or visual perceptions) or by intrapsychic pressure. Once activated, they demand satisfaction or release. Since some drives are linked to repressed memories, these can become active as well, and it is only in such instances that they may find their way back – are transformed into – consciously perceptible messages. The unconscious is thus in constant flux as it functions as a chaotic 'on' and 'off' of bodily and psychic drives; chaotic because triggered by unpredictable stimuli. The Ego in its mediator function can itself only be a dynamic function that moulds itself according to the demands of the Id and the Superego. Since human beings perceive their own identity as stable and unique, it is difficult to image the Ego as a fluid function rather than a stable entity. Still, one's identity is always, if ever so slightly, different, depending on where one is and with whom. Every social situation forces the individual to take on another role. The individual's identity thus constantly changes with every new role it takes on. At the same time, the socio-cultural environment also operates on the unconscious, the Id, via drives that are activated by outside stimuli. A person's identity, which the Ego-function forms from between the pressure zones of the Superego and the Id, is thus subject to and dependent on social circumstances that exert influence at any given moment. The Ego-function is therefore particularly dynamic.

The creative process of producing art is linked closely to the Ego's function of balancing out the Id and the Superego functions. Creative activities thus are Ego-strengthening and help to reduce psychic pressure. Freud often exemplifies his concepts by means of literature or art and frequently comments on the close connection between unconscious processes and the creation of art. Talking about the pleasure principle and the reality principle, he states:

> Art brings about a reconciliation between the two principles in a peculiar way. An artist is originally a man who turns away from reality because he cannot come to terms with the renunciation of instinctual satisfaction which it at first demands, and who allows his erotic and ambitious wishes full play in the life of phantasy. He finds the way back to reality, however, from this world of phantasy by making use of special gifts to mould his phantasies into truths of a new kind, which are valued by men as precious reflections of reality. Thus in a certain fashion he actually becomes the hero, the king, the creator, or the favourite he desired to be, without following the long roundabout path of making

real alterations in the external world. ("Formulations on the Two Functions of Mental Functioning" 224)

Art, Freud suggest here, is a route both of escape from the troubles of reality as well as a way back. The "reconciliation" of the pleasure principle and the reality principle that art represents, according to Freud, constitutes one reason for the healing powers of art. Also, artists can live out their instinctual drives in ways harmless to society. This is what Freud has termed 'sublimation'. Humanistic art therapy, let it be remembered, locates psychological conditions in the inability of a client to cope with the demands of reality. In the light of this, one could also say that in creating art, the demands of the pleasure principle and the demands of the reality principle are subjected to a process which transforms them into a state of mutual co-existence, or in more Freudian terms, mutual satisfaction. The demands of the reality principle are thus fused with those of the pleasure principle under the transformative pressure of the artistic process, the result of which is the work of art. Therefore, the work of art – the poem – is more than a balanced mixture of the demands of pleasure principle and reality principle; the transformative process has made it more than the sum of its parts. This notwithstanding, any piece of art always still contains the traces of its raw materials beneath the surface. This residual material of art's transformation prompts Kramer to define art as "retell[ing] a story of transformation" (39).[74] Art, according to Kramer,

> retells the story of transformation; it offers primarily the pleasure of witnessing the process. [...] Artist and audience travel together in two directions, from the primitive source of the creative impulse towards its final form, and again from the contemplation of form to the depth of complex, contradictory, and primitive emotions. In this adventure conscious, preconscious, and unconscious processes complement each other. (39)

The key word in Kramer's statement is "transformation." Creation of art is not, as is often claimed, a mere translation of unconscious material into a consciously acceptable and perceptible form. It is not a process of a one-to-one transfer of content. Rather, the original – unconscious – content is changed during the process of creation; it is turned into something different while yet retaining the essence of its original nature. Thus, the transformative process of poetic creation does not imply that once-hidden meaning suddenly lies open in the poem. Rather, unconscious influences are re-coded into language during the poetic process, entering the text more often than not in distorted and

---

[74] Not all sublimation is artistic in nature. Anger that is directed towards a supervisor at work, for instance, and which therefore cannot be articulated or acted upon, can be sublimated by being redirected towards another person. The instinctual drive causing the initial feeling of anger is thus given vent through another activity, i.e. it is sublimated. For Freud, art was a special form of sublimation superior to other forms. He considered the artist a person with "special gifts," a genius, and therefore sublimation via art was, for him, a route only few could travel (For a similar argument cf. Rank, *Art and Artist. Creative Urge and Personal Development*). This contention is no longer valid today. Every human being is endowed with a creative faculty and everyone is capable of experiencing and initiating a creative process.

hidden form such as symbols or verbal ambiguities. These are traces of the unconscious which, due to their nature as trace, form part – and not necessarily the final part – of a network of traces, a chain of supplementarity, that can be mapped in order to uncover relevant unconscious content.[75] Before turning to the poetic process in particular, however, it is necessary to address the structure of the unconscious and find out in which way it affects written texts and imprints these with additional, therapeutically valuable meaning.

The poetic artefact, it has been shown, retells the story of the transformation of internal libidinal drive motilities and external socio-cultural demands from the chaos of the threshold of their ever-changing pressure-zones into a seemingly stable product. It tells this story by means of veiled traces of this very process. These hidden traces are ingrained in the textual matrix of the poem, which, when read accordingly, may (re-) produce additional and/or original meaning. The textual traces of the sublimatory transformation are subversive instances that, on closer inspection, disrupt the message of the text, opening it up to further interpretations. They serve as pathways to encoded and sometimes encrypted messages from the unconscious. The finished poem, like any text, is thus only stable on the surface. For now, a discussion of the impact of the poem's inherent instability on the practice of poetry therapy will be postponed in favour of a close explication of the Freudian topography of the psyche.[76] This will provide the basis for mapping the interconnection between libidinal drives, sublimation, language and, eventually, poetry.

3.1 From the Freudian Unconscious to Lacan's 'Unconscious as Language'

The Ego, as mediator between Superego and Id, is also the function that facilitates sublimation. Drives are sublimated by the Ego into socially acceptable behaviour. Sublimation is thus a fundamental psychic function and not only reserved for art. Sublimation through art is only one means of sublimation. Kramer designates sublimation as

---

[75] This process is indeed more of a 'mapping' than a retracing since the traces do not necessarily follow a chronological structure but rather constitute nodes which can connect the most disparate of experiences and notions regardless of chronology.

[76] Cf., for now, Eco's statement regarding the openness and completeness of works of art: "A work of art, therefore, is a complete and *closed* form in its uniqueness as a balanced and organic whole, while at the same time constituting an *open* product on account of its susceptibility to countless different interpretations which do not impinge on its unadulterable specificity. Hence every reception of a work of art is both an *interpretation* and a *performance* of it, because in every reception the work takes on a fresh perspective for itself. Nonetheless, it is obvious that works like those of Berio or Stockhausen are 'open' in a far more tangible sense. In primitive terms we can say that they are quite literally 'unfinished': the author seems to hand them on to the performer more or less like the components of a construction kit." (*The Role of the Reader* 49; emphasis original)

processes whereby primitive urges, emanating from the id, are transformed by the ego into complex acts that do not serve direct instinctual gratification. In the course of this transformation, primitive behavior, necessarily asocial, gives way to activities that are ego-syntonic [...]. [Sublimation] embraces a multitude of mechanisms. These include displacement, symbolization, neutralization of drive energy, identification and integration. Always there is a threefold change: of the object upon which interest centers, of the desired goal, and of the kind of energy through which the new goal is attained. (28)

Sublimation is a complex psychic function which entails the participation of "a multitude of mechanisms." These mechanisms are necessary to affect the respective changes in "object," "goal," and "energy." The change "of the object" is occasioned by the function of the Superego according to the specific cultural circumstances present. The "desired goal" of the unconscious is altered by necessity of being blocked from the original goal by the Superego. The "kind of energy" to attain the new goal is then chosen by the Ego-function under the functional pressures of the Id and Superego. A forbidden sexual desire may in this way be sublimated by physical activity of another kind such as sport. The primitive urges or drives that are sublimated are granted gratification via an activity other than the one originally desired. This substitute activity is symbolic for the original, but forbidden activity. Sublimation thus works through "symbolization," and it is here that one can locate the key towards understanding the relationship between the unconscious and the conscious, between trace and text:

> If [Freud] teaches us to follow the ascending ramifications of the symbolic lineage of the text of the patient's free associations, in order to detect the nodal points [*noeuds*] of its structure at the places where its verbal forms intersect, then it is already quite clear that symptoms can be entirely resolved in an analysis of language, because a symptom is itself structured like language: a symptom is language from which speech must be delivered. (Lacan, "The Function and Field of Speech and Language in Psychoanalysis" 222-223)

Here, Lacan recalls that, according to Freud, the unconscious presents itself in symbolic fashion. Therefore, one has to follow "the symbolic lineage" of the client's text. This text can be one of free association, but may equally well be a written poetic text. Lacan grounds the effectiveness of psychoanalytic discourse in the fact that "a symptom is itself structured like language" and can therefore be resolved through language. Symptoms find expression in the client's text (spoken as well as written) as symbols and images, and it is by means of these that they can be discovered and faced. It is on the basis of this connection of symptoms with symbols that Lacan postulates that the unconscious is structured like language. Symptoms, Lacan argues, are symbolic for the actual (mental) illness. In their symbolic character they are akin to the linguistic sign, or to be more precise: the signifier. The signifier is also a symbolic representation of something mental, namely the signified. Lacan concludes that since symptoms of mental illness are structured like language – since they are signifiers of the actual problem – they are linguistic in nature, and since they originate from the unconscious, one can conclude that the unconscious itself is structured like language.

At first glance, the notion of the unconscious as structured like language goes against the classical interpretation of Freud's concepts. The Freudian unconscious is governed by the so-called primary processes, which are structureless. The Freudian unconscious knows neither time, nor space, nor order. It is a place where drives run wild and where no type of ordering principle reigns. Order is only imposed later on by the Ego and Superego functions when unconscious elements try to become conscious or crave satisfaction (cf. Freud "The Unconscious," especially 186-195). This strict separation between the chaos of the unconscious and the order of consciousness is reflected in traditional aesthetics where art is identified with the conscious functions and is perceived as inherently structural. According to this point of view, art is to follow organisational patterns that impose order and, consequently, art is perceived as being "exclusively shaped by the conscious and pre-conscious functions, the so-called secondary process" (Ehrenzweig 3). According to this understanding of the creation of art, the unconscious does not actively participate in it. The unconscious may provide the initial stimulus for the artistic process, but it does not manifest itself in the finished piece of art. If at all, the unconscious elements are subjected to the ordering principles demanded by art. Within traditional aesthetics, in order for art to be art, it has to be structured in a clear form and express the artist's full (conscious) control over the material. With the emergence of experimental forms of art and a consolidation of a postmodern understanding of art, this conception of art can no longer be upheld, of course. Today, art is seen as inherently unstable, harbouring virtually unlimited possibilities for interpretation. Psychologically, Lacan explains this – paradoxically at first – by endowing the unconscious with a structure, the structure of language. In doing so, Lacan establishes "a completely new definition of the psychoanalytic experience itself; he defined it as an experience of discourse. His formula, 'the unconscious is structured as language', has been repeated so often that it seems obvious. [...] Before Lacan, no one thought of locating the subject *within the very act of talking*" (Safouan 3; emphasis original). Quite surprisingly at first glance, Lacan insists that his radical reinterpretations of psychoanalytic principles are a 'return to Freud'. There is, however, legitimacy in Lacan's assertion: by closely reading Freud's original works in the light of structuralism (predominantly Saussure, Barthes, and Levi-Strauss), Lacan reinterprets Freudian theories in a new light.[77] Lacan's point of departure in re-reading Freud is the realisation that Freudian psychoanalysis anticipated the principles underlying structuralism. This is most predominantly so with respect to structural linguistics as pioneered

---

[77] In doing so, Lacan criticises the concepts of Ego Psychology as well as Object Relation Theory. On Ego Psychology, cf. Gertrude Blanck, *Ego Psychology: Theory and Practice*; Heinz Hartmann, *Essays on Ego Psychology. Selected Problems in Psychoanalytic Theory*. On Object Relation Theory, cf. Harry Guntrip, *Psychoanalytic Theory, Therapy, and the Self*, Frank L. Summers, *Transcending the Self: An Object Relations Model of Psychoanalytic Therapy* (especially Chapter 2) and Summers' *Object Relations Theories and Psychopathology: A Comprehensive Text*. Cf. also Joseph Smith, *Arguing with Lacan: Ego Psychology and Language* and Burgoyne, *The Klein-Lacan Dialogue*.

by Saussure, Jakobson and the Prague School. With regard to structuralist terminology, Lacan observes:

> Freud did not have this particular instrument at his disposal. But this historically motivated lacuna makes all the more instructive the fact that the mechanisms described by Freud as those of the primary processes, by which the unconscious is governed, correspond exactly to the functions this school of linguistics [the Prague School] believes determine the most radical axes of the effects of language, namely metaphor and metonymy – in other words, the effects of the substitution and combination of signifiers in the synchronic and diachronic dimensions, respectively, in which they appear in discourse. ("The Subversion of the Subject and the Dialectic of Desire" 676)

Lacan argues here that Freud discovered and understood the importance and the fundamental processes of language, and their centrality for the unconscious, but, since he lacked the descriptive instruments to phrase his insights accordingly, the close conceptual proximity between Freud's theories and structural linguistics has been overlooked. According to Lacan, Freud's concepts concerning the primary processes which govern the unconscious are the same as those elaborated by Saussure and Jakobson with regard to the fundamental properties of language. In the context of the present focus of delineating the ways unconscious content can negotiate its way into the conscious, the analogous nature between the primary processes and the functions of language deserve particular attention. In this respect, it is illuminating to consider what Freud says about the possibility of unconscious drives becoming conscious:

> An instinct can never become an object of consciousness – only the idea that represents the instinct can. Even in the unconscious, moreover, an instinct cannot be represented otherwise than by an idea. If the instinct did not attach itself to an idea or manifest itself as an affective state, we could know nothing about it. When we nevertheless speak of an unconscious instinctual impulse or of a repressed instinctual impulse, the looseness of phraseology is a harmless one. We can only mean an instinctual impulse the ideational representative [Vorstellungsrepräsentanz] of which is unconscious, for nothing else comes into consideration. (Freud, "The Unconscious" 177)

The *Vorstellungsrepräsentanz* is Freud's term for what Saussure has termed the 'signifier'. The way the "instinct attach[es] itself to an idea" in order to enter consciousness is precisely the same mechanism as delineated by Saussure with regard to the linguistic sign. Saussure's sign, as is well known, "unites [...] a concept and a sound-image. The latter [being] not the material sound, a purely physical thing, but the psychological imprint of the sound" (Saussure 66). Saussure's "sound image" is Freud's *Vorstellungsrepräsentanz*. Saussure's "concept," i.e. the signified, is equivalent to Freud's "instinct" which can never express itself in the consciousness unless linked to a *Vorstellungsrepräsentanz*. A signified can never be expressed save through its signifier. Saussure "call[s] the combination of a concept and a sound-image a *sign*" (ibid. 67; emphasis original) and by virtue of this parallelism it is possible to designate the combination, or better: the linkage of a drive motility with a *Vorstellungsrepräsentanz* as a symptom. Consequently, the symptom has the same properties as the Saussurean sign; in fact: it *is* the Saussurean sign. It is due to this connection that Lacan states of the symptom that it "is itself structured like language, a symptom is language from which speech must be delivered" ("The Function and Field of Speech and Language in Psychoanalysis" 223). It is here that Lacan locates the linguistic basis of Freud's theories. Psychoanalysis functions so well as a *talking cure* precisely because speech, that is, language, and psychological symptoms are structurally identical.

Repression serves as a perfect example to illuminate this vital contention of the identical structure of language and psychological symptoms further. For a memory or desire to be repressed, it is not enough to simply repress the instinctual aspect of it. Both Freud and Lacan clearly state that drives cannot become conscious, but need to "attach" themselves to a *Vorstellungsrepräsentanz*. Along the same lines, the signified is nothing – is unthinkable – without its signifier and both are only apprehensible as the complete sign. Repression thus does not affects the drive itself, but its *Vorstellungsrepräsentanz*. Repression is the repression of the signifier, because only by its means can the symptom become manifest in the consciousness and only by its repression can it be banned from conscious thought. For Lacan, "Freud's conception […] leaves no room for ambiguity at this point: it is the signifier that is repressed, there being no other meaning that can be given to the […] word *Vorstellungsrepräsentanz*" (Lacan, "In Memory of Ernest Jones: On his Theory of Symbolism" 598).[78] The instinct, that is, the signified, is not – at least not directly – affected by repression (or any other psychic mechanism) because it is by definition incapable of being conscious. Since the unconscious, according to Freud, is defined by "exemption from mutual contradiction, primary process (mobility of cathexes), timelessness, and replacement of external by psychical reality" ("The Unconscious" 187), it is impossible to repress a drive itself. This is first of all due to the "timelessness" prevailing in the unconscious, but equally because of the "mobility of cathexes." To wit, drives have the ability to "attach" themselves not only to one *Vorstellungsrepräsentanz*, but are characterised by a mobility to establish numerous such connections. It is in doing so that repressed drives can cross the threshold between the unconscious and the conscious in spite of a successful repression of their original signifiers. Freudian slips are the outcome of this process, as is the fact that every text contains a surplus of meaning. This surplus is conditioned by the mobility of cathexes of drives. Lacan thus postulates that "[s]tarting with Freud, the unconscious becomes a chain of signifiers that repeats and insists somewhere […], interfering in the cuts offered it by actual discourse and the cogitation it informs" (Lacan, "The Subversion of the Subject and the Dialectic of Desire" 676).

The above example of the process of repression pointedly elucidates Lacan's fundamental statement that the 'unconscious is structured like language' in the context

---

[78] There is a certain ambiguity in Lacan's writings as to his definition of the signifier in relation to Freudian concepts. Lacan defines both Freud's *Wahrnehmungszeichen* and the term *Vorstellungsrepräsentanz* as signifier although they are distinctly separate terms in Freud (cf. Arrivé 139-140 for a discussion of this topic). Since the identification of signifier with *Vorstellungsrepräsentanz* seems to me to be the predominant one in Lacan, I have used this term here.

of Freudian theory. The refashioning of Freud's "instinct" and *Vorstellungsrepräsentanz* in terms of structuralist linguistics constitutes a fusion of both fields and inevitably recentres psychoanalysis on the primacy of language. With this, Lacan asserts the primacy of language and speech even more rigorously than Freud does. This taking seriously of the language aspect in psychotherapy is also required in poetry therapy. This is the more so since language is at the very heart of both disciplines. An additional implication of the Lacanian refashioning is that it automatically puts the creator of language – the client – at the centre of the endeavour, a fact that fits the humanistic approach constituted for poetry therapy above. There are, however, a number of additional implications arising from Lacan's 'return to Freud' which affect the production of meaning and, by proxy, the nature of the (poetic) text as well as the client. It is therefore necessary to investigate these implications at some length.

3.2 The (post-)structural Unconscious and its Implications for the poetic Aspect of Poetry Therapy

With respect to the position of the individual, Lacan maintains that

> the subject as such is uncertain because he is divided by the effects of language. Through the effects of speech, the subject always realizes himself more in the Other, but he is already pursuing there more than half of himself. He will simply find his desire ever more divided, pulverized, in the circumscribable metonymy of speech. The effects of language are always mixed with the fact, which is the basis of the analytic experience, that the subject is subject only from being subjected to the field of the Other, the subject proceeds from his synchronic subjection in the field of the Other. (Lacan, *Four Concepts* 188)

The above quote shows the complex nature of and the wide-ranging implications resulting from the refashioning of Freudian concepts along structural linguistic lines. Lacan mentions effects on the subject, its division and subjection, the metonymy of speech, the realization in the Other, desire and the connection of all these with the "analytic experience." In order to understand the extent of the Lacanian refashioning it is necessary to know what each of the above terms denotes within the field of Lacanian psychoanalysis. This will be the central concern of the following pages.

Lacan, while admitting that there is an apparently fixed relationship between the constituents of the Saussurean sign, regards the sign as ultimately unstable and prone to a continual sliding of meaning even under the most strict socio-linguistic conditions. He locates this instability in the nature of the signifier. There is no fixture regarding the possible cathexis of drives and signifiers and, therefore, a signifier is never stable and can contain an unforeseeable surplus of meaning. The nature of the unconscious as essentially timeless and disordered provides the foundation for the contingent cathexes of drives to signifiers. The signifier is thus subject to a constant sliding precisely because it is affected by the contingent 'attachment' of drive motilities. These attached drive motilities can seep – in a scattered fashion – into any text and represent nodal point for the production of surplus meaning. The Lacanian signifier thus constitutes a reservoir of potentially limitless meaning.

Lacan states that the unconscious is structured like language. In this context, Derrida observes that "[l]anguage is a *structure* – a system of oppositions of places and values – and an *oriented* structure. [...] One will be able to call it a *polarization*. Orientation gives direction to movement by relating it to its origin as to its dawning" (*Of Grammatology* 216; emphasis original). The question that presents itself here is the following: what do Lacan and Derrida have in mind when they talk of 'structure' and, with regard to the topic at hand, how can the unconscious be a structure if it is timeless and disordered? To begin with, the concept of structure is and has always been a concept central to how human beings organise the world around them. They categorise, prioritise, and produce hierarchies; in short, human beings, somewhat artificially and arbitrarily, simplify the world and make existence manageable by organising it into structures. Derrida states that

> structure – or rather the structurality of structure – although it has always been at work, has always been neutralized or reduced, and this by a process of giving it a center or of referring it to a point of presence, a fixed origin. The function of this center was not only to orient, balance, and organize the structure [...] but above all to make sure that the organizing principle of the structure would limit what we would call the *play* of the structure. ("Structure, Sign and Play" 278; emphasis original)

According to Derrida, once a structure is set up, a centre is introduced to limit the theoretically endless structural possibilities, the infinite "play" which would otherwise result. This centre is, however, essentially arbitrary, designed to privilege one origin, one cause, at the cost of marginalising others. The introduction of a centre organises its structural field, but it favours monocausal explanations. Derrida proposes to re-think the manner in which structure has previously been defined and used.[79] He proceeds from the basic assumptions delineated above, but maintains that, though each structure has a centre, a fixed origin, this very centre does in fact not exist as "a fixed locus but a function, a sort of nonlocus in which an infinite number of sign-substitutions come into play" (ibid. 280). The centre of a structure is, in Derrida's view, a non-locus, because it is purely arbitrary and prone to be infinitely supplanted. It is arbitrary, because, as with the Freudian concept of the psyche, the centre of a structure is a function rather than a place. It is the function of the centre that upholds the structure and not the nature of the centre itself. This idea can be exemplified by taking a look at politics. The political system of an imaginary country which is organised according to constitutional democratic principles shall serve as an example. The position of the presidency in the constitution of that country is the centre of its political system; it is here that the legislature, the executive and the juridical branch meet. The office of the

---

[79] Derrida does not, as is sometimes argued, propose to abandon the concept of structure as a whole. This would presuppose a total paradigm shift in how human beings exist and perceive the world which is, of course, impossible.

presidency is thus the centre of the governmental structure of the country and it is here that the whole structure is anchored. This central position is occupied by an individual designated as president. The person of the president is the physical manifestation of the governmental function of the presidency who exercises that function's power. After a certain period of time, however, an election inevitably substitutes the person of the president with another person. Electing a new president does not, however, change the function of the presidency within the structure of the constitution of the country. The president – the human being occupying the office – is merely a temporary token of the presidential function; a token which is contingent and infinitely supplantable. Hence, while the presidency functions as the centre of the structure, it cannot ultimately be connected to one specific person. The centre is thus not a place, or locus, but a function that can be exercised in different manners.

The above has further implications. Since the individual filling the centre-function is interchangeable, it follows that the centre of a structure is never really completely part of the structure precisely because it is exchangeable. Whenever the element of a structure that embodies the function of the centre is exchanged – and this exchange is always a possibility as it is the function not the token that is structurally important – the interrelations between the nodes of the structure are slightly reshuffled – re-polarised – to accompany the change. The centre of a structure thus in fact decentres the structure rather than consolidating it. This can again be made clearer by means of the above example: following an election, the new president, though fulfilling the centre-function and thus guaranteeing the stability of the governmental structure, will have her own understanding of how to fill the role; the new president will manage her office differently from her predecessor within the limits set by the position she has been elected to. The new president inevitably constitutes a reorientation of the working habits within the government which can be conceptualised as a rippling effect on the governmental structure.

The centre-function sets up the limits of the "play" within a structure while it is at the same time bound by these limits. While the centre limits the endless possibilities of "play" within a structure, it remains impossible to define a structure and all possibilities of "play" in their entirety. There is thus no absolute centre that effectively and totally arrests the structural matrix, because of the possibility of exchange. This is a matter of supplementarity which defines the centre as fundamentally transitory. Essentially,

> the supplement supplements. It adds only to replace. It intervenes or insinuates itself *in-the-place-of*; it fills it as if one fills a void. [...] The sign is always the supplement of the thing itself. [...] [T]he supplement is *exterior*, outside of the positivity to which it is super-added, alien to that which, in order to be replaced by it, must be other than it. (Derrida, *Of Grammatology* 145; emphasis original)

Thus one cannot determine the centre of a structure because the centre is always transitory and that which replaces the centre is outside the structure and as such unknown. The position of the president is temporary and every single president is inevitably supplemented by another one. Since the new president is unknown until the moment of successful election, the new polarisation so to speak cannot be anticipated. Thus, the supplement of the centre is something that is added to the structure, because it has not previously been part of the structure. Once this supplement is added as centre, replacing another centre, this new addition reorients the structure, or, to speak with Derrida, it re-polarises it. Hence, there is always something missing from a structure, namely "a center which arrests and grounds the play of substitution" (Derrida, "Structure, Sign, and Play" 289).[80] In this manner, a final consolidation of the structure is endlessly deferred. By being endlessly deferred and thereby decentred, the centre as non-locus is the motor and governing principle of the structure. It simultaneously permits the play within its structure and closes off the play for "[a]s center it is the point at which the substitution of contents, elements, or terms, is no longer possible" (ibid. 279).

Lacan constitutes the unconscious as 'structured like language' and Derrida's notions about the structure and its centre can be applied here. In linguistic terms, the centre-function can be perceived as a signified that is expressed by varying signifiers. In language, Derrida implies, the concept of the signified serves as the centre in that it anchors the signifier, giving it a point of origin, reference and orientation. But language is, according to Saussure, a structure that is entirely differential, i.e. that is constructed and produces meaning through difference. Considering this essential feature of language, Derrida arrives at the conclusion that language is lacking a centre. He does not believe in the signified as a vehicle of meaning, much less a vehicle of stable meaning. In language, the substitution that is characteristic of the centre-function takes place in an arbitrary and unpredictable way. This effectively effaces the centre-function. The structure that is language is caught in a chain of deferral and supplementarity that negates any consolidation of the structure and, therefore, of meaning. The signified can consequently no longer be regarded as essential for the production of meaning in language. The constant deferral from signifier to signifier is in fact what produces meaning. The meaning produced by this process of signification is, however, an inherently unstable and decentred meaning. "The absence of the transcendental signified [the fixed point of origin in the "real" world] extends the domain and the play of signification infinitely" (Derrida, "Structure, Sign, and Play" 280). This (among many other concepts) is what Derrida denotes as *différance*.[81] The deferential nature of

---

[80] This endless deferral, the possibility of infinite substitution of the centre, however, does in no way postulate that any given structure is "an inexhaustible field" (Derrida, "Structure, Sign, and Play" 289). If this were so, conceptualising structures would not help human beings make sense of the world since there would be no simplification involved. Although we cannot define all possibilities of a structure's "play," this does not mean we cannot rule out certain possibilities.

[81] *Différance* was coined by Derrida and is deduced from the French word 'différer', which can mean both 'to differ' and 'to defer'. In spite of this seemingly rather simple dictionary definition, it is extremely difficult to explain the concept of *différance* without going into the intricacies of Derridean philosophy. The first thing to say is that the concept of *différance* is not a concept at all: "The word [*différance*] combines in neither

language means that, without a centre, meaning is never stable and always refers from one signifier to the next ad infinitum. Due to *différance*, human beings cannot come into contact with reality for they cannot escape language in whatever they do. Our world is therefore constructed through language. The objectivity we ascribe to our perception of the world as well as the stability of meaning we credit language with, is in

---

> the active nor the passive voice the coincidence of meanings of the verb *différer*: to differ (in space) and to defer (to put off time, to postpone in presence). Thus it does not function simply either as *différence* (difference) nor as *différance* in the usual sense (deferral) and plays on both meanings at once. [...] Derrida links the concept of *différance* to his play on the words *totalitarian* and *solicitation*. He sees structuralism as a form of philosophical totalitarianism, i.e. as an attempt to account for the totality of a phenomenon by reduction of it to a formula that governs it *totally*. Derrida submits the violent, totalitarian structural project to the counterviolence of *solicitation*, which derives from the Latin *sollicitare*, meaning to shake the totality (from *sollus*, "all," and *ciere*, "to move, to shake"). Every totality, he shows, can be *totally shaken*, that is, can be shown to be founded on that which it excludes, that which would be in *excess* for a reductive analysis of any kind" (Bass, "Translator's Introduction" in Derrida, *Writing and Différence* XVI). Bennington ventures a definition in his book *Jacques Derrida,* which I will quote in abbreviated form here (cf. 70-84): "*Différance* attempts to name: 1. not what Saussure calls differences in the system of *langue*, but the differentiality of being-different of those differences, their 'production,' the 'force' that maintains the system gathered in its dispersion, its *maintenance*. 2. the delay or lateness that means that meaning is always anticipated or else reestablished after the event [...] in which every present element (which is thus never really elementary or present) is stretched or spread between a 'past' and a 'future' which themselves will never have been present. 3. the possibility of any conceptual distinction [...]. The word or concept *différance* is thus itself spread out, *in différance*, plunged into what it attempts to name and understand. It follows that this 'word' or 'concept' can be neither a word nor a concept, naming the condition of possibility (and therefore impossibility) of *all* words and concepts. [This leads us to the concept of *trace* which, in Derrida, works in the same direction as *différance*.] Let us note that if these paradoxes are indeed produced by the application of a 'concept' to itself (*différance* is subject to *différance*), the result is not at all an interiority closed in upon itself, but a metonymic contamination, and therefore opening. [...] We can already name the *trace*. For if every element of the system only gets its identity in its difference from the other elements, every element is in this way marked by all those it is not: it thus bears the trace of those other elements. [...] Every trace is the trace of a trace. [...] [I]n every 'element' all that is 'present' is the other, 'absent' element, which must, for language to be possible, present this alterity *as* alterity. [...] 'Trace' attempts to name this entwinement of the-other-in-the-same which is the condition of the same itself, which would perhaps be the most general statement about what we are trying to understand here. [...] *Différance* is never pure. [...] It is always in between or in-the-process-of; never itself, never present. Let us attempt provisionally to think of it as a *force*, [...] the force that produces and shakes up form. But one quickly sees [...] a pure force would not be a force, it only becomes one faced with another force, resistance. *Différance* 'is' this relation, and thus precedes de jure any given force" (emphasis original).

fact only imaginary. It is something we have artificially postulated in order to make sense of the world.

It is not the world alone that is constructed through language, but, as Lacan postulates, so is the unconscious and, in fact, the human being as subject. For Lacan, the unconscious is "the sum of the effects of speech on the subject, at the level at which the subject constitutes himself out of the effects of the signifier" (*Four Concepts* 126). The unconscious is constituted, like in Freud's theory, not as a place, but as the effects and function of speech. Lacan translates Freud's notion into a linguistic conception of the unconscious that is constituted by unlimited signification, or, in Derridean terminology, a constant process of *différance*. In classical Freudian theory, the aim of psychoanalysis is to bring the chaotic desires and drives to conscious understanding so that they can be managed and ordered. For Lacan, the aim is, on the one hand, to stop the free play of signification, because only in this manner can stable meaning be created. On the other hand, Lacan's connection between symptoms and language implies that symptoms are a distortion in language originating from the unconscious. This distortion has to be resolved in language, i.e. normalised into the system of language. For both Freud and Lacan, this development from chaos/unlimited signification to order/stable meaning happens naturally as we progress from childhood to adulthood. Obstacles encountered during this process, like, most importantly, the inability to successfully overcome the Oedipus Complex, will lead to mental disorders in later life. I will not go into further detail here as to Freud's conception of this process, but it is necessary to concentrate on the refashioning of these Freudian concepts by Lacan, because the Lacanian reconceptualisation of the Oedipus Complex by means of the three realms of the Real, the Imaginary and the Symbolic basically sets up human social existence along linguistic lines. This will serve as the basis to interface psychotherapy and poetry within the broader complex of humanistic art therapy. In the context of interdisciplinarity between poetry and psychotherapy, social existence and interaction linguistically conceived has a unifying function with regard to the two disciplines involved in poetry therapy: it pertains to poetry due to its linguistic basis; at the same time, the realm of the Symbolic can be appropriated to conceptualise not only the regular social position and interaction of clients, but also and especially their social (inter-)dependence and their psychopathologies. The latter is of particular importance as humanistic art therapy concentrates on precisely this area.

3.3 From 'Being' to 'Meaning': The Real, the Imaginary and the Symbolic

For Lacan, the unconscious originates out of the transition from 'Being' to 'Meaning'.[82] This is the stage in human development during which the infant (Latin: 'infans' = 'not speaking') becomes a child, i.e. a speaking subject. The infant begins, like in

---

[82] For a concise summary of this point, cf. Easthope 89-100.

Freud, in a stage where it is inseparable from the mother and knows no distinction between itself and the world (cf. Lacan "The Mirror Stage" 75 passim). This is what Lacan calls the Real. "In the real, everything is simply itself [...]. The gaps and differences between the signifiers in language introduce lack and absence into the subject; the real, in contrast, has no holes in it" (Easthope 90). The Real is thus constituted as a psychic place of completeness and original unity. In the Real, there is only unity and no difference. At this stage, there is only need (for food, comfort, etc.) and the mother that satisfies the infant's needs. The biological condition of need knows no absence. This precludes, for the duration of the developmental phase of the Real, the original difference of presence/absence.[83] When the infant is gradually left alone for longer periods of time, the necessary separation of mother and infant entails the first experience of loss: through this loss of unity – of the Real – the infant begins to become an individuated person. The original difference of presence and absence shatters the state of the Real. Before, there was only 'Being'; now there is difference, and difference denotes 'Meaning'. The absence of the mother introduces difference into the world of the infant which forever closes off the realm of the Real. From the original state of the Real, of pure 'Being', the infant inevitably moves on into 'Meaning' by way of what Lacan calls the Mirror Stage.

At the age of between 6 and 18 months, the infant begins to distinguish between its body and the rest of the world. From need the infant moves into demand. While needs are satisfiable by objects (milk, the body of the mother, being changed, etc.), demand is always a demand for recognition by another, a demand for love. "Need is in the domain of the real, demand happens in the realm of the imaginary" (Easthope 93). The Imaginary denotes the subject's initiation into language which goes along with the constitution of the Ego-functions by means of recognition of the other. Demand is need that expresses itself in language and therefore it is addressed to the other: "demand annuls (*aufhebt* [in a Hegelian sense]) the particularity of everything that can be granted, by transmuting it into a proof of love, and the very satisfactions demand obtains for need are debased (*sich erniedrigt*) to the point of being no more than a crushing brought on by the demand for love" (Lacan, "Signification of the Phallus" 580). Lacan's reasoning here appears tautological at first, but in fact it links demand with language. "A young child in a shop tries to get his parents to buy sweets, then a toy, then an ice-cream [...]. The child is not concerned with the real objects (if it gets one it wants another) but rather with what getting them means" (Easthope 93), namely recognition. Demand manifests itself in the demand for a signifier, which is in essence

---

[83] The dichotomy of presence/absence was first located by Freud in his grandson's *fort/da* play. Little Hans threw away a ball attached to a string saying 'fort' (gone) when he had thrown it and 'da' (here) when he had retrieved the ball (cf. "Beyond the Pleasure Principle," especially 12-17, and Lacan, *Four Fundamental Concepts* 62-63; cf. also Easthope 34-36 for a summary account.). According to Freud, this game was a compensation for his mother's absence. It allowed the child to attain a certain level of mastery over the absence of things thus coming to terms with his mother being away.

an empty signifier easily exchanged for another, because it does not represent that which is needed, namely love. "[D]emand always fails to get what it wants" (ibid. 94), because its satisfaction is endlessly deferred. Demand asks for the particular but in fact seeks the universal, the acknowledgement and certainty of being loved. Since demand is beyond satisfaction it passes into desire. Lacan defines desire as "neither the appetite for satisfaction nor the demand for love, but the difference that results from the subtraction of the first from the second, the very phenomenon of their splitting (Spaltung)" ("Signification of the Phallus" 580). Demand is the demand for a signifier and as such it is subject to *différance*. Since demand seeks the particular but does so in language, which is universal, demand inevitably "annuls the particularity of everything." In this split, which falls into the Mirror Stage and coincides with the subject's initiation into the Symbolic Order – the precise process of which will be examined shortly –, desire is created at the point where need and demand are separated. Something of need, of the Real, of 'Being', is present as a trace in desire. Since a trace is always a trace of a trace, it is caught in a continuous sliding which can never be arrested. Desire can therefore never be satisfied and this perpetually constitutes a lack. Desire is therefore "a relation of being to lack" (Lacan, *Seminar II* 223). "Desire is an unconscious search for a lost object, lost not because it is *in front* of desire waiting to be refound but because it is already *behind* desire and producing it in the first place" (Easthope 97; emphasis original). The lack desire strives to fill is need which has been irretrievably lost in the Real in the course of the above split. It is therefore "*behind* desire;" it is the cause of desire and its motor. Desire, Easthope rightly points out, is the search for "a lost object." Lacan calls this object *objet petit a*. The 'a' stands for the French 'autre' – the other. The other has to be differentiated from the Other (with a capital 'O'). Whereas the Other denotes all the signifiers that are 'other,' which can be equalled to language as a whole, the other denotes the one signifier which the subject has chosen as its object of desire. The other is therefore a particular subset of the universal Other.[84]

Once the sense of the Other[85] has been introduced into the infant, it can never be removed. This coming to terms with the appearance of the Other is the condition of

---

[84] Cf. also Safouan: "The first point is that Lacan was always convinced that the human object cannot be identified with the object of knowledge. To him the idea of an object of knowledge is the result of a long tradition of occidental thought. For Lacan there is another, more primitive object: the object of desire. [...] [I]n our everyday experience desire is most often experienced as regret or nostalgia, or it is defined as 'that which I don't know,' or 'I didn't mean that,' or 'I don't know what I want,' or 'I wanted something else.' So you can even say that the object of desire as commonly experienced is always the Other thing" (8).

[85] On the 'o/Other' in Lacan, cf. Evans: "The 'other' is perhaps the most complex term in Lacan's work. [...] In 1955 Lacan draws a distinction between 'the little other' ('the other') and 'the big Other' ('the Other') [...]. 1. The little other is the other who is not really other, but a reflection and projection of the ego. [...] He is simultaneously the counterpart and the specular image. The little other is thus entirely inscribed in the

becoming an individuated subject. It is irreversible and inevitable. The process which brings the infant to a conception of its own wholeness is the Mirror Stage proper. The Mirror Stage initiates and enables the movement from the Real into the Imaginary and finally into the Symbolic.[86] The infant, knowing what the 'others' look like and perceiving them as whole rather than fragmented, eventually sees itself in the mirror. Seeing the mirror image, the infant can construct its own unity. It sees itself as unified and identifies the image in the mirror as 'I'. Thus, the mirror gives the infant a sense of an integrated body and of a self, a sense which is reinforced by the other persons who confirm that the being in the mirror is indeed the infant.[87]

> It suffices to understand the mirror stage in this context as an *identification*, in the full sense analysis gives to the term: namely, the transformation that takes place in the subject when he assumes [*assume*] an image – an image that is seemingly predestined to have an effect at this phase, as witnessed by the use of analytic theory of antiquity's term, "imago". [...] But the important point is that this form situates the agency known as the ego, prior to its social determination, in a fictional direction [...]. The total form of his body, by which the subject anticipates the maturation of his powers in a mirage, is given to him only as a gestalt, that is, in an exteriority in which, to be sure, this form is more constitutive than constituted. (Lacan, "Mirror Stage" 76)

Through the identification with its own mirror image, the infant's Ego is formed. The infant, by recognising the semblance as itself, internalises this semblance, which is unified and not fragmented, thus creating the Ego-functions that enables the infant to think of itself as 'I'. In truth, however, the infant's identification with the mirror image is a misrecognition. What the infant designates with 'I' is, in fact, not itself, but an image. The unified mirror image of the infant's body is external to the infant. It is a *gestalt*, which is to say that the tendencies of human perception towards *form* misconstrue a unity that is in fact not present. This is the reason why Lacan states that it is

---

imaginary order. [...] 2. The big Other designates radical alterity, an other-ness which transcends the illusory otherness of the imaginary because it cannot be assimilated through identification. Lacan equates this radical alterity with language and the law, and hence the big Other is inscribed in the other of the symbolic. Indeed, the big Other *is* the symbolic insofar as it is particularised for each subject. The Other is thus both another subject, in its radical alterity and unassimilable uniqueness, and also the symbolic order which mediates the relationship with that other subject" (*An Introductory Dictionary of Lacanian Psychoanalysis* 132-133). A closer examination of the concepts of the Symbolic and the Imaginary will be given in the main text shortly.

[86] It is important to keep in mind during the following discussion of the Imaginary that it is still pre-Symbolic, i.e. anterior to language. The Mirror Stage is part of the Imaginary while the Imaginary is a condition that persists even after the Symbolic Order has been established. The Imaginary is the realm in which the self is formed and kept.

[87] The mirror is not to be taken as a literal mirror. Lacan's mirror represents the feedback we get from other people regarding our behaviour and deeds; the responses to our actions from our social environment. Identity is constructed via a negotiation of what other people think of us, how we are 'mirrored' in their opinions. This is what the metaphor of the mirror denotes in Lacan's theory.

"more constitutive than constituted." The Ego, for Lacan, is therefore to some extent fantasy, based on an external image rather than an intrinsic whole. The nature of the Ego as an image marks it as essentially fictitious. This, in turn, makes it ideal. The Ego as deduced from the mirror image is an ideal Ego that allows the infant to completely identify with it. Since the Ego is an imaginary entity, it can accommodate all that the infant projects into it. It is perfect, a self that is whole and without insufficiency – a self-sustaining entity that has no lack or sense of absence.[88] The infant's identification with its own semblance during the Mirror Stage creates the fiction of a stable and unified whole that is able to compensate for the loss of the Real. Since the mirror image is drawn from the responses of the (social) environment of the infant, it necessitates a reorientation of the maturation towards the external and social. Consequently, the subject has to enter the Symbolic Order, the realm of language and speech and hence of human culture.

The Symbolic Order refers to the realm and structure of language that we must enter in order to become speaking subjects. The child's voluntary subjugation under the laws of language marks the entrance into the Symbolic Order. The place of language, which is the Symbolic, "is that of the Other, with a capital O, because here it is a matter of a different kind of otherness, which has nothing to do with vision and nothing to do with image or semblance, but which has everything to do with language and the talking subject" (Safouan 11). Safouan emphasises that the Other that is language is fundamentally different from the otherness encountered before. When the other was constituted in the Mirror Stage, it hinged on "image" and "semblance" in a manner that was anterior to language. The Other that is language is not Imaginary but Symbolic.[89] While it does not entail a renunciation of the Imaginary, the entrance into the Symbolic does require the infant's subjugation under its law:

> The symbolic function is [...] dissociated from all pleasure, made to oppose it, and is set up as the paternal place, the place of the superego. According to this view, the only way to react against the consequences of repression imposed by the compulsion of the pleasure principle is to renounce pleasure through symbolization by setting up the sign through the absence of the object, which is expelled and lost forever. (Kristeva, *Revolution* 149)

In order to pass from the Imaginary to the Symbolic, the child needs to encounter difference as it is the foundation of language. The Imaginary is still prelinguistic in nature, but it introduces into the child the concept of difference; with the formation of the

---

[88] Lacan in fact distinguishes two Egos: the ideal Ego and the Ego-ideal. Since this distinction is not essential to the present argument, I shall not pursue the matter further. Cf. *Four Fundamental Concepts* 144, where Lacan comments on the ideal Ego and the Ego-ideal, but does not provide a further explanation. Cf. also Lacan, *Seminar I*, Chapters IX-XI.

[89] The child does not forgo the Imaginary completely when entering language proper (the Ego is forever caught in the imaginary miscognition of its own existence and the fantasy of unity).

Ego, the dichotomy between self and other is established. With this dichotomy, the infant formulates the idea of 'Otherness' (capital 'O'). It knows the difference between itself and the Other, and from this the infant can deduce meaning, namely its own individuality as opposed to others. As we have seen in our discussion of Derrida, the structure of language is differential and with the discovery of the concept of difference in the Imaginary phase, the infant is ready to enter language. In addition to the original dichotomy of presence/absence, which introduced the concept of difference as such, the difference between the self and the other established in the Mirror Phase allows the child to produce meaning for the first time. It is this which marks its entrance into the Symbolic Order. "The function of the mirror stage [...] is to establish a relationship between an organism and its reality – or, as they say, between the *Innenwelt* and the *Umwelt*" (Lacan, "Mirror Stage" 78). The subject's 'Being' reorients itself towards the *Umwelt* and in order to successfully do so it requires language to express 'Meaning'. Language is the means to access the *Umwelt*. Without it, the subject would remain isolated and its identity would remain fragmented.

Because the child's desire is now mediated by a concern for the other via the *objet petit a*, the Ego "turns the *I* into an apparatus to which every instinctual pressure constitutes a danger, even if it corresponds to a natural maturation process" (ibid.). Necessary and inevitable as the subjugation under the rules of language is, it cannot be precipitated of the infant's own initiative, because, "[t]he very normalization of this maturation process is [...] dependent on cultural intervention" (Lacan, "Mirror Stage" 79). This "cultural intervention" is represented by the figure of the father. In order to keep up the idealised image of the Ego that underlies the subject, instincts and drives have to be kept in check and this is achieved by means of a subjectification under the law of the Symbolic Order. The Symbolic Order is perceived by Lacan as paternal and its structural rules of language are called 'The Name of the Father', or 'The Law of the Father'.[90] "The father represents a function of both power and temperament simultaneously; an imperative that is no longer blind but 'categorical'; and a person who dominates and arbitrates the avid wrenching and jealous ambivalence that were at the core of the child's first relations with its mother and its sibling rival" (Lacan, "Presentation on Psychical Causality" 149). In its function the figure of the father in Lacan is close to the Freudian one, if geared towards Symbolic structuring from the very start. The father is 'categorical' which means he sets up structures which the child will eventually take over via the road of the father's function of "dominat[ing] and arbitrat[ion]." The Symbolic Order is thus created through the Oedipus Complex. The Freudian father threatening castration becomes the structural order of the Symbolic.[91]

---

[90] For more detailed information on the Symbolic Order cf. Lacan, *Seminar I*, Chapter XVIII and *Seminar II*, Chapters III and XIX; "The Signification of the Phallus."

[91] The following description of the Oedipus Complex in Freud and Lacan will be deliberately reductive. A brief summary is, I believe, necessary, but I will not go into greater detail here.

In Freud, the Oedipus Complex institutes the function of the Superego in that the child subjects itself to the laws of society as represented by the father. From a condition of initial identification with the father, the child develops hostile feelings once the father is perceived as a rival for the love of the mother. The only way out of the conundrum for the child is to repress the incestuous feelings towards the mother and submit to 'The Law of the Father', which is done via a renewed identification with the father. This repression constitutes the original act of sublimation. The drive motility of the incestual desire is sublimated through a reorientation of desire and energy towards the father. The original identification with the father is reaffirmed through the internalisation of traits of his identity and personality. Other parts of the incestual desire are repressed, serving as the motor for future desires:

> [The Ego] borrowed strength to do this [i.e. to repress oedipal desires], so to speak, from the father, and this loan was an extraordinarily momentous act. The super-ego retains the character of the father, while the more powerful the Oedipus complex was and the more rapidly it succumbed to repression (under the influence of authority, religious teaching, schooling, reading) the stricter will be the domination of the super-ego over the ego later on – in the form of a conscious or perhaps of an unconscious sense of guilt. (Freud, "The Ego and the Id" 34-35)

The strength borrowed "from the father" denotes the identification with the paternal node of the oedipal triangle. It is here that Lacan refashions Freud, arguing that the identification exchanges a real father with a signifier, namely *the name of the father*. "It is in the *name of the father* that we must recognize the basis of the symbolic function which, since the dawn of historical time, has identified this person with the figure of the law" (Lacan, "Function and Field of Speech and Language" 230; emphasis original). 'The Name of the Father' is the parental metaphor which denotes the subjugation of the individual under the law of culture and society which has existed since the dawn of time.[92] The concept of 'The Name of the Father' establishes the phallus[93] in the unconscious as the signifier of the desire for the Other:

---

[92] Cf. Lacan: "The primordial Law is therefore the Law which, in regulating marriage ties, superimposes the reign of culture over the reign of nature, the latter being subject to the law of mating. [...] This law, then, reveals itself clearly enough as identical to a language order. For without names for kinship relations, no power can institute the order of preferences and taboos that know and braid the thread of lineage through the generations" ("Function and Field of Speech and Language" 229-230). In this case, Lacan borrows heavily from Levi-Strauss and structural anthropology. For a discussion of this topic cf. Wilden's "Lacan and the Discourse of the Other" in Lacan, *Speech and Language in Psychoanalysis* 249-270.

[93] The phallus is not a physical entity, nor to be confused with the male procreative organ. Lacan's notion of the phallus is perhaps his most criticised and the least well understood concept despite its obvious centrality. Cf. Easthope's sobering comment regarding the concept of the phallus: "The phallus is one of the most controversial notions in Lacan, and my own view is that if Lacan had known exactly what it was he would have said. Lacan wants the phallus to control two kinds of content: language [...] and at the same time sexuality. [...] He also wants it to be both present and absent, full and empty at

The demand for love can only suffer from a desire whose signifier is foreign to it. If the mother's desire *is* for the phallus, the child wants to be the phallus in order to satisfy her desire. Thus the division immanent in desire already makes itself felt by virtue of being experienced in the Other's desire, in that this division already stands in the way of the subject being satisfied with presenting to the Other the real [organ] he may *have* that corresponds to the phallus; for what he has is not better than what he does not have, from the point of view of his demand for love, which would like him to be the phallus. (Lacan, "Signification of the Phallus" 582; emphasis original)

The phallus is thus the symbolic representation of the object of desire which motivates the subject in speech. The phallus is the signifier for that which the mother lacks and, consequently, the child, in its striving to return to the state of the Real, desperately wants to be the phallus for the mother. In addition to orienting the subject's desire, Lacan denotes the centre of language by the term phallus in order to underline its patriarchal function. He states that "the phallus is a signifier, [...] the signifier that is destined to designate meaning effects as a whole, in so far as the signifier conditions them by its presence as signifier" ("Signification of the Phallus" 579). The concept of the phallus – which guarantees the laws governing the use of language – limits the free play of signification, thus giving structure and stability to the Symbolic Order.[94] The

---

once" (101). I am inclined to agree with Easthope here. The concept of the phallus smacks of Lacan's variant of Einstein's cosmological constant, with the difference that, unlike Einstein, Lacan never revoked his concept. Like with Einstein's addition, the phallus is an external addition to the system and, therefore, the phallus might be construed as a 'transcendental signified', something outside language which guarantees its structure. The 'transcendental signified' introduces the possibility of arresting the sliding of the signifier and thus enables the production of fixed meaning. Indeed, Derrida believes this to be the case with respect to Lacanian theory. He contends that "it was necessary to begin thinking that there was no center, that the center could not be thought in the form of a present-being, that the center had no natural site, that it was not a fixed locus but a function, a sort of nonlocus in which an infinite number of sign-substitutions came into play. This was the moment when language invaded the universal problematic, the moment when, in the absence of a center or origin, everything became discourse – provided we can agree on this word – that is to say, a system in which the central signified, the original or transcendental signified, is never absolutely present outside a system of differences. The absence of the transcendental signified extends the domain and the play of signification infinitely" ("Structure, Sign and Play" 280). For Derrida, the introduction of a 'transcendental signified' into Western thought was an ontological necessity arising from its logocentrism. Derrida "would not privilege a signifier into transcendence" (Spivak LXX), however. Lacan needs the phallus as a 'transcendental signified' in the context of his theoretical matrix, because he needs "the play of signification" to be arrested at certain points in order for meaning to emerge. Still, one has to wonder if the notion of the phallus does not pose more problems than it solves.

[94] In this context, the phallus does indeed function as a 'transcendental signified'. One could argue, however, that, given the phallus' origin in the Imaginary, it, too, is only imaginary and so is its function of arresting the sliding of the signifier. This accounts for the apparent stability perceived in language and, at the same time, would not essentially go against Derrida's denial of the 'transcendental signified'.

phallus is the signifier for the father and by extension the law that he represents. It is the repression of the phallus as signifier that animates the unconscious as language. Since the phallus is repressed and therefore beyond conscious reach, so is the father. The father is, however, taken on as a model of identification so that primary repression ultimately orients desire towards itself and thus inaugurates a lack in language. Since the phallus as signifier is repression beyond recovery, the desire for the phallus is invested into other signifiers which all turn out not to correspond to the phallus. Every signifier in language thus fails to be the phallus which inaugurates a perpetual lack in language. "The phallus is the privileged signifier of this mark in which the role [*part*] of Logos is wedded to the advent of desire" (ibid. 581). The phallus as "the privileged signifier" makes the Symbolic Order possible ("Logos") and invests language with desire and, in doing so, brings about the possibility for the subject to experience *jouissance*.[95]

Summing up, Lacan's theories constitute language as a Symbolic system that is erected over the chaotic and basically unstructured realm of signification that is the unconscious. The Symbolic realm that every human being enters in order to become a speaking subject is governed by the phallus, which structures the unconscious as language by means of repression. Since the phallus is repressed, however, it is also outside language as it resides in the unconscious which, though structured *like* language, is different from it. Safouan states that

> the phallus [...] is *articulated only in the unconscious*. I mean that speaking about the way it structures our relation to language, or to the Other as the place of language, or to the unconscious, is different than saying what it is. Like death, the phallus lies outside the field of representation; we only "represent" it through metaphor. [...] (1) there is no signifier that can tell us what we are and (2) this signifier is the phallus. (58; emphasis original)

The phallus thus takes on the form of a non-signifier in much the same way as the centre of a structure in Derrida is a non-locus. The phallus is a function of human language that orients it towards perpetual desire and which thereby links the Symbolic Order with the unconscious realm of the repressed signifier. The Symbolic Order that the child enters with the mastery of the Oedipus Complex is only the appearance of a stable structure. The structure of language superimposed over the chaos of the unconscious is based on an imaginary perception of unity. In other words, our entrance into language – Lacan's Symbolic Order – and the stability of meaning we apparently perceive in the use of language is i/Imaginary. Additionally, our desire for the phallus is

---

[95] The phallus and the Real appear very similar at first glance and indeed they are in that both are places of unity and the absence of lack. Also, and this is particularly important, they are inaccessible to the subject-in-language. The Real, which Lacan perceives as maternal, as the ground from which we spring, is lost to us once we have discovered the Other during the Mirror Stage. The phallus is the idea of the Father, the patriarchal order that rules culture and language. It is the centre which cannot be occupied by any part of the structure without collapsing the entire organization. It, too, is unreachable.

ultimately a desire to merge with the Other and become whole again. Such a state, a state that is *not* differential, excludes not only language, but the self. The desire for the phallus leads back to the chaos of the unconscious lurking beneath the Symbolic Order. Fulfilling the desire for the phallus would constitute an annihilation of language, the destruction of the Symbolic and thus a return to pure signification. This is the reason why the phallus is repressed. Paradoxically, the driving force of language – that which perpetuates its use –, namely desire, would, in fulfilment, lead to the annihilation of language.

3.4 Crossing the Bar: The Sliding of the Signifier, *Points de Capiton*, and the Production of Meaning

Having thus far established the structure of the unconscious as the structure of language and the implications for the subject's identity resulting from this, it is now time to zoom in on the production of meaning in the context of the unconscious' participation in the same. Within the humanistic therapeutic context of poetry therapy, the meaning clients ascribe to their lives and to particular events and experiences are important. The aim of the therapeutic process is to guide clients to reinterpret existing notions of meaning, construct new meanings and evaluate the process of meaning production that pertains to therapy. It is due to this that it is indispensible to take a close look at how Lacanian principles of meaning production function. This is vital for the main agenda of poetry therapy, namely to trace unconscious influences in the poetic text.

For Lacan, there exists "an 'autonomy' [...] of the signifier with respect to the signified" (Arrivé 126).[96] The identity of the Lacanian signifier depends not on its unity with the signified, but is present only in its difference from other signifiers.[97] In a Lacanian context, the signifier is thus no longer dependent on the signified in indissoluble unity; rather, the signifier is defined in isolation of the signified and this establishes two separate realms in language, namely that of the signifier and the signified.[98] While the two realms of the signifier and the signified are clearly divided in

---

[96] Lacan's theory of the signifier appears in its most systematic form in "Seminar on 'The Purloined Letter'" and "The Instance of the Letter in the Unconscious, or Reason since Freud."

[97] Lacan was influenced, among others, by Roman Jakobson here. Cf., for instance, Jakobson's *The Fundamentals of Language*, Chapter 1 and Part II.

[98] Cf. Lacan: "A psychoanalyst should find it easy to grasp the fundamental distinction between signifier and signified, and to begin to familiarize himself with the two networks of nonoverlapping relations they organize. The first network, that of the signifier, is the synchronic structure of the material of language insofar as each element takes on its precise usage therein by being different from the others [...]. The second network, that of the signified, is the diachronic set of concretely pronounced discourses, which

Lacan, they are not totally disconnected. Lacan has put the relationship between the signifier and the signified into the following matheme:[99]

$$\frac{S}{s}$$

This algorithm "is read as follows: signifier over signified; 'over' corresponding to the bar separating the two levels" (Lacan, "Instance of the Letter" 415). The capital 'S' representing the signifier symbolises the importance of the signifier over the signified. In addition to this, it also represents the fact that it is actually the signifier that constitutes our world rather than the signified and that, counter-intuitively, the signified is determined by the signifier.[100] Meaning is produced whenever a signified attaches itself to a signifier, i.e. when a drive connects to a signifier. The same idea has been elaborated by both Saussure and Freud before, but there is a crucial difference. For Saussure, signifier and signified are inseparable, which is to say that in a language one signified is attached to one signifier and this is how language works. Freud's position is similar in that he proposes that the subject's drives and psychic energies are attached to a signifier (Freud's *Vorstellungsrepräsentanz*).[101] The "bar" between 'S' and 's' has to be read as a barrier to be overcome in order for meaning to be produced.

The Lacanian signifier is diacritical in nature and can never exist in isolation, but always in relation, and in opposition to another signifier: $S_1 \rightarrow S_2$. 'S_2' refers both to the signifier that forms a relation to 'S_1' and to all other signifiers, because language is both particular and universal. In theory, a signifier can form a relation to any other signifier in the system of language. Practically, however, the semantic as well as other extra-linguistic factors limit the possibilities of signification. For Lacan, the relationship between signifier and signified is contingent, because they are separated by a bar ($\frac{S}{s}$) that resists the production of meaning. It is only in the instance of a signified crossing the bar that specific meaning is produced.[102] Lacan borrows from Jakobson

---

historically affects the first network, just as the structure of the first governs the pathways of the second. What dominates here is the unity of signification, which turns out to never come down to a pure indication of reality [*reel*], but always refers to another signification. In other words, signification comes about only on the basis of taking things as a whole [*d'ensemble*]" ("The Freudian Thing" 345).

[99] I am aware that Lacan's mathemes, their concept and use, are controversial to say the least. In spite of this, I have included those algorithms which I find useful in illustrating Lacan's ideas. I will consciously refrain from commenting or evaluating these algorithms with regard to their scientific, or psychoanalytic relevance and/or accuracy.

[100] Lacan borrows this notion from Levi-Strauss. (cf. Wilden's "Lacan and the Discourse of the Other" 248-262).

[101] It has to be noted that Freud's arguments are mainly concerned with the processes of repression while Lacan is concerned with the production of meaning in general. This is the reason why Freud does not pursue his argument further.

[102] The phrase "crossing of the bar" must not be taken too literally. It is not necessary for a signified to rise from the depth of the unconscious realm to a certain threshold that is the 'bar'. It has to be kept in mind that these are psychic and linguistic functions rather

the idea of the two fundamental axis of language and it is on these two axes that signifiers relate to each other and can produce meaning by forming a 'signifying chain'.[103] The first axis is the axis of combination which supposes a word-to-word connection ("The Instance of the Letter" 421). The second axis is the axis of selection which supposes a word for word substitution. It is in these two fundamental features of language – combination and substitution – that Lacan locates the possibility of crossing the bar. The axis of combination is metonymic and Lacan "designates as metonymy the first aspect of the actual field the signifier constitutes, so that meaning may assume a place there" (ibid.). The nature of the axis of selection is metaphoric. Metaphoric meaning does not come into being "from the juxtaposition of two images, that is two equally actualised signifiers. It flashes between two signifiers, one of which has replaced the other by taking the other's place in the signifying chain, the occulted signifier remaining present by virtue of its (metonymic) connection to the rest of the chain" (ibid. 422). Metaphor thus produces meaning that goes beyond the merely metonymic while remaining caught up in it. Metaphor eradicates the position of one signifier and fills the gap with another. This new signifier is integrated into the metonymic relationship of the signifying chain in question and thus produces meaning. Jakobson unequivocally asserts the importance of both functions in language, stating that "[i]n normal verbal behavior both processes are continually operative, but careful observation will reveal that under the influence of a cultural pattern, personality, and verbal style, preference is given to one of the two processes over the other" (Jakobson, "Two Aspects of Language" 60).

Lacan calls instances in the production and reception of language that constitute meaning *points de capiton*.[104] *Points de capiton* represent a successful crossing of the bar separating signifier and signified.[105] The term *points de capiton* has been translated into English as 'anchoring points,' 'quilting points,' and, in the most recent edition of *Écrits*, as 'button ties'. In those instances where I will not leave the term *points de*

---

than places. The crossing of the bar resisting the production of meaning thus always happens when meaning is produced. It represents the momentary nullification of a resistance.

[103] Cf. Lacan, "Instance of the Letter:" "The second property [the first is its differential nature] of the signifier, that of combining according to the laws of a closed order, affirms the necessity of a topological substratum, of which the term I ordinarily use, 'signifying chain,' gives an approximate idea: links by which a necklace firmly hooks onto a link of another necklace made of links" (418). A signifying chain thus facilitates connections between otherwise distinct elements producing a new element, which in the current case is meaning.

[104] It is important to keep in mind that *points de capiton* do not represent *the* meaning of a statement or utterance, but rather denote instances where meaning can be actualised. These actualisations are prone to change and revaluation.

[105] We can even trace the nucleus of Lacan's *points de capiton* already in Jakobson, who is well aware of "the influence of a cultural pattern, personality, and verbal style" ("Two Aspects of Language" 90) on the production of meaning.

capiton untranslated, I will, even if running the danger of adding to an already abundant terminological chaos, refer to *points de capiton* as 'juncture points'. This English phrase captures the essence of *points de capiton* that is most useful and important in the present discussion. *Points de capiton* are indeed juncture points in that they not only facilitate meaning, but also contain unactualised surplus meanings that can be accessed and actualised at this node. The sliding of the signifier over the signified, i.e. unlimited signification, is temporarily arrested at the *point de capiton* and meaning is produced by means of the metonymic and metaphoric processes along the two axes. Jakobson's axes also have a temporal dimension that attains importance if one wishes to discover how juncture points and consequently meaning are created out of the contexts of a person's life. The axis of combination is synchronically oriented in time. This means it is not possible to know the end of an utterance and thus its meaning before it has been finished. The axis of selection is diachronic on nature. It constitutes the array of all those words in a language that theoretically fit into the slot that is to be filled in the axis of combination. In order to select the appropriate word, the subject draws on the socio-cultural context of the utterance. This context includes, among many other factors, the personal history of the speaker and recipient, the cultural history and the actual communicative situation. Meaning that is established at a *point de capiton* need not be the ultimate meaning assigned to a signifying chain. The reader of a crime novel, for instance, has – if it is a well-written story – a number of hypotheses about who the murderer probably is and in which way the story will resolve its plotlines. Most of these hypotheses, each of which is a different actualisation of a *point de capiton*, or a network of the same, will be discarded before the end of the novel. The same process takes place in everyday communication and in every production of language. This is why even "coherent meaning can never exclude the effects of metonymy and metaphor. Unintended meanings are always excited and have to be actively denied" (Easthope 43). Unintended surplus meaning that is not denied may come to take the place of the consciously intended meaning. But even if this is not the case, unintended meanings always lurk in the shadow and can become manifest, especially in written texts, when the conditions actualise a different *point de capiton* or actualise a particular *point de capiton* in another way. "Indeed, there is no signifying chain that does not sustain [...] all attested contexts that are, so to speak, 'vertically' linked to that point" (Lacan, "The Instance of the Letter" 419). It is precisely this surplus of meaning poetry therapy is interested in.

The combination of linguistics and psychology that is present in Jakobson's essay on aphasia suggests further parallels between the two fields and, indeed, Lacan develops these implicit notions further,[106] namely by linking metonymy and metaphor to essential processes of the dream-work. Lacan explains:

---

[106] Jakobson advocates an interdisciplinary approach to the problem of aphasia in *Fundamentals* (69-71) and also draws on Freud (78; 95) and other therapists during his argument.

Verdichtung, "condensation," is the superimposed structure of signifiers in which metaphor finds its field; its name, condensing in itself the word *Dichtung*, shows the mechanism's connaturality with poetry, to the extent that it envelops poetry's own properly traditional function.[107] *Verschiebung* or "displacement" – this transfer of signification is [...] presented, right from its first appearance in Freud's work, as the unconscious' best means by which to foil censorship. What distinguishes these two mechanisms, which play a privileged role in dream-work, *Traumarbeit*, from their homologous function in discourse? Nothing, except a condition imposed upon the signifying material, called *Rücksicht auf Darstellbarkeit*, which must be translated as "consideration of the means of staging."[108] (ibid. 425)

Freud's process of condensation corresponds to the linguistic concept of metaphor while displacement is correlated to metonymy.[109] Lacan states that displacement is

---

[107] Lacan's etymology of the German word "Dichtung" is wrong. The noun "Dichtung" (poetry) derives from the verb "dichten," meaning "to write verse." The word is a loan word from the Latin "dictare" (to dictate, to speak a text for another person to write down), which is itself derived intransitively from the Latin "dicere" (to say). (cf. the entry on 'dichten' in *Kluge: Etymologisches Wörterbuch der deutschen Sprache* 198). The word "dichten," thus, has no etymological connection with the German "dichten," which denotes the process of sealing up something (or even "verdichten," i.e. to condense matter). This, however, is the meaning to which Lacan apparently refers in the above quote. Although Lacan has his etymology wrong, his argument remains sound. Poetry exhibits a strong connaturality with condensation and displacement.

[108] The translation of *Rücksicht auf Darstellbarkeit* as 'consideration of the means of staging' is not particularly felicitous. A better translation might perhaps be "regard for representability. In any case, I have chosen to stick to the German term.

[109] Cf. Freud's definitions of the terms of condensation and displacement: "The laws that govern the passage of events in the unconscious, which come to light in this manner, are remarkable enough and suffice to explain most of what seems strange to us about dreams. Above all there is a striking tendency to *condensation*, an inclination to form fresh unities out of elements which in our waking thought we should certainly have kept separate. As a consequence of this, a single element of the manifest dream often stands for a whole number of latent dream-thoughts as though it were a combined allusion to all of them; and in general the compass of the manifest dream is extraordinarily small in comparison with the wealth of material from which it has sprung. Another peculiarity of the dream-work, not entirely independent of the former one, is the ease with which psychical intensities (cathexes) are *displaced* from one element to another, so that it often happens that an element which was of little importance in the dream-thoughts appears as the clearest and accordingly most important feature of the manifest dream, and, vice versa, that essential elements of the dream-thoughts are represented in the manifest dream only by slight allusions. Moreover, as a rule the existence of quite insignificant points in common between two elements is enough to allow the dream-work to replace one by the other in all further operations. It will easily be imagined how greatly these mechanisms of condensation and displacement can increase the difficulty of interpreting a dream and of revealing the relations between the manifest dream and the latent dream-thoughts" (*An Outline of Psycho-Analysis* 167-168; emphasis original). The similarities between metonymy as a relationship of word-to-word and displacement as going "from one element to another" as well as metaphor as a relationship of word-for-word and

"the unconscious' best means to foil censorship" and the same is true of condensation. In contrast to the dream-work, metonymy and metaphor are limited by the *Rücksicht auf Darstellbarkeit*. This does not mean, however, that it is easy to spot displaced and condensed content. Rather the opposite. Since language exists as a "signifying material" that follows specific rules, the means of representability as such are limited and have to adhere to strict laws. This means that the unconscious content can be staged only within the limits set by the Symbolic Order. Since these limitations exist, however, unconscious content may be more strongly affected by displacement and condensation than in the dream-work. Signifying material that has crossed the bar has to adhere to the *Rücksicht auf Darstellbarkeit* and may be integrated in the Symbolic matrix at nodes that have no relation at all to the originary signifying material. This amplifies the processes of displacement and condensation. It may therefore prove more difficult to spot and decipher unconscious content in language than in the dream-work. It is essential for the therapist to be aware of the fact that, in language, the *Rücksicht auf Darstellbarkeit* has a more profound effect on the staging of unconscious content. When dealing with a linguistic text as opposed to the text of a dream, this has to be taken into consideration.

A point that is of particular importance for the present agenda is the fact that these processes exhibit, as Lacan states, a "connaturality with poetry." The psychic processes of condensation and displacement thus naturally appear, as metaphoric and metonymy functions, in poetry. It follows logically, then, that it is at metaphorical or metonymical instances in a poetic text that unconscious influences manifest themselves. Metaphors and metonymic expressions are thus *points de capiton* not only with regard to the production of meaning as such, but serve, especially in the poetic text, as junctures where unconscious meanings can be discovered and discussed in therapeutic sessions. So far, Lacanian theory has helped to constitute the way unconscious influences are produced and come into being alongside conscious patterns of language. What needs to be done now is to establish how exactly this process affects poetic texts and to which extent poetic language is particularly susceptible to surplus meaning. The correlation of metonymy and metaphor with displacement and condensation respectively, has provided a first headway towards the discussion of the problematic.

3.5 The dipartite Unconscious: Signification and the *Chora*

Julia Kristeva employs Lacanian terminology and concepts in order to trace the unconscious elements in texts, and especially poems. She states: "[i]f one is to account for

---

condensation as an element "stand[ing] for a whole number" of others are obvious. The concepts of condensation and displacement are ubiquitous in Freud's writing. I have chosen his definitions from *An Outline* because the text stems from the last period of Freud's life (1938) and it can be assumed that his concepts have advanced furthest here. Cf. also *The Interpretation of Dreams*, Chapter VI on the dream-work.

the production of a work, one needs to investigate the forces that bought it into being. Such forces are channelled through what shall be called a 'writing subject' rather than an author, for the latter term emphasizes the conscious intent of a writer who possesses *author*-ity over the meaning of his work" (*Revolution* 7). Kristeva takes a closer look at the structure of the unconscious and its relation to the Symbolic. She sets up the unconscious as a semiotic realm – in fact calling it *the Semiotic* – and puts it, if not fully in opposition, at least in a dialectical polarity to the Symbolic Order as conceived by Lacan.[110] She

> designate[s] *two modalities* of what is [...] the same signifying process. We shall call the first "*the semiotic*" and the second "*the symbolic.*" These two modalities are inseparable within the *signifying process* that constitutes language, and the dialectic between them determines the type of discourse (narrative, metalanguage, theory, poetry, etc.) involved; in other words, so-called "natural" language allows for different modes of articulation of the semiotic and the symbolic. [...] Because the subject is always *both* semiotic *and* symbolic, no signifying system he produces can be either "exclusively" semiotic or "exclusively" symbolic, and is instead necessarily marked by an indebtedness of both. (*Revolution* 23-24; emphasis original)

Kristeva's argument here contains echoes of both Lacan and Jakobson. She implicitly cites Jakobson's model of the functions of language when she states that natural language has different modes of articulation.[111] In contrast to Jakobson, for whom the respective functions of language are important with regard to their communicative effect, Kristeva is interested in how they are created and come into being in the first place. She consequently locates the creation of the "different modes of articulation" in the varying dominance of the Semiotic over the Symbolic and vice versa. In doing so, she extrapolates on Lacan. For Kristeva, the subject is "necessarily marked" by both the Semiotic, i.e. the unconscious, and the Symbolic. The function or the effect of the Semiotic on the mode of articulation is, according to Kristeva, poetic. This establishes a close connection between the unconscious and utterances in which the dominant function is poetic. Poetry and the unconscious are thus intricately linked. Along the same lines, poetry, as a genre, is differentiated from other forms of writing on the grounds of its close ties to the unconscious. "[Kristeva] assigns the communicative,

---

[110] For Kristeva the unconscious is "a more specific domain that she calls *le sémiotique* ('the semiotic') seen as one of the two components of the signifying process – the other being 'the symbolic.' While this division is not identical with that of unconscious/conscious, id/superego, or nature/culture, there are analogies here that could be usefully kept in mind. In all four instances there is a constant dialectical process at work, one that has its source in infancy and is implicated in sexual difference" (Roudiez 4; emphasis original). The differentiation between the two modalities is ultimately born out of Kristeva's own distinction of structuralism, which for her "posits [language] as a homogeneous structure" as opposed to semiotics, which, "by studying language as a discourse enunciated by a speaking subject, grasps its fundamentally heterogeneous structure" (Kristeva, "The System and the Speaking Subject" 24).

[111] Cf. Roman Jakobson's "Linguistics and Poetics."

systematic, homogenous and coherent aspects of signification to the *symbolic* (her definition of it); and reserves for the *semiotic* a range of linguistic effects particularly characteristic of poetic language" (Easthope 122). This is not only an invaluable insight for poetry therapy as a practical approach, but also sets up poetry therapy as a potentially uniquely effective writing-based therapy.

The Semiotic as conceived by Kristeva thus holds the key to understanding both the creation of poetry as such and the complexities of unconscious influences in poetry. Of the two modalities of the signifying process, the Semiotic is

> the one Freudian psychoanalysis points to in postulating not only the *facilitation* and the structuring *disposition* of the drives, but also the so-called *primary processes* which displace and condense both energies and their inscription. Discrete quantities of energy move through the body of the subject who is not yet constituted as such and, in the course of his development, they are arranged according to the various constraints imposed on this body – always already involved in semiotic processes – by family and social structures. In this way the drives, which are energy charges as well as 'psychical' marks, articulate what we call a *chora*: a non-expressive totally formed by the drives and their stases in a motility that is as full of movement as it is regulated. (Kristeva, *Revolution* 25; emphasis original)

Kristeva conceptualises the unconscious as a semiotic realm that is similar to Lacan's unconscious in that it is primarily chaotic and not infused by any organizing principle. Kristeva constitutes the Semiotic as the predominant state in early infancy – to be roughly equated with Lacan's 'Real'; following Lacan's process of maturation, the law of the Symbolic Order is eventually superimposed over the Semiotic with the advent of the Mirror Stage. More specifically, Kristeva grounds her conception of the Semiotic – the unconscious– on Freudian ideas, taking recourse to Freud's theory of drives and how they are made to conform to "family and social structures" during the individual's maturation process. Kristeva locates the place of instinctual drives quite logically in the somatic; she situates them in the physical body rather than merely in the psyche and calls this entity the *chora*. Kristeva "borrow[s] the term *chora* from Plato's *Timaeus* to denote [this] essentially mobile and extremely provisional articulation constituted by movements and their ephemeral stases" (ibid.; emphasis original). The Semiotic realm is thus inherently somatic in its nature, as it is created by, based on and functions through drives, which are defined as "energy charges as well as 'psychical' marks." These drives "articulate [...] a *chora*: a non-expressive totality." The oxymoronic nature of this statement (the drives articulate something which is non-expressive) deserves explication: "Although the *chora* can be designated and regulated, it can never be definitely posited: as a result, one can situate the *chora* and, if necessary, lend it a topology, but one can never give it axiomatic form" (Kristeva, *Revolution* 26; emphasis original). The *chora* has to be envisioned as an extremely ephemeral structure in the Derridean sense; a structure that can be given a certain topology, but which never consolidates into a form that could be mapped out.[112] This is the case because drives are indeed to a certain extent structured, but their activities are not, because these are contingent on external and internal factors that are constantly changing. Derrida's concept of the trace illuminates the function of the *chora* in Kristeva:

> Here the appearing and functioning of difference presupposes an originary synthesis not preceded by an absolute simplicity. Such would be the originary trace. Without the retention in the minimal unit of temporal existence, without a trace retaining the other as other in the same, no difference would do its work and no meaning would appear. It is not the question of a constituted difference here, but rather, before all determination of the content, of the *pure* movement which produces difference. The *(pure) trace is differance*. It does not depend on any sensible plenitude, audible or visible, phonic or graphic. It is on the contrary, the condition of such a plenitude. Although it *does not exist*, although it is never a *being-present* outside of all plenitude, its possibility is by right anterior to all that one calls sign (signified/signifier, content/expression, etc.) concept or operation, motor or sensory. (*Of Grammatology* 62; emphasis original)

Derrida contends that every presence includes absence by means of the trace[113] without which textual production is not possible: "The interweaving results in each 'element' – phoneme or grapheme – being constituted on the basis of the trace within it of the other elements of the chain or system. This interweaving, this textile, is the text produced only in the transformation of another text" (Derrida, *Positions* 24). Taking this into consideration makes clear how the above quote illuminates the nature of the *chora:* she is the cradle of the trace. If the "pure trace is differance," as Derrida states, and if it is "not the question of a constituted difference" and does "not depend on any sensible plenitude, audible or visible, phonic or graphic," the *chora* is indeed where the pure trace can be encountered.[114] The *chora* constitutes the rule of the drives during the state of the Real, a state of being that is non-expressive, but constitutive of the difference that is the basis of language. Traces of the *chora*'s motility pervade all language (which is, according to Kristeva, always indebted to the Semiotic as much as to the Symbolic) and all texts via *différance*.[115]

---

[112] I am aware of the fact that Derrida himself was very critical of the concept of *chora* (cf. Jacques Derrida, *Positions*). I nonetheless draw on Derrida here and later, because this study is not concerned with the philosophical implications of the concepts used, but their applications to understanding the creative poetic process.

[113] "Derrida, then, gives the name 'trace' to the part played by the radically other within the structure of difference that is the sign. [...] In spite of itself, Saussurean linguistics recognizes the structure of the sign as a trace-structure. And Freud's psychoanalysis, to some extent in spite of itself, recognizes the structure of experience itself to be a trace, not a present-structure" (ibid. XVII).

[114] Of course, since the *chora* is Semiotic and situated in the Real there is no chance for the subject-in-language to ever experience it. The pure trace is 'Being' and thus barred from the subject initiated into the Symbolic. It is present and can be experienced only as metaphorical or metonymical manifestations in a text; only as a trace of itself.

[115] The close connection that exists between the concepts of the Semiotic *chora* and the Derridean *trace* can also be seen in the following definition of the *chora*: "The *chora* is

The transitional process from the Semiotic to the Symbolic entails and constitutes interdependencies between the two realms, the most important of which is the 'thetic'. The 'thetic' originates in the Mirror Stage and gives direction and purpose to the Semiotic drive motilities:

> The thetic originates in the "mirror stage" and is completed through the phallic stage, by the reactivation of the Oedipus complex in puberty; no signifying process can be without it. Though absolutely necessary, the thetic is not exclusive: the semiotic, which also precedes it, constantly tears it open, and this transgression brings about all the various transformations of the signifying practice that are called "creation". [...] what remodels the symbolic order is always the influx of the semiotic. This is particularly evident in poetic language since, for there to be a transgression of the symbolic, there must be an irruption of the drives in the universal signifying order, that of "natural" language which binds together the social unit. (Kristeva, *Revolution* 62)

Kristeva's 'thetic' is established during the Mirror Stage with the discovery of the o/Other and the emergence of the Ego. It is completed with the Oedipus Complex and the final initiation of the subject into language. The 'thetic' is thus another term for the Symbolic break that establishes the subject in language. The 'thetic' is "structured as a break in the signifying process, establishing the *identification* of the subject and its object as preconditions of propositionality" (Kristeva, *Revolution* 43; emphasis original). The 'thetic' posits language as being oriented towards an object, thus giving it a *telos*. "The thetic is a moment of *positing,* a moment of *enunciation* or utterance. [...] The thetic thus produces both language and the speaking subject" (Moi 641; emphasis original). The teleological direction the thetic bequeaths on every enunciation is continually and inevitably disturbed by Semiotic influxes, which, by tearing open the Symbolic, create other teloi and/or disrupt the original one. Kristeva, having established the Semiotic as a second, independent concept alongside the Symbolic, argues that

> the subject, finding his identity in the symbolic, *separates* from his fusion with the mother, *confines* his *jouissance* to the genital and transfers semiotic motility on to the symbolic order. Thus ends the formation of the thetic phase, which posits the gap between the signifier and the signified as an opening up towards desire but also every act, including the very *jouissance* that exceeds them. (*Revolution* 46; emphasis original)

During Kristeva's thetic phase, drives are transferred to the Symbolic, i.e. linked to language. The "*jouissance* that exceeds" the possibility of this transfer remains unbound and free-floating in the Semiotic. Since these drives did not partake in the thetic positing of language, they do not adhere to the rules of the Symbolic. It is by means of these free-floating drives that the Semiotic generates surplus meaning, opening the Symbolic up, disrupting it, overcoming the resistance of the bar. Since the subject is produced through language and is denoted by the signifier *'I',* the *chora* both generates

---

> a modality of signifiance in which the linguistic sign is not yet articulated as the absence of an object and as the distinction between the real and symbolic" (Kristeva, *Revolution* 26).

and negates the subject. She[116] generates it through language, but the *chora* herself knows no signifier or signified, she is beyond and before signification and hence there cannot be meaning, however ephemeral and deferred, because difference is negated before the *chora*. Consequently, the subject, when it is confronted by the *chora*, is negated. Its mirror is broken and its imaginary unity lost. The subject, once it has entered language, cannot escape language without negating itself, it always upholds 'The Law of the Father'. Only through 'The Law of the Father', through subjugation under the rules of language, can the individual escape its own negation. In spite of this, there is still always the intrusion of the Semiotic, which involuntarily – and in most cases unknowingly – decentres the subject's language and thus the subject itself. Because unbound drive motilities are not thetic they have the tendency to interfere with the teleology of the enunciation, causing surplus meaning to be interwoven in the text. When activated, such drives cause "'distortions' of the signifying chain and the structure of signification" (Kristeva, *Revolution* 49). Any text is thus inevitably disrupted by "those drives that the thetic phase was not able to sublate [*reliever, aufheben*] by linking them into signifier and signified" (ibid.).

Drives that have not been linked to signifiers are thus what allows the unconscious to influence the process of language production through the incursions of the instinctual Semiotic into the realm of the Symbolic. This is the reason why Kristeva speaks of the *subject in process/on trial [sujet en process]*. To avoid its own negation, the *I* must evade confrontation with the *chora*. It has mostly done so by liking drives to language. This accounts for the relatively unproblematic everyday use of language. Since not all drives have been bound, however, the subject nonetheless remains on trial; fearing its own negation, it is forced to defend itself with every new incursion of the Semiotic into the Symbolic realm. The Semiotic has to be "understood as pre-thetic, preceding the positing of the subject. Previous to the Ego thinking within a proposition, no meaning exists, but here *do* exist articulations, heterogeneous to signification and the sign" (Kristeva, *Revolution* 36; emphasis original). The Semiotic *chora* is "pre-thetic," which means she does not articulate meaning and its articulation has no orientation as is necessary for communication. Primarily somatic as the *chora* is, she functions as the interface between 'Being' and 'Meaning', while rooted firmly in the first. The "*chora* is no more than the place where the subject is both generated and negated, the place where his unity succumbs before the process of charges and stases that produce him" (ibid. 28). The *chora* not only precedes signification but she remains at all times extra-linguistic. Its non-expressiveness notwithstanding, she contains and constitutes the nucleus of signification, the foundation of the Symbolic. The *chora* is formed in the context of drives and their stasis. Drives are differential in nature. They are either active or in stasis, either on or off, either 1 or 0. In this respect, the instinctual *chora* is basically linguistic. Through the differential nature of the

---

[116] In Kristeva's model, the Semiotic stands opposed to the Symbolic and since the Symbolic is inherently patriarchal, we have to envision the realm of semiotics as essentially matriarchal. Therefore, the *chora* is denoted by a female pronoun.

drives that constitute her, the *chora* becomes the herald of signification, mother to the two primordial forms of difference – presence/absence and self/other.

The Semiotic influx is thus another term for creativity in language. It is Semiotic motility that is active when language, and especially poetry, is being written:

> [The] semiotic, which also precedes it, constantly tears [the Symbolic] open, and this transgression brings about all the various transformations of the signifying practice that are called "creation". [...] what remodels the symbolic order is always the influx of the semiotic. This is particularly evident in poetic language since, for there to be a transgression of the symbolic, there must be an irruption of the drives in the universal signifying order, that of "natural" language which binds together the social unit. (Kristeva, *Revolution* 62)

The remodelling of the Symbolic through the Semiotic constitutes an inherently creative process, which can best be observed in poetry; in fact "[a]ll poetic distortions of the signifying chain [...] yield under the attack of the 'residues of first symbolizations' (Lacan), in other words, those drives that the thetic phase was not able to sublate [*relever, aufheben*]" (ibid. 49). Since not all drives have been successfully conquered by linking them with language, i.e. signifiers, and, due to the pressures exerted on the individual in the social reality, the *subject in process/on trial*, in order to preserve its unity and avoid its own negation before the *chora*, reacts with repression of the drives when confronted by them too harshly. These repressed conflicts then find a different way of expression through language and through poetic language in particular, namely by means of metonymic and metaphoric substitution. Kristeva describes this process in the following manner, which is vital to our discussion and deserves to be quoted in full:

> [I]n aesthetic productions, which do not involve transference, negation is not "conquered." Rejection operates in them and does not produce an "intellectual acceptance of the repressed" (in other words, it does not affect the passage of the repressed element into the signified, into the symbolic function). Instead it marks *the signifying material* with the repressed. [...] [T]he reintroduction of the symbol of negation into poetic language [...] *arranges the repressed element in a different way*, one that does not represent an "intellectual acceptance of the repressed," an *Aufhebung*, but instead constitutes a post-symbolic (and in this sense anti-symbolic) hallmarking of the material that remained intact during the first symbolization. This "material," expelled by the sign and judgement from first symbolizations, is then withdrawn from the unconscious into language, but is not accepted there in the form of "metalanguage" or any kind of intellection. [...] The semiotic device constructed by poetic language through the positing of language as a symbolic system constitutes a third-degree negativity. It is neither the lack of a "no" (as in the unconscious), nor a negative formula (a sign of the instituted symbolic function), nor negation-as-denial (symptoms of the neurotic ego idealizing the repressed), but instead a *modification of linguistic and logical linearity and ideality*, which cannot be located in any ego. Poetic rhythm does not constitute the acknowledgment of the unconscious but is instead its expenditure and implementation. (*Revolution* 163-164; emphasis original)

When the repressed enters the poetic text from the unconscious, it does so without being intellectually accepted, i.e. without being recognised by the writing subject. It is present in the matrix of the poetic text in such a manner that makes it an "expenditure and implementation" of the unconscious itself. This means that, more than other texts, the poetic text is defined by *différance*, and it is in following the play of signification, which manifests itself predominantly in verbal ambiguities and symbolic expressions – in the rhetorical figures of metaphor and metonymy – that the unconscious influences are unveiled and thus allow for an "intellectual acceptance of the repressed" in poetry therapy.

There are different levels in which the production of texts encourages unconscious participation, but what can be said with certainty is that the creation of poetry furthers this process more strongly than any production of prose texts. Poetic language is different from prose in that it follows the rules of language in a much looser fashion. In poetic writing, the subject is allowed to transgress the grammatical rules if it suits the poem. Also, as Jakobson famously put it, the poetic function of language "projects the principle of equivalence from the axis of selection into the axis of combination" ("Linguistics and Poetics" 358). In common language, the axis of combination is relatively fixed. It is that axis along which the words of, say, a sentence are aligned – horizontally, so to speak – according to the rules of a language so as to produce a correct utterance. The axis of selection, on the other hand, is freer: for every type of word that is required of a sentence, one has to choose a particular one to fill in the gap. One can choose the word from a whole surplus of synonymous or near-synonymous words. In short, the choices of expression can be much more individual and free. In poetic language, this freedom is transposed onto the axis of combination. This means that the rules of grammar – the rules of the Symbolic – are partly nullified. Poems can create their own structures, their own rules of combination. Since, according to Jakobson, poetic language refers back upon itself, the reader as well as the creator of poetry can deduce the rules of combination for each individual poem from its linguistic structure. Poetic language is much more flexible than prose language, because it refuses to be entirely subjected to 'The Law of the Father'. This gives room for creativity and the Semiotic faces less resistance from the otherwise rigid Symbolic structures of grammar and so forth. This is why poetry is particularly well suited to include unconscious influences, that is, facilitative to the crossing of the bar of those drives not bound during first symbolisation.

With regard to poetry written in the therapeutic environment, the question is how analysis can best spot unconscious material within the matrix of the text. Since the *chora* is the functional entity from which the openings in the Symbolic spawn, one has to wonder in how far the *chora* – especially considering its differential nature – is structural herself; for if the *chora* is indeed characterised *solely* by her differential nature, her influence in the Symbolic matrix of any text will be perfectly integrated and veiled from the subject. The Symbolic is based on difference as well, so that the differential influxes from the Semiotic cannot be noticed. Practical, textual experience, of course, shows that this is not the case. The openings in the Symbolic caused by the Semiotic influx from the *chora* are perceptible in texts, especially poetic texts, and thus cannot be purely structural.

Regarding the opening in a structure, Derrida states:

> [W]hen one comes to think that the opening of the structure is "structural," that is, essential, one already has progressed to an order heterogeneous to the first one: the *difference* between the (necessarily closed) minor structure and the structurality of an opening [...]. There are some givens which must be described in terms of structure, and others which must be described in terms of genesis. There are layers of meaning which appear as systems, or complexes, or static configurations, within which, moreover, are possible a movement and a genesis which must obey both the legality proper to and the functional significance of the structure under consideration. Other layers, sometimes more profound, sometimes more superficial, are given in the essential mode of creation and movement, that is, in the modes of primordial origin, of becoming, or of tradition; and these require that in speaking of them one use the language of genesis, supposing that there is one, or that there is only one. ("'Genesis' and Structure and Phenomenology" 155; emphasis original)

Derrida ascribes to the elements of a structure and especially to "the opening of a structure" a hybrid character in that the elements of a structure are both structural and productive. Structural in that they constitute "a form or a function organized according to an internal legality in which elements have meaning only in the solidarity of their correlation or their opposition" (ibid. 157); productive ("genesis") in that they precipitate and participate in "the search for the origin and foundation of the structure" (ibid.). This dual nature given to the opening of a structure – which in the context of poetry therapy is naturally the structure of poetic language – delineates the basic approach towards textual interpretation to be used in poetry therapy where it is equally important to focus on the text as artefact of the creative process and the participation of language in all its various manifestations. It is in language that the client's symptoms can be both discovered and treated. In the quote above one can trace a dialectic very similar to Kristeva's, where Derrida mentions "layers of meaning which appear as systems, or complexes, or static configurations" (the Symbolic, the thetic) and layers which constitute an "essential mode of creation and movement, that is, in the modes of primordial origin, of becoming" (the Semiotic, the *chora*). Considering this in the light of Kristeva's dialectical relationship of the Symbolic and the Semiotic, a first conclusion as to the manifestations of unconscious notions in poetic texts can be formulated: unconscious content can appear as strong metaphors or ambiguities in a text (genetic), but it can equally well appear as incorporated in the structural matrix of a text (structural). Therefore, the analysis within therapeutic sessions has to vary according to the text presented. It may be necessary to set up a structural matrix of a poem in order to ascertain the interrelations between the Semiotic openings and the Symbolic law; in another text it may be more fitting to try and break the thetic positing of the text's message by means of free association (genetic) with regard to specific elements of the text.

Thus, Semiotic traces in the poetic text have to be conceived of "as a 'second' return of instinctual functioning within the symbolic [following first symbolization at the closure of the thetic phase], as a negativity introduced into the symbolic order and as a transgression of that order" (Kristeva, *Revolution* 69). The influx of the Semiotic raises the danger of coming face to face with the *chora*, the danger of negation. This introduces a "negativity" into the textual matrix which cannot be filled. It is a negativity, because it cannot be brought in line with the thetic positing of the text. The poetic text, however, "does not relinquish the thetic even while pulverizing it through the negativity of transgression. Indeed, this is the only means of transgressing the thetic" (ibid.). Artistic transgression of the thetic by means of infusing unbound drives from the Semiotic is the reason for the healing powers of art. Instinctual pressures are released by this means, which results in a state of temporary mental relaxation. Also, by thus transgressing 'The Law of the Father', the subject is temporarily liberated from its suppression, which contributes to a feeling of freedom and equilibrium. In the end, "the semiotic we find in signifying practices always comes to us after the symbolic thesis, after the symbolic break, and can be analysed in psychoanalytic discourse as well as in so-called 'artistic' practice" (ibid. 68).

On the basis of the ideas and notions delineated above, Kristeva zooms in on the interrelations and interdependencies of the unconscious, the conscious and the poetic text by introducing the concepts of the *phenotext* and the *genotext*. According to Kristeva, every text is constructed from the interplay of *genotext* and *phenotext*. These are not distinctive unities within any given text, but can be conceived of as interconnected traces interwoven in the empirical text. As any "subject is always *both* semiotic *and* symbolic" (Kristeva, *Revolution* 24; emphasis original), every text represents a mixture of *phenotext* and *genotext*. The *phenotext* "encompasses the emergence of object and subject, and the constitution of nuclei of meaning involving categories: semantic and categorical fields" (ibid. 86). The split into object and subject as well as the constitution of semantic relations clearly marks the *phenotext* as Symbolic. In contrast to this, the *genotext* is close to the somatic, it "include[s] drives, their disposition and their division of the body" (ibid.), i.e. "semiotic processes" (ibid.). It is not purely Semiotic, though. Since those Semiotic processes that coalesce in the *genotext* do so as language, they are always already tainted by "the advent of the symbolic" and are represented in the context of "the ecological and social system surrounding the body" (ibid.). The *genotext* is thus never openly present in any text but requires analysis to be uncovered. Of special importance for poetry therapy is that the *genotext* is

> the only transfer of drive energies that organizes a space in which the subject is not *yet* a split unity that will become blurred, giving rise to the symbolic. Instead, the space it organizes is one in which the subject will be *generated* as such by a process of facilitations and marks within the constraints of the biological and social structure. (Kristeva, *Revolution* 86; emphasis original)

Since we know from Lacan that the subject lodges itself in the signifier and has existence only in the production of language, the central importance of the *genotext* for the identity of the subject in therapy cannot be overestimated. While the *phenotext* "serves to communicate, [...] obeys rules of communication and presupposes a subject of enunciation and an addressee" (ibid. 87) the *genotext* is a process rather than a structure and as such

> tends to articulate structures that are ephemeral [...] and non-signifying [...]. It forms these structure out of: (a) instinctual dyads, (b) the corporeal and ecological continuum, (c) the social organism and family structures, which convey the constraints imposed by the mode of production, and (d) matrices of enunciation, which give rise to discursive 'genres' (according to literary history), 'psychic structures' (according to psychiatry and psychoanalysis) or various arrangements of 'the participants of the speech event' (in Jakobson's notion of the linguistics of discourse). (ibid.)

The ephemeral structures thus delineated merge with the structures of the symbolic representation of the *phenotext*. A text generally favours and predominantly exhibits phenotextual elements, because its main purpose is to communicate, which necessitates as clear and unambiguous a message as possible. The dominance of phenotextual elements in texts depends on the genre of the text in question. Newspaper articles, business reports and so forth naturally suppress genotextual elements as their main aim is the clear and efficient communication of information. Letters, diaries, and other prose writing generally have a stronger participation of genotextual elements, which increases still in aesthetic and fictional texts such as novels, or fairy tales. Now, poetry, as opposed to prose, privileges the genotext like no other textual medium and it is here that one can locate the reason for the healing power of poetic writing. "Designating the genotext in a text requires pointing out the transfers of drive energy that can be detected in phonematic devices (such as the accumulation and repetition of phonemes or rhymes) and melodic devices (such as intonation or rhythm)" (Kristeva, *Revolution* 86). The *genotext* thus manifests itself in what are trademark devices of poetry: rhyme, rhythm, and repetition. It is therefore in poetry and its unstructured structurality that the *genotext* achieves dominance. Since the predominant function of poetic language is, according to Jakobson, not communication, but a reference back upon itself, a focus on its message for its own sake (cf. Jakobson "Linguistics and Poetics" 356), the *genotext* can assert itself more vigorously in poetry. Since poetic language is more dynamic and violations against the norm of the Symbolic are permissible, the Semiotic motility in poetic texts remains itinerant, containing a creative potential for the emergence of surplus meanings, which in turn provide access to unconscious desires, repressed wishes and problems.

The task of poetry therapy is to isolate the *genotext* in the poetic text written by the client. As already hinted at, the manifestations of the *genotext* in any given text are inevitably subject to the Symbolic representation necessary to produce meaning. Therefore, they appear, even in poetic texts, only as traces – symbolic traces distorted by the functions of metonymy and metaphor. The *genotext* can thus be traced by concentrating on the symbols and metaphors in the poetic text. The therapeutic environment in combination with the therapeutic experience and knowledge of the analyst facilitates – in conjunction with the client's wishes as conceived within the principles of humanistic art therapy – the discovery of unconscious content to be usefully exploited in the therapeutic sessions. Poetry therapy can make obvious these intrusions of the unconscious into language and, in doing so, clarify repressed desires, wishes and conflicts. Yet it is not enough to know that the unconscious affects statements. One has to find out more about the manifestations and the extent to which this happens in language and especially in poetic language and texts. It is necessary to know *how* the unconscious influxes of the Semiotic disrupt the structures of 'The Law of the Father' in a poetic text. When surplus meaning in a client's poem is not actualised by an appropriate context, it may well remain hidden to both the client and the analyst. This, in turn, hampers the effectiveness of poetry as a therapy. It is thus essential for the therapist to be able to spot juncture points even if they are not actualised through the context of the poem or therapy (yet); it is necessary to spot their potential for actualisation and then guide the client towards a context that allows the conscious actualisation of the untapped potential for meaning.

4. Textual Manifestations of the Unconscious: Figurative Language as the *Via Regia*

> In the act of writing, especially of writing verse, one is always convinced that what appears on the page is only a distorted fragment of what, somewhere or other inside you, wanted to appear and would have appeared too, if only we knew how to listen to it more subtly and widely and deeply, and record it more boldly. (Ted Hughes in his "Foreword" to S. Brownjohn's *What Rhymes with Secret?* 7 [qtd. in Bolton 197])

At the beginning of the previous century, Otto Rank developed a theory of (poetic) creativity, which, though indebted to Freud, goes beyond Freud's primarily libidinal theory.[117] At the onset of his central argument, Rank contends that poetic creation is comprised of "two separate phases, which have been called the conscious and the unconscious, but really correspond to the two processes of language-formation. The individual creative expression of an experience, and the collective communication of it" (275).[118] The individual aspect is necessary to make the poem the unique expression of its author while the collective aspect safeguards the dissemination of the poem in its target culture. Rank's theory thus accounts for the universality of poetry ("collective communication") expressed in "individual" language. In the further course of his argument, Rank refines his initial concept of creativity. He maintains that the creative process

> cannot be simply split into two phases, since in each of the two phases the individual and collective elements both mingle and oppose each other. It seems to me to be one of

---

[117] For a concise rendering of both Rank's theory and its conflicted relationship to Freud, cf. Ellen Handler Spitz, "Conflict and Creativity: Reflections on Otto Rank's Psychology of Art."

[118] The division into separate phases can be found in many subsequent works on creativity as can the notion of conscious reworking. Cf. Wallas, *The Art of Thought* (1926) for a near contemporary approach to Rank's. Wallas divides the creative process into four stages: (1) Preparation. The artist freely associates, thinks about a topic, collects information. (2) Incubation. Time elapses and the material undergoes internal elaboration and organisation. (3) Illumination. The artist discovers a 'solution' to the problem. This can be an intuition, a hunch or a true solution. (4) Evaluation. The artist evaluates the product as to its acceptability in the social environment. In *Applied Imagination* (1953), Osborn divides the creative process into seven stages, which simply further differentiate Wallas's four (especially stages 1 and 2). Three stages – hypothesis formation, hypothesis testing and communication of results – suffice Morris Stein (1974) for his theory of creativity. In this study, I will follow, mostly implicitly as theories of creativity concern us only peripherally, theories of creativity that work from a holistic – sometimes even synesthetic – approach as expressed, for instance, in Robinson's *Out of our Minds: Learning to be Creative* (2001), and Bolton's *The Therapeutic Potential of Creative Writing* (1999).

the most complex of all psychological problems to decide in what way the reciprocal action between the individual and the collective, which is inherent in language, comes out in poetic creation; but [...] we may suppose that the process is somewhat as follows: In an individual who reacts in language, a personal experience first of all finds its rough form in the traditional language stock, which is thereby permeated by the personality and individuality vitalized. On the other hand, the second stage, the verbal shaping proper, is, as it seems to me, a fresh collectivizing of what was originally expressed personally, with communication and understanding as its object. Put shortly, the first would be the expression of an individual state of feeling in the collective raw material of inherited language, the second a personal infusion into this linguistic raw material, necessitated by the social urge to communicate. (279)

The key insight expressed by Rank here is that the creative process is reciprocal rather than sequential, that is, the diverse processes that partake in creativity form dynamic, simultaneous relationships rather than following some fixed (chronological) sequentiality. What is particularly modern in Rank is the connection he draws between the individual and the collective within the creative process. The individual and the collective are intricately linked; they are interdependent and constantly negotiate their relationship. Based on this insight, Rank rightly re-conceptualises his two (previously sequential) stages of creativity as reciprocal. He comes to the conclusion that poetic writing entails a dialectical process of language formation which oscillates between a collective and an individual pole. This dynamic concept of poetic creativity brings Rank surprisingly close to Lacan and Kristeva. Indeed, it is possible to refashion his approach in their terms. Rank's "individual who reacts in language" is the Lacanian subject. Once initiated into the Symbolic Order, a person cannot but "react in language," because the subject's experiences are necessarily negotiated in the "traditional language stock," which is no more than another term for Lacan's Symbolic Order of language. While the individual's experiences are apprehended within the limits and the framework – the structure – of the Symbolic, the process of apprehension as such is influenced, first of all, by the unique and personal context of the experience – a pragmatic influence on the text to be produced – and, secondly, by the individuality of the Semiotic disposition of the person in question. Together these two factors constitute what Kristeva has termed the genotext. It is by means of this that the Symbolic Order is "vitalized" by the individual. The actual "verbal shaping" of the text, which involves the participation of the phenotext,[119] necessarily takes place in the Symbolic proper. In order to ensure "communication and understanding" the text is shaped according to the (universal) laws of language.[120] The negotiations between geno- and phenotext at

---

[119] It should be remembered that the phenotext does not equal the empirical text on the page. It is the process or the function of its shaping in conjunction with the genotextual elements present.

[120] With Jakobson one could argue that the individual's arrangement of words on the axis of combination is collectively determined by the rules of language, which constitutes Rank's "fresh collectivizing" of the individual's personal metonymic freedom on the axis of selection (though this is also mediated by pragmatic aspects).

points de capiton thus produce the actual textual artefact and it is at such juncture points that the personal experience is "collectivized" and the Symbolic Order experiences a "personal infusion."

The question answered above, if in a rather general manner, is how the creative process ends up producing an artistic artefact, namely the poem. For the present study, it suffices, in accordance with the principles of art therapy, to constitute the creative process as a healing activity per se. The question that is of main interest with respect to poetry therapy is therefore not so much *in which manner* the creative process works, but *how* one can trace the unconscious elements of the genotext in the poem. The implications that arise for poetry therapy from the relationship between creativity and therapy, the outcomes and effects of the interactions of these two processes, are of central interest here. Genotext and phenotext make up the material text, while their distinctive elements become almost indistinguishable. In order to rediscover or excavate those textual elements that function genotextually, psychotherapists can draw on the techniques and methods of their craft and apply these to the written poetic text with relative ease. Most effectively this can be done by exploiting the parallels that exist between the interpretation of texts in literary studies and the psychoanalytical analysis of dreams. The traces of the genotext in the poem take the form of linguistic and semantic ambiguities in and violations of the common standard of the Symbolic Order. As will be made clear in this chapter, this takes place, primarily, through metaphor and metonymy. In a similar fashion, the dream-work displaces and condenses aspects of our consciously apprehended reality, combining them in seemingly chaotic and unusual ways that require interpretation. On the following pages, the interpretation of dreams and of poetry will be conceptualised as sharing the same features and methods.[121] In this respect, the practice of interpretation serves as a linkage of therapy and literary studies. This chapter will thus serve as a transitional chapter, connecting the delineation of the first phase of poetry therapy in the preceding chapters to the in-depth discussion of the second phase which constitutes the bulk of the remaining part of this study.

4.1 Creativity, Dreaming and the Writing of Poetry

The violation of the Symbolic Order through genotextual traces is, generally speaking, more pronounced in poetic texts than in prose. Poetic language is a sub-code of language – as is prose –, but a sub-code which by its very nature is less restricted and restrictive with regard to the Symbolic. Consequently, it lends itself more readily to the

---

[121] This analogy is, of course, set up by Freud himself in the essay "Creative Writers and Daydreaming."

expression and influx of unconscious and creative impulses.[122] The practice of poetic writing thus becomes an "exploration and discovery of the possibilities of language; [...] an activity that liberates the subject from a number of linguistic, psychic, and social networks; [...] a dynamism that breaks up the inertia of language habits" (Roudiez 2-3). In short, poetic writing provides a feeling of liberation and freedom. In art therapy, it is precisely this sensation or mood which is constitutive of the therapeutic experience and which is usually called creativity. Creativity, however, is not simply pure liberation and freedom:

> Creativity is one of the major means by which the human being liberates himself from the fetters not only of his conditioned responses, but also of his usual choices. However, creativity is not simply originality and unlimited freedom. There is much more to it than that. Creativity also imposes restrictions. While it uses methods other than those of ordinary thinking, it must not be in disagreement with ordinary thinking – or rather, it must be something that, sooner or later, ordinary thinking will understand, accept, and appreciate. (Arieti 4)

Arieti contends that creative activities free the subject from "conditioned responses" and help pave the way towards unusual choices, i.e. to break free of one's established behavioural patterns. The rediscovery of one's freedom through creativity is exactly what was established as the aim of humanistic poetry therapy. The fact that in poetry therapy the creative responses are written textual productions poses the danger of curtailing the inherent freedom of creativity, however. The poems produced within the therapeutic experience are always necessarily bound by the 'The Law of the Father'.[123] Their nature as written texts consigns them to a more rigorous subjectification under the Symbolic than oral utterances, or even paintings or sculptures. The poem as a creative response in written language can consequently only be free within certain limits. Since poetry thus does not constitute unconditional freedom from the laws of the Symbolic, the breaking of "conditioned responses" by means of the client-poem is no uncomplicated matter and can only succeed if the normalising and curtailing factors of the Symbolic are recognised and taken into account.

---

[122] I contend that, fundamentally, prose does have the same inherent potential for creativity as poetry. However, the therapeutic potential is higher in poetry and it is specifically this potential which is relevant for poetry therapy. Poetry is more conducive to creative processes and facilitates these easier in the therapeutic context. Since prose is more tightly linked to 'The Law of the Father' – and is for the most part identical with it – unconscious influences do not easily cross the bar and, when they do, are not as readily discernable. Poetry and prose, as sub-codes of language, thus share at their basis the same potential for the influx of the Semiotic. In the actual practice of writing poetry (and of poetry therapy), however, it is poetic language which manifests unconscious influxes easier and which offers greater possibilities of freedom from the oppressive, phallocentric structures of the Symbolic Order. As a result, poetic language is in itself already therapeutic and, on a second plane, facilitative of the psychotherapeutic endeavour.

[123] While poetry allows for expressions less constricted by the Symbolic, it remains by nature a written text which necessarily adheres to the laws of the Symbolic.

A second point Arieti makes is that the creative expression "must not be in disagreement with ordinary thinking;" consequently, the poetic artefact, too, requires interpretation so that "ordinary thinking will understand, accept, and appreciate" it. When it comes to poetry therapy, this point constitutes a problem that is linked to the one discussed above. The poetic text is always already a censored text. Every text, being a means of communication, has to follow the laws of the Symbolic, even if its dominant function is poetic. It is only by (a minimal) adherence to 'The Law of the Father' that the message becomes intelligible. Every interpretation must thus take the communicative function into consideration. Viewed within the context of communication, an interpretation has to choose to proceed along one of two possible paths: first, it can draw its conclusions from the text as it is given – censored by the Symbolic with respect to its Semiotic influences – and assemble inferences and deductions from this surface level, thereby embedding the message in a socio-cultural context. This type of interpretation emphasises the communicative function that is already naturally apparent in the poem. Another approach is to consciously disregard the surface structure and embark on a search for hidden and marginalised content or, in a more technical jargon, for genotextual traces. Such an interpretation requires more (intellectual) work to uphold communication, because it has to construct a new communicable message from its findings. A conscious awareness of the centrality of the communicative function is particularly important here. It is obvious that it is the latter course poetry therapy needs to embark upon.

Regardless of the level of Symbolic adherence, every text bears the trace of its becoming – in the form of buried genotextual elements – and exhibits, beneath the superficially smooth surface, roughened spots and even cracks that stand in contradiction to what the text appears to communicate at first glance. These elements are what might be termed 'scars' of *points de capiton* that have, in addition to producing 'meaning' in accordance with the laws of the Symbolic Order, also experienced cathexes of the Semiotic. The poetic text, being of a more flexible nature than prose, is more open to such cathexes. In poems, to repeat what was said in the previous chapter,

> negation is not "conquered." Rejection operates in them and does not produce an "intellectual acceptance of the repressed" (in other words, it does not affect the passage of the repressed element into the signified, into the symbolic function). Instead it marks *the signifying material* with the repressed. [...] [T]he reintroduction of the symbol of negation into poetic language [...] *arranges the repressed element in a different way*, one that does not represent an "intellectual acceptance of the repressed," an *Aufhebung,* but instead constitutes a post-symbolic (and in this sense anti-symbolic) hallmarking of the material that remained intact during the first symbolization. (Kristeva, *Revolution* 163; emphasis original)

The poetic text is thus marked with the repressed. The "material that remained intact during the first symbolization" is material of the Semiotic drive motility that has remained free and has not been subjected to 'The Law of the Father'. In a process of second symbolisation during the creative act, this material re-enters the Symbolic

Order in the form of symbolic[124] language. In this sense, it is indeed "anti-[S]ymbolic." Within the Symbolic structure of the text, these elements – because of their "anti-[S]ymbolic" nature – are perceived as 'Other'. The second symbolisation thus introduces difference into the text. The 'otherness' of the material introduced during second symbolisation, i.e. in the process of poetic creation, manifests itself in the text in the form of images, symbols and metaphors:

> What is important is the version of the text, and that, Freud tells us, is given in the telling of the dream – that is, in its rhetoric. Ellipsis, pleonasm, hyperbaton or syllepsis, regression, repetition, apposition – these are the syntactical displacements; metaphor, catachresis, antonomasia, allegory, metonymy, and synecdoche – these are the semantic condensations; Freud teaches us to read in them the intentions – whether ostentatious or demonstrative, dissimulating or persuasive, retaliatory or seductive – with which the subject modulates his oneiric discourse. (Lacan, "The Function and Field of Speech and Language in Psychoanalysis" 221-222)

Lacan is talking about dream analysis here, but he is employing the vocabulary of literary studies, or, to be more precise, of "rhetoric." As Lacan emphasises, the "version of the text" is what is important. For psychoanalysis, this "version of the text" is the verbal utterance of the client and its "rhetoric." With "rhetoric" Lacan denotes those verbal features of the utterance that have rhetorical potential; those qualities that are clearly imbrued with ambiguity and/or emotional weight, aspects of an utterance that dissimulate. In poetry therapy, as opposed to the dream (or better: the telling of the dream), these elements of potentiality (a) abound to an even greater extent in rhetorical figures as enumerated above by Lacan, and (b) can be discerned better as they are part of a written text. Poetry therapy thus supplies the notions of dream analysis with an empirical space.

The rhetorical elements in the poetic text are indeterminate elements within the Symbolic structure and cause tensions in the textual matrix, because they threaten the Symbolic's primary function of unequivocal communication. Since the Semiotic otherness is located in indeterminate textual elements, these mark possibilities of interpretation, making the text dynamic. Arieti states that ordinarily

> we select words and put them in special orders for special purposes, whereas when we resort only to our imagination, we allow words to occur freely as in free association. The creative process differs from the ordinary functions of the mind insofar as it uses many kinds of symbols. It also uses the symbols in different contexts and proportions, so that these new, different contexts and proportions themselves become symbols of things never before symbolized or else symbolized previously in different ways. (39)

---

[124] I will use the term 'symbol' or 'symbolic' to denote the figurative elements in the poetic text, i.e. those elements charged with Semiotic content. I thus delimit the Lacanian "Symbolic" (capital 'S') from the rhetorical symbol. I shall not further differentiate between image, symbol, icon, etc., as their function in poetry therapy is basically the same.

The symbolisation that occurs during the creative process establishes "new, different contexts and proportions" for symbols and even sets up contexts for new symbolic linkages. This process of symbolisation in creativity can be linked with two key concepts of psychotherapy: free association and dream analysis. Free association draws connections between ordinarily unrelated content, producing from these connections new meanings and new contexts. Likewise, dream analysis mines the often chaotic landscape of the dream's symbolism for possible connections and parallels, thus creating new meaning. The symbolisation that occurs during the production of poetic texts creates a similar symbolic space: it infuses the textual matrix of the poem with dynamic potential and motility for the creation of new connections, contexts and meanings. As in dream analysis, the poetic text becomes inherently dynamic, because it is dealt with not as a univocal message, but as equivocal, and read for hidden, repressed or subjugated meaning. The infusion of Semiotic content is subject to the normalising tendencies of the Symbolic which are akin to the function of the Superego. In a similar manner, the dream work is limited in its expression by a minimal level of representability, which means that while dreams are chaotic and disrupted, the individual images have to have some root in reality. Unlike in dreams, however, the Semiotic infusion into texts is further censored by 'The Law of the Father'. There is thus a double censorship at work, namely from the Superego and, additionally and more generally, by means of the Symbolic.

On the basis of these apparent parallels between dream analysis and symbolisation during the creative process, poetry therapy combines deconstructive methods and techniques of dream analysis to probe deeply into the structure of the poetic text. This is a dynamic process which involves the poem intimately. These dynamics can best be conceptualised as a form of energy circulating within the confines of the text, but also beyond it. As a first step in outlining the parallels between dream analysis and interpretation in poetry therapy, the following brief excursion will constitute the effects of the genotextual elements as energy. Poetic texts are charged with what I would like to call 'Semiotic energy'. This form of energy can – in function as well as effect – be conceptualised along the lines of what New Historicism defines as 'social energy'. The term 'social energy'

> implies something measurable, yet [one] cannot provide a convenient and reliable formula for isolating a single, stable quantum for examination. We identify *energia* only indirectly, by its effects: it is manifested in the capacity of certain verbal, aural and visual traces to produce, shape, and organize collective physical and mental experiences. (Greenblatt, "The Circulation of Social Energy" 6).

This definition of social energy can be taken over for Semiotic energy as it is precisely the effects of the Semiotic influx in a text that interests the poetry therapist.[125] Also,

---

[125] Social energy is constituted as present in the entire realm of the synchronic semiotic productions of a given culture. Social energy is therefore a collective phenomenon and, according to the New Historicists, its circulation can become traceable only when a number of semiotic artifacts are read side by side. Semiotic energy does have collective

Greenblatt notes that social energy can only be identified indirectly. The same is true of Semiotic energy. Precisely because it is Semiotic, Semiotic energy cannot be represented directly in language, originating from the unconscious as it does. Like the traces of social energy, Semiotic energy traceable in a poetic text is "a subtle, elusive set of exchanges, a network of trades and trade-offs, a jostling of competing representations" (ibid.7) which the therapist has to open up into a discernable web of negotiating sign-functions. The New Historicists' semiotic approach to culture – "the notion of culture as text" (Gallagher/Greenblatt 9) – is another concept applicable to poetry therapy. Where the New Historicist works by "cast[ing] one's interpretative net broadly, to open the windows to the culture at large" (ibid. 13), the poetry therapist too has to take into consideration the entire universe of the text, but also the synchronic and diachronic hoard of the patient's experiences; only in this manner can a comprehensive network of Semiotic traces be apprehended. The text that is dealt with in poetry therapy is thus not only the material, poetic text, but also the text of the client's verbal and non-verbal utterances. The poetic text is, however, a major point of conversion of the other texts. Furthermore, in talking about the major modes of acquisition of cultural material between different cultural zones, Greenblatt isolates "Symbolic Acquisition" as one of the major modes (cf. *Shakespearean Negotiations*, mainly 10-17). In the light of the tendencies of unconscious content to manifest itself in symbolic and figurative language, this feature makes obvious that, indeed, Semiotic energy can be conceptualised along the lines of social energy. Greenblatt contents that in Symbolic Acquisition "a social practice or other mode of social energy is transferred [...] by means of representation" (*Shakespearean Negotiations* 10). Social energy thus functions is a way almost identical to the processes of the dream-work and the becoming conscious of repressed content established above for the negotiations between the Symbolic and the Semiotic. It is not surprising then that Greenblatt further differentiates Symbolic Acquisition into the following three types: (1) Acquisition through Simulation, (2) Metaphorical Acquisition, and (3) Acquisition through Synecdoche or Metonymy. (Cf. ibid. 10-11). In doing so, the delineation of social energy becomes almost identical to Freud's description of the functions of the dream-work. Consequently, the notion of Semiotic energy conceptualised on the basis of social energy fits congenially into the theoretical framework established so far and can be appropriated to elucidate and utilise the parallels between poetry and dreaming for poetry therapy.

Having defined Semiotic energy, it is now possible to focus more closely on the parallels of interpreting a text in poetry therapy and dream analysis. Both deal with symbols and how to exploit them productively in therapy. For poetry therapy, the interdependencies of first and second symbolisation are crucial. The chaotic liberty the subject experiences during the creative process – a liberty that is akin to both free association and the state of dreaming – incites those Semiotic charges that have not been

---

aspects as well in that – apart from the symbolic web generated from the text of the poem – the negotiations of Semiotic energy are followed in the context of the client's life, i.e. its extratextual, collective ties.

bound during first symbolisation to attach themselves to specific contexts and propositions thereby changing these or producing new ones. This process of second symbolisation, the charging of a text with Semiotic energy, it must be noted, takes place within the realm of the Symbolic Order established during first symbolisation. This has a threefold effect: (1) Second symbolisation is in most cases not permanent as is first symbolisation, i.e. it is much more contingent, being dependent on a specific context as well as the individual subject. (2) The effects of second symbolisation will be veiled by normalising tendencies of the Symbolic Order. The genotextual meaning can thus only be excavated by deconstructing the overt meaning of a text or phrase, by spotting a hidden ambiguity or consciously denying the 'established' interpretation of a symbol in favour of an interpretation more fitting the tropic context of the poetic text in question and the context of the client's individual life-story. (3) The signs of language (in the Saussurean sense), having been occupied, so to speak, with culturally determined semantic meanings during first symbolisation,[126] become overcoded when infused with Semiotic energy. Generally speaking one can say that signs either gain additional meaning through the process of displacement or become symbolic, i.e. their meaning becomes condensed thus adding ambiguity to a text. It can consequently be concluded that the functions of the second symbolisation partaking in poetic creation (displacement and condensation) are the same as in the dream-work. Symbols thus affect the text as a whole, adding a surplus of information which has implications for both the client and the interpretation.

The writing subject, in the process of creation, is unaware of the whole range of meaning brought about by the text it produces. In semiotic terms,[127] the outcome of the artistic process are "two excesses of redundancy (on expression and content planes respectively) [which] produce an *increase of informational possibilities*: the message has in effect become a source of further and unpredictable information, so that it is now semantically ambiguous" (Eco, *A Theory of Semiotics* 270; emphasis original). Due to this surplus of information, i.e. ambiguity of meaning, which is, with regard to the poetic text, primarily located in symbols and images, the conventional connection between the signifier and the signified is loosened up. The second symbolisation brought about in poetic writing thus influences the relatively stable connection established during first symbolisation. In other words, the drive charges which have become

---

[126] At this point it is necessary to be reminded of the following proposition made in the preceding chapter: Lacan determined that there is a constant sliding of the signifier over the signified and that meaning is therefore contingent, being produced at *points de capiton*. With the crossing of the subject from the Imaginary into the Symbolic, the process of first symbolisation arrests the sliding of the signifier to a certain extent, enabling the subject to use certain symbols – the signs, or words of a language – in a fixed manner so as to enable communication. Fundamentally, however, the process of first symbolisation does not stop the sliding of the signifier nor does it in any way impinge on the contingency of meaning. It does, however, set up rules, both semantic and pragmatic, that govern the processes on the axes of selection and combination.

[127] Semiotics as a text approach, not as a psychological function in the sense of Kristeva.

conventionally associated with particular signifiers during first symbolisation are disrupted by the introduction of new motilities by the Semiotic; their 'thetic' orientation is disrupted. In this manner they become charged with Semiotic energy. This energy increases the motility of signs with regard to the formation of meaning. The connection of signifier and signified thus becomes functional. Since the Ego, the Id and the Superego are not psychic places but psychic functions, the signs of language are no fixed constants,

> but only *sign-functions*. [...] A sign-function is realized when two *functives* (expression and content) enter into mutual correlation; the same functive can also enter into another correlation, thus becoming a different functive and therefore giving rise to a new sign-function. Thus signs are the provisional result of coding rules which establish *transitory* correlations of elements, each of these elements being entitled to enter – under given coded circumstances – into another correlation and thus form a new sign. (Eco, *Theory of Semiotics* 49; emphasis original)

The definition of the sign proposed by Eco here, namely as a function, refashions the concept of the Saussurean sign in a manner bringing it close to Lacan's concept of the production of meaning as $\frac{S}{s}$. For Eco, a sign-function is neither a physical entity, nor a fixed semiotic entity, but "rather a meeting ground for independent elements" (ibid.). The same is true of Lacan's concept of the signifier and signified being separated by the 'bar'. In the Lacanian system, meaning is produced at *points de capiton* which promote the appearance of meaning by virtue of contextual and intrapsychic conditions. Eco conceives of the sign-functions in an almost identical manner, stating that "it is not true that a code organizes signs; it is more correct to say that codes provide the rules which *generate* signs as concrete occurrences in communicative intercourse. Therefore, the classical notion of 'sign' *dissolves* itself into a highly complex network of changing relationships" (ibid; emphasis original), relationships which crystallise into meaning at the Lacanian juncture points. This happens, as Eco notes, only "under given coded circumstances" and it is precisely the unique code of poetic language that allows for the breaking up of conventional correlations. In *The Open Work*, Eco states that "the ambiguity of the aesthetic message is the result of the deliberate 'disordering' of the code, that is, of the order that, via selection and association, had been imposed on the entropic disorder characteristic of all sources of information" (67). The entropic disorder at the basis of all information must be read as Eco's rendering of Kristeva's notion of the Semiotic. The code is nothing but another term for the Symbolic, the rules that are upheld by 'The Law of the Father'. In poetry, the Semiotic is able to partly rewrite the code of the Symbolic through second symbolisation and, like the dream-work, the outcome of this second symbolisation is figurative content, the code of which is unknown and needs to be deciphered.

The ability of sign-functions to correlate to functives other than those ordinarily associated with it,[128] produces ambiguity. This ambiguity results from two processes:

---

[128] Eco's definition of a sign as being "the provisional result of coding rules which establish *transitory* correlations of elements" must not be taken as a referring only to artistic

(1) From an additional correlation of a sign-function which is a metonymic process. (2) Meaning is condensed when a sign-function changes its correlation due to contextual circumstances and this can be denoted as a metaphoric process. From the perspective of the applicability for poetry therapy, it becomes evident that, especially in the context of Lacan's identification of metonymy and metaphor with displacement and condensation, the genotext of the client's poem can be utilised therapeutically when concentrating on the figurative elements of the finished poem. The therapist's skills derived from the interpretation of dream imagery can be drawn upon here to great effect.

As in dreaming and in free association,[129] conscious control has to be relinquished for the Semiotic influxes to become manifest beyond what is easily censored by the Symbolic in ordinary language. This is, however, not to be confused with a trance-like state or hypnosis. The

> accessibility to the primary processes may require a state of passivity similar to dreaming; but the passivity cannot involve the artist's whole psyche. On the contrary, it contrasts with the increased alertness on the part of the psyche that deals with the secondary processes and presides over the artistic synthesis. Thus in the act of aesthetic creation, a complicated mental mechanism takes place that combines greater than usual passivity with greater than usual activity. The artist must put together many elements of different origins to make syntheses of higher orders – that is, to create artistic unities. (Arieti 185)

In a therapeutic environment, the state of passivity mentioned by Arieti always entails at the same time a state of activity. What is important is thus not so much passivity as relaxation. In poetry therapy, as in the other art therapies, relaxation is closely connected to playfulness. The mind, in being playfully active during artistic production,

---

use of language. It is ontological. Even though the rules of language seem stable, in fact they are only transitory as the fact of language change easily makes manifest.

[129] The method of free association is a Freudian technique which tries to access the repressed by going beyond structured thinking. Jung developed a similar technique called active imagination, which is closely connected with artistic expression in Jungian psychoanalysis: "Jung discovered what he would later call active imagination during a period of personal crisis after his relationship with Freud had been shattered in 1912-1913. [...] In opening himself to the childlike states of play, he found that the imagination has the ability to treat itself, and he used the arts as ways of 'giving shape' to different experiences he was undergoing. Images appeared spontaneously as he engaged different types of artistic expression. Rather than let reason control the therapeutic process, Jung gave 'the leadership to the unconscious' and formulated what he called the 'transcendent function', which integrates conscious and unconscious experience into a third state of adaptation and change" (McNiff, *Art Heals* 172-173). Similar techniques have been developed and practiced since the early days of psychoanalysis, including, in recent years, modes of psychic relaxation derived from Asian sources. I will not go into detail on any of these techniques as their implementation and effectiveness is dependent on the individual therapist's personal preference. It is the outcome of these techniques of psychic relaxation – a state of mind in which conscious interference is minimized and the client can thus approach a dream-like state – which are relevant for poetry therapy.

relaxes its conscious control which, on the one hand, breaks the client's fixation on the problems and, on the other hand, encourages a crossing of the bar of the Semiotic. Since the client's external context at the moment of the crossing is artistic, and a *point de capiton* is defined by its correlation of intrapsychic and external circumstances, the Semiotic will find expression in artistic form. Ehrenzweig notes that

> [c]reativity remains closely related to the chaos of the primary process. Whether we are to experience chaos or a high creative order depends entirely on the reaction of our rational faculties. If they are capable of yielding to the shift of control from conscious focusing to unconscious scanning the disruption of consciousness is hardly felt. The momentary absence of mind will be forgotten as the creative mind returns to the surface with newly won insight. (35)

Ehrenzweig suggests that the primary processes constitute a two-edged sword which, depending on the individual's predisposition, can induce either a feeling of chaos or of "high creative order." While the latter feeling is seen as beneficial and curative, the first one is clearly to be avoided.[130] Relaxation is the key. In dreams, relaxation happens naturally. The censorship of the Superego function is drastically reduced when dreaming, allowing for a harmless way of expressing and experiencing otherwise dangerous actions. Therapeutic writing, which is client writing that is carefully supervised and guided by the therapist in all stages, provides a safe, relaxing environment in which to exercise the client's creative impulse which is simultaneously a pressure release. Creativity, relaxation and the reduction of psychic pressures go hand in hand here. Consequently, before poetry therapy can be applied effectively, an atmosphere conducive to creativity has to be established and maintained. Only on this basis can clients "enter the flow of creative communication [and] it becomes easy and natural for the images to express themselves. [Clients] start to act like poets who move freely within a personified world where everything has the ability to speak and offer its unique perspective" (McNiff, *Art Heals* 92).

---

[130] While being concerned with creativity for its own sake, Arieti proposes "two kinds of prerequisites for the unfolding of the creative process. One kind may be designated as *contingencies*, a category that includes everything external to the creative person. A human being cannot originate new things out of nothing. [...] The second kind is much more specific. It refers to the psychological life of the individual, to anything that can be included under the category of *imagination* and *amorphous cognition*" (37; emphasis original). Arieti sees creativity as springing from a meeting of (communicative) context ("contingencies") and psychological predisposition ("*imagination* and *amorphous cognition*"). Although the term "*amorphous cognition*" cannot deny a close semantic relationship to "unconscious scanning," the dyadic notion of external context/internal predisposition, which is not set up as sequential, brings Arieti's concept close to Lacan's juncture points.

4.2 Poetry and Dreams: Semiotic Infusion – Symbolic Crystallisation

The process of poetic creation is non-sequential; it takes place in a state of active, ludic relaxation which has syncretistic or even synesthetic effects.[131] It joins heterogeneous experiences that participate in it: the amorphous Semiotic, the informational input from the outside world, the mental and physical reactions to both, and the actual hands-on technical process of producing the creative artefact. The poem therefore contains the experiences that partook in its becoming in a synesthetic manner. It is more than the sum of its parts and traces of the individual experiences are recoverable through the therapeutic process. The synesthetic nature of the creative process may also, at least partly, account for the healing powers ascribed to it by art therapy theory. Creativity is therapeutic, because its synesthetic nature provides a glimpse and a quasi-return to the ur-synesthesia of the Lacanian Real. The result of the synesthetic process has, however, to submit to a minimal representability that is the demand of the Symbolic Order. Since the Symbolic is differential in nature, the originally synesthetic creative outcome is divided up with its entry into the Symbolic. Synesthetic elements are separated into *different*, isolated fragments that fit into the structural order of the Symbolic. The result of this is that the originally synesthetic character of creativity becomes either completely veiled or that those aspects which conform to the censorship of the Symbolic are foregrounded. In poetry, the Symbolic process of differentiation and normalisation is counteracted by displacement and condensation of originally synesthetic elements into symbols. The same process can be found in Freud's notion of the dream-work. Dreams, Freud argues, are the *via regia* to the unconscious; dreams communicate via symbolism in the form of displacement and condensation, or in more literary terms, through metonymy and metaphor respectively.[132] McNiff also notes the parallelism between dreaming and artistic expression, arguing that "[t]he making of

---

[131] Synaesthesia is the phenomenon in which one sensory experience involuntarily triggers an experience in another sensory area. The most commonly known synaesthesia is the so-called colour-grapheme synaesthesia where letters and numbers are experienced as coloured. For a comprehensive account on the phenomenon of synaesthesia cf. Cytowic, *Synesthesia: A Union of the Senses*. Baron-Cohen/Harrison's *Synaesthesia: Classic and Contemporary Readings* considers synaesthesia in the context of art.

[132] On the interrelation of Jakobson, Freud and Lacan, cf. also Burke: "For Lacan, linguistic research led him to Jakobson's now famous distinction between metaphor and metonymy (the substitution of the part for the whole, i.e. the turf for horse racing) which he adapted, respectively, to Freud's characterisation of the dream process as condensation and displacement. This insight then allowed Lacan to begin his rereading of Freud from a linguistic perspective on the understanding that 'the unconscious is structured like language'. [...] Lacan stressed that it is not man as conscious subject who thinks, acts or speaks, but the linguistic unconscious that determines his every thought, action and utterance" (13). On metaphor and metonymy, cf. also Dirven, *Metaphor and Metonymy in Comparison and Contrast*.

artistic images can be likened to a waking dream" (*Art as Medicine* 131) and Crootof goes even further stating that

> the most remarkable similarity between poetry and dreams is in the fusion mechanisms that both employ. The figures of speech of poetic diction – metaphor, metonymy [...], and synecdoche [...] – and the processes of the dream world – condensation, displacement and symbolization – are so similar in their treatment of time, space and the things of reality that one is obliged to consider whether they are not basically the same mental operations. (46)

Indeed, the similarities traced so far between rhetorical tropes and dream images as well as between the processes of symbolisation and the dream-work strongly suggest that these are one and the same process. According to classical Freudian theory, dreams are a means of wish fulfilment. They serve as an outlet for psychic energy which would otherwise remain blocked and unsatisfied. Dreams thus follow the pleasure principle and by means of the dream-work, the primary processes transform unconscious content – which is essentially beyond representation – into a form that can be processed by the Ego and can thus find release. Freud distinguishes four elementary aspects of the dream-work: (1) Condensation, (2) Displacement, (3) Representability and (4) Secondary Revision (cf. Freud *Interpretation of Dreams*, [especially Vol. IV, 227-338; Vol. V, 339-508]; *An Outline of Psycho-Analysis* [165-171]). The same processes are at work in the production of verbal meaning by Semiotic infusions into the Symbolic.[133] The Symbolic is thus charged with Semiotic energy which affects the poetic text in manners almost identical to Feud's four aspects of the dream-work above: Semiotic cathexes produce metaphoric (number one above) or metonymic (number two above) effects. Since verbal meaning has to follow the laws of the Symbolic in order to be understandable, the Semiotic influx has to adhere to certain minimal rules of representability (number three above) and it is subject to the normalising tendencies of the Symbolic (number four above).[134] The representation of unconscious content in dreams, by means of the dream-work, and its representation in the poetic text, by means of the process of second symbolisation (i.e. the effects from the influx of Semiotic energy), are in fact the same process. Consequently, the psychological principles of dream analysis apply to the analysis of poetry and vice versa.[135] If the symbols in dreams follow the same principles of formation and representation as do

---

[133] Cf. Rycroft (1956, 1979, 1992) on the interrelation of creativity and the primary and secondary processes.

[134] Cf. also Ehrenzweig: "The process of (creative) symbol formation obeys the same rhythm. In order to symbolize another object, the symbolic image must interpenetrate with it in the undifferentiated matrix of image making. On being re-introjected into consciousness, the undifferentiated linkages will contract. The symbolic image alone catches the narrow focus of secondary revision and the other symbolized object remains repressed. But as long as unconscious linkage persists the symbolizing image will not be dissociated and remain imbued with unconscious meaning and reference" (193-194).

[135] Cf., for instance, Freud, "Creative Writers and Daydreaming."

those in poetic language, conceptions of symbols and metaphor used in literary studies are applicable to psychoanalysis as well. With respect to poetry therapy, this calls for an investigation into the nature of figurative language from the point of view of literary studies in order to broaden the poetry therapist's therapeutic knowledge and tools.

In the light of the above, the following pages will present an investigation of figurative language in the context of poetry therapy, outlining the knowledge required of the therapist in this field. I will begin with a brief discussion on the nature of the symbol broadly conceived. What will be said about the symbol in the following pages is valid for figurative language in general.

First and foremost, symbols are signs, and as such they have to follow the rules of all signs within the structure of language. This is the external nature of symbols which adheres to the regular rules of grammar. When it comes to content, however, symbols do not follow the Symbolic's inclination to unequivocal meaning. Rather the opposite. Symbols are evocative of meanings which go beyond the purely linguistic. "A true '*symbol*' creates a connection between conscious and unconscious. Its form expresses something that cannot be said more clearly, because it is not clearly understood" (Wallace 100). Though Edith Wallace refers to visual symbols here, her statements apply just as well to linguistic symbols. Symbols are, according to Wallace, denotative signs that lack a clearly defined denotation. Jungian psychoanalysis offers a similar definition. In distinguishing the symbol from the sign, Jung regards

> signs as images which refer to discoverable and specific events of fantasies in a person's past – the repressed material of the Freudian psychoanalysis. He regarded images as symbolic when they induced strong effects, yet defied complete or precise verbal description, Jung attributed symbolic status to images that Freud would have seen as resistant to interpretation because of unconscious defense mechanisms. (Edwards 83)

For Jung, symbols are images that defy precise description and induce strong effects. By defining symbols in this manner, it is possible to keep in mind their origin in the Semiotic, their nature as Semiotic energy and be mindful of their effects of introducing *différance* into the poetic text:[136] the literary symbol is never fixed; it is always ready to take on the connotations of the reader. The contingency of meaning is to a far greater extent part of the nature of the symbol than it is in words used non-figuratively. Whereas words are predominantly denotative, symbols are connotative in nature. Symbols are charged with meaning that is at once culturally defined and personally decentred. Even if a symbol achieves a provisional stability as a cultural symbol, this stability is immediately lost by the connotations the individual brings to it.[137] Symbols thus constitute and express – as best as is possible under the rule of the Symbolic – the

---

[136] The lack of precision is the inheritance from the unlimited signification in the unconscious and the strong effect harks back to the origins in the instinctual *chora*. The impossibility of representation of the synesthetic processes during creation also adds to the nature of the symbol and is, simultaneously, an agent and effect of *différance*.

[137] Cf. Eco's concept of the sign-function. Since the symbol is, of course, a sign, it, too, constitutes a function which is free to enter new correlations.

synesthetic legacy of the creative process.[138] In poetic texts, this feature is augmented by the influence of other symbols that generate additional possibilities of meaning. The symbol is the most 'free-floating' element within the Symbolic Order, the one least subject to 'The Law of the Father' and its phallocentric realm. Symbols constitute meaning from connotative relationships (mostly metaphorical and metonymical) to extra-linguistic sign-functions. This is to say symbols are signs that exist within the greater semiotic tissue of a culture or society and, simultaneously and reciprocally, the client's personal history and experience. Since non-linguistic signs – and consequently the meaning derived or constructed from these – follow different conventions and codes, these different principles of meaning production have an effect on the symbolic sign within the linguistic realm. It is decentred and enriched not only with possible meanings, but also with sign-functions alien to the Symbolic. This can provide symbols with a grammatical flexibility, allowing such symbols to appear in places that would normally be prohibited by the rules of a language. In a poetic text, which is grammatically more flexible in the first place, symbols therefore gain an increased motility.

The grammatical and semantic freedom exhibited by symbols is at once the basis and the effect of their close connection to the Semiotic. Symbols are not restricted grammatically and can appear everywhere in the text. They are mobile elements within the Symbolic matrix of the text, free to follow the play of signification. One can thus "see the emergence of a new conception of the symbol, one in which it is integrated into the chain of associations and does not reduce the subject to silence. The symbol therefore acquires the status of a product of the unconscious and becomes, by this token, an object which an analysis must work upon" (Arrivé 60). Symbols are thus obstacles to immediate understanding, but it is precisely this aspect which makes them ideal for therapeutic purposes as the process of making them understood is a therapeutic one. Because a symbol connects the conscious with the unconscious, part of what it expresses is always in the dark. Arrivé notes:

> The symbol, on the one hand, is seen as an already existing entity, "always already" created. And the silence which is observed about it can doubtless be explained by the sexual nature of the evoked content. But it can also be explained by the fact that one cannot, strictly speaking, say anything about such a symbol […] just as one cannot say anything, when discussing the words of language, about their relation between their form and meaning. (60)

---

[138] The *OED* gives three definitions of synaesthesia the second of which deals with the term in literature: "The use of metaphors in which terms relating to one kind of sense-impression are used to describe sense-impressions of other kinds; the production of synesthetic effect in writing or an instance of this." Although one has to be careful not to confuse synaesthesia, which is involuntary, with such cross-sensory metaphors as "biting wind" or "scorching sun," the definition makes clear the connection of synaesthesia and figurative language.

The symbol is "an already existing entity," because it is part of the cultural legacy of the Symbolic; that one cannot "say anything about [it]" is rooted in the symbol's affiliation with the Semiotic. The fundamental dynamics represented by Semiotic energy are thus accounted for. The Semiotic energy that is contained within the symbol lies dormant unless actualised and, once actualised, it decentres the symbol. The same is true about the social energy New Historicists locate in texts. The negotiations of social energy only become traceable when looked at in the context of a web of synchronic semiotic manifestations. Likewise, Semiotic energy only becomes productive for therapy if it is first of all recognised and, secondly, related to other occurrences of Semiotic energy, i.e. other rhetorical figures within the text. Poetry therapy therefore strives to create a web of symbols from the poetic text from which the negotiations of Semiotic energy can be deduced.

It has thus far implicitly been assumed that symbols occupy a foregrounded position in the fabric of the poetic text qua their nature as symbols. The supposition was that symbols are easy to spot elements in the matrix of the poetic text and can consequently be employed in poetry therapy with relative ease. During the therapeutic encounter, both clients and therapists can take recourse to symbols within the poem, but especially analysts, given their training in spotting and elucidating symbols in dreams, should be able to extract a web of symbolism from the matrix of the poetic text without too many problems. While dealing with and analysing symbols is at the heart of psychotherapy, there is still a difference between symbols in dreams, conveyed verbally, and figurative language in poems. In the telling of the dream, a symbol that defies understanding immediately stands out by the client's inability to incorporate it into the story of the dream. In the poetic text, a metaphor can – as will be made clear soon – go totally unnoticed without implicating the analysis of the poem's message. It is here that the training of the therapist may be insufficiently literary to spot figurative use whenever it is not obvious.[139] The nature of the Symbolic and its normalising tendencies aggravate this problem. I will continue to discuss this matter by means of a generic example, namely metaphor. Taking a look at metaphor will illuminate the problems and dangers hinted at above and produce an awareness of the same. Metaphor is the obvious choice here as it is a rhetorical figure that abounds in common language as well as poetic language and often goes unnoticed. Moreover, metaphor, or metaphorical processes, have already played a significant role in the previous chapter,

---

[139] Jaskoski, for instance, does not consider the traditional psychological training sufficient to spot symbols in the poetic text. She therefore includes the topic of 'Rhetoric' in her list of core literary competences a poetry therapist should possess (81-84). While I assume that any poetry therapist has developed – in the course of his or her core training or by means of further vocational training – a sufficient competence in the literary area to be able to discern the most common rhetorical figures, my argument will show that, in many cases, it may not be enough to have only a basic understanding of rhetorical figures. In this respect, Jaskoski's proposal is critical when it comes to the training of poetry therapists.

making it possible to draw parallels and to further elucidate the applicability and pervasiveness of these concepts in poetry therapy.

As Arieti succinctly states, "[p]oetry, of course, is not based exclusively on metaphor, but metaphorical language is one of its fundamental components" (136). The notion of metaphor and metaphoricality is essential to poetry and thus also to poetry therapy. According to Eco,

> [e]very discourse on metaphor originates in a radical choice: either (a) language is by nature, and originally, metaphorical, and the mechanisms of metaphor establishes linguistic activity, every rule or convention arising thereafter in order to discipline, reduce [and impoverish] the metaphorizing potential that defines man as a symbolic animal; or (b) language (and any other semiotic system) is a rule-governed mechanism, a predictive machine that says which phrases can be generated and which not, and which from those able to be generated are "good" or "correct," or endowed with sense; a machine with regard to which metaphor constitutes a breakdown, a malfunction, an unaccountable outcome, but at the same time the drive towards linguistic renewal. ("Scandal of Metaphor" 218)

The two alternatives presented by Eco above for the discourse on metaphor are not as "radical" as his argument might suggest. Eco's "radical choice" is, in fact, not inevitably a choice at all. Eco's (a) and (b) are not mutually exclusive and can be made to coexist when conceived chronologically. Eco's first proposition locates the origin of language in metaphor, a state which later became "discipline[d]" to "reduce [and impoverish] the metaphorizing potential." His second assumption is that language is a rule-based system that breaks down in the face of metaphor but is at the same time revitalised through this breakdown. Eco's first proposition is a rendering of the Mirror Stage during which the Semiotic and the chaotic, pre-linguistic world become systemised and language is instituted in the subject. Eco's second "choice" delineates the breaking of the Symbolic structure through the Semiotic influx, which, indeed, affects a revitalising of the Symbolic. The following discussion of metaphor will thus follow a combination of Eco's alternatives, which represents a rendering of Lacan's and Kristeva's psychoanalytical approach to language: Eco establishes metaphor as a disruptive element to the "rule-governed" structure of language. In the terminology of Lacan and Kristeva this is to say that metaphorical statements are charged with Semiotic energy and are inherently disruptive of the Symbolic Order. Furthermore, Eco contends that this very function of metaphor brings with it a "drive towards linguistic renewal." Linguistic renewal necessarily entails new denotative abilities, a plus in expressive possibilities and thus by proxy a plus in information.[140] It is precisely this

---

[140] Cf. Eco: "There can be no doubt that, at least, the final result of the Aristotelian proportion is a process very much like Freudian condensation, and that this condensation [...] can be described as far as its semiotic mechanisms are concerned in terms of the acquiring and losing of *properties* or *semes*, however one should want to call them" ("Scandal of Metaphor" 229; emphasis original). Any change of a term's properties leads to changes of meaning, or at least the range of possible meanings of any term in a variety of pragmatic circumstances.

which poetry therapy seeks to promote. Clients' use of metaphor or their metaphorically charged language can, when put in the context of both the poetic text and the metatextual framework of the client's life, take on new properties that lead to new information about the client's wishes and desires – new in the sense of previously unconscious.

What, then, precisely, is a metaphor? To answer this it is best to go back to Aristotle, who states: "Metaphor consists in giving the thing a name that belongs to something else; the transference being either from genus to species, or from species to genus, or from species to species, or on grounds of analogy" (*Poetics* 13).[141] Ricoeur notes that "metaphor takes the *word* as its unit of reference. Metaphor, therefore, is classed among the single-word figures of speech and is defined as a trope of resemblance. As figure, metaphor constitutes a displacement and an extension of the meaning of words; its explanation is grounded in a theory of substitution" (*The Rule of Metaphor* 3; emphasis original). Though he states, talking about the classical system of rhetoric, that metaphor is classed among the "single-word figures," Ricoeur does not state that metaphor is confined to the level of the word. It takes the "*word* as its unity of reference" as it must, but it is not confined to the word. This means that metaphorical statements are much more variable and can appear in various grammatical (dis)guises. This is further complicated by Aristotle's definition. From Aristotle's enumeration of metaphor's modes of transference it becomes clear that he sees metaphor as generic for the various species of rhetorical tropes.[142] This notwithstanding, there are two implications regarding the nature of metaphor that can be drawn from Aristotle's definition. The one reduces metaphor to a mode of comparison between two things. The other implication is that the "transference" of the name of one thing onto another adds new properties to the receiving term, which makes metaphor a creative rather than simply comparative mode of expression. Contemporary research on metaphor can be roughly divided into positions which represent one or the other of the above implications. Theories constituting metaphor as a mode of comparison are subsumed under the name *reductionism*, while those that see metaphor as creative go by the name of *interactionism*.[143] Generally speaking, it can be said that there is currently

---

[141] I take over Aristotle's definition from the *Poetics* rather than the *Rhetoric* because this "is justified by the fact that the *Rhetoric* – whether it was composed or newly revised after the *Poetics* was written – adopts, pure and simple, the well-known definition of metaphor from the *Poetics*" (Ricoeur, *The Rule of Metaphor* 13).

[142] Cf. Eco, "Scandal of Metaphor:" "The metaphor is defined as the recourse to a name of another type, or as the transferring to one object of a name belonging to another, an operation that can take place through displacements from genus to species, from species to genus, from species to species, or by analogy. Clearly, in laying the basis for a 'metaphorology', Aristotle uses /metaphor/ as a generic term" (221).

[143] For a summary and discussion of the theories of reductionism and interactionism, cf. Hausman's *Metaphor and Art* (especially 22-44) as well as Ricoeur's *The Rule of Metaphor* (in particular "Study 3," 65-100). Cf. furthermore Ayoob, "Black & Davidson on

a furious debate over whether the meanings of metaphors can be tied to speaker/author intentions; whether the meanings of metaphors are based on similarity, analogy, or dissimilarity; whether metaphor is a linguistic or ontological matter; whether metaphor violates linguistic rules or conversational norms; whether the meanings of metaphors can be literally paraphrased; whether an account of metaphorical meaning belongs in the domain of semantics as opposed to pragmatics; and even whether metaphor can be said to possess meaning at all. (Gibbs 576)[144]

These debates are only of interest at the moment in so far as metaphor's relation to the writing subject and the reader is concerned, and as a source of original and/or additional meaning in the poetic text. In the framework of classical rhetoric and, to some extent, reductionism, metaphor is seen as working by substituting one word through another via a "displacement and extension of meaning." Displacement, as has been shown, is Freud's term for the metonymic process of the dream-work and repression. In this light, metaphor would be a species of metonymy and not the other way around. At this point it is helpful to remember the fact that, in Freud, displacement and condensation – that is, metonymy and metaphor – are primary processes and any hierarchies we might impose on them can only be purely methodological. The same is essentially true of Jakobson's metaphorical and metonymical axes. Language, as his essay on aphasia clearly demonstrates, only works when both processes operate jointly. This is corroborated by Eco who states that "metonymical substitution is no different from the process Freud called 'displacement.' And just as condensation is involved with the process of displacement, so is metaphor involved [...] with these metonymical exchanges" ("Scandal of Metaphor" 244). For our purposes it is consequently best to conceive of metaphor and metonymy as co-influential in the production of figurative language. I will continue to use the term metaphor to denote this type of language, but it should be noted that this always implies metonymic processes as well.

Gibbs notes that the "interaction view is perhaps the most dominant theory in the multidisciplinary study of metaphor" (587). Max Black's interaction theory of metaphor is a prominent example and will work well within the theoretical framework of this study. Black argues that "when we use a metaphor we have two thoughts of different things active together and supported by a single word or phrase, whose meaning is a resultant of their interaction" (*Models and Metaphor* 38). This means that according to interactionism, metaphor is more than a vehicle of the poetic function of language foregrounding the artificiality of poetic language, nor is it limited to pointing out underlying relationships of meaning between the compared terms. Black, albeit implicitly here, grants metaphor creative and generative properties that result from the 'interaction' of its components. He states that the two *tertia comparationis* are "active together" which suggest a reciprocal or joined process of meaning production. Along

---

Metaphor;" Davidson, "What Metaphors Mean;" Black, "How Metaphors Work: A Reply to Donald Davidson;" "Metaphor," and Searle, "Metaphor."

[144] Although Gibbs essay is from 1991 and therefore a good 18 years old, the problems and topics contained in Gibb's essay continue to be hotly debated today.

the same line, there is a "resultant" emerging from the interaction, which, though produced by the two terms involved, is more than the sum of its parts, namely a figurative linguistic entity that semiotically behaves in a new manner.

Black's theory of interactionism distinguishes between the 'focus', or 'secondary subject', and the 'frame', or 'primary subject', of a metaphorical statement. The 'focus' denotes the word that is used figuratively, the 'frame' is the remainder of the statement that is to be read literally. According to interactionism, metaphorical meaning emerges from an interaction between the frame and the focus. Black

> postulates that a metaphor contains a primary subject and a secondary subject. The secondary subject is regarded as a system instead of a thing. In the act of creating and understanding a metaphor, an individual selects, emphasizes, suppresses, and organizes features of the primary subject by applying it to statements corresponding in structure and form with the secondary subject, reciprocally including change. (*Models and Metaphors* 168)

The interaction consists in the reciprocal (re)organisation of the primary and the secondary subjects which results in a change or extension of meaning. Black states that in a metaphor, the secondary subject influences one's perception of the primary subject by means of a "system of associated commonplaces," or implications (*Models and Metaphors* 40). Black constitutes a fundamental opposition for the focus and the frame, noting that the "duality of reference [between primary and secondary subject] is marked by the contrast between the metaphorical statement's *focus* (the word or words used nonliterally) and the surrounding literal *frame*" ("More about Metaphor" 27; emphasis original). Within the literal frame of a statement the focus thus appears as a distortion which incites the reader/hearer to construct a complex of associated implications which is then tested on the secondary subject. The reader/hearer is thus made aware of parallel features of the primary and secondary subject which reciprocally lead to a change of meaning in both participants and thus produces metaphor. In this way, those features of the primary subject are actualised which are commonly associated with the secondary subject. Although Black emphasises the fact that this relationship is reciprocal and the change in meaning affects both interacting parties – as it must since the meaning of a metaphor is the combination of both – it is clearly the secondary subject which is more central to the production of metaphorical meaning. This is why it is the focus of the statement.

Before a reader or hearer can construct the associated commonplaces that create metaphorical meaning, however, there has to be a perception of the possibility of figurative meaning. If the possibility of a metaphorical meaning is not recognised by a reader, the figurative properties are not actualised. There has to be a minimum amount of tension between the focus and the frame to denote the possibility of metaphor:

> An expression taken to be metaphorical is regarded as differentiating between two sets of properties in the intension or signification of its major terms. These two clashing sets of properties are [...] the "central meanings" (dictionary or accepted meanings) as distinct from its "marginal" meanings (remotely associated meanings). When a term is combined with others, there is a logical opposition between the central meaning of one

term and the central meaning of other terms. This opposition alerts us to the possibility that an expression may be a metaphor and that we need to shift from its center to its marginal meaning. (Hausman 32)

The tension between frame and focus signals to the reader that the word(s) may be used figuratively. The conflict is produced by the words' central meanings, which do not go together according to the usual rules of the Symbolic. Since the Symbolic is an *order*, there should ideally be no conceivable clash of meaning. The clash thus signifies a disruption of the Symbolic which necessitates a move to the peripheral meanings of the word(s) in order to solve the perceived paradox and to establish new or altered meaning(s). Metaphor conceived as an interactive process implicitly contains the possibility of not only creating meaning via pre-existing implications, but also of new and unexpected occurrences of meaning:

> The interaction theory of metaphor suggests that understanding metaphor creates similarity and does *not* simply emphasize preexisting but unnoticed aspects of the meaning or similarity relationship [...]. New meanings are made possible by the interaction of terms in a metaphor and not as a result of either shifting attention to marginal aspects of meaning or highlighting accidental properties of things. At least some metaphors involve the creation of new frameworks of connotation rather than the actualization of potential but unrealized connotations. (Gibbs 587; emphasis original)

Metaphors *create* a similarity and in doing so increase, to speak in Eco's terms, the informational potential of the associated terms, which brings about new meaning. In her critique of Black's concepts, Ayoob rightly argues that "Black gives us no reason for understanding why the focus of the metaphor is somehow more primary or accessible and able to make act upon the commonplaces of the frame" (58). By applying Lacanian concepts to Black's interaction theory, however, it is not only possible to answer this question, but also to emphasise the importance of a creative view of metaphor for poetry therapy. To begin with, we have constituted that metaphor comes into being through a tension between the focus and the frame; this tension disrupts the stable meaning of the frame and introduces a perceptible shift – a form of *différance* – into the statement. The focus is therefore a crack in the structure of the Symbolic frame and constitutes a Semiotic incursion. The entire statement is dislodged from its accorded position in the system of the Symbolic and (re)gains, to a varying degree, Semiotic motility. The focus is primary in this process, because it constitutes a *point de capiton*.[145] The appearance of juncture points is context-dependent and just such a context is here found as the basis of the production of metaphorical meaning.[146] It is

---

[145] Cf. also Ricoeur: "The level of the word is not just the intermediary level between those of the phoneme and syntagma; it is the connecting layer. From one side the first-level distinctive units presuppose the significant units of the lexical level" (*The Rule of Metaphor* 104). The word is the connecting layer that allows the Semiotic to affect the Symbolic Order.

[146] Cf. also Gibbs, who suggests "that metaphor understanding creates new ad hoc categories, ones with systematic entailments, [and] also provides a concrete model of the 'parallel implication complex' [...]" (594).

therefore wrong to say that figurative language is inviting unconscious influence; figurative language is figurative because it is based on the effects of the primary processes on language. Figurative language – symbols, images, metaphor, metonymy, and so forth – is the Semiotic embedded in the Symbolic. It is the unconscious yielding to the demand of minimal representability of the Symbolic while always striving to retain the maximum amount of its original motility and energy.

In order for metaphors to be effective – both as carriers of figurative meaning as such, but especially as part of the therapeutic process of poetry therapy – it is obviously necessary for metaphors to be recognised as such. Some forms of metaphor are not readily perceivable and may be taken for literal expressions. These types of metaphor demand an attentive reader or listener to be actualised. Especially with regard to poetry therapy it is important to note that metaphorical statements can take a number of guises. Commonly, the term metaphor is used for statements such as "Peter is a lion" or "Love is a battlefield." These kinds of utterance indeed appear to be more or less simple comparisons in which character traits of the one term are transferred onto the other along the lines established by Aristotle. There are, however, a number of other possible forms of metaphor which are more difficult to notice and not as readily apparent. Perrine (126-129) distinguishes four fundamental forms of metaphor:[147]

> ➤ "In Form 1 metaphors both the literal and the figurative terms are named. The most familiar type is a simple statement of identity following the formula 'A is B'."
> ➤ "In Form 2 metaphors, only the literal term is named, the figurative term must be inferred. […] Frequently, the metaphorical agent is the verb."
> ➤ "In Form 3 metaphors, only the figurative term is named, the literal term must be inferred. [These metaphors] can easily be mistaken for literal statements."
> ➤ "In Form 4 metaphors, neither the literal nor the figurative term is named; both must be inferred."

The first form, simple as it seems at first glance, also exhibits a greater variety than might be supposed. The "A is B" formula – Form 1 Metaphor – can, for instance, be realised via the genitive:[148]

---

[147] Perrine argues that "[u]nder the assumption that in all metaphors the concepts likened to each other are expressible as substantives, there are four possible forms of metaphor" (126). I would contend that there are potentially even more forms of metaphor that could be classified. In any case, I take metaphor only as a generic example for figurative language in general. It would therefore be a vain endeavour to try and establish an exhaustive catalogue at this moment. Perrine's four forms serve to create awareness as to where metaphor may lurk beneath the familiarisation of the Symbolic.

[148] I will give only as many examples for each of the four forms of metaphor as seems necessary to make clear its function and variety. The examples given here are not Perrine's, but have been chosen by me. For more examples cf. Perrine. I use excerpts from works of established poets here, because for the purpose of illustrating the use of metaphor these poems provide more readily accessible examples.

> Watching from a bluff the tiny, clear,
> <u>Sparkling armada of promises</u> draw near.
> (Larkin, "Next, Please" 5-6)

In this example from Larkin, the two important terms when it comes to metaphor are 'armada' (further specified by means of the adjective 'sparkling') and 'promises'. The comparison is realised via the of-genitive here. The term 'promises' is the literal term which is compared to a figurative "sparkling armada." The result is a notion of 'promises' as something grand, powerful and precious. Another possibility for a realisation of Form 1 Metaphor via the genitive is simple apposition:

> Come into the garden, Maud,
> For <u>the black bat, night</u>, has flown.
> (Tennyson, *Maud* 1-2)

Further possibilities include the use of a demonstrative adjective, the vocative, or the use of transitive verbs to transform the literal term into a figurative one. Also, the metaphorical meaning can become obvious through its context as is the case in the following quotation from Yeats' "Leda and the Swan:"

> A shudder in the loins engenders there
> <u>The broken wall</u>, the burning roof and tower
> And Agamemnon dead. (9-11)

The quotation is the beginning of the sestet of the sonnet and Leda, overcome by Zeus in the guise of a giant swan, here conceives Helen, an act which will lead to the "broken wall" of Troy, the city's destruction and ultimately the death of Agamemnon. In the context of the entire poem, however, the phrase "the broken wall" simultaneously evokes the loss of Leda's virginity. Without the entire context, the metaphorical meaning would not be discernible. Along similar lines, Form 1 Metaphor can also take the form of a self-reflexive metaphorical relationship of the kind "A is A_1" as can be seen in the following excerpt from *Lolita*:

> She was Lo, plain Lo, in the morning, standing four feet ten in one sock. She was Lola in slacks. She was Dolly at school. She was Dolores on the dotted line. But in my arms she was always Lolita. (Nabokov, *Lolita* 9)

Form 2 Metaphors have a similar range as Form 1 Metaphors. One can trace the most common mode in which the verb acts as the metaphorical anchor, for example, in the following lines.

> So through that <u>unripe</u> day you bore your head,
> And the day was <u>plucked</u> and tasted bitter,
> As if still cold among the leaves.
> (Larkin, "XXX" 1-3)

The verb 'plucked' in line two calls for the inference of a term such as 'flower', or 'fruit'. This is corroborated by the phrase "tasted bitter" indicating a premature harvest as well as the adjective "unripe day" in the first line. The phase "unripe day" is itself another Form 2 Metaphor in which the metaphorical anchor is an adjective. Further examples for Form 2 Metaphor can be found in the following lines:

> A look <u>contains</u> the history of man,
> And fifty francs will earn the stranger right
> To take the <u>shuddering city</u> in his arms.
> (Auden, "Brussels in Winter" 12-14)

The verb "contains" calls for the inference of "book" in the above context. The metaphorical connection is thus between "look" and "book," the latter of which, however, is not present in the text. The phrase "shuddering city" in the third line above is another example of a Form 2 Metaphor with an adjective as metaphorical anchor. "[S]huddering" is applicable only to living (human) beings, an attribute which is by inference transferred onto the city and, in this case, also extended onto the entire second and third lines.

The third form of metaphor is the inversion of Form 2 Metaphor. The literal term is absent and only the figurative one is named. As mentioned above, these metaphors can easily be mistaken for literal statements and are thus particularly context-sensitive.

> Yet pity for a horse o'er-driven,
> And love in which my hound has part,
> Can hang <u>no weight upon my heart</u>
> In its assumptions up to heaven.
> (Tennyson, *In Memoriam* LXIII)

Apart from the fact that "heart" is also in essence used metaphorically here, the metaphorical anchor is the figurative "weight" for which we have to infer something like "impede" or "detain." Since weight usually impedes motion, the figurative use here is hardly perceived. Another dense use of Form 3 Metaphors can be found in Larkin:

> Obedient daily dress,
> You cannot always keep
> That unfakable young surface.
> You must learn your lines –
> ("Skin" 1-4)

Here the literal term that is missing is 'skin' which is expressed metaphorically by means of the figural expression of "daily dress."

As to Form 4 Metaphors, Perrine contends that he "shall not pretend [to] have a long list of examples" (129) and indeed this form of metaphor is almost indistinguishable from common, non-figurative language. Since both terms have to be inferred it is difficult to point a finger on the metaphoricality of the statement. One example of this type of metaphor can be found in the poetry of Robert Southey:

> My days among the Dead are past;
> Around me I behold,
> Where'er these casual eyes are cast
> The mighty minds of old;

> My never-failing friends are they
> With whom I converse day by day.
> ("My Days among the Dead are Past" 1-6)

In this poem, the speaker is talking about his relation to the tradition of the poets of the past, how his study of these poets helped him become a good poet himself. Later in the poem, he contends that "with them/I live" (13-14) and that his "place with them will be" (20). The last line expresses his belief that he will be part of the great tradition of British poets. In this context, the first line of the poem constitutes a Form 4 Metaphor. In the line "My days upon the Dead are past," both the figural and the literal term have to be inferred. The lines should read "My life among the dead poets [the great, ancient masters of poetry] is over." The word "days" in Southey's line is therefore a synecdoche that calls for an inference of 'life'. The "Dead" mentioned also represents a metonymic displacement, either by means of ellipsis (of the term 'poets') or as a hyponym. The rhetorical figure of hyponym signifies a word that contains within it the meaning of (an)other word(s). In this sense, the word 'dead' encompasses all those who have ceased to exist. That the speaker is referring to the 'dead poets' has to be inferred from the context of the entire poem. Thus Southey's line "My days among the Dead are past" calls for an inference of the literal as well as the figural term and is a Form 4 Metaphor. As concerns poetry therapy, these forms of metaphor are negligible as the normalising and familiarising tendencies of the Symbolic have revised their Semiotic content to such an extent that they are all but useless as a means of retracing the genotext.

Although it is important to spot hidden metaphors like the above, it does not, of course, follow from this that every metaphorical statement is significant therapeutically. Not every symbol, metaphor or synecdoche in a client's poem is important in poetry therapy. Those figurative statements that are important, however, are characterised by a creative dynamic that has the potential to destabilise the entire message of a poem. It is therefore necessary to differentiate between metaphors that exhibit such an effect, or at least have the potential of doing so in a given (con)text, and metaphors that do not. Some metaphors that appear unimportant at first glance, might still be or become therapeutically important. Such metaphors can be denoted as 'frozen metaphors'. Frozen metaphors (words and phrases such as "the table's leg," "icy mood" or "heart of gold") inhabit common language to a great extent and generally go unnoticed as figurative meanings.[149] Hausman notes that "metaphors can be repeated. But if they can be repeated with stable significance that is isomorphic in many different contexts, then they must be frozen" (15). It can be assumed that at one point or other in the history of language, all metaphors were dynamic, creative metaphors, but "all usage tends to become habitual, and metaphor tends to resemble catachresis. The metaphor still remains a figure, for its purpose is not to fill a gap in signs. However, it appears in a

---

[149] The abundance of frozen metaphors in every language recalls Eco's statement above that "language is by nature, and originally, metaphorical, and the mechanisms of metaphor establishes linguistic activity" ("Scandal of Metaphor" 218).

more and more fixed and standardized fashion" (Ricoeur, *The Rule of Metaphor* 62). While it is true that metaphor may condition catachresis[150] and is prone to become habitual in this case, metaphor also stems from "an incentive to invention, as opposed to just being necessary [...], to breathe force and energy into discourse" (ibid. 63). While frozen metaphors are generally immobile with respect to the Semiotic, they do contain the potential of Semiotic motility. This is why I have refrained from using, as is often done, the term 'dead metaphor' to denote them. Frozen metaphors, especially in poetic texts, can become dynamic and creative again, and thus "breathe force and [Semiotic] energy into discourse." To take a rather blunt example: for a client who has been traumatised by the loss of an arm in a car accident, the commonly frozen metaphor of the 'armchair' may well attain a high Semiotic energy when it occurs in a poem. A poetic text facilitates the 'de-frosting' of frozen metaphors, because it

> always posits its own tropes as "first." Insofar as it obliges one to see them in a new manner, and arranges a quantity of correlations between the various levels of the text so as to permit an ever new interpretation of the specific expression (which never functions alone, but always interacts with some new aspect of the text [...]). Moreover, it is characteristic of contexts having an aesthetic function to produce *objective correlatives* which have an extremely "open" metaphorical function [...]. (Eco, "Scandal of Metaphor" 255; emphasis original)

Common metaphors are thus not dead, they are only frozen and under certain conditions they can indeed become un-frozen again and this is yet another aspect a poetry therapist should be mindful of.

For the practice of poetry therapy the following conclusion can be drawn with regard to the manifestations of the unconscious by means of the Semiotic influx of the genotextual elements of a text. (1) They can be traced in the figurative language of the poem. Symbols, as they are the most free-floating elements in the Symbolic Order, are the most obvious and potent means of representing the Semiotic in the Symbolic. The tendencies of the Symbolic towards familiarisation and normalisation do not affect symbols as easily as other parts of language. (2) Metaphor was used as a generic example for all types of figurative language and it was observed that there is a considerable variety in the possible manifestations of metaphor, many of which are not easily discernable from common language. In addition to this, metaphors – and consequently other figurative tropes – can either be frozen or dynamic. Frozen metaphors are embedded in the Symbolic structure of the poetic text in such a manner that they are often overlooked. They have the potential to become un-frozen again depending on the contextual circumstances of the client's individual poem and life. In poetry therapy, it is therefore imperative to search for frozen metaphors and ascertain their potential for

---

[150] With regard to catachresis, Ricoeur states that "catachresis refers to a situation in which a sign, already assigned to a first idea, is assigned also to a new idea, this latter idea having no sign at all or no other proper sign in the language. Consequently, every trope whose use is forced and necessitated, every trope that results in a pure *extension* of *meaning*, is a case of catachresis" (*The Rule of Metaphor* 62; emphasis original).

actualisation. Apart from frozen metaphors, the other examples above have shown that, in general, metaphors are not always as apparent as one would expect. The same is true for every type of rhetorical figure. Like any aspect of language, they are part of the Symbolic and necessarily subject to its normalising function. With regard to metaphor, another reason for this is the fact that, although the word functions as a metaphorical anchor, the metaphor as a whole can be a phrase, a whole sentence or an even larger linguistic unit. The longer the metaphorical statement, the more probable it is that the statement is not simply an enumeration of metaphors, but held together semantically by a controlling metaphor. The last example from the Larkin poem above is a case in point. Here, the controlling metaphorical anchor is the absent literal term 'skin' to which all other figures refer. The word, thus, is the beginning of metaphor, not its end: "The level of the word is not just the intermediary level between those of the phoneme and syntagma; it is the connecting layer. From one side the first-level distinctive units presuppose the significant units of the lexical level" (Ricoeur, *The Rule of Metaphor* 104). The production, identification and interpretation of metaphors all rest on the analysis of, firstly, the word and, second, on the lexico-syntactic context. For poetry therapy, the next step is to integrate these into the pan-textual matrix of the poem and finally to correlate this with the client's life, her condition during production as well as reception and her clinical diagnosis. (3) This can best be done by retracing the web of Semiotic energy in a manner akin to the way New Historicists do with social energy. Associated images that prevail in the figurative landscape of a poem constitute key images that guide the analysis.[151] Since Semiotic energy is attached to symbols and figurative language, the interrelatedness of these has to be analysed and made subject of the therapeutic discourse. (4) The creation of symbols (and by extension of figurative language) was constituted as a synesthetic process which is the basis of the healing effects generally ascribed to artistic processes by art therapy. Since artistic creation involves both the conscious (in a very relaxed state) and the unconscious and takes into account clients' past lives and experiences as well as their physical and mental condition during production, the feeling of unity that the synesthetic aspect of the creative process provides is reminiscent of the primordial feeling of the Lacanian Real. "Thus metaphorical knowledge is knowledge of the dynamics of the real. That definition seems rather restrictive, but it can be reformulated as: the best metaphors are those in which the cultural process, the dynamics itself of semiosis, shows through" (Eco, "Scandal of Metaphor" 234). Though Eco here is referring not to the "real" and "semiosis" in the sense of Lacan and Kristeva, the statement holds true if we read it this way. Metaphorical knowledge is the knowledge of the dynamic of the Real and

---

[151] Cf. Davis: "Key images are [...] important for patients who write poems about their experiences. A current illness, disability, or even a glass of water spilled on the bedsheets might be the occasion for the poem – but if the present moment elicits a key image or a cluster of images from the patient's past, the resulting poem will *feel* genuine and powerful to both poet and reader" (219; emphasis original).

the Semiotic. It is this dynamic, manifest in poetry through metaphor and symbolic language, which poetry allows privileged access to.

5. Revision and Reception: Negotiating the Interplay between Creation and Interpretation within Foucauldian Discourse

> Interpretation indicates the dominance of the conscious over the imaginary, and creation swaps the conscious by the imaginary. As these two activities interlink, they testify to something in the human makeup, which in the words of Anton Ehrenzweig could be called the ego-rhythm of structured focusing and oceanic dedifferentiation. At this juncture, the interplay between creation and interpretation could be conceived as a vantage point for opening up a perspective on the as yet widely unexplored territory of cultural anthropology. (Iser, "The Interplay between Creation and Interpretation" 395)

During the phase of artistic production, cultural and social influences enter the poem through the unconscious and this is particularly so in poetry:

> The artist, as it were, takes not only his canvas, his colours, or his model in order to paint, but also the art that is given him formally, technically, and ideologically within his own culture; this probably emerges most clearly in the case of the poet, whose material is drawn from the cultural possessions already circulating and is not dead matter, as is that of plastic art. (Rank 7)

It is precisely the fact that poets take their material from "cultural possessions already circulating" which is of central importance for the second phase of poetry therapy – the receptive phase – which this chapter will be predominantly concerned with. The preceding chapter has shown that unconscious influences in poetry are likely to be concentrated in figurative language.[152] The Semiotic influx manifest in figurative poetic language represents an original drive motility that seeks expression from the *chora*. It is important to keep in mind that the original drive motility is only *represented* by means of figurative language. It is not the original thing. In the light of this it has to be argued that figurative language distorts the Semiotic content as much as it ruptures and displaces the Symbolic. The Semiotic thus distorts and is distorted in language, and rhetorical tropes function as manifestations of this process. Interpretation is therefore always necessary to elucidate or excavate meaning:

> Once an emotion, feeling or experience is pushed away or left disregarded, it can rarely be brought back simply in the same form. Our mind plays tricks on us: offering it back in seemingly irrelevant bits and bobs, like jigsaw pieces of a window, or in code, as in puns or metaphors. These are images. [...] An image *is* important in itself. What would

---

[152] Of course, poetry, when considered as bound language, is structurally more formalised than prose. This, however, is only so with regard to form, not grammar and syntax. The repetitive nature of poetry when it comes to its linguistic makeup, be it formal verse or free verse, is in itself different from regular, prosaic language in common use. Within this verse structure, the laws of language can be bent or broken in order to accommodate the demands of poetic form. Instances of such bending or breaking constitute a rupture in the Symbolic.

seem to be perplexing is the way such a simple little thing can carry such a depth of emotion. Why expend storms of tears over such things so much later? It's because of what these images signify. Behind this seemingly trivial image there's a huge hinterland of emotional problem that hasn't been dealt with at all. Image exploration in writing can offer the necessary time and space to return to old pains – relatively safely. (Bolton 62-63; emphasis original)

Bolton describes the process of repression, stating that feelings which have been "pushed away" are irretrievable in their original form, resurfacing only in displaced or condensed "bits and bobs." Bolton's emphasis on the change between the original emotion, or feeling and its return as an image is particularly important in the present context. This has already been discussed in some detail in the previous chapter with the conclusion that the "most commonly used image in writing is the metaphor, in which one thing doesn't so much stand for another as carries over its essence, its smell and taste, to the other thing. [...] The original subject is magnified by its association with the metaphorical one" (Bolton 75). Laying down the figurative elements of (poetic) language as focal points for unconscious messages is one thing, there is, however, the problem of the normalisation of many of these images. The unconscious offers its content "in seemingly irrelevant bits and bobs, like jigsaw pieces of a window" and these are hard to discover and often harder to make sense of. The tendencies of the Symbolic towards codifying incongruous elements add to this.

Using clients' poems in poetry therapy is therefore a matter of the careful and shrewd actualisation of the hidden or dormant figurative potential pertinent to the individual client. This actualisation constitutes the second phase – the receptive phase – of my model of poetry therapy in which clients are confronted with their own creative outcomes and, in conjunction with the therapist, deconstruct the surface text of the poem in order to unveil hidden clues concerning their unconscious conflicts and relate them to their symptoms. This chapter will be concerned with the obstacles, fallacies and problems surrounding this receptive phase of poetry therapy. The second phase will be dealt with in close conjunction with what has been elaborated regarding the first phase (Chapter 3). It will focus on the processes of revision and (re)reading and the implications of these processes for the client as well as poetry therapy in general. In a second step, the interpretative process in poetry therapy will be conceptualised on the basis of narrative therapeutic principles. Additionally, socio-cultural forces will also be accounted for by means of Foucauldian theories.

In the model of poetry therapy proposed here, it is essential that the poems dealt with are produced by clients themselves.[153] Poetic creation originates, as all artistic

---

[153] I have noted the importance of client-created poems in Chapter 1. Chapter 1 concentrates on poems by clients in the context of the inherent healing potential of the creative act. In the present chapter, the therapeutic potential of the poems' language is at the centre of concern. On the importance of using language that is the client's and the cooperative nature of the therapeutic encounter that is also the basis of poetry therapy, cf. Carrey: "Using language people are familiar with and metaphors supplied by children to describe their problems often leaves them feeling relieved that someone has listened and

production, in a general creative urge, which demands expression. With the onset of poetic writing, "a personal infusion into this linguistic raw material" (Rank 279) takes place. This general assembly of creative drives is the genotext. At this stage, the genotextual infusion is no longer purely Semiotic, because to be consciously apprehensible it has to minimally conform to the laws of the Symbolic. Nonetheless, it is not fixed either, but a text in the sense of Derrida and Eco, consisting of an essentially limitless plurality of possible actualisations; a hoard of informational possibility. It is only in conjunction with the phenotext that the genotext consolidates into an empirical text. Even in this form, it remains – like the phenotext – a field or function of potentiality:

> The genotext is not linguistic (in the sense understood by structural or generative linguists). It is, rather, a *process*, which tends to articulate structures that are ephemeral (unstable, threatened by drive charges, "quanta" rather than "marks") and nonsignifying (devices that do not have a double articulation). It forms these structures out of: a) instinctual dyads, b) the corporeal and economical continuum, c) the social organism and family structures, which convey the constraints imposed by the mode of production and d) matrices of enunciation. (Kristeva, *Revolution* 87; emphasis original)

The keyword here is "process." The genotext is a process, which means that it is an amorphous, dynamic structural field, the interplay of biological, psychic and social factors joining forces to demand materiality in a text. Since everything connected with the unconscious can only gain materiality in and through language, the poetic text in poetry therapy is an artefact of this materialisation and constitutes a dynamic link between the creative forces of the first phase and the interpretative techniques and concepts employed in the second.

5.1 Communication vs. Understanding: The Process of Revision in Poetry Therapy

Talking about the processes of creative writing and revision in connection to figurative language, Bolton elucidates the importance of dealing receptively with one's own works:

> [T]he written image can be as clear as mud, in terms of personal meaning, until redrafting is undertaken. Redrafting is writing and rewriting to clarify and understand, to bring the writing closer and closer to what is in [the] mind, an artistic, crafting process, useful

---

> understood them and feeling more empowered to solve their problems. Using the traditional mental health approach (i.e. the therapist's solutions are best) reinforces people's dependency on external factors to solve their problems, which may lead them to feel less empowered and less in charge of their potential for change and growth in their lives. [...] [T]he language chosen in the therapeutic conversation not only conveys information but also actually co-constructs the reality between therapist and client. The language used to describe people actually speaks and writes them into the world in a manner that is either helpful or unhelpful to them" (86).

to borrow here. The writer will know if the image is worth exploring in this time-consuming way by the amount of energy (anger, fear, pain, joy, etc.) generated by re-reading the initial writing. The reworking of therapeutic writing creates communication back with the writer again. This is slightly different from the crafting of a poem intended for publication (for example), which is done in order to achieve a product which will communicate effectively with the reader/listener. On rewriting, sharper details of a memory come to mind (such as specific smells), errors are noted [...]. These details can make astonishing differences in comprehension of what the writing is telling the writer. Redrafting is a process of re-experiencing, or creeping back into the experience that led to writing in order to find the words that most closely evoke it. This pushes out the boundaries of the memory, extending and clarifying it to encompass colour, shape, texture, quality of light, sound, smell, heat, cold, taste, exactly what words and tone of voice, and so on. (25)

Bolton emphasises the establishing of a connection between the writer and the text here. For poetry therapy, this is important, because the poem is an integral part of the therapeutic process as a whole; the client has to work with the poetic artefact(s) for the entirety of the treatment. A personal connection to the poem is thus essential for therapeutic effectiveness. It is here that the strongest connection between the first phase of poetry therapy and the second phase can be located: the poem that originated from the client's own being during the first phase now becomes an external object that can be safely worked upon by its creator and can be evaluated. The conscious concern with the object creates a feeling of pride and achievement going hand in hand with the completion of the work. The 'meaning' of the poem as the 'author' has conceived it, creates a feeling of satisfaction and as a reader who is also the creator, the pleasure involved in the process of creation and of the obstacles overcome echo strongly with every re-reading. This pleasure forges and sustains an interest in the poem, its form and meaning, on the part of the client which can be drawn upon by the therapist to facilitate the therapeutic encounter. In this context it can be argued that the two phases of poetry therapy are connected by means of the nature of the becoming of the poem. Such a connection is facilitated through emotional investment in the text ("anger, fear, pain, joy, etc.") which is recalled in the process of revision and redrafting.

There is, however, a difference between the processes of redrafting or rewriting in a therapeutic environment as opposed to revising for publication. This difference can be conceived of as a difference in emphasis between communication and understanding. This is a difference that is important therapeutically as well. As Bolton rightly states, a poem intended for publication has to be carefully tuned for effective communication. This is its primary function. If the message[154] does not reach the reader, the poem is dead. Consequently, a poem that is consciously fashioned as an

---

[154] Of course, a poem does not have one, clear and definitive message. When I use the term message here, I mean to infer that a poem meant for the public usually exhibits the tendency of reducing at least some of its inherent ambiguities for the sake of the possibility of increased cultural dissemination. When I thus speak of 'message' in the above context, the term denotes this tendency towards disambiguation.

aesthetic object to be received publicly inevitably has to make concessions in order to communicate its message; it has to establish a context that allows the reader to receive the poem in a particular manner. In order to facilitate the contact between the poem and its readership, however, certain personal features will necessarily be marginalised and those that are hidden in the first place (like, for instance, frozen metaphors), will remain unactualised. Only in this manner can the poem's message – the one carrying the communicative weight – be sufficiently foregrounded.

In poetry therapy, the process of revising and redrafting has the goal "to clarify and understand, to bring the writing closer and closer to what is in [the client's] mind" (Bolton 25). Understanding in this sense requires access to Semiotic traces within the poem's text. Once these traces have been isolated, it is possible to construct (alternative) meaning(s) from the network of symbols. In setting up this network – that is, isolating figurative elements in the poetic text with possible therapeutic value – it becomes possible to delineate, at first roughly and later more finely, the negotiations of Semiotic energy within the Symbolic text. Access to the signifying potential locked in the poetic text is gained by means of a deconstruction of the surface meaning ascribed to the poem. Although the process of revision is time-consuming in its spotting, actualising, cross-referencing and questioning of marginalised and frozen tropes, it is indispensible: without this process, the Ego-strengthening effect of the creative phase would but be a fleeting feeling from which no enduring therapeutic progress could arise; the re-reading involved in revision and interpretation amplifies these Ego-strengthening effects. In turn, they become more permanent and, secondly, they help forge interest in the poem thus facilitating the basis for poetry therapy as such. Furthermore, the normalising tendencies of the Symbolic are undermined by the critical examination of the text and it becomes possible to construct meaning from previously unconscious materials. In therapy, the foregrounded message is thus neglected in favour of alternative, often subjugated, meanings. In poetry therapy, as opposed to publication, communication is not the primary function of the poem, rather it is a means of facilitating therapeutic understanding, namely by essentially being arrested and/or disrupted.

In poetry therapy, the primary function of the poetic text is to provide a means of understanding of the client's conflicts and problems. A poem created in a psychotherapeutic context aims at increasing the client's knowledge about herself. What is knowledge for the client-poet is not necessarily communication for the average reader. In fact, in order for therapeutic knowledge to become available in poetry therapy, the process of communication has to be arrested first. Poetry therapy thrives on the idiosyncratic nature of the client-poem as it constitutes an obstacle to communication. This produces a certain resistance to understanding as well as communication, a resistance that is at the centre of the therapeutic work. Therapeutic understanding thus comes about when the text stops communicating. In those moments before the client (and the therapist) discover a new focus, a new actualisation of the text, the text's previous meaning is negated. This means that communication breaks down and is temporarily disrupted. In order to re-establish communication, the client is forced to construct new/different meanings. This continuing process of actualisation increases the understanding of clients about themselves. It is the therapist's function to direct the client in this process by means of the guided deconstruction of the text, followed by a reconstruction along newly actualised *points de capiton*. By thus constructing poems anew through the act of reading, clients can be guided towards a critical examination of their productions in the contexts of their lives. Iser argues that meaning is not only dependent on a linguistic and culturally determined conditions and interpretations, but involves a process of the actual production of new signifieds, because

> the reader is compelled to transform a denotation into a connotation [...] for the signified which he has built up in turn becomes a signifier: it invokes his own concepts of perfection by means of this significant qualification [...], not only bringing them into the conscious mind but also demanding some form of correction. Through such transformations, guided by the signs of the text, the reader is induced to construct the imaginary object. It follows that the involvement of the reader is essential to the fulfilment of the text, for materially speaking this exists only as a potential reality – it requires a subject (i.e. a reader) for the potential to be actualized. The literary text, then, exists primarily as a means of communication, while the process of reading is basically a kind of dyadic interaction. (*The Act of Reading* 66)

Iser contends that while the denotation is in fact already the result of an act of interpretation (albeit one that is strongly implicated by socio-linguistic conventions), the connotation that the reader creates during the process of reading determines the actualisation of specific meaning(s) from the (potentially unlimited) s/Semiotic reserve a text represents. The latter process is one that requires the reader to be actively involved. It is creative in that it produces something new, namely new meaning. Applied to poetry therapy, the act of re-reading the poem constitutes another creative endeavour for the client. On an additional level, the process of re-reading facilitates the construction of alternative realities and new (or augmented) identities.[155] Eventually, the result is an altered perception of reality which can easily be adopted by clients, because these are perceived as originating from their own being in the form of the poem.

There are thus in fact two phases of poetic production. The first one in which the poem is created and consolidated as writing on a page and the second one in which meaning is constructed from this writing. The client as reader who is intimately aware of the poem's genesis, by re-reading and revising the poem, constructs a text that is different from the one originally conceived and originally remembered. The second

---

[155] On the connection of reading and therapy, cf. also Iser: "Now reading is not a therapy designed to restore to communication the symbols that have separated themselves from the conscious mind. Nevertheless, it does enable us to see how little of the subject is a given reality, even to its own consciousness. However, if the certainty of the subject can no longer be based exclusively on its own consciousness – not even through the minimal Cartesian condition of its being it because it can be perceived in the mirror of its consciousness – reading, as the activation of spontaneity, plays a not unimportant part in the process of "becoming conscious" (*The Act of Reading* 158-159).

phase of poetry therapy is thus the one in which the text is produced anew through reading. This production is not a stable one, however. The text cannot, as has been shown, be *one*, it cannot be seamlessly constructed and its meaning cannot be fixed. The actualisation of meanings from the poetic text is largely dependent on contextual implications of what clients believe they are supposed to find in the text. According to Iser, the literary text

> represents a reaction to the thought systems which it has chosen and incorporated in its own repertoire. This reaction is triggered by the system's limited ability to cope with the multifariousness of reality, thus drawing attention to its deficiencies. The result of this operation is a rearranging and, indeed, re-ranking of existing patterns of meaning." (*The Act of Reading* 72)

Iser constitutes literature as a tool of cultural diagnosis here, implying that literary texts strive towards a "rearranging" of ideological and cultural dogmata in order to affect a criticism of and ultimately a change in the structure of society. Indeed, Iser notes that the literary text

> takes the prevalent thought system or social system as its context, but does not reproduce the frame of reference which stabilizes these systems. Consequently, it cannot produce those "expected expectations" which are provided by the system. What it can and does do is set up a parallel frame within which meaningful patterns are to form. In this respect the literary text is also a system, which shares the basic structure of overall systems as it brings out dominant meanings against a background of neutralized and negated possibilities. [...] Although in structure basically identical to the overall system, the literary text differs from it in its intention. Instead of reproducing the system to which it refers, it almost invariably tends to take as its dominant 'meaning' those possibilities that have been neutralized or negated by that system. (*The Act of Reading* 71-72)

While the negation of "dominant 'meaning'" may be true for fictional texts intended for the public (and I believe this to be a somewhat naive generalisation), texts produced in poetry therapy are not essentially geared towards neutralising and negating the ideological system of their socio-cultural embeddedness.[156] Likewise, the client-created poem is a reaction of the individual client's thought system (which is an idiosyncratic representation of the thought systems prevalent in the client's culture) towards the "multifariousness of reality." Client poems predominantly express individual feelings and thoughts which refer only secondarily to the cultural context. Thus they are not primarily geared towards challenging ideological structures or even the status quo of the individual client's own life. In the beginning, client poems rather tend towards supporting and consolidating the status quo of their lives and identities.

The therapist's key task in the second phase is to guide the client to an actualisation of the poem which is conducive to the therapeutic endeavour. "The text must

---

[156] Naturally, poetic texts written by clients should be geared towards neutralizing the effects of ideology in order to be therapeutically useful. As will become clear in the course of this chapter, it is a central agenda of poetry therapy to turn the client's poem into such a text that challenges dominant truths.

therefore *bring about* a standpoint from which the reader will be able to view things that would never have come into focus as long as his own habitual dispositions were determining his orientation, and what is more, this standpoint must be able to accommodate all kinds of different readers" (Iser, *The Act of Reading* 35; emphasis original). The "standpoint" from which clients can actualise meanings relevant to their conditions is brought about by means of the therapeutic discourse centring on the poem. Within this context, every reading and every revision will unveil nuances in the poetic text which have gone unnoticed before, which in turn necessitate the actualisation of different aspects of the poetic text. In this manner, clients effectively turn into different readers every time the poem is approached

(Re-)tracing unconscious influences in this manner produces an increase in knowledge by means of temporarily arresting the poem's communicative function, which eventually enables clients to actively deal with their conflicts. "The constitution of meaning, therefore, gains its full significance when something *happens* to the reader. The constituting of meaning and the constituting of the reading subject are therefore interacting operations that are both structured by aspects of the text" (ibid. 152; emphasis original). This implies that in the "interacting operations" the poetic text functions as a means of (re)structuring and (re)negotiating client identities. The poem thus becomes a space of conversion from one identity to another; it constitutes an event through which the difference between two identities is at once posited, negotiated and constructed. It shatters and unites at the same time. With regard to identity, the writing of poetry as well as its interpretation constitutes a quest for a new identity within the vortex of the destruction of the old.

Generally, understanding requires interpretation of what is not (fully) apprehended or of notions which are in conflict with established structures of knowledge. This is precisely the reason why interpretation of a creative artefact is essential: creativity equals newness and is therefore prone to come into conflict with established structures. Interpretation works on the artefact of creativity in order to integrate this newness into existing frameworks. According to Kristeva, creativity in language is the restructuring of the Symbolic Order through the Semiotic *chora*. Creativity is therefore indeed, as art therapy and Kristeva propose, at the centre of the poetic process. "Creativity is basically an act of transgression, ranging from defamiliarisation through pattern breaking to scandal, simultaneously divesting creation of its various cultural notions as the crowning activity of man" (Iser, "The Interplay between Creation and Interpretation" 392).[157] Iser is right in stating that creativity by nature transcends normative values and discourses for without doing so, it would not constitute a creative act. The newness that creation represents demands interpretation which, Iser points out, is

---

[157] In seeing the act of creation as a mode of transgression, Iser renounces its Romantic heritage and simultaneously restores creativity to a central cultural position by setting it up as a dynamic process of socio-cultural reinvigoration. Creation thus loses its place as the "crowning activity of man," but gains new importance as a vital function in the processes of cultural adaptation and renewal.

"an attempt at translating events brought about by creation into existing frameworks for both their comprehension and manageability. Its cognitive operations are designed to control the uncontrollable" (Iser, "The Interplay between Creation and Interpretation" 392). According to Iser here, interpretation is brought to bear on creation in order to make it comprehensible and manageable. Inevitably, interpretation thus robs creation of its essential feature, namely its disruptive qualities and the newness it represents. The reader is liable to construct meaning which is to a great extent in line with the predominant understanding of the world and thus only requires a minimal – and thus manageable – adaptation of the latter. In attempting to bring creation into existing frameworks, associated modes of perception and understanding are brought to bear on the specimen of creativity and they are made subject to a process of normalisation. This is to say that those features which are beyond comprehension are marginalised or simply negated. In this respect, the

> two basic human activities creation and interpretation are not just opposed to each other, but are in constant interplay. Creation is never pure creation but always dependent on given contexts within which it occurs and by which it is conditioned. Although creation exceeds existing limitations and even scandalizes hallowed conventions, it nevertheless is unable to free itself totally from what it outstrips. In this respect creation is negative interpretation. Interpretation, in turn, is never pure cognition. Translating something which may range from the unfamiliar to the unavailable into given frameworks requires an imaginative leap at some point. In this respect, interpretation as a cognitive appropriation of the inaccessible is a guided creation. (ibid. 392-393)

The interplay between creation and interpretation is what the second phase of poetry therapy is all about. It is fashioned in terms of a reciprocal relationship of the Symbolic and the Semiotic. The Symbolic – through which clients necessarily have to pass in order to express their (conscious and unconscious) thoughts and desires – structurally exerts its normalising power on the Semiotic traces in the text, but also, and this is important, interpretatively when read by the client. At the same time, the Semiotic traces in the poetic text always constantly destabilise the Symbolic structure and can be retraced by means of careful interpretations. Interpretation, however, while necessary to human existence, marginalises a vast amount of elements of its subject matter; a fact that proves problematic in poetry therapy. It proves problematic, because interpretation is the necessary means or tool to retrace the Semiotic, but at the same time it is firmly embedded in Symbolic structures. Poetry therapy thus has to account for the fundamental tendency of interpretation towards normalisation, simplification and categorisation, before interpretation can be employed effectively.

Interpretation is a process that works in support of the Symbolic. In order to discover the unconscious conflicts of the client which have become inscribed in the text of the poem, it is essential to reduce the marginalising tendencies of interpretation to a minimum. This can be achieved first and foremost by a conscious awareness of the marginalising tendencies of interpretation and one's own cultural position as the interpretand. In poetry therapy, it is the therapist who has to cultivate this awareness and guide the client in the process of interpretation in such a manner that the meaning produced represents as much of the "scandalizing" potential of the poem as possible.[158] The poem constitutes "an annihilation of our cherished securities, and it tends to become scandalous the more entrenched our stabilities are" (Iser, "The Interplay between Creation and Interpretation" 394), but it is precisely these "stabilities" which have a constricting and unbalancing effect on the client's psyche. Therefore, an interpretation of the poem seeking to unlock rather than suppress its transgressive elements, functions to liberate the client's mind.[159] "Creation is basically 'decomposition,' as Beckett worded it, because we live in an interpreted world which stands in need of constant rearrangement in order to prevent it from lapsing into deadening immobility" (ibid.). It is precisely such a "deadening immobility" that clients are imprisoned in. From the point of view of humanistic art therapy, clients lack the ability to cope with life and are inhibited in their desire and ability of self-actualisation by outside forces impinging upon them from their surrounding community. Creation breaks up these structures while at the same time constituting an act of self-actualisation. As soon as the process of creation is over, however, much of what was produced by it is immediately made inaccessible by the normalising forces of language and those of interpretation. The social position of the individual brings with it associated morals, prejudices, experiences and thought patterns all of which converge in a biased world view and a blindness of clients as to the whole possibility of meaning that is inscribed in their poems; a blindness clients are unaware of, thus requiring the analyst as a guide. It is the analyst who must lift the veil from the client's eyes not only with respect to the surplus of meaning that has been unwittingly produced and the significance of it for the client's problems, but also with respect to the cultural position of the client. The second phase of poetry therapy thus constitutes an endeavour of interpretation that requires sensitivity to the dangers and problems inherent in the process as such, because it is heavily implicated by cultural factors. Only by questioning the act of interpretation itself, can interpretation in therapy result in the setting free, the liberation, of the essential function of creation. "Interpretation, then, becomes an endeavour to reap the fruits of this liberation" (ibid. 395). In order to truly "reap the fruits of [the] liberation" of the creative act, its artefact – the poem – needs to be given central importance in therapy by means of careful interpretation.

---

[158] Cf. also Jaskoski who contends that "the poem may function as a verbal focus for the client's projections, as the inkblot is a visual focus. Poems, however, must be referential and cannot be the purely 'neutral' forms that inkblots seem. Language totally without referent is symptomatic, not poetic. Poetry, therefore, cannot function in exactly the same way as abstract visual forms, or as music. It always carries content. For this reason, the therapist using poetry must be able to deal with the content of the poem as distinct from the client's projections into the text" (77).

[159] The client will be anxious to confront the disruptive elements contained in the poems, which has to be counterbalanced by the therapist. As long as the therapist acknowledges clients in the full complexity of their being, it is possible to counterbalance the fearfulness of clients in the face of their texts. (Cf. Chapter 2).

Coming back to the initial notion of communication, the dyad of client and therapist is supplemented by another entity in the receptive phase of poetry therapy, namely the poem, which actively partakes in the process of communication which is the therapeutic discourse. Only when the position of the poem as a vital part of therapeutic communication is understood and respected, can poetry therapy unfold its maximum efficiency as a therapeutic method. As was determined above, the poem affects and is affected by the therapeutic discourse. By temporarily arresting its communicative function and forcing the client and therapist to reactivate it via the construction of new or different complexes of meaning, the poem gives new directions to therapy. Like the client and the therapist, the poem has to be understood as an entity in the world which is subject to the same modes of repression and denial, which experiences the effects and dangers of transference and counter-transference, and which is capable of deceit and lying. "Viewed from this standpoint, the text itself is a kind of process, leading from interaction of structures to interaction with extra-textual realities, and ultimately to interaction with the reader" (Iser, "Current Situation of Literary Theory" 15). The interaction between reader and poem, client and work, under the guidance of the therapist, who is aware of the interpretative fallacies and cultural determinants partaking in the process, constitutes the dynamics of the second phase the poetry therapy. The act of interpretation is itself subject to forces of normalisation which I will conceptualise along the lines of Foucauldian discourse. The concept of the Symbolic and that of Foucauldian discourse thus constitute two fundamental and related problems when viewed in the context of poetry therapy's two phases of production and reception. This will be the centre of the following discussions, in which the associated dangers, complexities and fallacies indicated above will be explored in further detail.

5.2 Negotiating the Interplay of Creation and Interpretation in Poetry Therapy on the Basis of Narrative Therapeutic Concepts and within a Foucauldian Context

In order for the phase of reception to be effective – therapeutically – two factors are crucial. Firstly, there is the process of tracing unconscious influences in the poem and making these conscious und intellectually acceptable for the client. Secondly, there is the client as a person-in-the-world. This means that the client's embeddedness in his or her socio-cultural environment exerts a strong influence on the apprehension and interpretation of poems in therapy, but also on the acceptance of therapeutic conclusions resulting from the interpretative process. Clients approach the analysis of their poems based on unconsciously internalised views about poetry, the therapeutic situation in which the poems have been produced and are analysed, and, very importantly, about themselves. The psychotherapeutic discourse between the three nodes of poetry therapy (client – poem – therapist) is a manifestation of and participates in the overall discourses of the society in question. The subject's relationship to and its position in language is thus further complicated. In the process of interpretation in poetry therapy, the normalising function of the Symbolic with regard to the linguistic or formal aspects of the poem has to be taken into account. In addition to this, influences – both positive and negative – of a society's discourses have to be consciously acknowledged and taken into consideration. This goes for discourse in general, but also for those discourses pertaining to the discipline of psychotherapy as well as those important to the individual. This chapter will predominantly be concerned with outlining procedures how to take into account the cultural implications of discourse on poetry therapy.

One conclusion of Chapter 3 has been that writers do not hold *author*-ity over their own language which is why Kristeva prefers the term 'writing subject'. For the receptive phase of poetry, a parallel problem presents itself with regard to the client's participation in the interpretation of poetry in therapy. The forces of discourse, in which the client is inevitably embedded, necessarily determine the subject in its use of discourse. They do so without the subject noticing, i.e. unconsciously. The subject-in-discourse is thus very much like Lacan's subject-in-language. The individual is suffering from and is determined by the constrictions of the Symbolic and discourse respectively. Discourse therefore takes as central a position in poetry therapy as the Symbolic does, which calls for an equally exhaustive critical discussion. I will define discourse and examine its implications on poetry therapy by means of Foucault, who ascribes to discourse an all-pervading socio-cultural influence and power. He states:

> I am supposing that in every society the production of discourse is at once controlled, selected, organised and redistributed according to a certain number of procedures, whose role is to avert its powers and its dangers, to cope with chance events, to evade its ponderous, awesome materiality. In a society such as our own we all know the rules of *exclusion*. The most obvious and familiar of these concerns what is *prohibited*. We know perfectly well that we are not free to say just anything, that we cannot simply speak of anything when we like or where we like; not just anyone, finally, may speak of just anything. (*Discourse* 216; emphasis original)

Discourse is the very state of social existence which determines the subject through its totality. Every member of a society is constantly but unwittingly perpetuating and strengthening certain discursive formations. According to Foucault, human beings cannot escape the influence of discourse for

> [d]iscourse is not the majestically unfolding manifestation of a thinking, knowing, speaking subject, but, on the contrary, a totality, in which the dispersion of the subject and his discontinuity with himself may be determined. [...] It must now be recognized that it is neither by recourse to a transcendental subject nor by recourse to a psychological subjectivity that the regulation of its enunciations should be defined. (Foucault, *Archaeology* 55)[160]

---

[160] In this context, cf. also Derrida on the condition of the subject-in-language, the connection between the *I* and speech, and the relationship to discourse in the Foucauldian sense: "I must first hear myself. In soliloquy as in dialogue, to speak is to hear oneself.

In the light of this, therefore,

> we must understand by [discourse] the totality of things said, the relations, the regularities, and the transformations that may be observed in them, the domain of which certain figures, certain intersections indicate the unique place of a speaking subject and may be given the name author. 'Anyone who speaks', but what he says is not said from anywhere. It is necessarily caught up in the play of an exteriority. (ibid. 122)

Foucault uses the term "speaking subject"[161] which, one must assume, parallels Kristeva's 'writing subject' and has equally drastic implications on the individual as the creator of his/her own statements. The individual, Foucault argues, never speaks truly individually. It is always implicated and partially determined by the sociocultural factors of discourse. Inevitably, this brings up the question of authorship and in how far the subject-in-language and in-discourse can claim *author*-ity over its statements. While the subject's place within the overall flow of discourse – and when compared to a society's major discourses – is marginal and highly ephemeral, the amalgamation of statements by a certain individual can be demarcated to a certain extent and therefore ascribed to that one, specific individual. The 'speaking subject' thus occupies a place in discourse that becomes specific enough in the flow of discourse to be isolated. Within a Foucauldian context, 'author' is a function of discourse that

---

> As soon as I am heard, as soon as I hear myself, the I who hears *itself*, who hears *me*, becomes the I who speaks and takes speech from the I who thinks that he speaks and is heard in his own name; and becomes the I who takes speech *without ever cutting of* the I who thinks that he speaks. Insinuating itself into the name of the person who speaks, this difference is nothing, is furtiveness itself: it is the structure of instantaneous and original elusion without which no speech could ever catch its breath. [...] Henceforth, what is called the speaking subject is no longer the person himself, or the person alone who speaks. The speaking subject discovers his irreducible secundarity, his origin that is always already eluded; for the origin is always already eluded on the basis of an organized field of speech in which the speaking subject vainly seeks a place that is always missing. [...] It is first – but without meaning anything else – the cultural field from which I must draw my words and syntax, the historical field which I must read by writing on it. The structure of theft already lodges (itself in) the relation of speech to language. Speech is stolen: since it is stolen from language it is, thus, stolen from itself, that is, from the thief who has always already lost speech as property and initiative" (*Writing and Difference* 177-178; emphasis original). Derrida contends here that the subject's identity is always already elided in the expression of language. It is caught in an "irreducible secundarity." Since the subject speaks into a cultural field and takes language from it (i.e. discourse and the Symbolic, respectively), it never truly possesses language, existing only in the cut between (cf. Lacan). The argument that is elaborated by Derrida here parallels Lacan's concept of the Mirror Stage. As "I must first hear myself," to constitute myself in the text (and, in fact, *as* text), so the child in Lacan has to see itself in the mirror first, taking the unfragmented image for itself, before the emergence of the Ego functions can begin. As a result of this, the persona that speaks in language is never the subject as such. It is a secondary construct which only secondary authority over the text produced.

[161] So does Derrida. Cf. FN 160

allows for the amalgamation of statements.[162] This does not mean, however, that the statements themselves are idiosyncratic expressions of the subject in question, because the "psychological halo" (Foucault, *Archaeology* 98) of these statements is precisely not located in the mind of the speaking subject, but is controlled by "the enunciative field" (ibid.). While the discursive space delineated by such statements is related back to an empirical origin that might be termed 'author', this 'author's' statements are always linked to those discursive formations they share borders with. Statements thus transcend the subject and the subject's complete control. Such a concept of authorship is obviously radically different from the classical one and drastically curtails the possibility of individual self-actualisation in language, because "the rules of formation operate not only in the mind or consciousness of individuals, but in discourse itself; they operate therefore, according to a sort of uniform anonymity, on all individuals who undertake to speak in this discursive field" (Foucault, *Archaeology* 63). In participating in discourse, the subject consequently cannot freely express its individuality. It is partly consigned in its utterances to a "uniform anonymity" which negates at least some of the individual's uniqueness and results in a demand for conformity.[163] Herein lies the danger of discourse when it comes to psychopathological conditions: discourse precludes complete self-actualisation and, on a second level, it exerts constricting power over the individual and it does so without the individual being aware of it.[164] The forces of discourse curtail the client's essentially multifaceted, contingent and in many respects prismatic possibilities of self-actualisation, forcing the individual to

---

[162] Foucault defines the author as "a certain functional principle by which, in our culture, one limits, excludes, and chooses; in short, by which one impedes the free circulation, the free manipulation, the free composition, decomposition, and recomposition of fiction" ("What Is an Author" 119).

[163] Demand opens the possibility of lack, because if the demand cannot be answered, the individual will feel it 'lacks' what is necessary. The subject is thus faced again with the primordial situation of the breaking of the Real which instituted lack and demand before the Imaginary phase. If the subject thus fails to conform, if it fails to answer the demands of society, it will feel it lacks that part which would have allowed it to answer the demand. This feeling of lack is linked to the primordial lack experienced during the Real. Consequently, a failure to answer to social demands recreates the original situation of the shattering of the Real. This is something the subject wishes to avoid at all cost, because this entails fear, isolation and abandonment (cf. Chapter 3 and Kristeva's notion of the 'subject on trial').

[164] The concept of 'authorship' in the classical sense is essential for poetry therapy since it designates control. Especially in art therapy, a re-centering of clients via regaining control of their life is fundamental and this cannot be achieved without claiming authorship – and thereby responsibility – for the works of art that constitute the centre of art therapy. For the time being, I will not deal with this problem critically, but I will assume that, despite the implications of Foucauldian and Lacanian concepts, the possibility of authorship as demanded by art therapy does exist. Chapter 6 will deal in detail with the problem of authorship – which is in essence a problem of harmonising post-structural concepts with traditional ones.

construct an identity that does not, or as little as possible, conflict with the taboos set up by a society's discourses. Individuals, it must be concluded, are subject to constrictions through discourse in much the same manner as through the Symbolic. The individual's urge towards self-actualisation as understood in humanistic art therapy is thus inhibited on two fronts: the Lacanian Symbolic and Foucauldian discourse.

Since, according to Foucault, discourse pervades every aspect of life, the effects of discourse are not only a problem for poetry therapy, but for psychotherapy in general, relying as it does on the client's verbal expressions within the therapeutic dialogue. Poetry therapy, with the poem as an additional verbal element to account for, is, however, particularly in need of a way to acknowledge and negotiate the effects of discourse. The psychological school of narrative therapy has assimilated Foucauldian concepts into its therapeutic approach to account for its effects on the individual. Ideas and methods of narrative therapy can therefore be fruitfully integrated into poetry therapy to facilitate a break of discursive normalisation. Also, the concept of narrative identities has recently come to the fore in both psychotherapy and literary studies, which makes it an ideal interdisciplinary concept to work with in poetry therapy. Hence, the narrative approach combines in an almost ideal fashion the areas of therapy, literature and concepts of humanistic art therapy and thus interfaces congenially with poetry therapy. Appropriating the narrative approach for poetry therapy has the further advantage of providing poetry therapists with a method that has been developed in the therapeutic field and to which they can thus more easily adapt. The techniques of narrative therapy will augment the practice of the receptive phase of poetry therapy in that it is based on postmodern concepts, employing deconstruction and an awareness of the individual's discursive embeddedness to break through both the normalisations of the Symbolic and the ideological subjugation under discourse. In this way, narrative psychology can serve as an interface to bring together psychotherapy, poetry and Foucauldian theories for the second phase of poetry therapy. As a first step, some fundamental aspects of narrative psychology need to be elucidated, before I will continue by delineating Foucauldian concepts within the context of narrative therapy.

Narrative therapy constitutes narrative as fundamental to social existence and human perceptions of reality. In this respect, narratives share the basic premise of Foucauldian discourse. "In narrative psychology, narratives are not regarded as merely literary forms but as a fundamental way of organising human experience and as a tool for constructing models of reality" (Neumann/Nünning 4). Like discourse, narratives constitute a "fundamental way of organising human experience." Also, like discourse, narrative is not limited to a specific form of expression. Although the parallels drawn above between narrative therapy and literary studies might suggest the use of written stories in narrative therapy, this is not the case. Rather, narrative therapy works from the assumption that human beings organise their lives by casting them into stories, narrative accounts that are told (mainly verbally) and circulated. Primarily, narrative therapy is concerned with spoken narratives, i.e. with spoken discourses. Fundamentally, the practice of narrative therapy entails, first of all, a comprehensive mapping of the client's life-story by the therapist. The same is a necessary prerequisite for poetry therapy. The life-story of a client is usually acquired during the first sessions of therapy which basically consist of clients recounting their respective lives. The therapist follows the dominant narrative and considers it in the light of the problems and conflicts voiced by clients during the sessions. In this manner, the therapist acquires a narrative account of the client's past experiences within which the therapeutic discourse and the poems produced are evaluated and interpreted. The approach of narrative therapy thus tackles mental illnesses and psychological conflicts by means of a close reading of the client's life-story, which also forms the basis and context of the therapeutic method of poetry therapy, particularly as it is conceived of along interdisciplinary lines and as a humanistic art therapy.

Theories of narrative therapy postulate the construction of identities via the narration of an overall life-story. It is through perpetual narration of the life-story that the subject's identity is fashioned. In short, identity is expressed through a dominant narrative which integrates smoothly with the reigning discursive formations around the client. "Stories are transmitted largely through socially meditated language and social interaction within specific cultural and historical contexts. The meanings that we attach to events are thus never singular, individual, or simply subjective, never outside the social, but have shared or intersubjective meaning within a cultural nexus of power and knowledge" (Brown/Augusta-Scott, "Introduction" IX). It is in one's life-story that all of life's influences, past, present, and future, come together and participate in the formation of identities.[165] Clients' identities are constructed according to their roles or positions in the world. Furthermore, these self-images, or identities, are created, strengthened and perpetuated through the stories human beings tell about themselves every day. It is through narrating experiences that people establish and sustain their social connections, and it is in narrating stories that they construct their selves.

---

[165] Even though this has long been accepted as the standard view of identity, it should be emphasised again that (a) human beings do not have inherent identities and (b) that identities are never stable. Rather, human beings carry a store of identities with them which are subject to change depending on social contexts. Since life takes place in different social environments, there are identities for each respective occasion. John Storey explains that a person "may be in one moment a supporter of Manchester United, at another a university professor, at another a father, and in another a friend. Each of these moments has an appropriate mode and context of articulation; that is, depending on context, our identities form particular hierarchies of the self. In particular contexts, the identity 'in dominance' may be one thing, in another context it might be something quite different" (80). Identities are the roles we play in society and they are specifically constructed to serve this need for social 'roleplaying'. Since they are flexible, they can be changed – augmented, adapted or even discarded – depending on social circumstances. Cf. Neumann/Nünning who state that "as narrative psychology has pointed out, narrative and identity seem to be so closely intertwined that they constantly feed into and mutually constitute each other [...]. Indeed, the very possibility of identity is intimately tied to the notion of narrative and narratology – not only as descriptive of the self, but, more importantly, as fundamental to the construction of the subject" (3).

"Personal narrative simultaneously is born of experience and gives shape to experience. In this sense, narrative and self are inseparable. [...] We come to know ourselves as we use narrative to apprehend experiences and navigate relationships with others" (Ochs/Capps 21). Life narratives not only establish relations, they also help to understand and "navigate relationships." These are not only interpersonal and intra-personal relationships (that is, relationships between shifting social identities that exist in a person), but also relationships between events.[166] All these encounters and experiences, while basically cultural and therefore collective, are perceived as singular by the individual and are incorporated into life-stories that coalesce into narratives that represent the unique tales of the seemingly idiosyncratic events of a particular life in progress:

> In striving to make sense of life, persons face the task of arranging their experiences of events in sequence across time in such a way as to arrive at a coherent account of themselves and the world around them. [...] The success of this storying of experience provides persons with a sense of continuity and meaning in their lives, and this is relied upon for the ordering of daily lives and for the interpretation of further experience. (White/Epston 10)

In giving the individual the impression of causality, a life-story serves to create connections between events that are in many cases contingent, thus producing meaning where none exists.

Life-stories shape identities, allow plans to be made and connect the individual with its community by means of a shared and intertwined history. "Accordingly, single occurrences must be interpreted in light of larger configurations of events or sequences, whereas developing an understanding of larger configurations and connections requires making sense of a single event" (Neumann/Nünning 5). Narrative in the context of psychology is thus defined by its chronology in that events are storied and become a storehouse of experiences that are drawn upon to navigate the present and plan the future. "The essential order imposed by narrativization upon the universe of our experience is temporality, which implies the structure of past, present, and future, with the concomitant chronology" (ibid.). Human beings thus align their experiences on a chronological chain which constitutes the backbone of the life narrative, imposing order by setting up connections of cause and effect. As human beings we

> organize our experience and our memory of human happenings mainly in the form of narrative – stories, excuses, myths, reasons for doing and not doing and so on. Narrative is a conventional form, transmitted culturally and constrained by each individual's mastery and by his conglomerate of prosthetic devices, colleagues, and mentors. Unlike the constructions generated by logical and scientific procedures that can be weeded out by

---

[166] In this respect, cf. Huntington: "[I]dentities are defined by the self, but are the product of the interaction between the self and others. How others perceive an individual or group affects the self-definition of that individual group. If one enters a new social situation and is perceived as an outsider who does not belong, one is likely to think of oneself that way. [...] Alternatively, [individuals] may react against that characterization and define themselves in opposition to it. External sources of identity may come from the immediate environment, the broader society, or political authorities" (24).

falsification, narrative constructions can only achieve 'verisimilitude.' Narratives, then, are a version of reality whose acceptability is governed by convention and 'narrative necessity' rather than by empirical verification and logical requiredness, although ironically we have no compunction about calling stories true or false. (Bruner 4)

Life-stories, because they are narratives, have no inherent value of true or false. They "can only achieve 'verisimilitude'" and come to be an accepted version of reality by this road. Values of true and false are ascribed to narratives on the basis of their verisimilitude. Verisimilitude comes about and is maintained as long as there is no conflict with dominant discourses outside the life-story. Life thus storied does not follow a path of "empirical verification and logical requiredness," but is structured by postulations of cause and effect that do or do not make sense within the overall narrative.

Discourse aims at the construction of a smooth, socially concurring dominant life-story, which, while complex in itself, excludes disruptive elements as well as elements which do not fit the dominant plot of the life-story. The dominant life-story of every individual is thus a normalised account in which disruptive elements are repressed and experiences which have been excluded from it do not partake in the discursive materiality[167] of the life-story.[168] This discursive materiality is, in turn, dependent on language and thus the Symbolic. Consequently, a life-story is also subject to the entrenchments of 'The Law of the Father' and its normalising functions. The text of the client's life-story is consequently in fact more complex than the life-story that becomes manifest in discourse. The client consequently possesses a virtual life-story that, though multi-faceted and mosaic, is always only partly expressed (and in a twice censored way) in language. Experiences of the virtual life-story which would disrupt the veil of verisimilitude of the storied narrative remain repressed.[169]

The therapist is well aware that the story told is only one realisation of an unlimited number of potential stories within the client's hoard of experiences. In contemporary, modern societies "persons are constructed as objects and are encouraged to

---

[167] The term 'discursive materiality' denotes the power of discourse as it become effective in the real, material world. Potentialities within discourse can only become effective if they are taken up in speech; the 'discursive materiality' of discourse are thus those aspects of discourse which are articulated via statements. Repressed aspects of an identity thus never enter into the narrative of the life-story and remain hidden.

[168] With regard to the interplay of repression, narrative and therapy, cf. also Ochs/Capps: "Narrative activity is crucial to recognizing and integrating repressed and alienated selves. Posttraumatic stress disorder, for example, arises when an experience is too devastating to incorporate into one's life-story. Such experiences invade present lives in the form of somatic sensations or fragmented memories, i.e. flashbacks, but are not narrativized into a coherent sequence of events and reactions associated with a past self. [...] Many therapeutic interventions strive to develop a narrative that articulates the dissociated events and reconciles them with subsequent past, present and future selves" (30).

[169] In poetry, these repressed parts of the life-story are frequently concentrated in frozen metaphors. The 'defrosting' of these metaphors thus equals a making conscious of the repressed.

relate to themselves, their bodies, and to other persons as objects. This is a fixing and formalizing of persons. In western societies, these objectifying practices are pervasive" (White/Epston 66). White and Epston argue that the condition of the human being as a social animal can become oppressive in our modern, highly regulated and institutionalised world, meaning that the cultural lenses the individual employs in seeing itself can become highly constricting tools of self-surveillance. Like many fundamental concepts of narrative therapy, the cultural determination of the subject – via, among other things, cultural lenses, is based on Foucault.[170] Narrative therapy argues that

> our personal identities are constituted by what we "know" about ourselves and how we describe ourselves to persons. But what we know about ourselves is defined, for the most part, by the cultural practices (of describing, labeling, classifying, evaluating, segregation, excluding, etc.) in which we are embedded. [...] Thus, in the social domain, knowledge and power are inextricably interrelated. [...] [Michael] White draws heavily from the philosophical analysis of modern history by Foucault. Indeed, one of the most important original contributions [...] is White's analysis of Foucault's perspective and its relevance to therapy. (Tomm VIII)

In taking recourse to Foucault, narrative therapy exposes an underlying problem of humanistic art therapy: while humanistic concepts of therapy locate the client's problems in a lack of self-actualisation and control over life, they fail to fully enquire as to the root of this fact. Seeking the reasons for the client's psychological imbalance predominantly in the psyche itself does not do justice to the complexities of the field. Poetry therapy can circumvent this blind spot by taking Foucault's theories into consideration. Poetry therapy considered in the context of narrative therapy thus requires a closer investigation of Foucault's theories within a broader context of psychotherapy and literary studies.[171]

5.3 The Appropriation of Foucauldian Discourse for Poetry Therapy

The appropriation of Foucauldian theories for poetry therapy establishes a theoretical awareness of the socio-cultural embeddedness of clients, the effects of this embeddedness on the therapeutic endeavour as such and on the actual poetry produced within

---

[170] For detailed information on Foucault's theories and concepts cf. Foucault's *The Archaeology of Knowledge*, *Discourse on Language*, *Discipline and Punish*, *Madness and Civilization* and *The Order of Things*. Cf. also Rabinow's *The Foucault Reader*, especially Chapters II and III.

[171] The application of Foucault's theories in poetry therapy also strengthens the connection of poetry therapy to contemporary literary theory which appropriates Foucault most predominantly (but not exclusively) in the practice of New Historicism. For a summary introduction into the connection between Foucault and New Historicism, cf. Selden, Widdowson, Brooker, *A Reader's Guide to Contemporary Literary Theory* 178-196. Cf. also Veeser, *The New Historicism,* Greenblatt, *Shakespearean Negotiations* and "Towards a Poetics of Culture" and White, "New Historicism: A Comment."

this setting in particular. In addition to this, the following discussion of Foucault will supply the practice of poetry therapy with new concepts and methods to be integrated into the discipline; these are much needed therapeutic tools that account for discursive effects relevant for the therapeutic practice. When it comes to poetry therapy as an artefactual expressive art therapy based on humanistic, narrative principles, the notion of Foucauldian discourse is essential, because it represents a theoretical framework within which the client's socio-cultural embeddedness can be conceptualised on the basis of language. In addition to this, discourse is closely linked to the Symbolic which enables an interface of both notions by way of the centrality of language to therapy. Discourse clearly pertains to the whole range of poetry therapy and, quite importantly, gains its materiality, literally, in the poem and in the statements exchanged during the actual therapeutic session.

Foucault contends, as was noted, that the modern state is organised by discourse, arguing that every cultural practice within a society is being performed, controlled, and dominated by and through discourse. This pervasive nature of discourse ultimately stems from and is perpetuated by the human need to use language; in short, to communicate and interact socially. This happens by means of statements uttered. Here is Foucault's definition of 'statement':

> [A Statement] always has borders peopled by other statements. These borders are not what is usually meant by 'context' – real or verbal – that is, all the situational or linguistic elements, taken together, that motivate a formulation and determine its meaning. They are distinct from such a 'context' precisely in so far as they make it possible. [...] The psychological halo of a formulation is controlled from afar by the arrangement of the enunciative field. [...] At the very onset, from the very root, the statement is divided up into an enunciative field in which it has a place and status [...] it is always part of a network of statements, in which it has a role, however minimal it may be, to play. (*Archaeology* 97-99)

Furthermore, a statement

> is always an event that neither the language *(langue)* nor the meaning can quite exhaust. It is certainly a strange event: first, because on the one hand it is linked to the gesture of writing or to the articulation of speech, and also on the other hand it opens up to itself a residual existence in the field of a memory, or in the materiality of manuscripts, books, or any other form of recording; secondly, because, like every event, it is unique, yet subject to repetition, transformation, and reactivation; thirdly, because it is linked not only to the situations that provoke it, and to the consequences that it gives rise to, but at the same time, and in accordance with a quite different modality, to the statements that precede and follow it. (Foucault, *Archaeology* 28; emphasis original)

Thus, according to Foucault, statements constitute the nucleus of discourse. Although a statement constitutes first and foremost a speech act, it is also an event that has implications beyond the linguistic realm. This is the empirical power inherent in discourse. Statements do not exist autonomously from the cultural-semantic situation in which they are formulated. Discourse can open up "to itself a residual existence in the field of a memory;" also, it is "unique, yet subject to repetition, transformation, and reactivation" and, very importantly, "linked [...] to the situations that provoke it, and to the consequences that it gives rise to." This shows that discourse affects individuals in their intimate thought processes ("memory"), has the ability to take on a life of itself ("transformation") and has the potential to exert power in the real, material world ("consequences").

Although discourse permeates every cultural practice as well as the individual's life, it is not totally free in its dissemination. Every single statement is part of a whole semantic field of statements that are all related to one another. Consequently, the form and status of any new statement depend on the nature of its relation to other statements as well as the manner of its position and participation in the historical reality. This is as true for the highly evanescent statements uttered in a pub as of the statements that make up a poetic text. Statements are thus constrained in their freedom by neighbouring statements. The dissemination and flow of statements (and therefore of discourse as a whole) is thus always negotiated within certain limits, limits that originate from within discourse itself. Furthermore, statements can coalesce into larger, more regulated and regulating units which Foucault denotes as *discursive formations:*

> Whenever one can describe, between a number of statements, such a system of dispersion, whenever, between objects, types of statement, concepts, or thematic choices, one can define a regularity (an order, correlations, positions and functionings, transformations), we will say [...] that we are dealing with a *discursive formation*. [...] The conditions to which the elements of this division (objects, mode of statement, concepts, thematic choices) are subjected we shall call the *rules of formation*. The rules of formation are conditions of existence (but also of coexistence, maintenance, modification, and disappearance) in given discursive division. (ibid. 38; emphasis original)

Statements that have grouped together in discursive formations and have generated rules of formation, have an additional regulating function in the overall flow of discourse and affect the dissemination and organisation of other statements and other discursive formations. In a society, therefore, discourse becomes regulated by means of discursive formations, but also through what Foucault calls 'disciplines'. Disciplines are discursive formations that are held together through the formulation of rules of discursive practice which have become codified and can be clearly identified and demarcated. These rules tame the chaotic tendencies of discourse even further and allow for a categorisation of statements into disciplines. Thus, disciplines "constitute a system of control in the production of discourse, fixing its limits through the action of an identity taking the form of a permanent reactivation of the rules" (Foucault, *Discourse* 224). Consequently, "the production of discourse is at once controlled, selected, organised and redistributed according to a certain number of procedures, whose role it is to avert its powers and dangers, to cope with chance events, to evade its ponderous, awesome materiality" (ibid. 216). Without these discursive entities, discourse – and by implication human culture – would be an amorphous and chaotic amalgamation of statements. The rules inherent in discourse therefore facilitate order and in this respect form the basis of any social system. This is the constructive and positive quality of discourse in a society, working towards order and a reduction of chance events.

Foucault places the concept of power at the centre of his theories and argues "that we predominantly experience the positive or constitutive effects of power, that we are subject to power through normalising 'truths' that shape our lives and relationships. These 'truths', in turn, are constructed or produced in the operation of power" (White/Epston 19). These 'truths' are constituted through discursive power relations and function as signposts in the dissemination of discourse. In this way discourse has the power to influence individual subjects. Additionally, such propositions of truth represent the discursive manifestations of the Lacanian Phallus, facilitating structure, but themselves always elusive, deferent, unstable and ultimately unreachable. Due to what Foucault terms our "will to knowledge" people accept these propositions of truth without scrutinising them.

> Knowledge of all sorts is thoroughly enmeshed in the clash of petty dominations, as well as the larger battles which constitute our world. Knowledge is not external to these fights; [...] the 'will to knowledge' in our culture is simultaneously part of the danger and a tool to combat that danger. [...] Where religions once demanded the sacrifice of bodies, knowledge now calls for experimentation on ourselves, calls us to the sacrifice of the subject of knowledge. Foucault confronts this challenge, this threat, by refusing to separate knowledge from power. (Rabinow 6-7)

Knowledge and power are thus bound together in the way that knowledge is both a means of subjecting the individual under a certain discursive power and of fighting such a regime of power. Culture implies the dominance of certain discourses, the existence of discursive taboos and of censorship, and since knowledge is intricately bound to discourse it partakes in the above and is therefore never innocent. The more powerful discourses become ever more oppressive, because they automatically marginalise other discourses. This process is particularly strong in modern societies which are structured by means of institutions. Discursive power, according to Foucault, invests itself in the institutions of the state and in doing so it is perpetuated in all cultural practices that intersect with those institutions. Therefore, the discourses that are perpetuated most strongly are those that have become firmly institutionalised through science and the state. "[T]his will to truth, like the other systems of exclusion, relies on institutional support: it is both reinforced and accompanied by a whole strata of practices [...]" (Foucault, *Discourse* 219). The institutionalisation of certain dominant discourses in a modern society represents a dangerous concentration of discursive power. The effect of this aggregation of discursive power is a certain normalisation of the discursive landscape where counter-discourses are suppressed. In this context, it is therefore possible to ascribe to the process of the institutionalisation of discourse the same function, namely that of superimposing an ordering structure over an otherwise chaotic realm, as to the constitution of the Symbolic Order over the Semiotic. Foucault notes that it is

> on the basis of [...] contradiction that discourse emerges, and it is in order both to translate it and overcome it that discourse begins to speak; it is in order to escape the contradiction, whereas contradiction is ceaselessly reborn through discourse, that discourse endlessly pursues itself and endlessly begins again: it is because contradiction is always

anterior to discourse, and because it can therefore never entirely escape it, that discourse changes, undergoes transformation, and escapes of itself from its own continuity. Contradiction, then, functions throughout discourse, as the principle of its historicity. (*Archaeology* 151)

Discourse, according to Foucault, is based on contradiction and, to be more precise, contradiction which is "anterior to discourse." Contradiction denotes difference, which means that discourse, like language, is differential in nature. The difference at the heart of discourse equals the amorphous difference of the *chora*. In the same way that the *chora* as the motor of the Semiotic is always anterior to language, the difference from which discourse emerges is "anterior to discourse." In a manner equal to signification, Foucault's discourse "pursues itself and endlessly begins again," which endows discourse with the qualities of the Semiotic. According to Lacan, "the unconscious is that part of concrete discourse qua transindividual, which is not at the subject's disposal in re-establishing the continuity of his conscious discourse. This disposes of the paradox presented by the concept of the unconscious when it is related to an individual reality" ("The Function and Field of Speech and Language" 214). The unconscious is here conceived by Lacan as one function of language. It is all that is not consciously accessible by the individual in concrete speech or writing. Hence, the unconscious is that which is unrepresentable in Symbolic terms. The same is true for discourse: the existence of dominant and institutionalised discourses censors all statements which do not conform to the prevailing rules of formation. This prohibits the emergence of discursive formations from marginalised statement and effectively equals repression. Discourse and the Symbolic are thus structurally identical in their fundamental makeup: both aim at normalisation and level difference while at the same time they are disrupted and reinvigorated by that very difference they seek to annul.

Since every cultural system and practice is entangled with and basically originates in discourse, this includes, naturally, psychotherapy as well as poetry. When it comes to the receptive phase of poetry therapy, the above implies that knowledge extracted from the poetic text via interpretation is also an inherently discursive matter. Interpretation, it was determined, leads to understanding, leads to an increase in (therapeutical) self-knowledge. This knowledge is, however, liable to be constructed along discursively conformist lines, which marginalises other types of knowledge and thus implicitly limits the client's full self-actualisation. Interpretation, therefore, has to probe deeper and become self-questioning in order to break the discursive normalisation. These normalising effects of power prove particularly problematic when it comes to the cultural practice of (poetry) therapy, which seeks to challenge the discursive formation that is the client's life-story.

With regard to poetry therapy those discursive effects that curtail self-actualisation are of central importance and the effects from discursive processes of exclusion are among the most damaging to the therapeutic process. In order to motivate the client to take a positive and flexible stance in life again (poetry therapy's main aim), it is necessary to know and chart the extent of discursive curtailment so that it can be navigated and eventually broken up in therapy. A prerequisite for this is to be aware of and to be able to identify techniques and strategies of discursive curtailment. The techniques and strategies employed by modern societies to channel discourse according to a certain ideological dogma are "techniques of social control, 'of subjugation', techniques for the 'objectification' or 'thingification' of persons, and for the objectification of the bodies of persons" (White/Epston 24). A person's inherent drive for self-actualisation is curtailed by these techniques in a manner that the individual remains unaware of. Through techniques of objectification, "relations are established between institutions, economic and social processes, behavioural patterns, systems of norms, techniques, types of classification, modes of characterization; and these relations are not present in the object" (Foucault, *Archaeology* 45). Since "these relations are not present in the object," they are not perceived by the individual who therefore fails to recognise its own subjugation. White and Epston maintain that in "western societies, these objectifying practices are pervasive" (66); they are so pervasive, in fact, that individuals not only remain oblivious to their own objectification, but are active in their own subjugation. White and Epston describe this process in the following way:

> When conditions are established for persons to experience ongoing evaluation according to particular institutionalized "norms", when these conditions cannot be escaped, and when persons can be isolated in their experience of such conditions, then they will become the guardians of themselves. In these circumstances, persons will perpetually evaluate their own behaviour and engage in operations on themselves to forge themselves as "docile bodies." (24)

The term "docile bodies" does not refer to the physical aspect of the individual, but mainly to its mental disposition. It denotes a state in which the individual passively subjects itself to all normalising practices effective in a society. "For Foucault, culture is regulated through strategies or techniques of power that regulate or discipline its members through the construction and internalization of dominant truths or discourses. [...] Such strategies of power engage individuals in active self-surveillance and in processes of normalization of the self" (Brown/Augusta-Scott, "Introduction" XXIV). This process is termed 'subjectivation' by Foucault and works by means of (primarily) three modes of objectification of the subject, which denote "modes by which, in our culture, human beings are made subjects" (Foucault, qtd. in Rabinow 7).

The first mode of objectivation is "somewhat cryptically called 'dividing practices' [in which] the subject is objectified by a process of division either within himself or from others" (Rabinow 7-8). The isolation of lepers in the Middle Ages is one fitting example for this mode of objectification. The discursive patterns of the second mode of objectification, scientific classification, are closely connected to the first one, though working independently on the subject. This is a more abstract mode of "for example, the objectivizing of the speaking subject in *grammaire generale*, philology and linguistics [or] the objectivizing of the productive subject [...] in the analysis of wealth and of economics" (Rabinow 8-9). This third mode "looks at those processes of self-formation in which the person is active" (ibid. 9), which Foucault denotes with the term 'subjectivation'.[172] This third mode is essential for the effectiveness of the entire process, because 'subjectivation' denotes the individual's willing participation in the modes of objectivation, which "initiates an active self-formation" (ibid. 11) on the basis of institutionalised and dominant forms of discourse. Foucault's "modern system of power is one that not only renders persons and their bodies as objects, but also recruits persons into an active role in their own subjugation, into actively participating in operations that shape their lives according to the norms and specifications of the organization" (White/Epston 71). The encompassing materiality of discourse thus determines to a large extent the individual's life and, through discourse, its pragmatic use of language and thus its identity.

The objectifying and normalising effects of discourse delineated by Foucault's theories not only unwittingly guide and even dictate the individual's social identities and life-story, but affect therapy in a similar manner. Therapy as a cultural practice is part of the regulatory battery of every cultural system. In the modern state it is a highly institutionalised form of discourse. Therapy is

> for Foucault, a modernist strategy or mechanism of power. Therapy relies upon the modes of objectification of the subject delineated by Foucault, whereby under the gaze of science and classification, we come to understand ourselves 'scientifically'. Power and knowledge are not separate from the formation of the subject. Therapy is a socially legitimized arena for turning our gaze inward, disciplining the docile body, and ensuring we are self-containing. Dividing practices of traditional therapy include medicalization, labelling, stigmatization, and pathologization. Systems of classifying and labelling individuals rely upon the nexus of truth and power, legitimized by "experts" such as therapists, and are often dividing practices of strategies of power that determine which people are normal or abnormal, good or bad, strong or weak, moral or immoral. (Brown/Augusta-Scott, "Introduction" XVII)[173]

Therapy is here cast among the "dividing practices" and can therefore "invoke conservatizing, normalizing, and regulating processes of self in its operation as a social strategy of power" (ibid. XVII). Subjectivation is a double-edged sword. On the one hand, it is a necessary process of social control and individual identity-formation. On the other hand, subjectivation can come into conflict with necessary or desired changes in a subject's life and/or identity. In the latter cases, one can speak of negative subjectivation, which no longer fits the changed circumstances of a person's life and has therefore become 'other'. Since part of the individual's own self has becomes alienated, it experiences a conflict. The individual needs to reorganise its identity and life – via a new process of subjectivation – so that the alienated aspect no longer pertains intimately to its being. Poetry therapy is a means to this end. However, this function of

---

[172] Not to confuse the reader: indeed, the entire process is called 'subjectivation'; however, Foucault also denotes the third mode with the same term. The essential position of the third mode, 'subjectivation', for the modes of objectivation becomes clear in that the entire process takes its name from it.

[173] Cf. the implications of labelling in Chapter 2 which, as becomes clear here, are discursive.

therapy as a device of channelling discourse along established lines naturally complicates poetry therapy's aim of deconstructing even these tendencies of normalisation. Generally speaking, psychotherapy represents a discursive formation around scientific knowledge that has normalising functions: it establishes what is normal and what is abnormal, what is considered socially acceptable and what deviant, and, perhaps most importantly, what is madness. While therapy is an institutionalised form of discourse and thus working in support of ideology, it is also an inherent function of therapy to disrupt existing structures and go beyond them wherever this is deemed necessary. Therefore, the power of therapy can also be employed to challenge the established subjectivation and initiate change, thus solving conflicts in the client's identity. A constant awareness of therapy's and the client's embeddedness in discourse is, however, indispensible for this to be successful.

Also, the interplay between dominant discourses and marginalised ones is representative of the fundamental dichotomy between repression and revolution, of the negotiation between the Symbolic and the Semiotic by means of Semiotic energy. On the macro-scale, discourse has the same function on culture that, on the individual scale, language has on the subject: discourse thus constitutes itself in a twin existence of continuous repression and, to take over Kristeva's term, revolution. As subjects-in-language and in-discourse, clients are intricately entangled in this dichotomy. "The cut made by the signifying chain is the only cut that verifies the structure of the subject as a discontinuity in the real. If linguistics enables us to see the signifier as the determinant of the signified, analysis reveals the truth of this relationship by making holes in the meaning the determinants of its discourse" (Lacan, "The Subversion of the Subject and the Dialectic of Desire" 678). What Lacan is stating here is that it is the very nature of the subject to disrupt the normalising tendencies of discourse. Counter-intuitively, the true nature of the subject is a fragmented one. Human nature is thus in fact a state of discontinuity and fragmentation and human beings are merely conditioned to believe otherwise. This is why the normalising effects of the Symbolic and of discourse prove oppressive. In poetry therapy, this breaking open of the Symbolic has to be combined with an acknowledgement of the subjugating discourses, because this (at least partly) neutralises the subjugating effect and power. This facilitates a revitalisation of the client's cultural motility and the Semiotic energy. The poem represents the empirical means towards this revitalisation, but it is in the psychotherapeutic dialogue[174] about and with the poem that the actual revitalisation is achieved.

As with the life-story at the centre of narrative therapy, poems are essentially

> transmitted largely through socially mediated language and social interaction within specific cultural and historical contexts. The meanings that we attach to [poems] are thus never singular, individual, or simply subjective, never outside the social, but have

---

[174] When I speak of dialogue, here and on the following pages, I refer to the dialogue between client and therapist, but also to the dialogue that develops between the text and the client, the therapist and the text and any combination of the three entities.

shared or intersubjective meaning within a cultural nexus of power and knowledge. (Brown/Augusta-Scott, "Introduction" IX)

Poems thus have to be read in their dependence on cultural influences as well as on subjective influences from the individual that creates it. The nature of the individual's identity as a cultural discursive construct provides the basis for change in the client and for an undermining of the powers of dominant discourses: the individual's fundamentally fragmented state as well as the perpetual process of negotiation between a society's discourses constitute therapeutic entrance points. The fact that discourse is continually negotiating the borders of discursive disciplines and formations allows marginalised discourses to come to the surface, much like the Semiotic becoming manifest in the Symbolic. In fact, it is this inherent destabilisation of every discourse by marginalised ones which, in the long run, negates all rules of prohibition and taboo. Brown and Augusta-Scott argue that "the process of subjectification [sic] involves both power as constraint and domination and power as productive and constitutive. Thus, in making ourselves into subjects within the context of culture, we are both constrained and creative" (ibid. XVII). Foucault describes the manifest discourse as "the repressive presence of what it does not say; and this 'not-said' is the hollow that undermines from within all that is said" (*Archaeology* 25). Discourse thus exists as a twofold entity – manifest discourses and counter-discourses. Counter-discourses, the 'not said', are exactly what psychotherapy seeks to discover by means of the therapeutic discourse. Poetry therapy in its multi-discursiveness (between client-therapist, client-poem, therapist-poem, and the trinity of client-therapist-poem) establishes a network of counter-discourses that can challenge those repressive and normalising discourses pertaining to the life-world of the client.

Poetry therapy can set up a network of counter discourses by relating the poem to the dominant discursive entity in the client's life, the life-story. Consequently,

> practitioners must actively deconstruct and re-author oppressive stories and, in turn, the power and power relations embedded within them. [...] Narrative therapy in this sense involves the deliberate shifting of the oppressive, and often dominant, discourses and the reconstruction of counterdiscourses that are themselves sites of social resistance. This does not, however, involve simply erasing client's stories and replacing them with narrative therapists' reconstructed accounts. [...] Narrative therapy, then, is interested in the construction of stories, rather than inherent truths. Client's stories are multiple, shifting, discontinuous – not inherently real, true, or immutable. (Brown, "Situating Knowledge and Power" 6)

Since clients' life-stories do not represent nor contain "inherent truths," but represent constructions based upon normalising and dominant cultural discourses, they are essentially changeable.[175] Along the same lines, the contingency of meaning inherent in

---

[175] The life-story is only changeable within limits, of course. Events and experiences in life have happened and cannot therefore be simply erased. What can be changed, however, are the conclusions drawn from a life's experiences and events. Conclusions which, for instance, impact negatively on the client's identity or the plot of the life-story can be reinterpreted, thus changing the effect.

the production of poetic texts – the negotiations of pheno- and genotext – is also connected to this topic. The same goes for the virtual text of the client's life-story and the associated text(s) of the therapeutic discourse and dialogue. These do not furnish, as an ultimate outcome, a new, irrevocable truth; neither does poetry therapy aim at providing or constructing such a truth for the client to internalise. This would only lead to new obstacles in self-actualisation. Rather, the life-story as well as the therapeutic process offer possibilities for alternative constructions of reality; they constitute a pool of fragments to choose from, which, when regarded as useful by clients, are integrated into their reality. To recognise this is the first step; to appropriate it – via the constructions of alternative stories and knowledges – is the second.

Only in recognising its own fallacies can poetry therapy constitute an "effort to challenge the discursive practices of power and knowledge that have become problematically embedded within people's lives" (Brown/Augusta-Scott, "Introduction" XVII). In receiving and discussing the client's poem in relation to the life-story, the therapist has to be aware that

> this storying experience is dependent on language, in accepting this premise we are also proposing that we ascribe meaning to our experience and constitute our lives and relationships through language. When engaging in language, we are not engaging in a neutral activity. There exists a stock of culturally available discourses that are considered appropriate and relevant to the expression and representation of particular aspects of experience. (White/Epston 27)

While in Lacan the factor of unreliability concerned the production of meaning, the unreliability of language in the current context concerns primarily its reception. Narrative therapy, in taking conscious recourse to Foucault in the actual practice of its therapeutic approach, propagates a deconstructive mode of interpretation which serves both phases of poetry therapy. Firstly, it facilitates an interpretative approach which guards against and disrupts the effects of institutionalised forms of discourse.[176] Based on this, the actual practice of interpretation of client poems is opened to probe deeper for the Semiotic energy contained in the textual matrix. To facilitate this, dominant meaning that emerges from the superficial reading of the text is undermined by localising incongruities in the overt message which are then subjected to deconstructive close readings. In this way, the displacements and condensations of the Semiotic in the Symbolic are automatically taken into account during the analytical process. By thus appropriating the general method of narrative therapy for the second phase, poetry therapy's methodological foundation of working with the client poem receptively is brought into the compass of postmodern literary and psychological theory. In its focus on the contingency of meaning, the narrative approach of poetry therapy is fundamentally postmodern and aligned with deconstruction:

> [p]ostmodern narrative therapy represents a fundamental divergence from modernist psychotherapy perspectives. Unlike psychotherapy grounded in modernist constructions of knowledge, power, truth, knowledge, experience, emotion, reason, self, and identity,

---

[176] Also, this approach is inherently literary in its use of close reading and deconstruction.

the postmodern lens that shapes narrative therapy means these central foundational constructs to therapy are interrogated rather than taken as is. (White/Epston XV)

This postmodern approach guarantees an inherent scepticism and inquisitiveness regarding all forms of generalisations, categorisations, ideologies and systematisations; in its continuous self-questioning it works against the effects of the Symbolic and of dominant discourses. This unrelenting (self-)questioning during the reception of poetry results in the accumulation of propositions of meaning, the result of which is a hoard of potential *points de capiton* only some of which can be actualised at one time. Such an actualisation, ideally, results in what Derrida terms a 'signifying structure':

> The writer writes *in* a language and *in* a logic whose proper system, laws, and life his discourse by definition cannot dominate absolutely. He uses them only by letting himself, after a fashion and up to a point, be governed by the system. And the reading must always aim at a certain relationship, unperceived by the writer, between what he commands and what he does not command of the patterns of the language that he uses. This relationship is not a certain quantitative distribution of shadow and light, of weakness and of force, but a signifying structure that critical reading should *produce*. (Derrida, *Of Grammatology* 158; emphasis original)

As no writer can hope to fully dominate or command language use, so the reader, even, or maybe particularly so, the author-client as reader, cannot hope to bring into understanding all that is "unperceived by the writer" in the textual artefact. Any reading thus "*produce[s],*" that is, generates a 'signifying structure'. For Derrida, a structure is always only a temporary construct dependent on its centre function (the non-locus). Any setting up of a signifying structure thus constitutes only a partial and function-dependent actualisation of the virtually endless pool of (semiotic) possibilities. For poetry therapy this has the following consequences: since, according to Derrida, the aim of a reading is the production of a signifying structure which is the becoming present of aspects of the text the writer commands and does not command (i.e. the connections between the conscious realisations and the unconscious traces) on the basis of a certain centre-function that temporarily stabilises this structure, poetry therapy has to approach the client-texts in a manner that elucidates centre functions – and in doing so produces signifying structures – which actualise problem-relevant areas of the overall textual matrix. These centre functions are to be drawn from one or more *points de capiton* surrounding instances of figurative language.

5.4 Breaking Discursive Normalisations: Externalisation and 'Unique Outcomes'

People's interpretations of experiences take place, as Payne notes, "through cultural and social lenses" (21), rather than through "biological or psychological factors" (ibid.). In essence, he refashions the dyad of the Symbolic and the Semiotic in terms of macro-cultural factors and concepts. The function of the Symbolic for the individual being (initiation of the subject into its social environment and the setting up of certain limits and mechanisms of control within this environment), is mirrored by the function of discourse on the cultural plane. Along the same lines, the fate of the Semiotic in common speech as well as written texts (namely a displacement of its traces and a burying of the same beneath a layer of Symbolic normalisation) runs parallel to the fate of marginalised voices in the negotiations of Foucauldian discourse. As a consequence, clients seeking help in poetry therapy are fundamentally hampered in two ways: (1) Clients are restricted in their verbal actualisation by the Symbolic, because it is constrictive and suppressive of the Semiotic influences. (2) Clients are inescapably subjected under the rules of discourse. This means they are effectively blind to marginalised forms of discourse or likely to discard them as unimportant or peripheral to their state.

While these two factors normally remain largely unperceived and unproblematic, they become influential when there is a disturbance of the individual's psychological condition. The result is a feeling of a loss of control over one's own life, which, according to narrative psychology and art therapy, can be diagnosed as being at the heart of many, if not most, mental conditions.[177] In order to account for this in the therapeutic endeavour,

> one aim of narrative therapy, from the earliest possible moment, is to assist the person to regain her sense of control over her life. This is one of the reasons for systematically and persistently inviting her to *name the problem*. [...] When persons come to therapy, problems have gained power over them, so naming the problem can be morale-boosting. But it is more than a symbolic step towards regaining some sense of control, helpful though this may be. It is a means of clarifying problems and normalizing[178] them – both of which contribute to a person's sense that he can position himself differently in relation to the problem. (Payne 42; emphasis original)

The fundamental concepts of narrative therapy summarised by Payne here revolve around identification and integration, which corresponds to the basic principles of poetry therapy as an artefactual expressive art therapy, which employs the poems as an artefact of the client's verbal expressions. This, in turn, offers a palpable object of study, which can be used to *"name the problem"* and, once named, or identified, it

---

[177] To recount briefly: humanistic art therapy is based on treating clients in their entire multidimensionality as human beings. The humanistic approach to therapy thus moves away from symptom-oriented treatments and instead embeds clients' symptoms in their life world. In this respect, one can draw parallels to narrative therapy. Similarly, the humanistic approach is founded on the belief that psychological conflicts are to a great extent caused by an impairment of self-actualisation. Narrative therapy now provides an explanation of the causes of these impediments.

[178] The word 'normalizing' is not to be understood here in the sense of leveling or downplaying of the problems. Rather, narrative therapy aims at integrating problems – once identified – into the life-story of clients so that these are no longer alien (or repressed) aspects, but rather an acknowledged, unproblematic – and therefore 'normalised' – part of the overall life-story.

serves as a fixed reminder used to slowly integrate the problematic plot into the client's life-story.

Coming back to the understanding of clients according to the foundations of art therapy as "not 'mentally ill', but rather as encountering specific problems in their efforts to cope with life – as a result of intrapsychically or environmentally caused conflicts" (Rubin, *Approaches to Art Therapy* 344) – the effects of institutionalised discursive formations that serve as normalising practices have to be regarded as among the ultimate cause for the client's internal conflicts. Since the condition as a 'docile body' is by definition unconscious, so are the conflicts between the urge for self-actualisation and the subjugation through discursive practices. These conflicts are perceived in the instinctual Semiotic, the *chora*. Through the *chora*, which is differential in nature and anterior to symbolisation, conflicts enter the process of signification, which is the precondition of language, before finally seeping into the text of the writing subject through the break of the Symbolic structure by the Semiotic. During the process of writing, while creativity is utilised, there is a feeling of pressure-release, of overcoming obstacles and a liberation from constraint, but once crystallized in a text, the client's conflicts, which have participated in the process of creation, have re-entered the realm of Symbolic normalisation and are additionally subject to marginalisation and suppression of discourse in the process of reception and interpretation. On the Symbolic plane, the creative synaesthesia has been divided and the Semiotic traces have become displaced into figurative elements, or immobilised and trapped in, for instance, frozen metaphors. On the discourse plane, the client's docility causes the reading of the text to proceed along well established discursive lines, automatically marginalising therapeutically important content:

> Although individuals are active participants in the creation of their stories, these stories draw upon available social discourses and therefore consist of both subjugated and dominant knowledges. Importantly, as our experiences exist within a field of knowledge and power, no story is outside power. […] Self-stories of experience are constructed through a selective process, including what information is left out. Influenced by larger stories around us, self-stories of experience are unable to embody the full complexity of lived life, its gaps, contradictions, and silences. First-voice stories, or self-stories, then, are not inherently "truer" than other stories and thus cannot be privileged as beyond inquiry. (Brown/Augusta-Scott, "Introduction" XXVIII)

What is stated here with regard to the text of the person's life-story is equally true for the poem used in a therapeutic environment. The client's interpretation of the poem is shaped by the "selective process" intent upon upholding a coherent life-story: "unable to embody the full complexity of lived life," the interpretation of the poem needs to correspond to the life-story. The poem's meaning constructed by the client will tend to supplement the apparent 'truths' clients deduce from and for their life-stories. This constitutes a self-perpetuating and consolidating circular movement that needs to be broken.

The schism between the signifying potential of the Semiotic traces embedded in the client's poem and the extent to which they are noticed and actualised in the therapy session can be great indeed. Iser notes the gap between signifying potential and produced meaning as well, stating:

> The incongruity between discovery and disposition can generally only be removed through the emergence of a third dimension, which is perceived as the meaning of the text. The balance is achieved when the disposition experiences a correction, and in this correction lies the function of the discovery. The reader begins to negate his disposition – not in order to revoke it, but temporarily to suspend it as the virtualized base for an experience of which he can only say that it seems self-evident, because he has produced it himself through his own discoveries. (*The Act of Reading* 218)

Iser conceives of the act of reading as a sequential chain of theses – or dispositions – on the part of the reader. These theses are subject to continuous revision as the reader assembles the "third dimension, which is perceived as the meaning of the text" from this information gathered. While this process accounts for the dynamic process of reading, allowing for the fact that every reading is essentially a new experience based on new, or different discoveries made by the reader, Iser's theory does not account for the normalising tendencies of discourse. The guided reading of poetry therapy thus necessitates a fourth dimension which not only constructs and negates on the basis of the textual discoveries, but probes these discoveries themselves for evidence of displacement or condensation, for effects of *différance*, and discursive normalisation. This fourth dimension is the therapist who constructs meaning in conjunction with the client by always questioning the client's and her own interpretation of the poem.[179] The therapist guides clients towards a new point of view allowing them to come to an intellectual acceptance of the conflicts arising from their cultural-discursive embeddedness and their own problematic identity construction.[180]

The therapist inhabits another key function of discourse, namely that of commentary. Commentary by its very nature precludes silence and consequently counters

---

[179] On the position and function of the therapist in the context of her classical role, cf. Brown: "Rather than the traditional position of the expert, all-knowing therapist or its mirror twin, the 'not-knowing therapist', I will argue that both the therapist and the client are 'partial knowers'. As such, both bring knowledge and agency to the conversation. While I agree with abandoning the idea of the 'all-knowing' therapist and minimizing power differences in the therapeutic alliance, I argue that a 'not-knowing' stance is not effective for challenging oppressive social discourses or, subsequently, for deconstructing negative identity conclusions or rewriting alternative identities" ("Situating Knowledge and Power" 4).

[180] In this respect it deserves notice that therapists have to take care not to affect the consolidation of a disordered state which would be as paralysing to the client as the dominant discourses' normalising powers. In short, therapists have to be careful not to become agents of negative subjectivation. A self-consciousness about their own position and actions is thus of particular importance for therapists. The therapist, therefore, has to be careful not to cut clients off completely from the discursive net they are entangled in. What the client needs is an altered life-story (re)integrating problematic and repressed storylines, not a completely new life-story.

discursive marginalisation. In this way, commentary helps to revitalise discourse and to bring it into flux again. Foucault states regarding commentary:

> I would like to limit myself to pointing out that, in what we generally refer to as commentary, the difference between primary and secondary text plays two interdependent roles. [...] [I]t permits us to create new discourses as infinitum: the top-heaviness of the original text, its permanence, its status as discourse ever capable of being brought up to date [...] creates an open possibility for discussion. On the other hand, whatever the techniques employed, commentary's only role is to say *finally*, what has silently been articulated *deep down*. It must [...] say, for the first time, what has already been said, and repeat tirelessly what was, nevertheless, never said. (*Discourse* 221; emphasis original)

Foucault ascribes to commentary two vital functions within the play of discourse. Firstly, commentary creates new discourses and, secondly, it unearths the deeper meaning of existing discourses. Needless to say, these two functions are essential for poetry therapy, especially when considered as a cultural practice. In her function as commentary, the therapist is able to make the client sensitive to alternative discourses or implant new ones. Doing so breaks the hold of the dominant discourses and leads the client toward a heightened state of self-actualisation and self-knowledge. At the same time, the commentary function of the therapist gives voice to what "has silently been articulated *deep down*," which is to say that the therapist's comments work to make conscious the problematic nature of the client's situation and the problem-saturated discursive formations at the heart of this. Additionally, commentary reduces the chaotic contingency of discourse and can serve to erect a structure from within the discursive entanglements of the client's life-story which provides a new system of order.

> Commentary averts the chance element of discourse by giving it its due: it gives us the opportunity to say something other than the text itself, but on condition that it is the text itself which is uttered and, in some ways, finalised. The open multiplicity, the fortuitousness, is transferred, by the principle of commentary, from what is liable to be said to the number, the form, the masks, and the circumstances of repetition. (Foucault, *Discourse* 221)

The therapist functioning as commentary can thus give new direction and strength to the client in that it enables a repositioning of the client in relation to the problem(s), which helps to separate these from the client's self.

Commentary is, of course, discourse itself. It springs from discourse, works through discourse and relates to its various disciplines and formations. However, commentary implies that it has power over the text it comments upon; that it speaks from a position of authority. Poetry therapists hold such a position with regard to the texts of their clients by virtue of their psychotherapeutic and literary training and experience. They function as authority figures which, on the one hand, empowers their discourses, but also makes them powerful agents of a new subjectivation motility, because subjectivation, to recount the idea, "takes place through a variety of 'operations on [people's] own bodies, on their own souls, on their own thoughts, on their own conduct'. These operations characteristically entail a process of self-understanding *but one which is mediated by an external authority figure, be he confessor or psychoanalyst*" (Rabinow 11; emphasis mine). Poetry therapy seeks to break up structures established by a previous process of subjectivation; it does so by initiating a new process of subjectivation. Consequently, the notion of subjectivation is essential to the work of the therapist. Since the third mode of objectivation, subjectivation, is the key to the entire process, poetry therapy has to initiate a new subjectivation motility in the client. The therapist, conceived of as the discursive agency of commentary, facilitates this by simultaneously strengthening and re-channelling the client's text. The client is led from a state of docility into one of activity. While this process entails dangers, the function of the therapist as an "external authority figure" is necessary, because such a position is essential in initiating a new, positive process of subjectivation. This new process of subjectivation is able to amend or partly replace the structure of an old, constricting one. In this manner the process of subjectivation is utilised therapeutically. The position of the therapist and its discursive representation as the function as commentary enable precisely this.

The poetic artefact as well as the therapist thus constitute two vantage points external to normalisation. Although equally caught in the general normalisations of discourse, the therapist, in working with the client's life-story, does take on an outside perspective that allows for the necessary amount of objectivity. This (relative) objectivity is conveyed to clients via the critical discussion of their poems. In the critical examination of the poetic text the therapist guides the client towards the text's ambiguities, and its symbols as manifestations of the unconscious conflicts are discussed and reinterpreted in the light of self-actualisation, personal growth and the life-story.

The question that presents itself here is how exactly to break the hold of discourse in the actual practice of poetry therapy if it is truly so pervasive and encompassing. For narrative therapy, the solution is as follows:

> Within narrative therapy, the spoken problem identity is not considered a "fixed state," nor is it located within the body of the person. Instead, the problem identity is viewed within the context of intricate negotiations that take place inside complex fields of power and discourse. Because of this, a narrative therapist attempts to render transparent the status of identity-based politics in the life of the problem and to highlight the effect these discursive practices have had on the person's life and how the person has historically responded. (Madigan 139)

The position of the individual is considered, firstly, as not "fixed" and, secondly, a person's identity is culturally determined rather than originating from the person's body.[181] A person's identity is thus the result of a sequence of 'historical' positionings

---

[181] Although the individual's life-story provides some sense of stability, it does by no means negate the possibility of other stories altogether. Cf. Ricoeur, *Time and Narrative*: "In the first place, narrative identity is not a stable and seamless identity. Just as it is possible to compose several plots on the subject of the same incidents (which, thus,

"within the context of intricate negotiations that take place inside complex fields of power and discourse." This sequentiality provides meaning by orienting life teleologically in time from birth towards death. Traditional concepts of narrative (and to some extent also the postmodern approach of narrative psychology) consider sequentiality as a crucial and fundamental ordering principle of human existence; a sequential alignment of experiences provides a structure for the client's life-story, provides thetic orientation, and in doing so facilitates the construction of a (seemingly) fixed identity.[182] Consequently, poetry therapy that employs theories of narrative therapy aims at constructing a life-story, i.e. a historical sequentiality of the client's lived experience, which integrates problematic events as seamlessly as possible.[183] While this entails a disruption of the previously dominant life-story in the practice of narrative psychology, poetry therapy disrupts the sequentiality of the client's life-story in a much more fundamental way by virtue of the genre of poetry. Poetry is less sequential than, for instance, diaries or any kind of traditional narrative writing; in fact, poetry is not inherently sequential at all. Due to its increased number of figurative elements, poetry tends towards the episodic, thus rather breaking up sequentiality than supporting it. The nature of the poem as episodic also reflects the subject's fragmented state more closely than any sequential structure. This accounts for a greater potential for the materialisation of unconscious content. Any sequential order can only be artificially imposed on unconscious content and would necessarily lead to normalising changes in the original content. In poetry, no (rigorous) sequentiality is imposed, which means that the unconscious traces, while displaced, can be discovered in a more original

---

should not really be called the same events), so it is always possible to weave different, even opposed, plots about our lives" (248).

[182] Cf., for instance, Neumann/Nünning: "Through narrativization, heterogeneous and potentially ever-fluctuating experiences are transformed into a more or less coherent form, suggesting closure of one's life and relative stability of one's (diachronic) identity. Self-narratives bridge the temporal and cognitive gap between former, experiencing I and the present, narrating I. [...] Identity, thus seen, is not rooted in any kind of psychological continuity, it rather emerges from the relative unity of character and action imposed by the unity of narrative" (6). Cf. also Ricoeur, *Time and Narrative*: "[P]sychoanalysis constitutes a particular instructive laboratory for a properly philosophical inquiry into the notion of narrative identity. In it, we can see how the story of a life comes to be constituted through a series of rectifications applied to previous narratives, just as the history of a people, or a collectivity, or an institution proceeds from a series of corrections that new historians bring to their predecessor's descriptions and explanations. [...] The same thing applies to the work of correction and rectification constitutive of analytic working-through. Subjects recognize themselves in the stories they tell about themselves" (247).

[183] Although methods and techniques from the area of narratology are applied to the life-story, when I talk of narrative, narrative writing, plot devices and the like here, I do not refer to concepts, traditions and techniques of the genre of narrative. I do not speak of narrative in a narrow, literary sense, but take narrative to mean, more broadly, the telling of events in a more or less coherent, sequential manner.

form. These displaced traces can be reactivated and used in the re-authoring of the client's overall life-story. They disrupt the verisimilitude of the problematic life-story, which has to be rewritten along the lines suggested by the plot devices excavated from the poetic text. Only by rewriting the life-story can it be re-endowed with the label of 'truth'.

Taking the above into consideration, it is possible to say that the dominant life-story of any client originates from two archival repositories: the individual archive of the unconscious and the "historically and culturally transmitted repertoire or archive of stories, which serve as idealised models for the elaboration of our own experiences" (Neumann/Nünning 9).[184] The cultural archive partakes in the modes of objectivation. Stories that have become part of the cultural archive become "idealised models" which serve as blueprints according to which individuals shape their own life-stories. Those experiences not storied remain in the individual archive of the unconscious as repressed experiences and can be actualised in support of therapy's aim of re-authoring. The less sequential nature of the poem constitutes an ideal matrix from which to excavate these as yet unstoried experiences of clients. This is even more so as a second strain of cognitive theory challenges the belief that human beings rely (solely) on sequential narratives for making sense of the world and constructing identities.[185] These theories conceive of the meaning making process episodically. Life episodes from which meaning can be constructed become manifest in people's use of visually saturated metaphors:

> In contrast to narratives, which unfold a (temporal) sequence of events, metaphors or the ekphrastic descriptions of images freeze or arrest the chronological flow and – due to their visual quality – evoke manifold associations, which are not reducible to narrative representation. They embody a sort of amalgam, in which past, present, and future intermingle in manifold ways. (Neumann/Nünning 11)

Episodic structuring of experience is understood as spatial in contrast to the temporal matrix established by the sequentiality of narrative. The poem as a confined textual space interfaces congenially with the concept of episodic meaning conceived of as spatial. Contrary to the chronological nature of sequential structuring, the space of the poem is bereft of chronology and therefore closer to the Semiotic. In the light of Freudian and Lacanian psychoanalysis it can safely be argued that an episodic structuring of

---

[184] For the idea of literature and/or narrartive as an archive of cultural knowledge, cf. also: Hinchman/Hinchman, *Memory, Identity, Community: The Idea of Narrative in the Human Sciences*; Astrid Erll et al. (ed.). *Literatur – Erinnerung – Identität. Theoriekonzeptionen und Fallstudien*; John Niles, *Homo Narrans: The Poetics and Anthropology of Oral Culture*; Moritz Baßler, *Die kulturpoetische Funktion und das Archiv: Eine literaturwissenschaftliche Text-Kontext-Theorie*; Birgit Neumann, "Kulturelles Wissen und Literatur."

[185] Cf. especially: Lakoff/Johnson. *Philosophy in the Flesh: The Embodied Mind and Its Challenges in Western Thought* and *Metaphors We Live By*; Turner, *The Literary Mind*; Fauconnier, *Mappings of Thought and Language* and Strawson's "A Fallacy of our Age."

experience is closer to the concept of a timeless and chaotic unconscious than that of narrative. The prevalence for metaphoric imagery in episodic structuring corroborates this. However, there is no need to see both concepts as mutually exclusive. An expressive artefactual poetry therapy appropriating a narrative psychological approach within the broad conceptual framework of humanistic art therapy is able to fuse and make use of both sequential as well as episodic structural elements: the re-authoring process as a whole will follow narrative principles as outlined above while the localisation and interpretation of resurfaced experiences will disregard temporality and be episodic. Every such localised experience represents an episode in the client's life which is linked to other experiences present in the poetic text thus fashioning a web from which sequential elements can be extracted to re-author the life-story. The nature of the poem as a material artefact supports this process and thus becomes central in poetry therapy. Since the poem's text constitutes a space upon the sheet of paper, client and therapist can move freely within this space in search of episodes.

Two techniques employed by narrative therapy are crucial in the identification and activation of possible counter-discourses via episodic instances of meaning and in unifying the diverse concepts thus far delineated: (1) Externalisation and (2) 'Unique outcomes'. 'Unique outcomes' emerge from the life-story as it is narrated sequentially by the client during therapy. When clients are asked to recount their life-story, the therapist listens carefully for any contradictions in the story or signs of discontinuity, which represent what the narrative therapists have termed 'unique outcomes':

> These events that contradict the problem-saturated story (often of the person's identity) are referred to as *unique outcomes*. Unique outcomes are the entry points for re-authoring alternative stories. These unique outcomes, or exceptions to the problem stories, are at the heart of developing new life stories and help in the development of supports for the enactment or living of a preferred story. [...] Through deconstruction and reconstruction, narrative therapy enables the resurrection of the alternative or previously disqualified story. (Brown/Augusta-Scott, "Introduction" XXXIV; emphasis original)

The localisation of unique outcomes is thus the first therapeutic step in narrative therapy. On this basis of isolated unique outcomes, the second therapeutical step is the process of externalisation:

> "Externalizing" is an approach to therapy that encourages persons to objectify and, at times, to personify, the problems that they experience as oppressive. In this process, the problem becomes a separate entity and thus external to the person or relationship that was ascribed as the problem. Those problems that are considered to be inherent, and those relatively fixed qualities that are attributed to persons and relationships, are rendered less fixed and less restricting. (White/Epston 38)

Externalisation works to

(a) free persons from the problem-saturated descriptions of their lives and relationships, (b) encourage the generation or resurrection of alternative and more rewarding stories of lives and relationships, and (c) assist persons to identify and develop a new relationship with the problem. In so doing, the practices foster a new sense of personal agency; with this, persons are able to assume responsibility for the investigation of new choices in their lives and pursue new possibilities. In the process, they experience a newfound capacity to intervene in their world. (ibid. 65)

Externalisation is a therapeutic prerequisite for the deconstruction of oppressive stories and dominating knowledges.[186]

Externalisation and the discovery of unique outcomes allow the therapist to initiate in the client what Foucault calls "the insurrection of subjugated knowledges" (*Society* 7).

> In contrast to modernist practices of naturalizing experiences and thereby authorizing clients' interpretations of events in their lives, the postmodern influence on narrative therapy recognizes that as experience stories are socially constructed, they cannot be inherently authoritative or self-legitimizing. From a postmodern narrative view, these experience stories include both subjugated and dominant knowledge. (Brown, "Dethroning the Suppressed Voice" 181)

Taking a postmodern approach to psychotherapy, narrative therapy deliberately displaces clients in order to re-centre them in a more active and less conflicted life-story, a life-story they have consciously reworked and restructured so as to internalise it. Externalisation of problem-saturated parts of the life-story precedes this internalisation of alternative storylines:

> The externalization of the problem-saturated story can be initiated by encouraging the externalization of the problem, and then by mapping of the problem's influence in the person's life and relationships. [...] When unique outcomes are identified, persons can be invited to ascribe meaning to them. Success in this ascription of meaning requires that the unique outcomes be plotted into an alternative story or narrative. (White/Epston 16)

White and Epston state that unique outcomes have, simultaneously, a "historical, present or future location" (ibid.). They are, with regard to the overall life-story of the client, timeless, thus exhibiting the fundamental feature of the unconscious. In this respect, unique outcomes signify instances of episodic meaning. This is the reason they appear as alien aspects within the life-story as narrated by the client. The life-story in its discursive materiality is a hoard of sequential meaning and thus subject to the rules of sequentiality. Unique outcomes as instances of episodic meaning are elements that do not fit these rules and therefore run counter to the dominant meaning expressed in the life-story. Unique outcomes are thus facilitative of deconstruction. Once unique

---

[186] Cf. also Brown/Augusta-Scott: "The process of deconstruction involves externalizing the problem and the socially constructed discourses that shape the problem, and it helps the client to take a position on these stories. Towards this end, unique outcomes are stalled initiatives (times when the problem story has not dominated people's experiences), are identified as an entry point for creating alternative stories. [...] Deconstruction begins with externalizing the problem, which includes feelings, problems, practices, and interactions. [...] This process of separating the person from the problem often separates the person from problematic identity conclusions and dominant social discourses. Externalization or externalizing turns the problem into an object outside the person, emphasising that the person is not the problem" ("Introduction" XXX-XXXI).

outcomes have been identified, the person's dominant life-story is deconstructed, in the Derridean sense, and re-authored to include the events around the unique outcomes. Re-authoring – while still not granting authority over the new text both in the sense of Kristeva and in the light of Foucauldian discourse[187] – actively involves clients in refashioning their lives in a more positive manner:

> Re-authoring, then, involves developing a more helpful story, one that allows for life outside of the problem. In re-authoring or rewriting the story, the emphasis is on opening up other options and possibilities. While in the process of deconstructing the problem, narrative therapy uncovers the influence of the problem on the person; in the rewriting of more helpful stories, narrative therapy explores the influence of the person on the problem – in the past, present, and future. (Brown/Augusta-Scott, "Introduction" XXXIV)

The relations of power between the client and the problem are of intimate concern for poetry therapy. Externalisation via the poem helps clients to deal with problems, because these are no longer felt to intrude too intimately upon their own identity and freedom. Nonetheless, the poem has to maintain a certain connection to the client's life so that the externalised problem can be referred to the client's life-story and current condition. In his manner, therapeutic insights gained can be integrated into the person's personality and history in the context of the experiences from which they have emerged. The interplay of identifying unique outcomes and externalisation described above takes place in the threshold between the dominant discourses or knowledges and the subjugated ones. The

> performance of meaning around unique outcomes can also provide a basis for the identification of the subjugated knowledges. Again, the identification of these unique outcomes can be facilitated by the externalization of problems. [...] Thus, in therapy, as persons embrace these unique knowledges, we can witness, as Foucault puts it, the "insurrection of the subjugated knowledges." (White/Epston 32)

Externalisation not only works to strengthen and activate subjugated knowledges, it also marks those dominant discourses associated with the unique outcome as oppressive. Thus, externalisation paves the way for alternative interpretations of the externalised unique outcome, for a re-authoring of those aspects of the life-story identified as problematic.[188] Other than traditional narrative therapy, poetry therapy, in working

---

[187] Cf. also Brown: "Despite the preference for one story over the other, neither escapes social construction. All such accounts are discursive. What is not seen is that it is possible to advance a preferred position or story without naturalizing or essentializing it. The therapist and client can work together on re-authoring a more positive identity without resorting to the claim that they are discovering the real self. [...] Seeking a thicker description of people's stories means including that which has been disqualified, marginalized or suppressed, but that does not mean that inclusion necessarily needs to be either privileged or naturalized. The tension between resurrecting and dethroning the suppressed voice is at the heart of his work" ("Dethroning the Suppressed Voice" 189).

[188] Cf. White/Epston: "The externalization of the problem helps persons identify and separate from unitary knowledges and 'truth' discourses that are subjugating them" (30).

with a material text, is able to produce a thick description[189] of the client's text. By constructing a network, or web, of unique outcomes, client and therapist arrive at a thick description of the poetic text, which represents a charted crystallisation of the client's unconscious state and conflicts.

Having identified and externalised the problem, clients can deal with it actively and thus gain renewed control over their lives. This new agency can be channelled into all areas of life and re-establish a reciprocal relationship between client and society. In poetry therapy, the poem as an artefact of the creative process of the client can perform this function amiably. Externalising the problem has already taken place in the production of the poem and need not be specifically addressed by the therapist.[190] Externalisation happens not only regarding a specific unique outcome, but, one can assume, a whole cluster of potentially important unique outcomes is externalised in the poem.[191] The poem in poetry therapy *is* the external representation of the problem-saturated story. Because of this, the therapeutic work of reintegrating the problem and the active participation on the part of the client is not only more easily facilitated, it is in fact the natural outcome of poetry therapy. Clients in poetry therapy thus automatically externalise their problems and the fact that they do so in writing rather than in evanescent speech, increases the therapeutic impact of externalisation. The poem originates from the client – as the problem or symptom does – but it is clearly not part of the client anymore. In the poem, problems and symptoms have crystallised into a verbal artefact that can be subjected to whatever treatment the client envisions. The relations of power have been reversed: it is no longer the problem that has power over the client; the client is now in a position to affect the problem, namely through an interpretation challenging the Symbolic and dominant discursive elements of the text.

> This does not mean, it has to be noted here, that the newly discovered, or reconstructed discourses contain in any sense more 'truth': "Externalizing internalized dominant discourse often allows for suppressed or subjugated knowledge to emerge. However, [...], I will argue that resurrecting the suppressed voice is not the discovery of the real, unencumbered self. As such, it should not be privileged as natural or as providing an authoritative foundation" (Brown, "Dethroning the Suppressed Voice" 177).

[189] 'Thick Description' in the sense of Ryle and Geertz. For further information on the concept of thick description, cf. Ryle, "The Thinking of Thought," "Thinking and Reflecting" and Geertz, *The Interpretation of Cultures: Selected Essays*, especially the essay "Thick Description: Toward an Interpretive Theory of Culture" (3-30).

[190] In the case of more specific problems, of course, the therapist may want to specifically externalise the problems inherent in a symbol or image, but, generally speaking, the poetic symbols are already externalised to a great extent.

[191] It should be briefly noted here that in poetry therapy the sequence of identification of unique outcomes and externalisation is reversed. This is, however, inconsequential to the effectiveness of poetry therapy. First of all, externalisation and unique outcomes as methods are effective in their own right and not depended on a certain sequence. Secondly, a second phase of externalisation can always be added in therapy should it be deemed necessary by the therapist.

place or argument due the decentring effects associated with their origin from the Semiotic. In spite of this twofold problem, there is one place towards which the internal conflicts tend to gravitate, namely figurative language. It is the joined task of the therapist and the client to uncover the symbols and images in a poem and, by putting them into relation with each other, to (re)construct meaning from them, i.e. to set up a 'signifying structure' that serves as an interpretative framework. In poetry therapy, where the externalisation occurs before the identification of unique outcomes, the deconstruction of the text is at the same time a search for unique outcomes and a utilising of the same. As the poem includes a number of unique outcomes, these can be connected in therapy in order to construct a network of knowledge that can stand up to the subjugating discourses constricting the client's life. The flow and potency of the Semiotic energy is thus tapped into and can be charted and utilised. Since the poem is external to the client, it is possible to keep the emotional distance necessary to engage with it intellectually. Also, this allows clients to question the surface meaning and break the cycle of discursive subjugation. The episodic nature of unique outcomes in poetry is particularly conducive to this as it is (a) closer to the nature of the unconscious, i.e. the Semiotic content, and (b) not (yet) constrained by sequential needs of a coherent narrative. In this way, the isolation of unique outcomes from the textual matrix allows for the fashioning of counter-discourses. To speak in terms of literary theory, this isolation affects a defamiliarisation of the unique outcomes before the background of the normalised structures of the poem.[194] This effect of defamiliarisation, or foregrounding, is something traditional narrative therapy cannot accomplish as its text is spoken language which is ephemeral. In poetry therapy, the client can visualise and experience the identification of unique outcomes in working with the poem. This increases both the client's participation and the conscious impact of the therapeutic session. The poem also serves as a reminder of the therapeutic progress whenever the client re-reads it outside the therapy session. The defamiliarisation that is achieved through the poem works towards a re-quickening of the client's general attitude towards life. Crawford situates the concept of defamiliarisation in a broader context which elucidates this connection. Talking about Shklovsky, Crawford states that "the theory of defamiliarization oppose[s] life to death, the vital to the fossilized, created fullness to eroded emptiness, a graphic image to effacement and the empty algebraic symbol, aesthetic perception to habitual recognition, the lively force and beauty of a word at its coining to worn stereotype and dead metaphor" (209). The necessity of first recognising and then reanimating "dead" metaphors in poetry therapy has already been noted (cf. Chapter 4); defamiliarisation is now constituted as simultaneously the means

---

[194] On 'defamiliarisation' and 'foregrounding', cf. especially Mukarovsky's "Standard Language and Poetic Language," and *Word and Verbal Art.* Cf. also Shklovsky's "The Resurrection of the Word" (1914). For the concepts of Russian Formalism in general, cf. Bann/Bowlt, *Russian Formalism. A Collection of Articles and Texts in Translation* as well as Tobin's *The Prague School and its Legacy in Linguistics, Literature, Semiotics, Folklore, and the Arts.*

of reanimation and the effect of the same. In the context of unique outcomes and the construction of alternative life-stories, defamiliarisation is the outcome of successful externalisation. Defamiliarisation does, in fact, not simply represent a displacement of aspects of the Symbolic: due to its unfamiliar nature, it arrests communication and thus is conducive of new meaning. Furthermore, it constitutes a return to, not a pre-Symbolic level of meaning (which would be an impossibility), but, for lack of a better expression, a proto-Symbolic stage of signification. Shklovsky's "theory, and its rhetoric, neatly invert a common-sense dichotomy, since for Shklovsky it is the aesthetically given referent of language which rhetorically is named as the 'real' object re-represented and perceived in all its fresh originality – instead of the object referred to by our practical, daily, or even scientific discourse" (Crawford 210). Defamiliarised aspects of language escape the automatisation of linguistic processes that is standard language and bring forth their "fresh originality," that is to say their original meaning. It is precisely this which is needed in poetry therapy, an escape from the normalising of the Symbolic and it is this which the externalisation of unique outcomes provides.

The subject only truly knows its structure in discontinuity, which is represented in textual *différance* of various manifestations in the subject's speech and writing. This means that although the client's fragmented nature can be made explicit in the poetic text and the constructions of identity can be changed via the augmented life story, essentially the client's claim to conscious authorship of the poem produced has to be denied on the grounds of discursive and Symbolic implications. It is necessary to postulate at least some authority in the receptive phase of poetry therapy in order to re-centre the client in a new sense of autonomy and self-actualisation. To be able to situate poetry therapy as a humanistic art therapy, some concept of 'author' is needed, a concept that can be maintained even in the face of the post-structural notions elaborated thus far. Therefore, the next chapter will deal with finding a way of harmonising these postmodern concepts with the traditional concept of the 'author' required by humanistic art therapy.

6. Re-negotiating Textual *Author*ity in Poetry Therapy: The Function of the Author, 'Writing', and the Palimpsest

> What else than a natural and mighty palimpsest is the human brain? Such a palimpsest is my brain; such a palimpsest, O reader! is yours. Everlasting layers of ideas, images, feelings, have fallen upon your brain softly as light. Each succession has seemed to bury all that went before. And yet in reality not one has been extinguished. (De Quincey, *Suspiria de Profundis* 144)

The previous chapters have shown in how far the idea of the individual and its self-determination – the control over one's actions and, especially, one's language – is ultimately more suggestive fiction than fact. From Freud's fundamental insight that 'we are not masters in our own house' and the imaginary nature of the Ego to the more radical notions of Derrida and Lacan that the 'I' exists only in language which is essentially always already caught in *différance*, the idea of an active, self-contained and independent being has been constantly undermined. With respect to the broader social dimension, the Foucauldian concept of discourse has disclosed the nature of identities as socio-cultural constructions and their reliance on reiterated narrative structures. The above concepts have emerged as relevant for a model of poetry therapy that has been (a) divided into two phases, a (mainly) creative first phase and a (mainly) receptive second, and (b) situated within contemporary post-structuralist (literary) theory. The division into two phases has partly veiled a problem that becomes obvious when poetry therapy is again thought of as a unified practice: the notions taken from post-structuralist literary and psychotherapeutic theory, which have been shown to be central for poetry therapy, stand in conflict with poetry therapy as based on principles of humanistic art therapy. The humanistic approach aims at re-centring the client by offering orientation, security and a firm footing in life via the discovery of new (absolute) truths about the client's life. Contrary to this, post-structuralism negates the idea of objectivity and absolute perspectives. While, in general, poetry therapy seeks to empower clients through the active reconstruction of life-stories around unique outcomes, both the first and the second phase, though tapping into the fundamental healing potential of the creative act, efface rather than strengthen the client's self. Poetry therapy within a humanistic art therapy approach thus calls for a maximum of self-actualisation and a strengthening of Ego functions, and at the same time theorises the self-contained Ego into non-existence.

Generally speaking, the strong, self-contained and creative Ego humanistic art therapy calls for can be likened to the figure of the author traditionally conceived. In this sense, it stands in direct contrast to semiotic and other reader-oriented approaches. The conflict between humanistic principles and post-structuralist notions in poetry therapy is thus tied to the client-as-author and it is here that it must and can be resolved. In dealing with this dilemma, I will, on the following pages, zoom in on the problem by briefly retracing the development in literary theory and criticism from an author-centred approach to what Barthes famously called 'The Death of the Author'. In a second step, the author will be 'resurrected' for poetry therapy via a critique of Barthes's principles and a closer delineation of the function of the author-figure in poetry and poetry therapy.

The traditional view of the author was one of God-like power over the work and, consequently, literary criticism, before the linguistic turn, was largely author-centred:

> With the author all differences and conflicts are neutralised; polysemia is cancelled. Like the God of Christianity, the author does not equivocate or beguile: man, as Milton and the Bible tell us, only fell from grace with the advent of ambiguity. The 'Author-God' of criticism is thus the univocal, absolute subject of his work: he who precedes, directs and exceeds the writing that bears his name. Correspondingly, then, the liberation of the text from its author is to reiterate the liberation of the world from God. (Burke 24)

Predominantly in the 19th century, knowledge about the author and the author's intentions used to provide guidance to textual criticism. The importance of the author in traditional criticism lies in its function of disambiguation. The empirical author and the author's life were called upon to illuminate the work, that is, to disambiguate the text. The aim of such a disambiguation was to generate and validate the one true interpretation of the text. It was assumed that the author wrote firmly within and in order to support the dominant values of 'high culture' in the society. Clearly, the author functioned as a transcendental signified that was able to ground the literary text firmly in dominant, ideological discourses, arrest the process of unlimited semiosis and allow for (seemingly) unambiguous readings to be established. Such a concept of the author is indeed reminiscent of the all-powerful nature of the Christian God.[195] In the same manner as the God of the Bible has inaugurated the law of nature and set limits to life

---

[195] Cf. Burke: "The author is to his text as God, the *auctor vitae,* is to his world: the unitary cause, source and master to whom the chain of textual effects must be traced, and in whom they find their genesis, meaning, goal and justification. The author thus becomes, in Derrida's words, the 'transcendental signified' and attains the supernal privilege of being at once the beginning and end of his text. [...] The text is read as natural theologians read nature for marks of design, signs of purpose. [...] *Post hoc, ergo propter hoc,* the old fallacy is enshrined as the universal law of literary causality" (23; emphasis original). From the point of view of Foucauldian discourse, the author function allows discursive formations to come into being and consequently participates in the consolidation of certain dominant discourses: "The author's name serves to characterize a certain mode of being of discourse. [...] The author's name manifests the appearance of a certain discursive set and indicates the status of this discourse within a society and a culture" (Foucault, "What Is an Author?" 107). Foucault differentiates between authors in this sense and "founders of discursivity [who] have established the endless possibility of discourse" (ibid. 114) such as Freud and Marx.

and existence, the author conceived of as a transcendental signified has created the rules and limits that govern the meaning of a literary work.[196] Barthes notes that

> [t]o assign an Author to a text is to impose a brake on it, to furnish it with a final signified, to close writing. This conception is quite suited to criticism, which then undertakes the important task of discovering the Author (or its hypostases: society, history, the psyche, freedom) beneath the work: once the Author is found, the text is "explained," the critic has won [...]. ("Death of the Author" 1132)

The liberation from the 'Author-God' has done away with what was felt to be the oppressiveness of dogmatic readings. While Barthes' argument for a reader-oriented textual approach is certainly valid and well founded, his analogy between God and the author, while persuasive,

> is askew in one very broad sense. The attributes of omnipotence, omnipresence, of being the first uncaused cause, purpose and end of the world are all affirmed a priori of the Christian God: they inhere in his definition, without them He is not God. Not so for the author though: we can, without contradiction, conceive of authors who do not issue 'single theological messages', who do not hold a univocal mastery over their texts. There are indeed even conceptions of authorship that are determinately anti-theological. (Burke 25)

Burke argues against Barthes' central thesis here, noting that the function and position of the author as delineated by Barthes is only one critical stance among many. Depending on the critical approach, the author can be constituted and function as oppressive and limiting, but this is in no way an essential and pervasive feature. There have always been interpretations that made do without recourse to the author, for example when the author is not known. Along the same lines, there have always been branches of literature that have primarily taken the reader and the reader's reactions into account. It is one central aspect of rhetoric, for instance, to set up textual strategies that have certain well-planned effects on the reader/listener which are removed from any involvement of a specific author-figure. This argument invalidates the centrality which Barthes attributes to the parallelism between the author and the Christian God; in fact, there is good reason to believe that Barthes' "Death of the Author" participates as much in the construction of the author-God as in its deconstruction. Still, while the importance and menace of the omnipotent author-God may be overemphasised, it is useful to follow the arguments leading to the author's 'death' before turning to the question of why there is not only no need for the death of the author, but why the author remains in many ways a necessary and essential aspect of dealing with texts.

As with the emancipation of the world from the Christian God, the introduction of ambiguity into the text at the expense of certainty brought in its wake fear, loss of direction and what modern information theory calls entropy; in short, that which is

---

[196] Cf. Foucault: "[The author] is a certain functional principle by which, in our culture, one limits, excludes, and chooses; in short, by which one impedes the free circulation, the free manipulation, and free composition, decomposition, and recomposition of fiction" ("What Is an Author?" 118).

commonly referred to as chaos.[197] With the anchor cut loose – the transcendental signified lost – the text becomes a boundless ocean and those approaching a text find themselves lost in a small boat adrift upon that ocean. With "The Death of the Author" a text thus becomes a structureless structure that is not intrinsically ordered, but has to be given form from an external, previously unrelated source, i.e. the reader. While this concept of textuality congenially integrates itself in the two phases of poetry therapy as delineated above (especially so with regard to the second phase in which new constructions of clients' life-stories can only function on the basis of such an understanding of textuality), it negates a humanistic approach. The total chaos that an unrestricted textual space represents might, in addition, heighten client anxieties and/or negatively affect other emotional states. At the same time, the introduction of a transcendental signified – the resurrection of the 'Author-God' – negates any semiotic text approach. In order now to make possible an integration of the two-phase model of poetry therapy into the conceptional framework of humanistic art therapy, the figure and function of the author in relation to poetic writing and its reception needs to be scrutinised more closely.

6.1 The Need for Resurrection:
The Death of the Author and Poetry Therapy

In the second decade of the 20th century, T.S. Eliot proclaimed his impersonal theory of poetry,[198] which can be read as the first step in the development towards a reader-oriented understanding of literature and the diminishing importance and eventual death of the author as a consequence thereof: Eliot's theory was influential in the emergence of the American New Criticism with its focus on the text as a unique and complete whole to be interpreted without reference to biographical or historical contexts. When the ideas of the New Criticism began to mingle with those of the Russian Formalists, which are based on a model of communication and influenced by Saussurean linguistics, the reader emerged as the site for the construction of the meaning of a text. This process was also later advanced by the growing awareness of the theories of Lacan, Derrida and Foucault in the English speaking world. At the beginning of this chain (which should not be confused with its origin) is Eliot, whose impersonal theory of poetry is directed against the Victorian poetics predominant at this time, poetics which

---

[197] Cf. Burke: "No longer reduced to a unilateral system of conformities with the 'world', no longer reduced to a 'single message', the text is opened to an unlimited variety of interpretations. It becomes, in short, *irresponsible*, a ceaseless braiding of differences in which any sense of 'the truth of the text', its original meaning in the world, is overrun by untrammelled significative possibilities. This is the message – indeed the single message – of 'The Death of the Author'" (43; emphasis original).

[198] For more detailed information on the philosophical background underlying Eliot's theory, cf. Mowbray Allan's *T.S. Eliot's Impersonal Theory of Poetry*.

he considered a continuation of Romanic poetics with its emphasis on individuality, lyricality and heightened emotions.[199] Such poetics seemed out of place in an age of science, mass production, mechanised warfare, Einstein and Heisenberg. In the context of Romantic poetics, Eliot comments that

> 'emotion recollected in tranquillity' is an inexact formula. For it is neither emotion, nor recollection, nor, without distortion of meaning, tranquillity. It is a concentration, and a new thing resulting from the concentration, of a very great number of experiences which to the practical and active person would not seem to be experiences at all; [...] These experiences are not "recollected," and they finally unite in an atmosphere which is "tranquil" only in that it is a passive attending upon the event. [...] Poetry is not a turning loose of emotion, but an escape from emotion; it is not the expression of personality, but an escape from personality. (*Tradition* 43)

Eliot's argument is clearly directed against what he considers to be a focus on the emotional in Romantic and Victorian poetry. One might see in Eliot's phrase "escape from personality" an idea akin to the externalisation in narrative psychology, but Eliot goes further, stating that the "progress of an artist is a continual self-sacrifice, a continual extinction of personality" (ibid. 40). The infusion of individuality into the poem is thus regarded as essentially undesirable by Eliot, who wants poems to be as impersonal as possible; poetry should be universal rather than individual. Eliot not only seeks to minimise the individual aspects in the final poem, but ascribes to the individual a seemingly passive part in the creation of poetry. He states that the role of the author during poetic creation is

> that of a catalyst. When [two gases] are mixed in the presence of a filament of platinum, they form sulphurous acid. The combination takes place only if the platinum is present; nevertheless the newly formed acid contains no trace of platinum, and the platinum itself is apparently unaffected; has remained inert, neutral, and unchanged. The mind of the poet is the shred of platinum. (ibid. 41)

Eliot's analogy of the creating mind as a catalyst implies that the process of creation does not affect the author at all, nor does it endow the finished poem with traces of the author's personality, unconscious or otherwise. As the acid in Eliot's example "contains no trace of platinum," so the poem contains no trace of the poet's individuality.[200] Eliot thus establishes a theory of poetry that implicitly negates the use of poetry in therapy. Eliot's poetics strives for objectivity and transfigures the poet into a prophet through whom the essence of the age is voiced. This view of poetry, which, as noted earlier, stands at the beginning of the development towards a reader-oriented textual approach, both negates the author as an individual and raises the poet to a position of

---

[199] Cf. Timothy Steele's *Missing Measures: Modern Poetry and the Revolt against Meter*, especially Chapters 1 and 5.

[200] I am well aware of the fact that Eliot is more subtle than this, saying that only the great artists and poets achieve the desired level of impersonality. This implies that lesser poets, or clients as amateur poets, inscribe their personalities into the poems. This is, however, of secondary importance for the present discussion.

messianic prophet. Eliot can accomplish this by splitting the traditional author-God into the human being who is responsible for the actual writing – the empirical author – and the agency which speaks through and in the poem: the poet-persona.[201] For Eliot, the author is only passively involved in the creation of the content of the poem. The literary tradition of the past and its relationship to the author's present are mediated by the author's mind without being affected by it. This process thus

> involves, in the first place, the historical sense, which we may call nearly indispensable to anyone who would continue to be a poet beyond his twenty-fifth year; and the historical sense involves a perception, not only of the pastness of the past, but of its presence; the historical sense compels a man to write not merely with his own generation in his bones, but with a feeling that the whole of the literature of Europe from Homer and within it the whole of the literature of his own country has a simultaneous existence and composes a simultaneous order. This historical sense, which is a sense of the timeless as well as of the temporal and of the timeless and of the temporal together, is what makes a writer traditional. And it is at the same time what makes a writer most acutely conscious of his place in time, of his own contemporaneity. (Eliot, *Tradition* 38)

The "historical sense" required cannot "be inherited, and [one] must obtain it by great labour" (ibid.). The fruits of that labour, the knowledge that has become lodged in the author's mind, is that part of the author which participates in the creation of the poem; this, however, is not the empirical author, or the author's psyche, but, for Eliot, the true and objective representation of the relationship between past (literary) tradition and contemporary culture. It is the poet-persona speaking, not the author. Based on Eliot, one can differentiate three entities involved in the creation and construction of a poem's meaning: (1) The author, who is the physical entity responsible for the black marks on the page. (2) The poet-persona, who shapes the meaning of the poem as it is scripted by the empirical author according to rules and influences beyond the latter's understanding and (conscious) participation. (3) There is the speaker of the poem, the lyrical I, which is an ephemeral entity that emerges via the construction of the reader.[202]

Eliot's poet-persona is vital for the current discussion, because it takes on a mediating function between the empirical author and the speaker as constructed by the reader. Particularly interesting from the point of view of poetry therapy is the fact that

---

[201] Cf. also Foucault: "It would be wrong to equate the author with the real writer as to equate him with the fictitious speaker; the author function is carried out and operates in the scission itself, in this division and this distance" ("What Is an Author?" 112).

[202] Interestingly, Foucault also separates the author into three (discursive) functions: firstly, "the 'I' refers to an individual without an equivalent who, in a determined place and time, completed a certain task; in the second, the 'I' indicates an instance and a level of demonstration which any individual could perform provided that he had access to the same system of symbols [...] We could also locate [...] a third self, one that speaks to tell the works meaning, the obstacles encountered, the results obtained, and the remaining problems; [...] the author function operates so as to effect the dispersion of these three simultaneous selves" ("What Is an Author?" 112-113).

Eliot's poet exhibits striking qualities of the unconscious. The poet-persona inhabits the "historical sense" and is characterised by "a sense of the timeless" as well as a "simultaneous existence," both fundamental features of the Freudian and Lacanian unconscious. These are also fundamental features of the Christian God. One can therefore argue that Eliot's poet-persona is the seat of Barthes' author-God and that this persona has, quite rightly, been demolished by modern literary criticism. Since the poet-persona is to a great extent displaced by partaking in the nature of the unconscious, it cannot serve as an anchor for textual meaning, cannot be elevated into transcendence, and it, too, cannot be posited as the locus of the client's Ego and identity. This fact does not, however, negate the client as a human being and a psychological entity when it comes to the poem produced in therapy. "The renunciation of the author-God does not do away with the idea of authorship nor impede the creativity of the author and the intensity of his engagement with and within his text" (Burke 49). The trinity of author-poet-speaker consists of interdependencies which can be nullified but never totally denied. For literary studies, for instance, the author and the poet are without relevance.[203] A semiotic understanding of texts presupposes a reader-oriented approach. Consequently, modern literary criticism and interpretation are based upon models of communication. An interpretation of a text is thus the actualisation of the ephemeral voice of one speaker from the theoretically unlimited possible speakers within the text. In this respect, it is irrelevant who wrote the text in question and also whether or not there was a particular intention implied. It is equally irrelevant whether or not the author's unconscious displaced intended meaning, or to which extent. The communication of messages between the text and the reader is important. This, indeed, is the death of the author. It can never be denied, though, that there is a physical entity, the empirical author, responsible for shaping the text and writing the letters on a sheet of paper, or on the computer screen. Equally, it is a truism that, in doing so, the person's unconscious – the poet-persona in the author – partakes in the creative process, co-shaping it to a significant extent and inscribing itself into the matrix of the text. The empirical author and the poet-persona can be methodologically denied importance and relevance, but it does not follow from this that these functions do not exist nor that they are not effective during the creation of a text.

The above shows that the client as a creative agency can remain a central node in poetry therapy despite the negation of the author by (post-structuralist) literary theory. In following Burke's argument from *The Death and Return of the Author*, it is possible to further illuminate how the author can be resurrected for poetry therapy. Burke states:

---

[203] Ultimately this boils down to the question of approach. Literary biographies, for example, even in the postmodern age, draw connections between the empirical author and the works in order to reciprocally illuminate the person and the text. Literary criticism has for the most part subscribed to the 'death of the author', but between these two extremes is a spectrum of textual approaches as diverse as there are critics.

> The death of the transcendental subject is consectaneous with the death of the subject of knowledge, is in turn consectaneous with the death of the author as a formal principle of textual meaning which is again consectaneous with the disappearance of the psychological signified. This chain of associations is the 'philosophical' grounding of the death of the author. What it states, at base, is that the denial of the *cogito* erases all forms of subjectivity and predicates thereof. (107; emphasis original)

The logical chain presented by Burke here is by now familiar. If there is no transcendental signified anchoring the meaning of a text, this text cannot contain some irrevocable truth. The knowledge contained in the text is displaced by *différance*. Since this is so, that which is found in the text cannot be safely related to the author which makes the author useless as a "formal principle of textual meaning." This, the argument runs, in turn forbids any psychological connections to be established between the text and the empirical being that is the author. This syllogism, as Burke notes, is the "'philosophical' grounding" of the death of the author. When it comes to poetry therapy, however, it is precisely the psychological connection between the author and the text which is essential. It has already been established above that within the methodological concepts established for poetry therapy, the phrase 'the death of the author' does not apply to the author as the physical, human being, but the poet-persona. If thus the "philosophical" 'death of the author' equals the 'death of the poet-persona' in poetry therapy, it is necessary to re-establish and reconfigure the connection between the empirical author and the poem thus to bring the author back to life for poetry therapy. The above chain thus holds true – with all its implications – only for the poet-persona (as a clearly discernable and analysable entity) within poetry therapy. This makes it possible to retain the psychological connection between empirical client and poem as a creative artefact.

Poetry therapy's *cogito*, the client's self or Ego, principally shares the majority of features with the philosophical *cogito*, the denial of which, Burke states, "erases all forms of subjectivity and predicates thereof" (107). Poetry therapy's *cogito* is imaginary in the sense that it is not real. It does not possess presence that can be objectively validated. It exists only in and through language and then only in *différance*. It is constructed from the outside (Lacan/Foucault) and susceptible to changing influences. In contrast to the context of philosophy, however, the *cogito* is not erased in poetry therapy, but its nature as a construction is made explicit. Every manifestation of the Ego in language is transitory – which is one reason why life-stories are constantly reiterated in order to give them existence and coherence – and inevitably displaced by Semiotic influences. The Semiotic is an outside influence from the point of view of the client's Ego, because it stems from the Real, ephemerally articulated in the instinctive *chora*, which is external to the Imaginary and the Symbolic. On a second level, every utterance in language participates in discourse and as all discourses are epistemically determined, so is the Ego. Thus, the client's self is articulated through language and meaning which is changeable, but which also exerts its influence on everything that emerges from the client. It is the last aspect which differentiates the *cogito* in poetry therapy from the *cogito* of philosophy as delineated above. Though neither objectively true, nor real, the client's *cogito* becomes manifest as a constructed identity to which the client as a human being refers all experiences and thoughts. In this way, the *cogito* indeed functions as a transcendental signified via the client's identity. It is therefore not the author who becomes a transcendental signified, but rather the author's psyche constructs an imaginary transcendental signified in constant negotiation with the environment. "To be conceived in transcendental terms the author must be emptied out of all psychological and biographical content: a personalised, psycho-biographically constituted transcendental subject is unthinkable" (Burke 107). Poetry therapy's author is not bereft of his or her psycho-biographical content; rather the opposite. The poet-persona, however, is psychologically empty as it represents a virtual entity inscribed into the text. In the discussion of Eliot's impersonal theory of poetry, the poet-persona emerged as the impersonal site of literary tradition working through the empirical author, taking up the latter's emotions and feelings – emotions and feelings that were regarded as common to all human beings, as part of the human condition – to transform these into poetry, but doing so at an instinctual, unconscious, pre-Symbolic and therefore genotextual level. The poet-persona shares many features with the unconscious and is therefore basically a Semiotic, *choric* entity that organises the poetic text genotextually. In this sense it is anterior to Symbolic language. The poet-persona thus lacks all "psychological and biographical content," because it precedes or always remains outside the Imaginary and therefore the Ego.

The empirical author remains, at least during the creative phase, a catalyst in Eliot's sense. The poet-persona acts through the author and inscribes itself into the text as Semiotic influxes and disruptions of the Symbolic structure of the poem. The transcendental function traditionally ascribed to the author takes the form of the poet-persona from which the client-as-reader constructs a speaker from within the entire realm of the therapeutic discourse with the poem at the centre. The poet-persona, however, is not a transcendental function that reintroduces absolute authorial control over the text. It is transcendental no longer strictly in the Kantian sense, but in the more original sense in that it is beyond the empirical author's control, that it exceeds the conscious apprehension of the empirical author. It becomes clear "that the denial of an absolute authorial centre implies not the necessary absence of the author, but a redistribution of authorial subjectivity within a textual *mise en scène* which it does not command entirely" (Burke 184; emphasis original). The "redistribution of authorial subjectivity" is the scattering of Semiotic traces in the client's poem. During creation, the poet-persona displaces the Symbolic structure of the text through the scattering of Semiotic traces. The poet-persona that is inscribed into the text, precisely by being inscribed into the text, becomes a separate, externalised entity which takes over the space of the text. This, in turn, disrupts the empirical author's control over the text and the text itself becomes ambiguous beyond the empirical author's power to disambiguate. It is then the role of the reader to construct meaning from the text. The poet-persona inscribed in the text facilitates and influences the construction of meaning via the creation of a speaker by the reader. The author-God of traditional criticism is "thus constituted [as] neither a locus of forces nor a psychobiographical site, but a metaphor for the text operating at the most consistent and plausible level of interpretation" (Burke 109). In poetry therapy, the power of the author-God is redistributed into the three entities of empirical author-poet-speaker.

To summarise: the post-structuralist concepts appropriated in the previous chapters make it difficult to retain the idea of a psychological entity – the client – for poetry therapy. If the post-structural concept of text negates the author, how can these notions be employed by poetry therapy to find traces of the author in the poetic text? By posing three different entities – the empirical author, the poet-persona and the speaker – it becomes possible to treat the text along post-structuralist lines, while retaining the notion of an empirical being whose unconscious is inscribed within the semiotic tissue of the poem. Effects of displacement and *différance* are thus taken into account and at the same time linked to the psyche of the client. On this basis, further notions can be developed.

In both phases of poetry therapy, the author is and remains the seat of psychobiographical knowledge, which includes the Ego-functions and the client's identity, both of which exert influence on the poem during the first phase. Also during this phase, the poet-function constitutes the agency of the unconscious, undermining the conscious s/Symbolic structure erected by the empirical author. In the second phase, the client-as-reader approaches the text with the aim of uncovering surplus meaning around unique outcomes. The client's identity and Ego are intimately involved in this process and in the course of it they experience a reconstruction. The unity of the trinity author-poet-speaker is fragmented and displaced into textual functions which in part equal the psychological functions of Ego, Id and Superego. In taking part in this fragmentation during the second phase of poetry therapy, clients notice their originally fragmented state and can partake in the liberation of parts of their psyche. The speaker of the poem, representing an externalised aspect of the client, is subjected to a reconstruction and eventually re-integrated into the client identity and life-story.[204] Within this conceptual framework, "the empirical author acquires an important function. Not so much to understand the text better, but certainly in order to understand the creative process. To understand the creative process is also to understand how certain textual solutions come into being by serendipity, or as the result of unconscious mechanisms" (Eco, *Interpretation and Overinterpretation* 84-85). The deepened insight into the creative process heightens the effectiveness of creativity in poetry therapy by putting the client-as-author firmly at the centre of the therapeutic process. Additionally, the

---

[204] At this point I find it necessary to stress once more – as I have done already in the introduction – that I do *not* expect clients to be familiar with any of the theories expounded in this study. Even the discovery of the client's fragmented nature need not necessarily be made explicit. It is, however, essential for the poetry therapist to understand the close connection between psychotherapeutic processes and poetic ones. Only when the therapist understands and is able to follow the negotiations between client and text can poetry therapy be practiced efficiently.

client as the empirical author can provide a subjective account of the intention of the poem in question. This subjectivity is explicitly desired in poetry therapy and does not stand in indissoluble contrast to the idea of a reader-oriented textual approach or a semiotic understanding of the text. Author and reader unite in the person of the client. The possible fallacies originating from this have been elaborated upon in detail in the previous chapters.

The conflation of author and reader has advantages for poetry therapy, the most pertinent being that this makes possible an easier delineation of what Eco calls the *intentio operis*. The *intentio operis* functions as the playing field of poetry therapy. It is in no small way shaped by the author's intention and a creative interpretation. Eco states that

> [o]ne could object that the only alternative to a radical reader-oriented theory of interpretation is the one extolled by those who say that the only valid interpretation aims at finding the original intention of the author. In some of my recent writings, I have suggested that between the intention of the author (very difficult to find out and frequently irrelevant for the interpretation of a text) and the interpretation of the interpreter who (to quote Richard Rorty) simply 'beats the text into a shape which will serve his purpose', there is a third possibility. There is the *intention of the text* [...] or *intentio operis* as opposed to – or interacting with – the *intentio auctoris* and the *intentio lectoris*. (Eco, *Interpretation and Overinterpretation* 25; emphasis original)

Since texts are subject to the Symbolic, they are bound to use and follow the linguistic and pragmatic rules of language. A text that negates these rules no longer communicates, it arrests communication indefinitely. Adherence to 'The Law of the Father' thus automatically produces a certain textual coherence – which can vary from text to text and, as noted before, is less dominant in poetry. The *intentio operis* emerges from within this context. It interacts with the *intentio auctoris* and the *intentio lectoris* in that it is dependent on both to become properly actualised. From the interaction of the author – *intentio auctoris* – and the *intentio lectoris*, the reader's interpretation, emerges the function of the *intensio operis*, the intention of the text. In fact, the poet-persona is the *intentio operis*. In this sense, the intention of the text is genotextual as it takes part in the production of the meaning of a text. While it displaces the Symbolic, it nonetheless co-constructs the text that emerges, co-creating the possibilities of meaning in the text. The *intentio operis*, for Eco, serves as a guard against overinterpretation. In the context of poetry therapy, the *intentio operis* makes sure that the interpretations remains within the realm of the client's life-story. As was noted in the last chapter, the client needs an altered life-story and not a completely new one. The *intentio operis* facilitates this. In poetry therapy, the *intentio operis* presents itself in the unity of geno- and phenotext. It co-constructs the first level of meaning that is encountered in the second phase. The *intentio operis* takes the shape of a normalised account of the client's problematic life-story that is creatively displaced. This is precisely what makes it a useful tool in therapy. It is the familiar textual space in which the defamiliarising effects of the Semiotic can be discovered and unique outcomes be pinpointed. The *intentio operis* thus facilitates the deconstructive approach of poetry therapy via speakers that challenge the obvious, apparent meaning of the poem. Since the respective speaker as a construction of the reader is an externalised part of the client, it facilitates a deconstruction of parts of the established life-story and the construction of new ones within the broader context of the problem-saturated narrative.

If we apply the above to the two-phase model of poetry therapy, it is possible to return to a humanistic view of the subject. Utilising figurative language within the poem to deconstruct its surface meaning and gain access to unconscious, subjugated knowledges is no longer a process of a 'writing subject' but a 're-authoring' with all the implications of the term. Clients are able to regain *author*-ity over the text by intentionally deconstructing it, decentring it consciously thereby accepting the nature of their existence as basically decentred, breaking for an instance the mirror of their own delusions, making apparent the conflicts that are caused through their imaginary identification.[205] This leads to a refashioning of the self and a process of readjustment to the conditions of reality is instigated. By reconstructing their own creations as critical readers, Kristeva's 'writing subjects' become authors again, successfully rising against the subjugation of language and discourse to regain a sense of control and power over their own life.[206] The client initiates a new motility of self-actualisation (which is in fact a further process of subjectivation) which consequently enables persons to cope with life through a positive and active attitude towards it. By introducing the trinity of author-poet-speaker, which unite in the person of the client, it is thus possible to retain a humanistic approach even in the face of a post-structuralist theoretical basis. The humanistic assumptions are not negated, but they are conceived of as constructions that are viable to change. Though mere constructions, they constitute truths and fixtures for the clients and work as such in the humanistic therapeutic context. Post-structurally, the humanistic assumptions are perceived as the mere construction they are and this makes it possible to undermine and change them.

6.2 The Extension of the Concept of 'Writing' in Poetry Therapy

The above remarks concerning the author, while conceptually essential for the two-phase model of poetry therapy proposed here, serve another important function, namely a preparatory one for the following discussion on the concept of writing.

---

[205] Again, I do not expect client's to be familiar with Lacan, Derrida or Kristeva. When I state that clients *intentionally* deconstruct a text, I am referring to the fact that the client is aware that s/he is re-structuring his/her life and that by thinking about the poems clients can come to a new and different understanding of their lived life and present situation.

[206] Of course, this sense of control and power is also only imaginary and a result from the change that is brought about in the client's perception of reality. This is secondary, however, to the self-actualisation that takes place and which is crucial to the client's healing process.

'Writing' as conceived in the context of poetry therapy naturally has to denote the empirical marks on the page that are produced by the client in writing the poems within the therapeutic setting. 'Writing' in a post-structuralist context, however, goes beyond the traditional concept of the term and may, as will become obvious in the course of this chapter, be taken as a metaphor for the entire enterprise of poetry therapy. To begin with, it has been noted throughout this study that poetry therapy (and other writing-based forms of therapy for that matter), possesses certain advantages when it comes to therapy precisely because they employ written language. The function of externalisation is probably the most prominent example to be mentioned here. Why 'writing' in the traditional sense has these properties becomes clear when 'writing' is understood in the context of, once again, Derrida's philosophy of language.

For Derrida 'writing' is much more fundamental than simply black markings on a surface. In order to get to grips with Derrida's refashioning of 'writing', it is first necessary to understand that he strives to reposition it within the history and tradition of Western philosophy, which he calls logocentrism:

> [L]ogocentrism designates thought centred upon the logos, whereby logos designates not only the word of God, science and logic, but the broad conceptual system of Western metaphysics: the thing in itself, essence, origin, pure consciousness, identity, presence, being as presence. Where Derrida's thought here goes beyond Heidegger is in asserting that the metaphysical determination of being as presence could only have been produced as the outcome of the repression of writing, and that logocentrism is therefore the prior condition of onto-theology, the latter being produced as an effect of the valorisation of the logos or fully self-present meaning. (Burke 119)

Derrida gives the name logocentrism to the entire history of metaphysics since Plato, because of the prevalence given to the spoken word.[207] The spoken word is presence, which, according to logocentric thinking, denotes living speech and consequently 'Being'. 'Writing' is absent speech and consequently signifies death. In other words,

> [l]ogocentrism [...] is the repression of writing in favour of speech, a repression that Derrida regards as the founding subterfuge of metaphysics. Writing, he contends, has always been perceived as dangerous because it betokens absence in the same way that speech betokens presence. In speech the speaker must be present to the interlocutor; in writing, the writer may be absent from the reader; speech is associated with the breath of life, writing with the waste of death, the corpse of words. (Ellmann 211)

---

[207] Although Derrida's concepts are well known in literary studies, one cannot expect the same from psychotherapy. Therefore, I will clarify some fundamentals here. Derrida has a number of different names for the history of metaphysics; logocentrism is only the most commonly known, which is why I will use it predominantly. With the history of metaphysics Derrida means to denote the fundamental principles that organise Western (philosophical) thinking. He also simply uses the term 'metaphysics' to denote this. Other terms prominently used by Derrida in this context are 'phallocentrism', which puts emphasis on the patriarchal element dominant in Western culture and, particularly significant for the privileging of speech over writing, the term 'phonocentrism' is used by Derrida specifically in the context of his critique of Saussure's work, a critique I will deal with in more detail shortly.

'Writing' is put in opposition to speech and since speech is privileged, writing is naturally denigrated as not only less perfect, but actually dangerous. 'Writing' is the Other of speech.[208] Since the philosophy of presence constitutes the dominant discourse within Western culture, 'writing' has been marginalised and denounced as dangerous.[209] The traditional argument is as follows: spoken language is a representation of mental processes, of ideas (in the Platonian sense) present in the speaker. Written symbols represent the words of spoken language and are therefore representations of representations. Consequently, writing is twice removed from pure, or ideal thought. Speech is therefore to be preferred to writing as a means of expression and discourse, because it is closer to the original *logos*.

Derrida directs his critique of the privileging of speech over writing towards structuralist thinking as the (then) prevalent expression of the opposition:

> Structuralism attempted to rescue language from the oblivion to which Western metaphysics had consigned it, but failed to pose the question of writing. For Jacques Derrida this omission was not just a simple oversight, but the last and latest reinforcement of a metaphysics of presence (as old as Plato) which had always and everywhere repressed the written sign and modelled language according to metaphors of self-presence and vocalisation. In order to uncover and contest this repressed, Derrida devoted himself [...]

---

[208] Derrida borrows from and continues (not without deconstructively reworking) one of Heidegger's central philosophical premises, namely that, in privileging 'presence', Western thinking has neglected to enquire into the condition of this privileging. One of Derrida's primary philosophical agendas is to do just this and deconstruction is for him first and foremost a tool to achieve this. Burke notes: "Derrida himself insists that his project is to be understood as a continuation of [Nietzsche's and Heidegger's] critiques, particularly so in the case of Heidegger whose rereading of the history of philosophy functions as a continually invoked pre-text for the Derridean deconstruction. Following upon Nietzsche's identification of all metaphysical systems with the theological question, Heidegger came to conceive of metaphysics as onto-theology, the determination of being as presence. From Parmenides and Plato onward, says Heidegger, being has been conceived as a simple unity, a fully self-present origin and ground. [...] Heidegger explicitly sought this prior (and ungrounding) ground of being in what he called the ontological difference, or the difference between being and beings. What the thought of being as presence neglects is that being in the abstract is not the same as the things-that-are, that existence is not one and the same as existents. Being is something toward which beings maintain a relationship, onto whose promise they open. The difference is both spatial and temporal. 'Spatial' because whilst we can say that beings are here and there, being itself is never anywhere, but beyond and transcendent of beings; 'temporal' because being is conceived as the timeless essence of beings whilst beings themselves are always subject to their season in that they can pass in and out of existence at any time" (117).

[209] It is certainly true that the philosophical discourse has lost is former prominence. Historically, however, the philosophical discourse was among the most influential and most widely disseminated, and the subjugation of writing as opposed to speech was able to proliferate into virtually every other form of discourse and become fundamental to Western thinking as such.

to show that every attempt to subordinate writing to the immediate expressiveness and full self-presence of speech was obliged to presuppose a prior system of graphicity entirely at odds with the declared intent. (Burke 116)

Simply put, Derrida proposes a system of writing that predates the emergence of speech as a "full self-presence."[210] In *Of Grammatology*, Derrida investigates and eventually deconstructs the traditional oppositional hierarchy of speech and writing, theorising that writing is not in fact a derivative of speech, but is to be given equal importance in the emergence of language. Derrida does so by first delineating the origins of the subjugation of writing and then deconstructing the oppositional hierarchy via close readings of various structuralist texts by Saussure, Lévi-Strauss and other texts from earlier periods by Freud and Rousseau. Derrida's investigation into the opposition between speech and writing is essential to poetry therapy, because it will shed light on the importance and function of writing in therapy and enhance the concept of writing to be further appropriated later. Writing/speech is in fact only one token of a chain of oppositions including such pairs as life/death, us/them, A/Z, 'I'/Other, Real/Symbolic, Ego/Id, conscious/unconscious, and so forth.[211] It is immediately obvious that these oppositions are central not only to Western culture, but naturally and particularly to psychotherapy and thus poetry therapy. Derrida's critique regarding the privileging of speech in Western philosophy can be applied to any of the above oppositions, which means that it touches upon and affects the central concerns of poetry therapy as conceived in this study. On the following pages, I will focus on Derrida's critique of Saussure's *Course in General Linguistics* for the obvious reasons that, first of all, it has the most relevance to poetry therapy and, secondly, because Saussure has already been dealt with (cf. Chapter 3).

---

[210] It has to be noted that this does not insinuate that writing is the more important manifestation of language. Derrida does not deconstruct the predominance of speech to put writing in its stead. Language is and develops from an interplay between writing and speech.

[211] Derrida wants the opposition between speech/writing to be not only one in a chain of oppositions fundamental to Western thinking, but, while not endowing it with a transcendental status, accords the speech/writing dichotomy with an originary significance. This is somewhat problematic for the philosopher, because "what Derrida, for all his labours, cannot establish is why the opposition speech/writing is anything more than one opposition among others why, that is, it should have inaugural and all-institutive status within the history of metaphysics. It is easy enough to follow Derrida in seeing that the speech/writing opposition is related to the opposition presence/absence which Heidegger regarded as constitutive of all metaphysical thought, but it is not clear why it should do so as the condition of the metaphysical condition rather than as an effect" (Burke 136). For poetry therapy, it is inconsequential whether or not the opposition speech/writing is or can be established to be in any way inaugural. The importance for poetry therapy lies in the concept of writing that emerges from Derrida's concern with the matter, and the fact that it is put into relation to oppositional pairs which, too, are at the core of poetry therapy.

Saussure's adherence and propagation of the primacy of speech is obvious virtually everywhere in the *Course*. Therefore, one example shall suffice here. Chapter VI of the "Introduction" of Saussure's *Course in General Linguistics* is entitled "Representation of a Language by Writing" and it is argued there that writing enjoys a certain prestige which it is not due precisely because it is merely a representation of language (in the sense of present speech) rather than the real thing:

> Language and writing are two distinct systems of signs; the second exits for the sole purpose of representing the first. The linguistic object is not both the written and the spoken forms of words; the spoken forms alone constitute the object. But the spoken word is so intimately bound to its written image that the latter manages to usurp the main role. People attach even more importance to the written image of a vocal sign than to the sign itself. A similar mistake would be in thinking that more can be learned about someone by looking at his photograph than by viewing him directly. (Saussure 23-24)

Saussure states unambiguously here that the spoken word is to be not only the preferred object of linguistics, but its sole object. The privileging is obvious.[212] In order to justify this, Saussure compares writing to photography, stating that people prefer the living face of a person that is viewed "directly," i.e. unmediated, to a photograph of the face. While this is certainly true, it does not follow from this that photographs are not usefully employed by people for the sake of recognising other people. What is more important for our present discussion, however, is that Saussure clearly separates writing from speech, constituting them as "distinct systems of signs." For Saussure, as we have noted numerous times, a sign is the unity of the signifier and the signified. It unites an outside with an insight. The signifier is the external representation (be that a letter of the alphabet, or a phonetic symbol or a sound wave) of an immaterial concept, the signified. Derrida notes of Saussure's concepts: "the word (*vox*) is already a unity of sense and sound, of concept and voice, or, to speak a more rigorously Saussurean language, of the signified and the signifier. [...] [Writing] must necessarily operate from already constituted units of signification, in the formation of which it has played no part" (*Of Grammatology* 31). Saussure thus regards writing as not only twice removed from the original thought, but also as essentially a form of representation alien to speech and, by implication, also to life, dynamics, and presence. It is from this assumption that Saussure derives a danger inherent in writing. Writing, Saussure argues, covers up the originary nature of speech, because "people pay more attention to visual impressions simply because they are sharper and more lasting than aural impressions; that is why they show a preference for the former. The graphic form manages to force itself upon them at the expense of sound" (Saussure 25). The danger of writing according to Saussure is that it dissimulates the truth about language, namely that speech and speech alone is the closest possible representation of thought, of the *logos*. Saussure is

---

[212] Saussure continues his argument by constructing a history of writing on the following pages of the chapter which strives to show the undue attention given to writing rather than to speech. Like Barthes with the author-God, Saussure has, to a certain extent, to first create the problem that he means to solve.

thus propagating a logocentric theory of language. Derrida summarises the attitude of the *Course* with regard to writing, stating:

> Writing, a mnemotechnic means, supplanting good memory, spontaneous memory, signifies forgetfulness. [...] Forgetfulness because it is a mediation and the departure of the logos from itself. Without writing, the latter would remain in itself. Writing is the dissimulation of the natural, primary, immediate presence of sense to the soul within the logos. Its violence befalls the soul as unconsciousness. (*Of Grammatology* 37)

It is from here that Derrida begins his deconstruction of Saussure's concept of writing. For our present purpose it is most important to note Derrida's further comment on the violence of language mentioned above: "Deconstructing this tradition will therefore not consist of reversing it, of making writing innocent. Rather of showing why the violence of writing does not *befall* an innocent language. There is an originary violence of writing because language is first, in a sense I shall gradually reveal, writing" (ibid.). Derrida's argument here clarifies just how well his deconstructive approach in general and the revised concept of writing which will be elucidated in the following fit with the model of poetry therapy proposed here. First of all, Derrida contends that his deconstruction will not reverse the phonocentric hierarchy. This is important as such a reversal would be hard to reconcile with the basic Freudian and Lacanian theories expounded so far. Language and the spoken word are primary tools for the psychotherapeutic endeavour. Rather than reversing the hierarchy, Derrida will show how language is in fact writing, but a concept of writing that is conceived not traditionally but has much in common with a semiotic understanding of language. Thus Saussure's separation of speech and writing is negated and language incorporates writing along with speech as essential constituents. Writing and speech no longer constitute two separate systems.[213] They are a natural part of language.

Derrida also notes that writing and consequently language is not innocent in the first place, a realisation that coincides with the concept of language elaborated in Chapter 5 within the context of Foucault. Along the same lines, Derrida neither denies that there is a "violence of language" nor that it does "befall" language. In this context, Derrida assumes that, for Saussure, the violence of language "befalls the soul as unconsciousness." Since Derrida reads Saussure as implying that the violence of language is writing, namely a violation or disruption of the direct connection of speech to *logos*, one can also read that "[writing] befalls the soul as unconsciousness." There is thus a connection drawn between writing and the unconscious. Since the unconscious is traditionally conceived of as diametrically opposed to the *logos*, Saussure denounces writing for subverting, interfering and disrupting the otherwise clear, straight path of speech, i.e. *logos*. The connection between writing and the disruption of *logos* that both Saussure and Derrida acknowledge accounts for the therapeutic effectiveness of writing-based therapies in general. Writing *is* the unconscious in that it does to *logos*

---

[213] Cf. Chapter 4 in which the commonly perceived dichotomy of prose and poetry is resolved by organizing them as part of one system of language.

what the Semiotic does to the Symbolic. By employing writing, writing-based therapies incorporate unconscious processes intimately into their approach in the first place which, naturally, help to make them effective as a therapy. One could (briefly) read this by means of Kristeva. The written text is constituted by the interplay of the pheno- and the genotext. The Semiotic acts through and is present in the text by means of the genotextual elements which constantly threaten to rupture the Symbolic surface of the text. This can be interpreted as the violence of writing, especially when this is connected to the unconscious as is the case in Saussure. I will not go further down this road as it will only lead us to another manifestation of the principal process of Semiotic influx that has already been exhaustively dealt with. It is sufficient at this point to realise the close proximity of these concepts. It is more helpful at this juncture to delve into the concept of writing delineated by Derrida as it will clarify the central function of writing for poetry therapy.

While Derrida is not entirely successful in proving the originary status of the speech/writing dichotomy, he is able to deconstruct the prevailing assumption that writing is a representation of speech and consequently secondary. Burke summarises Derrida's line of thought as follows:

> Metaphysics could not have begun to install the thought of presence at the origin without having always already repressed the primacy of the signifier over the signified, the primacy of the sign representing presence-in-its-absence over presence itself. [...] This recognition then prepares the way for the second phase of Derrida's attempt to pass through and beyond the Heideggerian deconstruction. If the forgetting of writing, the sign, or 'trace' as Derrida often calls it, is the precondition of the epoch of metaphysics [...] then the liberation of the signifier will unleash a pre-originary difference still more pristine than that between being and beings. Whilst it must be that all metaphysics rests upon the privileging of the *phonē* via the erasure of writing, then the breaching of all metaphysics will consist in propagation of writing as a difference which precedes ontological difference as the unthought of metaphysics; a writing which, as we know, is thought as *différance,* a differing and deferring (non)principle which produces not only the illusion of presence, but the very possibility of differentiation in the first place. (Burke 119; emphasis original)

In a first step, Derrida argues that in order for logocentrism to set up presence as originary and as, indeed, the *logos,* the "primacy of the signifier" needs to be repressed first. This, however, presupposes its existence thus making writing not secondary, but contemporaneous with speech. There is consequently no basis for setting up the hierarchy of speech over writing: both exist always already in a non-oppositional relationship. This is why writing "does not *befall* innocent language." It is part of language. Derrida notes that

> the violence by which writing would substitute itself for its own origin, for that which ought not only to have engendered it but to have been engendered from itself – such a reversal of power cannot be an accidental aberration. Usurpation necessarily refers us to a profound possibility of essence. This is without doubt inscribed within speech itself and [Saussure] should have questioned it, perhaps even started from it. (*Of Grammatology* 39-40)

Derrida argues here that Saussure blames writing for "substituting itself for its own origin," meaning that writing has become looked upon as more permanent and trustworthy than speech. Derrida now argues that if speech was truly the originary form of language, it implies that speech had been "engendered from itself." He is extremely wary of this argument because it implies a unique cause rather than a dynamic development, or process between writing, broadly conceived, and speech. Furthermore, Derrida comments that, given that writing indeed usurped the position of speech, this "reversal of power" cannot be (a) accidental and (b) without a fundamental necessity. Consequently, this reversal was from the very start "without doubt inscribed within speech." One has to carefully take note of Derrida's use of the word 'inscribe'. In saying that the function of writing is "*inscribed* within speech" (emphasis mine), he effectively lodges writing *within* speech, negating all separation between the two concepts. Writing is part of speech and both are not separate systems of language; rather they are two manifestations of language that always reciprocally engage each other and which cannot function properly without the other. This is an important insight for the practice of poetry therapy. Since writing is not ancillary to speech, but rather stands in a reciprocal relationship with speech when it come to constituting language as a whole, writing not only gains a more central importance generally, but poetry therapy as a writing-based therapy can no longer be seen as merely ancillary to methods of therapy based solely on speech. The poetic writing that happens in poetry therapy and that is taken up in the therapeutic discourse, contributes essentially to the meaning production within the therapeutic endeavour. If writing is indeed, as Derrida convincingly maintains, inextricably lodged within speech, the explicit employment of writing in therapy – and especially poetic writing with all its unique properties delineated in the previous chapters – increases therapeutic effectiveness by, among other things, increasing the participation of language.

When talking about the "primacy of the signifier," Derrida goes along with Lacan in situating the functioning of language and its importance for both the individual and culture in general not in the sign, but in the signifier and its continual *différance*. The signifier, being the material manifestation of the sign, is that part of language which interacts with the world, with beings and 'Being', and preconditions these concepts in the first place. Therefore, the "liberation of the signifier" will instigate a difference which is more "pristine" and precedes the "ontological difference" between speech and writing, it is the very condition of its existence. Derrida calls this a "pre-originary difference" which is reminiscent of the difference that exists in the *chora*, which is pre-thetic and yet the precondition of all later difference, predominantly of self/other and Semiotic/Symbolic. Concerning writing, Derrida states:

> Now we must think that writing is at the same time more exterior to speech, not being its "image" or "symbol," and more interior to speech, which is already in itself a writing. Even before it is linked to incision, engraving, drawing, or the letter, to a signifier referring in general to a signifier signified by it, the concept of the *graphie* [unit of a possible graphic system] implies the framework of the *instituted trace*, as the possibility common to all systems of signification. (*Of Grammatology* 46; emphasis original)

The graphic signifier that is found in writing constitutes an "instituted trace" implying that it has acquired a certain stability and common sanction comparable to the concept of the Symbolic in Lacan. It is, however, still subject, as was noted throughout this study, to *différance*. Graphic writing systems are thus only one manifestation of what Derrida terms "ache-writing" and which is, in the full sense of the word, inscribed in all aspects of language. Derrida elaborates:

> I would wish rather to suggest that the alleged derivativeness of writing, however real and massive, was possible only on one condition: that the "original," "natural," etc. language had never existed, never been intact and untouched by writing, that it had itself always been a writing. An arche-writing whose necessity and new concept I wish to indicate and outline here; and which I continue to call writing only because it essentially communicates with the vulgar concept of writing. (ibid.56)

Writing in the Derridean sense is thus the condition of *différance* which breaks up the established notions of logocentrism. The very word '*différance*' is a symbol for this function. As mentioned already, *différance* joins the differing and deferring aspects of language. There is no audible difference between the words *différance* and *difference*. It requires writing to distinguish the two words. Thus Derrida's coinage *différance* negates Saussure's contentions that (a) writing is an unnecessary, secondary addition to speech and (b) that speech and writing are two distinct systems of language. The spoken word in fact requires the function of writing to work properly.

In going beyond the traditional concept of writing, Derrida's notion of 'arche-writing' constitutes signification in general as a mode of writing. Lacan based the psychology of human beings on the functions of language, showing that the perception of ourselves and the world depends on difference. Derrida now argues that the psyche and through it the perception of our identity and the world as a whole, is based on *différance*.[214] Spivak summarises:

> Something that carries within itself the trace of a perennial alterity: the structure of the psyche, the structure of the sign. To this structure Derrida gives the name "writing." The sign cannot be taken as a homogeneous unit bridging an origin (referent) and an end (meaning), as "semiology," the study of signs, would have it. The sign must be studied "under erasure," always already inhabited by the trace of another sign which never appears as such. "Semiology" must give place to "grammatology." [...] "Writing," then, is the name of the structure always already inhabited by the trace. This is a broader concept than the empirical concept of writing, which denotes an intelligible system of notations on the material substance. This broadening, Derrida feels, is accomplished by

---

[214] 'Trace', '*différance*', and 'arche-writing' are used interchangeably by Derrida and all denote the same (non)concept. Cf. Spivak who notes: "Now there is a certain difference between what Heidegger puts under erasure and what Derrida does. 'Being' is the master-word that Heidegger crosses out. Derrida does not reject this. But his word is 'trace' (the French word carries strong implications of track, footprint, imprint), a word that cannot be a master-word, that presents itself as the mark of an anterior presence, origin, master. For 'trace' one can substitute 'arche-writing' ('arche-écriture') or 'différance'" (Translator's Preface to *Of Grammatology* XV; emphasis original).

Freud's use of the metaphor of writing to describe both the content and the machinery of the psyche. (Translator's Preface to *Of Grammatology* XXXIX)

Particularly important in the above quote is, of course, the reference to Freud and the psyche. The concept of writing[215] as refashioned by Derrida encompasses the entire sphere of human existence. Writing in the traditional sense is at the centre of poetry therapy, but, as becomes clear with Derrida, it pertains to the entire process. Essentially, this is why writing-based therapies work so well: they add to a process that is already essentially a writing – a retracing of the trace – another, an empirical, level of writing thereby potentiating the original process. Therapeutic approaches that creatively employ written language tap into the potential of writing in both Derrida's sense and the vulgar sense. Poetry therapy mines this potential particularly well due to the unique properties of poetry delineated in Chapters 4 and 5. The Derridean notion of writing is, first of all, intricately connected with the creative phase and the associated Lacanian concepts. In this context, Derrida's "trace of a perennial alterity" signifies the inevitable displacement of the subject and the subject's language through the Semiotic, the Semiotic being the dynamic motility of the Real, the other that ultimate knows no alterity. Since the second phase is mainly concerned with changing clients' attitudes towards life through a deconstruction of the text of the poem, the pertinence of the deconstructive approach is evident. However, writing in the Derridean sense is linked to Freudian concepts in a more general sense and thus gains even more importance. "*From now on, starting with the Traumdeutung (1900), the metaphor of writing will appropriate simultaneously the problems of the psychic apparatus in its structure and that of the psychic text in its fabric*" (Derrida, *Writing and Difference* 206; emphasis original). Freud's use of the metaphor of writing for the psychological apparatus and its function is taken by Derrida as a deliberation of the concept of 'archewriting'.[216] Dreams once again serve as the link between Freudian concepts and writing. Freud proposes that

---

[215] As the above quote suggests that "the sign must be studied 'under erasure'," so the term 'writing' has to be considered as being used 'under erasure' from now own. Thus, rather than differentiating between empirical writing and 'arche-writing', between traditional concepts of writing and *différance*, I will continue to use the term 'writing' to denote Derrida's "broader concept" which includes the "empirical concept of writing." The term 'under erasure' – originally coined by Heidegger – is attached to conceptual terms when they no longer sufficiently define their concept but remain necessary because these concepts simply cannot be thought of in other terms. Not to solve but make conscious this paradox, terms are put 'under erasure.' Spivak explains: "Since the word is inaccurate, it is crossed out. Since it is necessary, it remains legible" (Translator's Preface to *Of Grammatology* XIV). I will continue to use the notion of 'writing' under erasure without specifically marking it.

[216] For a detailed account, cf. Freud's "A Note Upon the 'Mystic Writing-Pad'" (1925) and Derrida "Freud and the Scene of Writing" in *Writing and Difference* (196-231). I will go into more detail later in this chapter.

> [i]f we reflect that the means of representation in dreams are principally visual images and not words, we shall see that it is even more appropriate to compare dreams with a system of writing than with a language. In fact the interpretation of dreams is completely analogous to the decipherment of ancient pictographic script such as Egyptian hieroglyphics. (Freud, "The Claims of Psycho-Analysis to Scientific Interest" 177)

Of course Freud is arguing firmly from within the framework of a logocentric point of view, suggesting that speech and writing are different systems of language. Derrida cites this passage (in *Writing and Difference*) to expound the fact that Freud already conceived of the functioning of the human psychological apparatus as a form of writing. At the heart of the connection of Derrida's 'arche-writing' and the Freudian metaphor of the psyche as writing is the unconscious. As was shown in Chapter 3, the unconscious – timeless and without structure – influences all parts of the psyche and of human thinking. It does so via the trace that a/effects conscious thought and conscious action. In this manner the unconscious inscribes itself into every action and thought. Since it thus 'inscribes' itself into thought, it is indeed a form of writing, a pre-originary difference that is not posterior to speech. Writing, in the narrow sense of empirical inscription of marks upon a surface, represents and exercises the pre-originary difference; one can state with Foucault that empirical writing gives the trace discursive materiality. In doing so, it creates a space in which functions of the unconscious – the trace – begin to play. Empirical writing is thus close to the unconscious, a characteristic that is emphasised by means of poetry's tendency towards episodic meaning. A further investigation into the 'trace' is necessary to gain a deeper understanding of the possibilities of poetry therapy.

According to Derrida, the trace negates origin. "The trace is not only the disappearance of origin – within the discourse that we sustain and according to the path that we follow it means that the origin did not even disappear, that it was never constituted except reciprocally by a non-origin, the trace, which thus becomes the origin of the origin" (Derrida, *Of Grammatology* 61). Although the trace is defined here as the "origin of the origin," this does not mean that the trace is originary in a chronological sense. Indeed, Derrida does specifically not introduce a diachronic element into his concept of the 'trace', or 'arche-writing'. To do so would inevitably privilege the anterior with respect to the posterior, thus reintroducing logocentric dichotomies. Derrida elaborates on this in the context of Freudian theories:

> No doubt life protects itself by repetition, trace, *différance* (deferral). But we must be wary of this formulation: there is no life present *at first*, which would *then* come to protect, postpone, or reserve life in *différance*. The latter constitutes the essence of life. Or rather: as *différance* is not an essence, as it is not anything, it *is not* life, if Being is determined as *ousia*, presence, essence/existence, substance or subject. Life must be thought of as trace before Being may be determined as presence [...]. [Freud] complies with a dual necessity: that of recognizing *différance* at the origin, and at the same time that of crossing out the concept of *primariness*. [...] To defer (*différer*) thus cannot mean to retard a present possibility, to postpone an act, to put off a perception already now possible. That possibility is possible only through a *différance* which must be conceived of in other terms than those of a calculus or mechanics of decision. [...] The

irreducibility of the "effect of deferral" – such, no doubt, is Freud's discovery. Freud exploits this discovery in its ultimate consequences, beyond the psychoanalysis of the individual, and he thought that the history of culture ought to confirm it. (*Writing and Difference* 203; emphasis original)

Similar to Lacan, who credits Freud for the discovery that 'the unconscious is structured like language' in the absence of any knowledge of Saussure, Derrida here credits Freud for nothing less that the discovery of the trace at the heart of everything human. The consequences of Freud's discovery go "beyond the psychoanalysis of the individual" and Derrida's aim is to chart and illuminate the implications arising from this. For the present context it is particularly important to note that the fundamental features in the theories of Lacan and Derrida – the structure of the unconscious as language and *différance*, trace, arche-writing, respectively – both meet in the Freudian discovery of psychoanalysis. Derrida basically describes the condition of unlimited semiosis, a never-ending chain of signification – signifier referring to and then being replaced by another signifier – which can also be found in Lacan. It is the Lacanian unconscious. Lacan attempts to arrest this process by the introduction of a transcendental signified (the Phallus) and the Symbolic as a regulating structure. In Derrida, there is no Phallus, no transcendental element to govern signification; there is also no origin, because the origin as such is also nothing but a trace leading to another trace, and without end.[217] This basically chaotic non-structure which is suggested by the concept of writing as an inscription of the trace and which, lacking a proper origin, is non-thetic and thus bereft of chronology, equals the nature of the unconscious as delineated by Lacan and Kristeva.[218] This parallel can be further elucidated by means of Freud, to whom Derrida returns frequently. Like in Lacan, Freud's dream theory is of particular importance for Derrida:

> It is here that the Freudian break occurs. Freud doubtless conceives of the dream as a displacement similar to an original form of writing which puts words on stage without

---

[217] Cf. also Burke on Derrida's negation of the concept of the transcendental in the activity of writing and reading: "Intention is to be recognised, and respected, but on condition that we accept that its structures will not be fully and ideally homogeneous with what is said or written, that it is not always and everywhere completely adequate to the communicative act. There will be times at which crevices appear in its hold, at which language resists, or wanders away from the speaker's determinate meaning. Consequently, though the domination of intention over the textual process is to be rigorously refused, intention is not thereby cancelled but rather lodged within a broader signifying process. Intention is within signification, and as a powerful and necessary agency, but it does not command this space in the manner of an organising *telos* or transcendental subjectivity" (140).

[218] In addition to this, the network that the trace inevitably constitutes might also be interpreted as an image of a neural network and thus be representative not only of contemporary psychoanalytical but also of neurological research. Likewise, the network of traces is only another way of denoting the network of Semiotic energy that can be apprehended from the poem's textual matrix.

becoming subservient to them; and he is thinking here, no doubt, of a model of writing irreducible to speech which would include, like hieroglyphics, pictographic, ideogrammatic, and phonetic elements. But he makes of psychical writing so originary a production that the writing we believe to be designated by the proper sense of the word – a script which is coded and visible "in the world" – would only be the metaphor of psychical writing. This writing, for example the kind we find in dreams which "follow old facilitations," a simple moment in a regression toward a "primary" writing, cannot be read in terms of any code. It works, no doubt, with a mass of elements which have been codified in the course of an individual and collective history. But in its operations, lexicon, and syntax a pure idiomatic residue is irreducible and is made to bear the burden of interpretation in the communication between unconsciousnesses. [...] The absence of an exhaustive and absolutely infallible code means that in psychic writing, which thus prefigures the meaning of writing in general, the difference between signifier and signified is never radical. Unconscious experience, prior to the dream which "follows old facilitations," does not borrow but produces it own signifiers; does not produce them in their materiality, of course, but produces their status-as-meaningful (*signifiance*). Henceforth, they are no longer, properly speaking, signifiers. (Derrida, *Writing and Difference* 209; emphasis original)

Derrida locates in the dream-work "an original form of writing." What Derrida describes is in fact nothing but a paraphrase of the Lacanian unconscious and the becoming manifest of the unconscious in a text according to Kristeva. Derrida argues that the processes underlying the dream-work cannot be read "in terms of any code." They thus remain anterior to meaning like Kristeva's *chora*. The dream-work is non-thetic while prefiguring, as the *chora* does, "the meaning of writing in general." Empirical writing is thus only "a metaphor of psychical writing." Writing as commonly understood is thus an instance of those ontological metaphors which are "so natural and so pervasive in our thought that they are usually taken as self-evident, direct descriptions of mental phenomena. The fact that they are metaphorical never occurs to most of us" (Lakoff/Johnson, *Metaphors We Live By* 28). Derrida insists that the processes of the dream-work cannot be read or defined by any code, and this accounts for the defamiliarisation that is perceptible around unique outcomes. Unique outcomes are Lacan's juncture points and they constitute the displacement caused by the effects of *différance*, of the trace. Unique outcomes are central to the re-authoring of client's life-stories which in turn requires a certain alienation from the original identity which is represented in and by the life-story. As our identity is constructed through the other, so must the new identity by means of the re-authored life-story. The 'trace' consequently has to be inhabited by the other in order to facilitate therapeutic change. Derrida, indeed,

> gives the name 'trace' to the part played by the radically other within the structure of difference that is the sign. [...] In spite of itself, Saussurean linguistics recognizes the structure of the sign as a trace-structure. And Freud's psychoanalysis, to some extent in

spite of itself, recognizes the structure of experience itself to be a trace, not a present-structure." (Translator's Preface to *Of Grammatology* XVII)[219]

The trace thus inscribes the radically, wholly other into meaning and this is why meaning is essentially unstable. The network of unique outcomes which is to be constructed from the client poem – via a network of figurative language – emerges from the context of the individual client's life-story and socio-cultural context. Meaning in poetry therapy, or any activity for that matter, cannot be constructed from itself. In essence, "no meaning can be determined out of context, but no context permits saturation. [...] When a text quotes and re-quotes, with or without quotation marks, when it is written on the brink, you start, or indeed have already started, to lose your footing. You lose sight of any line of demarcation between a text and what is outside it" (Derrida, "Living On" 67). Derrida remarks that context is necessary while at the same time contextual information can never "saturate" meaning, it can never lead to a final, ultimate and unchangeable truth.[220] Poetry therapy is a form of (re)writing that permits and includes

---

[219] Cf. also Miller who states: "For Derrida the other in question in a poem's benediction is entirely different, 'wholly other'. The consequences of accepting such a notion are not trivial. Something wholly other is frighteningly alien, unassimible. Nevertheless, Derrida argues that a poem comes from such a wholly other and speaks for it" (171).

[220] Cf. also Derrida's further comments: "If we are to approach a text, it must have an edge. The question of the text, as it has been elaborated and transformed in the last dozen or so years, has not merely 'touched' 'shore,' [...] all those boundaries that form the running border of what used to be called a text, of what we once thought this word could identify, i.e., the supposed end and beginning of a work, the unity of a corpus, the title, the margins, the signatures, the referential realm outside the frame, and so forth. What has happened, if it has happened, is a sort of overrun [*débordement*] that spoils all these boundaries and divisions and forces us to extend the accredited concept, the dominant notion of a 'text', of what I still call a 'text', for strategic reasons, in part – a 'text' that is henceforth no longer a finished corpus of writing, some content enclosed in a book or its margins, but a differential network, a fabric of traces referring endlessly to something other than itself, to other differential traces. Thus the text overruns all the limits assigned to it so far (not submerging or drowning them in an undifferentiated homogeneity, but rather making them more complex, dividing and multiplying strokes and lines) – all the limits, everything that was to be set up in opposition to writing (speech, life, the world, the real, history, and what not, every field of reference – to body or mind, conscious or unconscious, politics, economics, and so forth). Whatever the (demonstrated) necessity of such an overrun, such a *dé-bordement*, it still will have come as a shock, producing endless efforts to dam up, resist, rebuild the old partitions, to blame what could no longer be thought without confusion, to blame difference *as* wrongful confusion!" ("Living On" 69-70; emphasis original). The context-dependence of the text – the text that is the client in therapeutic discourse – is also recognised widely in humanistic art therapy. McNiff, for instance, states that "[n]othing creative exists in complete isolation. Artists, like Shamans, draw their medicine and inspiration from highly individuated relationships to familiars – themes, figures, methods, styles, and materials – that interact with the artist throughout the creative process" (*Art Heals* 84). Josef Garai contends that "[t]he art therapist must constantly check back with the client to see if she is attuned to that person's symbolic messages. The therapist must never

a number of contexts from which to draw in the elaboration of meaning. The discovery and application of the trace, the other, to the client's text – the poem and the text 'written' by the client during his participation in the therapeutic discourse as a whole – adds to this text, it is supplemented to the text – the life-story – of the client. Chapter 5 has made it clear that in poetry therapy a re-authoring of the client's life-story does not supplant one story with another. The existing life-story is refashioned according to the principles of humanistic art therapy. The concept of the supplement elucidates how this is to be understood within a post-structuralist framework. The supplement, Derrida remarks, "adds itself, it is a surplus" (*Of Grammatology* 144). If the supplement is a surplus, this suggests that it is something external to the thing it is added to. Indeed, Derrida argues that "the supplement is *exterior*, outside of the positivity to which is it super-added, alien to that which, in order to be replaced by it, must be other than it" (ibid. 145). The supplement is thus the other, it is the trace which, once discovered and appropriated, represents surplus meaning, adding new layers to the text. However, the "supplement supplements. It adds only to replace. It intervenes or insinuates itself *in-the-place-of*" (ibid.). This is the nature of the Semiotic influx within the matrix of the Symbolic of any text. The Semiotic, the other, the real, displaces common Symbolic structures, it "insinuates" additional meaning, an agency which "intervenes" by suggesting change, difference and surplus meaning.

It is this intervention the trace orchestrates which, in poetry therapy, is manifest in the re-authoring of the life-story. The supplement is thus both increase and substitution, both organic and external. It is an external revelation that is added to and welcomed into the client's life-story which is in turn refashioned while remaining firmly the client's. Also, "Derrida points out that the very presence of a supplement implies a deficiency within the origin to be alleviated. Thus the supplement resembles Lacanian desire in that both originate in lack, and both proliferate symbolic substitutes for a lost plentitude" (Ellmann 221). There is thus a need to re-author the client's life-story because it lacks that which is supplemented in poetry therapy.

The above shows that Derridean and Lacanian theories can be integrated into poetry therapy, especially into one based on humanistic principles, without introducing contradictions in any way.[221] If writing is as fundamental to language as Derrida

---

[221] jump to premature conclusions about their meaning, derived from the 'universal' symbolism of psychoanalytic or mythological theories. She must keep in mind the specific symbolic meaning of the message for this client at this particular stage of life, in the context of his or her life history and experience" ("Humanistic Art Therapy" 155).

Cf. also Ellmann: "Both theorists belong to the structuralist tradition and both make difference – specifically the differential nature of the linguistic sign – the cornerstone of their convictions. Lacan believes the self to be constituted in and by language, which differentiates the 'I' from the 'not I'. The new born infant has no self because it is oblivious to difference, adrift among sensations, appetites, phantasmagoria. Its accession to language entails a loss of this ineffable experience of being, giving rise to an insatiable desire for a complement to fill the lack within the self: insatiable because no object could alleviate the longing for undifferentiated being, for the 'oceanic feeling' that

proposes, if language indeed is writing, the nature of writing is also fundamental to both the unconscious and the Symbolic. Writing understood in this sense is able to bring about a unity of otherwise separate (or separately thought) forms and levels of language. The Derridean notion of writing thus facilitates a unification of the separate parts of poetry therapy:

> If writing is *inaugural* it is not because it creates, but because of a certain absolute freedom of speech, because of the freedom to bring forth the already-there as a sign of the freedom of the augur [...]. The revelatory power of true literary language as poetry is indeed the access to free speech [cf. Kristeva], speech unburdened of its signalizing functions by the word "Being" [...]. It is when that which is written is *deceased* as a sign-signal that it is born as language; for then it says what it is, thereby referring only to itself [cf. Jakobson], a sign without signification, a game or pure functioning, since it ceased to be *utilized* as natural, biological, or technical information, or as the transition from one existent to another, from a signifier to a signified. And, paradoxically, inscription alone – although it is far from always doing so – has the power of poetry, in other words has the power to arouse speech from its slumber as sign. By enregistering speech, inscription has as its essential objective, and indeed takes this fatal risk, the emancipation of meaning [cf. Foucault/2nd phase] – as concerns any actual field of perception – from the natural predicament in which everything refers to the disposition of a contingent situation. This is why writing will never be simple "voice-painting" (Voltaire). It creates meaning by enregistering it, by entrusting it to an engraving, a groove, a relief, to a surface whose essential characteristic is to be infinitely transmissible (Derrida, *Writing and Difference* 12; emphasis original)

Derrida contends that writing, or the trace, inaugurates "free speech." This is to say that writing frees language from the presence of the originator. Meaning is no longer bound to presence but it is "enregister[ed]" and "engrav[ed]" and thus "infinitely transmissible." This freedom is especially present in literary language and here particularly so in poetry. When Derrida constitutes that "revelatory power of true literary language as poetry is indeed the access to free speech," he comes close to Kristeva whose understanding of poetic language as intertextual indeed frees it from the control of any type of 'author' in the traditional sense. Referring back to Jakobson, Derrida bases the emancipation of language in poetry on the fact that it is self-referential thus forgoing any immediate, external reference. The lack of the latter constitutes the "fatal risk." Poetry, which is the inscription of the trace, "has the power to arouse speech from its slumber as sign." It possesses this power because it goes beyond the limits of the Symbolic and it is inscribed with the power to negotiate the boundaries and channels of Foucauldian discourse. By being self-referential, poetry frees the signifier from

---

> Freud attributed to speechless infancy. (Freud, 1930, pp. 64-65,72). Henceforth, all the subject's satisfactions will be incomplete, for desire is condemned to seek symbolic substitutes to fill in or figleaf over this fundamental lack of desire. [...] Put this way, Lacan's account of desire, – as the drive to fill the unfillable lack – prefigures Derrida's concept of the logic of the 'supplement' and even seems to steal the latter's thunder" (211. Ellmann's reference to Freud is to "Civilisation and its Discontents" in *Complete Psychological Works*).

its association with the sign, referring it back to itself rather than a signified. The self-referential function of poetry throws clients back upon their own beings and their own consciousnesses. Emerging from the interplay of the geno- and phenotext, the poem contains and thus refers back to Semiotic influxes and constitutes a space where Semiotic energy is circulated and can be reactivated (for example, by means of defrosting frozen metaphors). Poetry's "power to arouse speech from its slumber as sign" is not always active, of course; rather, it is one of the central aims of poetry therapy to excavate and reinvigorate this power in the process of therapy.

The trace links and unites the two phases of poetry therapy by linking and uniting the Semiotic and the Symbolic, by weaving together the fabric of the pheno- and the genotext, and by merging the individual with the cultural.[222] Poetry therapy thus becomes a form of writing, specifically of rewriting of the client's life-story. While the latter has already been established for poetry therapy in Chapter 5, it now becomes clear how *all* of poetry therapy is a rewriting and not only the process of empirically revising a poem. The latter is what provides poetry therapy's particular edge when compared to other writing-based therapies. Poetry, by being particularly susceptible to Semiotic influxes, emphasises and makes cognisant the 'trace' while at the same time both externalising it and temporarily arresting it. The network of 'traces' thus isolated in the client poem – traces which due to the nature of poetry are particularly charged with Semiotic energy – are then related to the more ephemeral network of traces drawn from the traditional therapeutic discourse. Poetry therapy thus brings together layers of traces, of writings, that all pertain to the client's life and which reciprocally supplement each other. The client is the medium where traces drawn from the poem, the therapeutic discourse and the life-story are re-inscribed. The above implies what semiotics as a field of study presupposes, namely "that we come to think of our social and cultural world as a series of sign systems, comparable with language. What we live among and relate to are not physical objects and events; they are objects and events with meaning" (Culler 25). Poetry therapy is thus at its heart a semiotic practice which strives to isolate, construct and determine meaning from a diverse number of sign systems such as dream images, body language, and, most predominantly, poetic language.

6.3 Poetry Therapy as Palimpsest

Derrida's deconstructions of logocentrism have brought to light the fundamental semiotic structure of the psychoanalytical endeavour to which poetry therapy, in contrast to the traditional *talking cure*, adds the layer of writing and, more specifically, the layer

---

[222] Cf. Culler, whose understanding of semiotics is close to the principles delineated above: "The general implication of this method, which has become a fundamental principle of structural and semiotic analysis, is that elements of a text do not have intrinsic meaning as autonomous entities but derive their significance from opposition which are in turn related to other oppositions in a process of theoretically infinite semiosis" (29).

of writing in verse which, as has already been established, partly nullifies the barriers between the Semiotic and Symbolic, the unconscious and conscious and further cultural barriers pertaining to dominant and subjugated discourses. It is because of this that poetry therapy needs to take its literary side seriously. Culler's definition of a literary work makes obvious how the theoretical concepts that have been shown to be central to a truly interdisciplinary poetry therapy meet in the poem. Literary texts, according to Culler,

> are to be considered not as autonomous entities, 'organic wholes,' but as intertextual constructs: sequences which have meaning in relation to other texts which they take up, cite, parody, refute, or generally transform. A text can be read only in relation to other texts [cf. Kristeva's theory of intertextuality], and it is made possible by the codes which animate the discursive space of a culture [cf. Foucault/Eco]. The work is the product not of a biographically defined individual, about whom information may be accumulated, but of writing itself [cf. Derrida]. To write a poem the author had to take on the character of the poet, and it is that semiotic function of poet or writer rather than the biographical function of author which is relevant to discussion of the text. Literary studies experienced what Barthes called 'the death of the author' but almost simultaneously it discovered the reader, for in an account of the semiotics of literature someone like the reader is needed to serve as centre [cf. Chapter 6.1]. (38)

Poetic texts thus constitute an empirical space that unites poetry therapy's diverse theoretical concerns. In other words, using poetry in therapy adds another layer to the semiotic process that is therapy, a layer that is in itself already a space of semiotic potential. Poems

> differ from everyday speech: they are not only more structured, but – through their overdetermination – they also reduce the predictability of the individual parts of speech. In everyday speech there is an increasing degree of redundance as the parts of speech become more and more predictable, but in literary speech the opposite is true. The reduction of predictability in overdetermined texts brings about a structure of different semantic levels which may be related to one another in a variety of ways. In this sense, the term "overdetermination" – originally taken from dream-psychology – may fairly be applied to literary texts, but there is one vital fact that must be borne in mind [...]. It follows that an "overdetermined text" causes the reader to engage in an active process of composition, because it is he who has to structure the meaning potential arising out of the multifarious connections between the semantic levels of the text. (Iser, *The Act of Reading* 48-49)

In the apprehension of their own texts, clients-as-readers make use of the overdetermined state of the poem with the help of the therapist and inscribe, in a reciprocal process, their lives into the poem and the poem into their lives. As human beings,

> we react to what we ourselves have produced, and it is this mode of reaction that, in fact, enables us to experience the text as an actual event. We do not grasp it like an empirical object; nor do we comprehend it like a predicative fact; it owes its presence in our minds to our own reactions, and it is these that make us animate the meaning of the text as a reality. (ibid. 129)

The poem is, due to its overdetermination, a vault of potential meaning that owes its actualisation to "its presence in our minds and to our own reactions."

It has been established that the *intentio operis* serves as a guard against overinterpretation, that is, against exploiting the overdetermination of a poetic text beyond its reasonable limits.[223] "Readers do not have the freedom to read as they will. Poetic signs form patterns that cannot be ignored" (Culler 94).[224] This works two ways, however, to limit the possibilities of interpretation, but also to facilitate the detection of unique outcomes:

> Reading a poem is a quest for unity, and unity is achieved or perceived only when the reader abandons the apparent referential or representational meaning of the discourse and grasps the unifying feature or factor that the various signs of the poem express indirectly. There are thus two stages of reading. In the initial or 'heuristic' reading, readers comprehend linguistic signs in a primarily referential fashion; they assume that the poem is the representation of an action or a statement about objects and situations. But they encounter difficulties, or, as Riffaterre calls them, 'ungrammaticalities': some signs give bizarre or contradictory results when interpreted referentially. [...] These difficulties give rise to a second, 'retroactive' or 'hermeneutic' reading in which the obstacles that arose when one tried to read mimetically become the keys to a new reading. (Culler 81)

The two stages of reading Culler proposes here can also be found in poetry therapy. The so-called 'heuristic' reading leads to the conscious intention of the client. It signifies what the client wishes to say in the poem. This reading does not yield any new information for use in therapy. The 'retroactive' or 'hermeneutic' reading constitutes poetry therapy's deconstruction of the first reading via the discourse of client and therapist with the poem as a third active party of communication. Riffaterre's "ungrammaticalities" constitute juncture points around which the therapeutic discourse will isolate unique outcomes. During the therapeutic session, the focus on "ungrammaticalities" leads to the construction of another set of significations:

> The ungrammaticalities spotted at the mimetic level are eventually integrated into another system. As the reader perceives what they have in common, he becomes aware that this common trait forms them into a paradigm, and that this paradigm alters the meaning of the poems, the new function of the ungrammaticalities changes their nature, and now they signify as components of a different network of relationships. This transfer of signs from one level of discourse to another, this metamorphosis of what was a

---

[223] In the extreme, an overinterpretation would lead to the construction of a completely independent speaker-persona in the poem; one that is not connected to the client's identity and life-story. A re-inscription of such a character into the life-story and identity could institute a case of schizophrenia.

[224] Culler also regards literature as a whole as a particularly potent semiotic realm, arguing that "[l]iterature is the most interesting case of semiosis [...]. In so far as literature turns back on itself and examines, parodies, or treats ironically its own signifying procedures, it becomes the most complex account of signification we posses" (35-36).

signifying complex at a lower level of the text into a signifying unit, now a member of a more developed system, at a higher level of the text, this functional shift is the proper domain of semiotics. Everything related to this integration of signs from the mimesis level into the higher level of significance is a manifestation of *semiosis*. (Riffaterre 4; emphasis original)

Riffaterre constitutes the discipline of semiotics as a study of the functional shift of signs from one system to another. He sets up a hierarchy here in that he considers the mimetic or heuristic level of signification – the system of signs, sign-functions and sign-relations that produces meaning at this level – as lower than "the more developed system" that emerges from the so-called retroactive meaning. The move from one level to the other entails, according to Riffaterre, a "functional shift" that changes the sign-relations and thus produces new meaning. In reinterpreting a text there is naturally a functional shift as there cannot be new meaning without the emerging of new or different relations between the signs involved. To introduce a hierarchy, however, constitutes a logocentric fallacy on the part of Riffaterre. There is no basis for privileging the meaning constituted in the retroactive reading. In fact, both meaning complexes constitute two layers of meaning that emerge from the same hoard of semiotic possibilities. Also, the second reading is inevitably coloured by the first reading. Likewise, the first reading does not simply disappear; it continues to exist, but is invested with and invests itself in the knowledge of the second possible reading. In poetry therapy, these interpretations of the poetic text are further connected to the texts of the client's life-story and those of the therapeutic discourse. Poetry therapy thus deals with texts that exist in a close intertextual relationship according to Kristeva's definition of the term: "Coined by Julia Kristeva, the term 'intertextuality' means that texts are tissues of quotation, shaped by the repetition and transformation of other textual structures" (Ellmann 215). In this sense, 'intertextuality' represents the amalgamation of knowledge that makes meaning possible. Relevant meaning does not emerge from the subject, but rather from the texts involved; "the notion of *intertextuality* replaces that of *intersubjectivity*, and poetic language is read as at least *double*" (Kristeva, "Word, Dialogue, and Novel" 66; emphasis original). In poetry therapy, the poetic text is indeed read *double* as has been noted. It only acquires its relevant meaning, however, when the intertextual connections to the other texts pertaining to the therapeutic process are made obvious. Kristeva's concept of intertextuality, as broadly conceived as it may be, charges Derrida's trace with meaning. Derrida only establishes the trace as always already there, as permeating all modes of signification, installing difference everywhere. Kristeva's concept of intertextuality suggests how meaning emerges from the inscription of the trace.[225] Meaning is born from the intertextual connections which knit *different* texts into a meaning making complex.

---

[225] Cf. also Culler's remarks on this concept of intertextuality which underscores the similarity between the notion and Derrida's trace as well as its cultural permeation: "Discursive conventions can only originate in discourse; everything in *la langue*, as Saussure says, must have first been in *parole*. But *parole* is made possible by *la langue*, and if

When looking at poetry therapy as a whole with its appropriation of various semiotic systems, different kinds of writing, verbal and written texts, the concept of 'intertextuality' appears as the logical means to bind them all together. There is, however, a setback in conceiving of poetry therapy as an intertextual practice. The concept of intertextuality – as the name clearly suggests – supposes separate textual spaces that form an intertextual matrix. This matrix connects these spaces by reciprocal quotations, pastiche, parody, commentary and so forth. In spite of this connecting function of intertextuality, there is inherent in the concept a basic tendency towards separation and schism. This study seeks an integrated concept of poetry therapy in which the two disciplines of poetry and psychotherapy share in its practice in a truly interdisciplinary fashion, and where the therapeutic process is conceptualised, conducted and perceived as a unified whole. To try and unify poetry therapy solely on the basis of intertextuality poses dangers and may easily lead to unwanted separations or privileging of the individual intertexts present. This can be avoided by conceiving of the relationship of the texts of poetry therapy not merely as intertextual, but as palimpsestuous. "There is [...] a productive relationship between the concept of the palimpsest and the concept of intertextuality as coined by Julia Kristeva and as it functions in poststructuralist theory" (Dillon 85):

> I would argue that another, more productive analogy is that of the palimpsest, according to which the geno-text corresponds to the infinite possibilities of palimpsestuous textuality, the pheno-text to the 'singular' text which is marked by and cut through by those possibilities, and which bears the trace of the virtual entities that it *could have been*. The plurality of the geno-text, of palimpsestuous textuality, constantly operates in, disrupts, and yet engenders the meaning of any text – this is the specificity of the text, of writing, as opposed to the work or the book. (ibid. 87; emphasis original)[226]

> one attempts to identify any utterance or text as a moment of origin one finds that they depend upon prior codes. [...] 'Intertextuality' thus has a double focus. On the one hand, it calls our attention to the importance of prior texts, insisting that the autonomy of texts is a misleading notion and that a work has the meaning it does only because certain things have previously been written. Yet in so far as it focuses on intelligibility, on meaning, 'intertextuality' leads us to consider prior texts as contributions to a code which makes possible the various effects of signification. Intertextuality thus becomes less a name for a work's relation to particular prior texts than a designation of its participation in the discursive space of a culture: the relationship between a text and the various languages or signifying practices of a culture and its relation to those texts which articulate for it the possibilities of that culture" (103; emphasis original).

[226] It is unclear whether Dillon consciously refashions the concept of the phenotext to represent the "singular" empirical text, or if this is a misunderstanding of the concept of the phenotext on her part. In any case, her concept of geno- and phenotext as different textual realms essentially goes against her later argument, namely that in palimpsestuous textuality there is no originary text, but only overlappings of texts the dynamics of which create potential for meaning. The definition of the phenotext used so far in this study is therefore much more pertinent for the palimpsest and I will continue to refer to the phenotext in his manner, as a textual function rather than the "singular" text.

By employing the metaphor of the palimpsest here, Dillon refashions the concept of intertextuality and takes into account the Semiotic nature of the genotext. The concept of the genotext as a field of s/Semiotic potentiality embodies congenially the notion of "palimpsestuous textuality." This textuality "constantly operates in, disrupts, and yet engenders" other texts – texts which need not necessarily have any close relationship to each other – transferring its palimpsestuous nature onto these associated texts. Rather than being merely intertextual, poetry therapy reveals itself as a palimpsestuous process from which new texts and meanings can be "engendered." In accordance with the post-structuralist approach to poetry therapy delineated in this study, the concept of the palimpsest is to be preferred to that of Kristeva's intertextuality. "[T]he palimpsest presents us with another global concept of this experience [of intertextuality], a more appropriate one than intertextuality since, while retaining the emphasis on the textual, it distances itself – by the very interrelatedness of the texts that constitute it – from the confusion with source study" (Dillon 85). By conceiving of the inevitable intertextuality in terms of the palimpsest, the logocentric implications are minimised. Palimpsestuous intertextuality is non-thetic as well as bereft of temporality. This precludes the setting up of hierarchies and the negation of temporality evinces the nature of the unconscious. Before going into any more detail, a brief definition of the term 'palimpsest' will pave the way.

The OED has the following relevant entries for 'palimpsest':

1. Paper, parchment, or other writing material designed to be reusable after any writing on it has been erased. *Obs.*
2. A parchment or other writing surface on which the original text has been effaced or partially erased, and then overwritten by another; a manuscript in which later writing has been superimposed on earlier (effaced) writing.

Palimpsests have been preserved from antiquity and the Middle Ages where parchment and paper were in short supply. The shortage of material to write upon prompted writers to scrape off the original text in order to use the parchment or paper again. Sometimes commentaries were added to the older text, or the older texts were preserved alongside a new text written on the margins of the parchment.[227] A palimpsest can thus be defined as an empirical textual space which is home to two or more textual entities which co-habit that space.

The study of palimpsests as archaeological objects is, like poetry therapy, necessarily interdisciplinary, requiring experts in ancient languages, parchment production, chemistry and physics (to make the erased text reappear by means of chemical substances or technology). Palimpsests

> embody and provoke interdisciplinary encounter, both literally [...] and figuratively. The palimpsest cannot be the province of any one discipline, since it admits all those terrains that write upon it to its body; nor, indeed, does the palimpsest have a province

---

[227] For a summary history of palimpsests, cf. Dillon, *Palimpsest: Literature, Criticism.* Chapter 2.

of its own, since it is anything other than that which offers itself at first sight, the literal meaning of province. (Dillon 2)

The essential interdisciplinary nature of palimpsests can be extended into a concept that is capable of embodying at the same time the inter(textual)relations between the disciplines and theories pertaining to poetry therapy and their distinctiveness. Dillon locates the origin of the use of the palimpsest as a concept, as a figure or metaphor, in Thomas De Quincey's 1845 essay on "The Palimpsest;" she states that "[c]oupling 'palimpsest' with the definite article 'the' (for the first time in a non-specific sense), De Quincey's essay *inaugurated* [...] the substantive concept of the palimpsest" (1; emphasis original). Since this inauguration of the concept, "the figure of the palimpsest is invariably found in areas of research which insist upon the interdisciplinary nature of their work" (ibid.). The palimpsest lends itself as a conceptual metaphor according to which poetry therapy can be thought in post-structural and yet integrative terms. "[T]he palimpsest [is] a figure for interdisciplinarity – for the productive violence of the involvement, entanglement, interruption and inhabitation of disciplines in and on each other" (ibid. 2).

The metaphor of the palimpsest can also be found in psychology and psychoanalysis. To begin with, the palimpsest conceptualises the timelessness of the unconscious in its textual space. Dillon contends that

> [t]he 'present' of the palimpsest is only constituted in and by the 'presence' of texts from the 'past', as well as remaining open to further inscription by texts of the 'future'. The presence of texts from the past, present (and possibly future) in the palimpsest does not elide temporality but evidences the spectrality of any 'present' moment which always already contains within it 'past', 'present', and 'future' moments. (37)

The palimpsest is the simultaneous presence of all the texts that inhabit it as well as all the texts that will be inscribed upon it in the future. The spatial cohabitation of texts compels interrelations to be formed, interrelations that give rise to new texts emerging from them. All these texts within the space of the palimpsest are always already inhabited by the trace and thus defy temporality. In this respect, the palimpsest indeed "elide[s] temporality" precisely because of its spectral nature as trace. Like the unconscious, the palimpsest is thus essentially timeless and, if not wholly un-thetic, fundamentally contingent and unstructured. There is no limit and no structure in the way new texts or new meanings can emerge from the overlappings, displacements and condensations between the inhabiting texts. It thus mirrors the condition of dreaming and facilitates a function similar to the dream-work. De Quincey was the first to draw a parallel between the nature of the palimpsest and the human psyche. Friedmann argues that "like a palimpsest, both psyche and literary text are layered, with repressed elements erupting in disguised form onto the manifest surface of consciousness, of a text" (239). A palimpsestuous relation between the psyche and a literary text consequently establishes "an unconscious accessible to interpretation through a decoding of its linguistic traces and effects" (ibid. 369). The link between the palimpsest as an essentially literary concept and the psyche lies in the "decoding of [their] linguistic traces and effects." The obvious parallelisms to the concept of poetry therapy elaborated in the previous chapters need not be further discussed at this juncture. Suffice it to say here that Lacan, Foucault, Derrida, and Freud are all encompassed by the palimpsest of poetry therapy. As to the nature of the palimpsest, Dillon contends that "just as the underlying layers of palimpsests are susceptible to resurrection by the atmosphere and chemical or digital reagents, the layers of the palimpsest of the mind are ever-ready for revival and resurrection [...]" (28). Dillon paraphrases De Quincey here, but she might also have paraphrased Freud. In "A Note upon 'The Mystic Writing Pad'" Freud compares the psychic apparatus to the "Mystic Writing Pad," a children's toy which

> is a slab of dark brown resin or wax with a paper edging; over the slab is laid a thin transparent sheet, the top end of which is firmly secured to the slab while its bottom end rests on it without being fixed to it. [...] To make use of the Mystic Pad, one writes upon the celluloid portion of the covering-sheet which rests on the wax slab. For this purpose no pencil or chalk is necessary, since the writing does not depend on material being deposited on the receptive surface. [...] If we lift the entire covering-sheet – both the celluloid and the waxed paper – off the wax slab, the writing vanishes and, as I have already remarked, does not re-appear again. The surface of the Mystic Pad is clear of writing and once more capable of receiving impressions. But it is easy to discover that the permanent trace of what was written is retained upon the wax slab itself and is legible in suitable lights. Thus the Pad provides not only a receptive surface that can be used over and over again, like a slate, but also permanent traces of what has been written, like an ordinary paper pad: it solves the problem of combining the two functions *by dividing them between two separate but interrelated component parts or systems*. But this is precisely the way in which, according to the hypothesis which I mentioned just now, our mental apparatus performs its perceptual function. ("A Note upon 'The Mystic Writing Pad'" 228-230; emphasis original)

Essentially, the 'Writing Pad' is a surface upon which one can write again and again. By applying pressure to the surface, marks – words – are inscribed into the surface. These marks can be erased again by lifting off the covering sheet. However, the "permanent trace of what was written" remains imprinted upon the lower wax surface. For Derrida, Freud's use of the 'Writing Pad' as a metaphor for the psychic apparatus, signifies arche-writing or the trace. Similarly to Lacan, who believes Freud to have discovered the nature of the unconscious as language – and thus the nature of language as such – parallel to Saussure, Derrida sees in Freud a precursor of his own concept of the trace.[228] Derrida states that in Freud "[p]sychical *content* will be *represented* by a text whose essence is irreducibly graphic. The *structure* of the psychical *apparatus* will be *represented* by a writing machine" (*Writing and Difference* 199; emphasis original). Psychic processes are thus a form of writing, a network of traces. This network of traces can in turn be conceptualised as the palimpsest (of the mind). The 'Writing Pad'

---

[228] Cf. *Writing and Difference*: "The irreducibility of the 'effect of deferral' – such, no doubt, is Freud's discovery. Freud exploits this discovery in its ultimate consequences, beyond the psychoanalysis of the individual, and he thought that the history of culture ought to confirm it" (203).

constitutes a palimpsest: it is a textual space in which different and possibly unrelated texts meet – texts are erased and replaced, others are superimposed upon previous texts.[229] The 'Writing Pad', being a metaphor for psychic processes, is thus itself a metaphor for the palimpsest. The palimpsest is therefore to be found at the heart also of Freudian psychoanalytic writing.

When Dillon draws the insight from De Quincey that "just as the underlying layers of palimpsests are susceptible to resurrection by the atmosphere and chemical or digital reagents, the layers of the palimpsest of the mind are ever-ready for revival and resurrection" (28) there is, in addition to the above mentioned parallel to Freud's 'Writing Pad', an implicit relation to what has been introduced as 'frozen metaphors'. As was noted before, frozen metaphors are once lively metaphors that have been familiarised to such an extent that they no longer appear as metaphors. In short, they have become regular aspects of the Symbolic and lost their Semiotic motility. Another type of frozen metaphors is a metaphor that lies (Semiotically) dormant in a client poem until actualised in the context of poetry therapy. Frozen metaphors represent another underlying layer of poetry therapy's palimpsestuous text. They point at and/or signify buried juncture points which have been repressed and can be excavated for use in therapy.

> This so-called 'underlying' layer of the palimpsest is, in fact, like the crypt: [...] The palimpsest does not conform structurally to a psychoanalysis of surface and depth, latent and manifest. The palimpsest of the mind is not structurally akin to Freud's first stratified topography of the unconscious, preconscious and conscious systems. Rather, the palimpsest presents a complex structure of cryptic incorporation. [...] [T]he palimpsest of the mind has more in common figuratively with Freud's second topography, in which the mind is haunted by the ghostly figures of the Id, the Ego and Superego. (Dillon 29)

---

[229] While the palimpsestuous structure of the 'Writing Pad' is not explicitly mentioned by Freud, he does invoke the 'palimpsest' as, interestingly, a metaphor for the dream-work. In a footnote added in 1909 to *The Interpretation of Dreams* he states "[i]t is hard to credit the obstinacy with which readers and critics of this book shut their eyes to this consideration and overlook the fundamental distinction between the manifest and latent content of dreams. On the other hand, nothing in the literature of the subject comes so near to my hypothesis as a passage in James Sully's essay 'The Dream as a Revelation' (1893, 364). The fact that I am only now quoting it for the first time is no sign of disparagement: 'It would seem then, after all, that dreams are not the utter nonsense they have been said to be by such authorities as Chaucer, Shakespeare and Milton. The chaotic aggregations of our night-fancy have a significance and communicate new knowledge. Like some letter in cypher, the dream-inscription when scrutinized closely loses its first look of balderdash and takes on the aspect of a serious, intelligible message. Or, to vary the figure slightly, we may say that, like some *palimpsest*, the dream discloses beneath its worthless surface-characters traces of an old and precious communication'" (*Complete Works,* Vol. IV 135; my emphasis). On this subject matter, cf. also Dillon 135, the note number 7 for Chapter 2.

Dillon states that the metaphor of the palimpsest is closer to Freud's "second topology" of the psyche.[230] Indeed, the palimpsest cannot be akin to Freud's first topology because this topology still follows a certain sequential organisation which cannot be made to agree with either the second topology or the post-structural concept of the palimpsest. What is more important for the present discussion is Dillon's introduction of the concept of the crypt for the underlying layers of the palimpsest. As we noted above, frozen metaphors constitute one such layer which contains important material in the context of poetry therapy. In this sense, frozen metaphors in texts represent what Abraham and Torok have termed 'the crypt'.[231] These authors designate as 'the crypt' the psychic mechanism which encapsulates repressed thoughts or memories. The 'crypt' is created by the process called 'incorporation' which stands in opposition to the psychic function of 'introjection':

> The authors distinguish between two modes of psychic internalization, 'introjection' and 'incorporation', the first of which augments the ego while the second splits it apart. Introjection is the means by which the ego is enlarged through the extension of its primal auto-erotic instincts into object-love. Introjection does not simply take the object in, but overcomes the repression of the drives awakened by the object and reabsorbs them into an expanded ego. This labour is accomplished by means of language, which always bears the stigma of the lack from which it stems, for the infant resorts to words only when the things it wants are unavailable. The empty mouth, deprived of food, fills up with words. Incorporation, on the other hand, occurs when 'words fail to fill the subjects void and hence an imaginary thing is inserted into the mouth in their place. (Abraham and Torok, 1994, 111-115, 127-9). [...] Destructive though it ultimately is, incorporation appeals to the ego as an easier alternative to introjection. [...] Incorporation creates a 'crypt' within the ego in which the object and the passions it aroused are held in quarantine. (Ellmann 230-231. Ellmann's reference to Abraham and Torok is to "*Mourning or Melancholia:* Introjection *versus* Incorporation" in *The Shell and the Kernel*[232])

Introjection is a slow and costly process for the Ego, but in the end introjection overcomes and transmutes repression into acceptance by enlarging the Ego through the acceptance of the repressed. In essence, therefore, it is a process of introjection which poetry therapy ultimately seeks to induce: the reauthoring of life-stories through the integration – the introjection – of unique outcomes. Incorporation represents an easier

---

[230] This is the psychic model used throughout in this thesis, consisting of the conscious and unconscious systems which are inhabited by the three functions of the Id, the Ego and the Superego. Freud used this second model until the end of his life. It can therefore be safely assumed that it constitutes the final outcome of his theorising.

[231] For a detailed account of the concept of the 'crypt' and its application in psychotherapy, cf. Abraham/Torok's "*Mourning or Melancholia:* Introjection *versus* Incorporation," *The Shell and the Kernel*, and *The Wolf Man's Magic Word: A Cryptonymy*. The latter work also contains a foreword by Derrida, "Fors: The Anglish Words of Nicholas Abraham and Maria Torok" (xi-xlviii), in which he deals critically with the concepts around the 'crypt'.

[232] The essay also appeared under the title "Introjection-Incorporation: *Mourning* or *Melancholia*" in Lebovici and Widlöcher.

alternative for the Ego since it constitutes a simple quarantining of the psychic object within the 'crypt'. The content of the 'crypt' is inaccessible and thus repressed. In contrast to the classical Freudian understanding of the repressed, however, the content of the 'crypt' is not unconscious. It is imprisoned as part of the Ego itself which causes a split in the Ego. Part of the Ego is under lock and key, but the Ego is well aware of this and, constantly seeking access to the 'encrypted' object, the Ego is continually weakened and unbalanced.[233]

The interesting aspect of the theory of the crypt for poetry therapy – the one that will lead back to the concept of the palimpsest – is that the process of incorporation is characterised by a loss of figurative language. Abraham and Torok state:

> Crypts are constructed only when the shameful secret is the love object's doing and when that object also functions for the subject as an ego ideal. It is therefore the *object's* secret that needs to be kept, *his* shame covered up. Yet the love object's mourning does not proceed in the usual way with the help of words used figuratively. This is so because if the metaphors that were used to shame the object somehow reemerged in the course of mourning, the ensuing loss of the ego ideal, their guarantor, would nullify them in their role as metaphors. The cryptophoric subject's solution, then, is to annul the humiliation by secretly or openly adopting the literal meaning of the words causing the humiliation. [...] The above makes clear that *the crucial aspect of these fantasies of incorporation is not their reference to a cannibalistic stage of development, but rather their annulment of figurative language.* (*The Shell and the Kernel* 131-132; emphasis original)

Abraham and Torok also call incorporation an antimetaphor precisely because it negates the figurative use of language.[234] As was noted above, frozen metaphors have lost their figurative potential. Taken in his sense, frozen metaphors can be conceived as *encryptions* of repressed object-cathexes which can be freed or re-mobilised in order to make them accessible to introjection. Introjection in this sense is another word for a re-authoring of the client's life-story. In the same manner as introjection constitutes a reintegration of the repressed into "an expanded ego," re-authoring integrates marginalised aspects of the life-story situated around unique outcomes into a refurbished and extended life-story; a life-story which is integrative rather than cryptic. The fact that frozen metaphors play a part in both processes signifies a close relation between re-authoring and introjection. This in turn adds another layer to the palimpsest

---

[233] Freud's concept of incorporation is based on a regression to infantile fantasies and desires, which cause the object to be incorporated to be repressed beyond the reach of the Ego, which, culturally determined by the Superego, shies away from infantile rawness. In Freud, the Ego itself is thus kept separate from the incorporated object and there is no Ego-split. (cf. Freud, "Mourning and Melancholia").

[234] Cf. also Ellmann: "According to Abraham and Torok, fantasies of incorporation are characterized by *'their annulment of figurative language'*. This process, also designated as 'demetaphorization' or 'cryptonymy', serves to protect encrypted objects from intruders, even from the ego itself, which is demoted to the status of cemetery guard" (231; emphasis original).

of poetry therapy. At the same time, re-authoring and introjection signify the process of subjectivation which is still another layer. Frozen metaphors constitute an unactualised layer of the empirical poetic text as well as the palimpsestuous text of poetry therapy. At the same time, frozen metaphors generate yet another, an en*crypt*ed layer that needs to be broken up – de*crypt*ed –, transformed and integrated through introjection. The reactivation of Semiotic energy in frozen metaphors constitutes the actualisation of surplus meaning for the sake of therapeutic knowledge on one plane, while simultaneously it represents the isolation of unique outcomes for the re-authoring of the client's life-story and the initiation of introjection on two other planes. This shows the palimpsestuous nature of poetry therapy where distinct layers are nevertheless interrelated, orchestrating a true fusion of the literary and the psychological disciplines involved.

Poetry therapy can be conceived of as a palimpsest because it houses numerous texts within its space. The practice of poetry therapy is a space where numerous forms of writing meet, overlap and interrelate. Since poetry therapy, in contrast to the traditional *talking cure*, deals with empirical writing in the form of poetry in addition to writing in the Derridean sense, the metaphor of the palimpsest is even more fitting. In the context of the palimpsest and Derrida, Davidson coins the noun "palimtext" in order to transpose the concept of 'trace' onto actual writing. He explains:

> I would like to retain post-Structuralism's emphasis on writing as trace, as inscription of an absence, but emphasize the material fact of that trace, an inscribing and re-inscribing that, for lack of a better term, I have called a "palimtext." By this word I mean to emphasize the intertextual – and inter-discursive – quality of postmodern writing as well as its materiality. The palimtext is neither a genre nor an object, but a writing-in-progress that may make use of any number of textual sources. As its name implies, the palimtext retains vestiges of prior writings out of which it emerges. Or more accurately, it is the still-visible record of its responses to those earlier writings. ("Palimtexts" 78)

By coining the term 'palimtext' Davidson wants to designate material texts and make obvious their structure as a palimpsest, but he contradicts himself in what precisely a 'palimtext' is supposed to be. According to Davidson, a 'palimtext' is "neither a genre nor an object," but at the same time, it "retains vestiges of prior writings out of which it emerges." It is here that he implicitly negates the post-structural emphasis on writing as trace which he seeks to emphasise.[235] Derrida's concept of the trace specifically denies the existence of any form of origin. If a 'palimtext' thus "emerges" out of prior writings, these prior writings unavoidably constitute its origins, instituting a temporality and a thetic chain of cause and effect. Any text is inhabited by traces of other writings, but these are non-thetic, non-hierarchical and contemporaneous. Thus, what the term 'palimtext' actually brings back is the traditional view of intertextuality and interdiscursivity, putting one text in the centre and elucidating its meaning by making explicit the quotations of other text within its textual tissue. Such an understanding of

---

[235] My critique on Donaldson's concept of the 'palimtext' here is based on Dillon's (Chapter 4 of her book), appropriating it for poetry therapy.

the palimpsest presupposes a meaningful connection between the texts of the palimpsest, which goes against the very nature of what palimpsests constitute:

> Davidson coins the word 'palimtext' in order to combine 'post-structuralism's emphasis on writing as trace, as inscription of an absence' (p.78) with 'the material fact of that trace, an inscribing and re-inscribing' (p.78): 'the palimtext is neither a genre nor an object, but a writing-in-progress that may make us of any number of textual sources' (p.78). [...] Davidson is mistaken here, however, in appealing to the propriety of the name, for, since there is no necessary relationship between the texts that co-inhabit the space of a palimpsest – one text is not derived from one another, one does not serve as the origin of the other – the palimpsest does not *properly* figure the relationship between a text and its sources, including its own earlier drafts. (Dillon 47; emphasis original)

The texts that make up a palimpsest need not be related in any way. Often it is pure chance that brings these texts together. This is why the palimpsest does not "figure the relationship between a text and its sources." The same is true about the texts – the s/Semiotic systems – that inhabit the space of the practice of poetry therapy. The centre of this practice – in line with the humanistic approach – is the client. The client is the parchment upon which is inscribed the inherently multilayered text of the lifestory. The client becomes inhabited by the text of the analyst as well, a text that is also again inscribed by the trace of the analyst's life-story which has no connection to the client's. Then there is the poem which stands in a closer intertextual relationship to the client in that it does indeed originate from the client. The poem constitutes a material, thetic outcome of the client's Semiotic reactions during creativity; it is a commentary on the other texts of the palimpsest. The poem thus occupies a special position in the palimpsest that is poetry therapy; it is its latest layer and its empirical space.

Poetry therapy as palimpsest constitutes what Davidson terms a writing-in-progress. "The process of palimpsest production is one of layering – of erasure and superimposition [...]. The palimpsest is a space in which two or more texts, often different and incongruous, coexist in a state of both collision and collusion. [...] the space that marks their difference" (Dillon 47). There is no stable text in poetry therapy and the illusion of a stable text – the life-story and identity of the client – is deliberately shattered. This is the process of erasure necessary to superimpose another writing. It is erasure in the sense of Derrida in that the other writing remains legible but 'under erasure'. It is in the difference between these two layers of the palimpsest that new meaning emerges, meaning which eventually leads the client into healing. The manifestation of this difference is the poem to which I will ascribe the term 'palimtext' as coined by Davidson. The poem is the foil that enables the reading of the palimpsest in its entirety, it is the Symbolic – and therefore cognoscible – expression of the palimpsestuous writing that is poetry therapy.[236] In this respect the poem serves as a focal

---

[236] Dillon makes a point of coining the new adjective "palimpsestuous" to replace "palimpsestic," arguing: "According to *The Oxford English Dictionary*, the official adjective from 'palimpsest' is 'palimpsestic', meaning: 'that is, or that makes, a palimpsest'. In contrast, 'palimpsestuous' does not name something as, or as making, a palimpsest, but

point, because it manifests a palimpsestuous organisation where numerous texts inhabit the same space.[237] Derrida states that "[literature and criticism] should have a form that is both rigorous and capable of taking account of the essential possibility of contamination between all these oppositions" (Derrida, "This Strange Institution called Literature" 52). The same is true for the relationship between poetry and therapy: the metaphor of the palimpsest provides a conceptual framework that fashions a state of simultaneous closeness and separation between poetry therapy's literary and psychological disciplines. A palimpsestuous poetry therapy preserves the distinctiveness of both its participating disciplines and the individual texts employed (both empirical and other), while providing a space for their reciprocal contagion and interdependence. A palimpsestuous poetry therapy is thus a non-structure in which elements are brought together by a practice external to them (the therapeutic practice and, within this, the poetry, already again a palimpsestuous organisation); these elements are put into relation to each other because they share the space of the same idiosyncratic discursive formation, a formation that emerges uniquely for every client. "Identifying the signifying complexes at work in these [textual elements] discloses the disruptive and founding presence of palimpsestuous textuality in each of them, and provides a new way of understanding their complex textuality" (Dillon 87). Since these signifying complexes that share the palimpsestuous space of poetry therapy emerge uniquely for every client, they turn clients into "founders of discursivity" (Foucault, "What Is an Author?" 114) of their own therapeutic encounters, making them authors in the humanistic sense.

Conceiving of poetry therapy along the lines of the palimpsest has another (favourable) implication on its practical application: it enhances the participation of the creative faculty. Poetry therapy thus returns to its humanistic core. "Since the texts of

---

described the type of rationality reified in the palimpsest. Where 'palimpsestic' refers to the process of layering that produces a palimpsest, 'palimpsestuous' describes the structure that one is presented with as a result of that process, and of the subsequent reappearance of the underlying script" (4). I will take over "palimpsestuous" in this manner. On the relation between Davidson's 'palimtext' and the palimpsestuous concept her book proposes, Dillon states that "Davidson's 'palimtextual' reading corresponds to palimpsestuous reading which seeks to trace interwoven relations between the layers that constitute the fabric of a text. Palimtextual or palimpsestuous reading does not reduce the text to a single layer but takes all of a texts layer into account and respects 'the degree to which poem are a temporal process of making and remaking, of response and contention' (Davidson 1989, p. 93)" (48. The reference to Davidson is to "Palimtexts.").

[237] The function of the poem as a focal point is not to be confused with setting the poem up as centre. According to the humanistic approach the client is at the centre. However, the client in poetry therapy is a person whose identity is partially displaced and whose life story is being rewritten in and through the process of therapy. The client's being is thus in flux, essentially making the client a non-centre at the centre of the therapeutic encounter. The client is the main concern of therapy, but since therapy by definition induces change and temporary instability with regard to the factors mentioned above, clients can only be non-centres in the Derridean sense.

the palimpsest bear no necessary relation to each other, palimpsestuous reading is an inventive process of creating relations of where there may, or should, be none. As such, it always runs the risk of being false or fictitious. Palimpsestuous reading is caught up in the palimpsestuous intimacy of security and insecurity" (Dillon 83). It is the fictitious character of palimpsestuous texts which invites a creative response and thus allows the construction of new meaning complexes. Since this creates "relations of where there may, or should, be none," poetry therapy does not arrive at therapeutic conclusions via deduction, but rather through a process of inference, or abduction.

> Whereas deduction is reasoning in which a conclusion is drawn from a set of premises and in which the conclusion necessarily follows from those premises, according to Charles Sanders Peirce, abduction (also called 'retroduction' or 'hypothetic inference') is reasoning 'which depends on our hope, sooner or later, to guess at the conditions under which a given kind of phenomenon will present itself. (1958, p.248). Whereas in deduction the conclusion should be logically valid, in abduction evidence is used to reach a wider conclusion by a method of inference to the best possible explanation. (Dillon 67. The reference to Peirce is to "To F.A. Woods on 'would be' (1913)")

Dillon contends that the strategy of abduction, while more risky, "is necessary in the reconstruction of the underlying texts of [the] palimpsest" (ibid.). Part of abduction consists of invention which is creative. This is a valid form of arriving at conclusions in poetry therapy, because the aim is to re-author clients' life-stories and to enable them to refashion their identities. Both life-story and identity are constructions and as such principally arbitrary. It is irrelevant whether or not the refashioned constructions are more or less true than the originals. All that matters is that they empower the client to lead a happier and more balanced life. Abductive reasoning is the more productive in this respect as it "is an act of invention that comprises a process of discovery […] and an act of creation or original contrivance – the ingenious production of a new text that, consequently, runs the risk of being false or fictitious" (ibid. 68), but which actively re-inscribes clients into their individual lives. This is the aim of poetry therapy and the means to achieve it.

7. Poetry Therapy and the Question of Form: Free Verse and/or Formal Verse

> The poet who writes 'free' verse is like Robinson Crusoe on his desert island: he must do all his cooking, laundry and darning himself. In a few exceptional cases, this manly independence produces something original and impressive, but more often the result is squalor – dirty sheets on the unmade bed and empty bottles on the unswept floor.
> (Auden, *The Dyer's Hand* 22)

Having thus far delineated a theory of poetry therapy based on post-structuralist concepts – concepts of deconstruction and *différance* – little concern has been given to how the formal aspects of a poem might be relevant for and be influential in the therapeutic encounter. The formal character of the client poem has been dealt with peripherally in the discussion on metaphor and metonymy in Chapter 4 and was also touched upon in the context of figurative language. Other than that it has been left unaddressed. This has been done deliberately in order not to obscure the discussion of other central ideas. Since the formal aspect is important for the effectiveness of poetry therapy, however, this chapter will address the formal aspect directly, concentrating on the question of formal verse vs. free verse in poetry therapy. I will begin with a few general remarks about form, particularly form and language, and form and poetry.

It should not be underestimated how great the impact of form on meaning actually is. Form is not something that simply serves as a container for its content. It is commonplace aesthetic creed that form should correspond to content. This, however, is a somewhat limited point of view, because "form is *constitutive* of content and not just a reflection of it. Tone, rhythm, rhyme, syntax, assonance, grammar, punctuation and so on are actually generators of meaning, not just containers for it" (Eagleton 67; emphasis original). Form always influences content and the expression of the same. Eagleton continues his argument as follows:

> In everyday language, too, 'content' is the product of 'form'. Or, to put it more technically, signifieds (meanings) are a product of signifiers (words). Meanings are a matter of how we use words, rather than words being a matter of conveying meanings which are formed independently of them. [...] In everyday speech, it seems as though the word is the obedient transmitter of the meaning. It is as though it evaporates into it. If language did not conceal its operations in this way, we might be so enraptured by its music that, like the Lotus Eaters, we would never get anything done. [...] Ordinary language, like history for Nietzsche or the ego for Freud, operates by a kind of salutary amnesia or repression. Poetry is the kind of writing which stands this inversion of form and content, or signifier and signified, on its feet again. (68)

In Eagleton's emphasis on the inversion of the traditional relation between signifier and signified, one can trace the influence of Lacanian theories and Derrida. The form of the poem is, according to Eagleton, what differentiates it from "ordinary language," because it lifts the veil from the fact that it is form which defines content. By using traditional forms such as metre and rhyme in poetry therapy, this general feature outlined by Eagleton can be utilised to increase the effectiveness of therapy. "The poetic text is multi-systemic, in the sense that each of its formal aspects [...] constitutes a separate system within it" (Eagleton 52). Metre adds another system to the text, which thus becomes overcoded. Since form defines content, overcoded form denotes content that is equally overcoded, that is, saturated with additional meaning (with Semiotic, i.e. unconscious content). This, in turn, increases the usefulness in therapy, because poetry, precisely by being overcoded, "activates the full body of the signifier" (ibid. 53). In *The Open Work,* Eco defines works of art in general by the ambiguity of the message that is communicated. This ambiguity is due to the overcoding of artistic texts and Eco links this with Jakobson's poetic function:

> Any work of art can be viewed as a message to be decoded by an addressee. But unlike most messages instead of aiming at transmitting a univocal meaning, the work of art succeeds precisely insofar as it appears ambiguous and open-ended. The notion of the open work can be satisfactorily reformulated according to Jakobson's definition of the "poetic" function of language. Poetic language deliberately uses terms in a way that will radically alter their referential function (by establishing, among them, syntactic relationships that violate the usual laws of the code). It eliminates the possibility of univocal decoding; it gives the addressee the feeling that the current code has been violated to such an extent that it can no longer help. The addressee thus finds himself in the situation of the cryptographer forced to decode a message whose code is unknown, and who therefore has to learn the code of the message from the message itself. The addressee will find himself so personally involved with the message that his attention will gradually move from the signified to which the message was supposed to refer, to the structure itself of the signifiers, and by so doing will comply with the demands of the poetic message, whose very ambiguity rests on the fact that it proposes itself as the main object of attention. (196-197)

In contrast to most forms of communication, art communicates in ambiguous messages. It is thus 'open' to a variety of interpretations. What Eco calls "most messages" can, in the case of poetry therapy, be equated to prose messages, which aim at univocal meaning. The messages of poetry are equivocal, regardless of form. However, what Eco states about the 'poetic function' here supports the thesis that formal verse is an effective and suitable medium for poetry therapy. The poetic function inevitably leads the addressee (read: client) "from the signified to which the message was supposed to refer, to the structure itself of the signifiers." The "emphasis of the message on its own self" (Jakobson, "Linguistics and Poetics" 356) causes the client to focus increasingly on the signifiers, on the structure of language itself, and the features of metrical verse support this more effectively than the looser rhythms of prose or free verse. The use of formal verse thus promises therapeutic advantages.

In spite of the above, poetry therapy as expounded in the previous chapters is not immediately associated with formal verse; in fact, formal verse is a form of poetry that is nowadays often regarded as outdated by both poets and readers. Most poetry produced and read today is in free verse, which has all but replaced formal verse as the preferred mode of poetic writing. The Modernists, spurned by "that general revolution in the arts that occurred at the end of the nineteenth and the beginning of the twentieth century" (Steele, *Missing Measures* 6), abandoned the device of traditional metre in a desire to overcome the dated, "vague and overly decorative lyricality of much Victorian verse" (ibid. 34). This inaugurated a sea-change in poetry from which emerged what has become known as 'free verse' or *vers libre*. "The revolt against meter is perhaps the most striking feature of the Modernist revolution in poetry, and free verse is probably the most significant legacy of that revolution" (ibid. 29).[238]

Contemporary notions of formal verse emerged from a discursive field which favoured free verse over formal verse. This sheds doubt on the validity of these notions. "Free verse, the creation of an older literary revolution, is now the long-established, ruling orthodoxy" (Gioia 159). In other words, the discourse of free verse has become the dominant, institutionalised one while that of formal verse is marginalised.[239] The diminished status of formal verse often precludes its use in poetry therapy simply for the fact that it does not figure as a valid form of poetry. When considering the neglect and misunderstanding of the poetic side of poetry therapy that has been diagnosed in the previous chapters, the lack of knowledge about formal verse is the more hazardous for it corroborates the marginalisation of the poetic side of poetry therapy. A more thorough understanding of free verse and formal verse and their differences will have two implications for poetry therapy: firstly, therapists will not be negatively predisposed towards client poems written in formal verse, and, secondly, therapists become aware of the additional benefits formal verse and formal structures can bring to poetry therapy and of the fallacies inherent in free verse.

---

[238] It should be noted that formal poetry as such has not stopped being written, which is evidence that the diminishing numbers of poems written in traditional metre and the decline of knowledge about metre that goes along with this, are not based on a loss of appeal of rhyme and metre, nor on some fundamental flaws of metrical verse. Thus it cannot be argued that the reign of free verse is based on some inherent defect or artificiality of formal verse. In fact, it is notable that many of the foremost poets following the high Modernists have continued to write (at least part of) their poetic works in formal metre: "Even in the past one hundred years or so, when many writers have challenged the efficacy or legitimacy of traditional versification, meter has remained an instrument of undiminished value and has been brilliantly employed by a wide range of modern and contemporary poetry" (Steele, *All the Fun* 1). Among the more prominent examples of poets writing in metre are W.H. Auden, Philip Larkin and Seamus Heaney.

[239] Cf., for instance, Dana Gioia who argues with regard to poetry in the USA that "[b]y 1980 there has been such a decisive break with the literary past that in America for the first time in the history of modern English most published poets could not write with a minimal competence in traditional meters [and] most of the craft of traditional English versification has been forgotten […]. These young poets have grown up in a literary culture so removed from the predominantly oral tradition of metrical verse that they can no longer hear it accurately" (165-173). Gioia's assessment of the situation of formal verse in the USA is true for contemporary poetry in general.

There are two most widely held misconceptions about formal verse which are, not surprisingly, also the most damaging to the understanding of metrical poetry. The first of these misapprehensions is that formal verse is monotonous and something that is superimposed over the natural cadence of language, the latter being implicitly equated with that of prose. This argument is based on the assumption that metrical poetry is bereft of variety and therefore monotonous. The regular and repetitive pattern of formal verse is given as a reason for this persistent notion. The second misconception predominant today is that formal verse is constrictive. This is to say, formal verse forces the poet to adhere to a strict, predetermined framework or structure. This, in turn, is said to make poetry counterproductive to the poet's immediate expression of feelings, because the imaginative energy is entrapped in the metrical framework. The consequence of these two misconceptions is that formal verse is seen as uncreative; it is merely a craft rather than a form of art. Gioia states that "[f]orm, we are told authoritatively, is artificial, elitist, retrogressive, right-winged [...]. None of these arguments can withstand critical scrutiny, but nevertheless, they continue to be made so regularly that one can only assume they provide some emotional comfort to their advocates" (159). Gioia is right when he states that the arguments constantly being brought forth against formal verse cannot "withstand critical scrutiny." The first step to rectify these misunderstandings will therefore be an analysis of the nature and origin of these two misapprehensions of formal verse via a discussion of free verse. The nature of formal verse will thus be made clear before the backdrop of the discussion of free verse. Following this, I will also point out possible fallacies of using free verse in therapy. As a further step, I will link the rhythmical and repetitive nature of formal verse to some of the key concepts established in the previous chapters to show that formal verse can indeed be, maybe counter-intuitively, more liberating than free verse.

7.1 Free Verse: The Modernist Legacy and its Implications for Poetry Therapy

It is easy to miss the extraordinary quality of the Modernist revolution against metre, its unique position in the history of verse and the momentous shift in poetic tradition it signifies. The omnipresence of free verse makes it hard to imagine a poetic world where free verse did not exist. Steele is able to elucidate the singularity of the Modernist revolution by putting it in its historical perspective. He states:

> If a reader of Roman poetry had fallen asleep in 45 B.C. and had awakened twenty-five years later to find at his bedside Horace's *Epodes* and the first three books of *Odes*, he might well have been astonished on unrolling the scrolls. The poet's material and presentation of it would have seemed most unusual. Yet the reader, at least the educated one, would have recognized the verse forms. If he had wished, he could have traced in his mind their continuity all the way back to the misty beginnings of Greek iambic and melic poetry. Similarly, if an English reader had fallen asleep in 1775 and had awakened a quarter of a century later to find the *Lyrical Ballads*, he might well have been

startled by the subject and manner of "Tintern Abbey" or "Her Eyes Are Wild." He would, however, have had no difficulty determining that the first was in conventional blank verse and the second mainly in rhymed iambic tetrameters. If a reader had fallen asleep in 1900 and awakened in 1925 to find Ford's *On Heaven*, Eliot's *The Waste Land*, and Pound's *Draft of XVI Cantos*, it is likely he would have been very confused by the versification in the books. (*Missing Measures* 55)

The above quote captures perfectly the feeling of genuine strangeness of what the Modernists inaugurated. The dominance of free verse and the associated (and often polemical) critical notions of the Modernists upon which much of the theoretical discourse about free verse is (still) based, has obscured the uniqueness of the Modernist revolution.[240] The negative notions regarding formal verse originally emerged and have been consolidated through the polemics of the Modernist movement's effort of validating their then-radical mode of writing in free verse

Free verse, or *vers libre*, is, considered from the point of view of prosody and traditional poetics, a contradiction in terms. 'Verse' cannot, by definition, be 'free' in the sense of 'without a metre'. Verse has to follow a certain pattern in order to be different from prose. Definitions of poetry, unsatisfactory as they are, generally agree that poetry is defined by rhythm and metre. It is not surprising therefore that both words are evoked in definitions of free as well as formal verse. What is important is that poetry entails rhythm *and* metre: both are necessarily part of poetry. Eagleton states that "[m]etre is a regular pattern of stressed and unstressed syllables, whereas rhythm is less formalised. It means the irregular flow of the verse, its rippling and undulations as it follows the flexing of the speaking voice" (135). While Eagleton's explanation does not provide a definition of poetry on the basis of metre and rhythm, it does delineate the fundamental difference between rhythm and metre as such, namely that metre is, first and foremost, "a regular pattern" as opposed to rhythm which is characterised by "the irregular." This distinction provides the basis for a careful delineation of the difference and the respective functions of metre and rhythm in free and formal verse respectively. Eagleton's statement suggests the following: metre provides a regular and, on the whole, fixed pattern within which the language of poetry is crafted. The rhythm of a poem emerges from within this structure and is to a certain extent predetermined by the linguistic fashioning of the text. In the performance of the poem, by the idiosyncratic pronunciation of the person reading the poem, rhythm becomes expressed.

---

[240] Steele's example is, while catchy, not free of polemics itself. As one of the leading poets and theorists of the American *New Formalist* movement, he is naturally biased towards formal verse. In this respect, *Missing Measures* constitutes a conscious attempt to undermine the foundations of free verse in order to initiate nothing short of a counter-revolution of formal verse. I believe that, despite this bias, the arguments presented by Steele in the book serve to break up misunderstandings concerning formal verse and its relation to free verse. Steele is undoubtedly an expert in verse – both practically as well as theoretically – and his arguments are, though biased, sound. The fact that he is cited, for instance, by both Beth Bjorklund and Eleanor Berry is a case in point for his standing.

This expression is, in turn, based upon and caught up in the particular flow of speech unique to every language. In this respect, rhythm is indeed less formalised, but that does in no way separate it from metre when it comes to poetry. Rhythm is essentially part of poetry; it is both the basis of metre and the vehicle of its performance. "Meters themselves are abstractions from or selections of certain patterns of speech in a language. Ancient and modern writers alike testify that metrical systems establish themselves gradually by trial and error. Writers do not sit down and invent them. They are invented, so to speak, by the languages they serve" (Steele, *Missing Measures* 27). Metre thus brings to the fore fundamental features of language and it is this which gives a poem its aural qualities. The poetic metres of any language develop organically from that language and constitute a foregrounding of basic patterns – the rhythm – inherent in the language and its non-poetic uses. The rhythm that is experienced in the performance of the poem is therefore not some kind of superimposed rhythm, but an enlivening of the already inscribed rhythms of a language which is given emphasis by means of the increased regularity of the metrical patterns, which, in turn, are and must be modulated through real speech.

When it comes to the rise of free verse, the Modernists were forced to delimit free verse from traditional verse while at the same time proving that it is indeed a form of poetry and not simply prose written out as verse. Steele convincingly locates the Modernists' dislike of and reasons for the abandonment of metre in the confusion of metre with scansion and of idiom with metre which also holds the key to the Modernists validation of free verse:

> With the best of motives and intentions, [the modernists] objected to the diction and attendant subject matter of Victorian verse. Yet they identified Victorian poetry with the metrical system which the Victorians used but which was not itself Victorian [...]. Hence, the modernist attack on Victorian idiom led to an attack on meter and to the suggestion that metrical composition was outmoded in the same manner that Victorian style was outmoded. (*Missing Measures* 34)

The Modernists equated idiom with metre and, consequently, they abandoned traditional metrics along with what they considered a stale and outmoded poetic idiom. This conflation of metre, idiom and scansion originated within the general atmosphere of experimentalism, *avant garde* and cultural change of the Modernists' time (cf. especially Chapter 2 of Steele's *Missing Measures*). The abandonment of metre was born out of this context, a development which was aggravated by the practice of reading poetry out aloud. Poems were performed in a manner that was to emphasise the metrical pattern, a habit of reading which resulted in an extremely unnatural performance, which distorted and overshadowed the fact that metre is based on the natural flow of language.[241] The origin of the connection drawn by the Modernists between metrical

---

[241] The "Poetry Archive" Webpage has a recording of Alfred Lord Tennyson reading his poem "The Charge of the Light Brigade." Though the recording is understandably poor, it still gives a good impression of the Victorians' manner of reading poetry (http://www.poetryarchive.org/poetryarchive/singlePoet.do?poetId=1569).

verse and notions of inflexibility and monotony can thus be traced to the Victorians' emphasis of scansion as a didactic tool. Hence, the generation that would grow up to be the Modernist poets was regularly exposed to poetry that was bereft of its natural cadences and rhythmic variability. The following anecdote from Ford Maddox Ford elucidates this point. When poets read aloud, Ford remembers,

> the most horrible changes came over these normally nice people. They had, all, always, on these occasions the aspects and voices, not only to [sic] awful High Priests before Drawing Room altars – but they held their heads at unnatural angles and appeared to be suffering the torture of agonizing souls. It was their voices that did that. [...] A long rolling stream of words no-one would ever use, to endless monotonous, polysyllabic, unchanging rhythms [...]. (157)

It is reasonable to believe that Ford's experience is not singular, but that most of the Modernists had suffered through similar hardships in their youths. In their minds, the performance of poetry according to the abstraction of metre on the grounds of scansion made scansion and metre synonymous.

The identification of scansion with metre is at the heart of Eliot's polemic against metre. In "The Music of Poetry" he states that "when it came to applying rules of scansion to English verse, with its very different stresses and variable syllabic values, I wanted to know why one line was good and another bad; and this, scansion could not tell me" (108). Eliot's line of reasoning here is to be understood as follows: in analysing the metres of English poetry, he found that English verse does in fact exist in a state of variety as regards stress and syllable value. As a consequence, scansion could not help him know the nature of a poem, because scansion obscures the dynamic and flexible quality at the heart of poetry. Eliot failed to differentiate between metre and scansion here, blaming metre itself for his inability to see why "one line was good and another bad." Eliot's 'failure' lies in the application of scansion to a question it was never designed to answer. Scansion is not meant to tell good poetry apart from bad. It is meant to elucidate the metre of a poem. What scansion can identify is a predominant metre of a line or poem; it can tell which metre is predominant in a poem and whether or not the metre is 'perfect' or exhibits variation. This, however, has no bearing on whether a line is good or bad. A line of poetry can be metrically perfect but still generally considered to be bad.[242] Due to the overemphasising of the patterns of stress by the Victorians the Modernists perceived metre as lacking "rhythmical distinction." As a consequence, Modernist poets sought to distinguish their poetry from that of the Victorians by breaking away from metre completely. While the underlying reasons for the Modernists' abandonment of metre are questionable, the arguments made

---

[242] Cf. Steele, *Missing Measures*: "The [Victorian] method of reading and scanning [...] obscures [the natural rhythmic] quality in English meter and [...] the understandable hostility to the method came to be directed at meter itself. Ultimately that hostility led to the idea that the only way a poet can give rhythmical distinction to his verse is to violate meter. It led to the idea [...] that skillful versification involves departure from the norm rather than variation within it" (62).

on this basis have become commonly accepted.[243] The need of the Modernists to establish the nature of free verse as (a) verse and (b) different from formal verse is at the heart of this matter. It becomes clear that the Modernists were compelled to define metre differently in order to validate their use of free verse.

In order to successfully supplant formal verse with free verse it was necessary for the Modernist poets to come up with a system of prosody different from the traditional one. Such a prosody would presuppose a fundamental change in the structure of language itself, which is, naturally, an impossibility.[244] In trying to advocate free verse

---

[243] The move away from formal verse has to be taken with even more suspicion when one considers remarks such as Eliot's, who freely admits that he has "never been able to retain the names of feet and meters or to pay the proper respect to the accepted rules of scansion" ("The Music of Poetry" 108). How much of this statement is polemical is unclear and certainly Eliot was an accomplished poet who in his adolescence had experimented with traditional metrical forms. In his biography of Eliot, Peter Ackroyd describes him at the age of around twelve as "a young poet who adopts the formal organization and tone of the work he has admired [...]. In his early poetry he becomes charged with the style of the poet who 'possesses' him, as if he could only find himself within another" (27). Eliot's statement therefore rather suggests a conscious denigration of the "accepted rules of scansion" – and, by implication, of metre – for reasons other than inherently poetic ones. Rather, Eliot's, and to a lesser extent also Pound's, notions about verse, while probably rooted in a dislike developed in early adolescence, are predominantly part of their effort to establish themselves and their poetic ideas in the literary landscape of their time. In any case, the misconceptions about formal verse that were introduced, whether being true (mis)conceptions or part of a rhetorical strategy of persuasion, have continued to be perpetuated and still abound in contemporary critical and non-critical circles.

[244] The Modernist hope for the emergence of a free verse prosody is actually based on the belief that the prosody of formal verse has always been an artificial adjunct to living language. According to this argument, metre is not only artificial to English, being a forced adaption of the English language to the rules of versification of Greek poetry, but the rules of Attic versification themselves were believed to be artificial. This belief was based on the study of ancient Greek prosody by Antonius N. Jannaris. Beyers summarises Jannaris' argument as follows: "Jannaris remarks that the Attic dialect is a 'merely historical *abstraction*, that is an *artistic* language which nobody spoke but still everybody understood.' (4). [...] Thus, the received prosodic system was based on an appraisal of a language no longer current. [...] That is, later prosodists surveyed Attic poetry, described what they read, and then turned their descriptions into prescriptions for future poetry. [...] Traditional English versification is quite a remove from [...] a natural feel for rhythm. [...] Jannaris provided the Moderns with a theoretical justification for the idea that poetic rhythm is created solely from the poet's sense of rhythm, as well as for the corollary that the traditional rules of versification are arbitrary structures under which poets mistakenly believed they had to 'labour'" (20-22. Page numbers in the quotation refer to Jannaris' book; emphasis original). It is easy to see how Jannaris' theory presupposes that once the artificially imposed structure of metre is removed, a new and more natural prosody is bound to constitute itself. The fact that free verse is still without such a prosody invalidates Jannaris' argument. (Beyers also maintains that Jannaris' theories contain the seed for a counter-critique on free verse along yet another line. Cf.

and constitute it as a form of valid poetry, it was, however, imperative for the Modernists clearly to differentiate free verse from formal verse. They set out to do so by basing the poetics and prosody of free verse on rhythm. In short, the Modernists set out to prove that free verse was indeed a true form of 'verse' by "substituting, in prosodic theory, *rhythmos* (rhythm in a broad sense) for *metron* (metrical arrangement in particular)" (Steele, *Missing Measures* 99). In the light of the intertwined nature of metre and rhythm delineated above, it is immediately clear that such a substitution will not and cannot generate a new system of versification. The reasons are the following: poetry consists of or is defined by a combination of metre *and* rhythm. The basis for prosody in poetry is metre (which is itself based in the rhythms of the language it serves) to which rhythm is added as the actual performance of the metrical structure in speech. This rhythm emerges automatically as it is the natural cadence of language. Rhythm alone therefore cannot serve as the basis for a prosody of poetry as rhythm alone is the cadence of prose. Common prosaic speech acts follow a certain rhythm that is unique to every language and modulated within limits by the person uttering a specific speech act. When the inherent rhythm of a language is heightened by means of a regular pattern, one produces a metrical pattern. This means that if metre is taken away, one is left with rhythm, one is left, again, with prose. If one thus substitutes, as the Modernists did, rhythm for metre as the prosody of free verse, one ends up with prose. The Modernist definition thus manages to differentiate free verse from formal verse, but it does so at the expense of blurring the – in any case always already fuzzy – distinction between prose and verse. Free verse is thus defined differently from formal verse, but it is defined in a manner that makes it dangerously similar to prose.

Having thus managed to differentiate, albeit on wrong grounds as was shown, free verse from formal verse, the Modernists faced the following problem: free verse is different from formal verse, but it is now liable to the accusation that it is nothing but prose written out as verse. As a next step, it was thus necessary to prove that free verse, while different from formal verse in lacking a metrical pattern, was still a valid form of verse. Eliot's definition of free verse in the conclusion of his "Reflections on Vers Libre" elucidates how this was tackled. In this essay, Eliot argues that "for *vers libre* we conclude that it is not defined by absence of pattern or absence of rhyme [...]; that it is not defined by non-existence of metre, since even the worst verse can be scanned; and we conclude that the division between Conservative Verse and *vers libre* does not exist" (36). Eliot defines free verse in the negative. He begins by implying that free verse is not bereft of "pattern" and "rhyme." Eliot is right in stating that there are patterns in free verse.[245] This however does not necessarily mean that these are *metrical* patterns. Eliot's first definition is thus only seemingly sound. Eliot's second argument is supposed to show that free verse is fundamentally metrical and therefore

---

22-23). This notwithstanding, at the beginning of the previous century, Jannaris' ideas made the emergence of a free verse prosody a distinct possibility in the eyes of the Modernists.

[245] Rhyme is no essential feature of poetry and can be disregarded here.

rightly carries the denotation of 'verse' as opposed to prose on the grounds that every line can be scanned. In the attempt to come up with a vindication of free verse as, simultaneously, a form of verse and something new and inherently different from traditional verse, Eliot, and by implication the Modernists, set up an argument which is essentially a paradox. Free verse, the Modernists argue, is free because it does not follow the traditional metrical system. As a consequence, free verse is liberated from the mannerisms and ideological ballast the Modernists attributed to formal verse. At the same time, the Modernists emphasise that free verse is indeed a form of verse. They do so by stating that every line can be scanned. The Modernists, who have wrongly conflated verse and scanning, can thus establish the following simple, but only seemingly logical chain: (1) Everything can the scanned. (2) What can be scanned is verse. (3) Free verse can be scanned, therefore it is proper verse and consequently poetry and not prose. This argument puts forth what Steele has termed the 'unavoidable-feet theory'. Steele gives the Modernists' identification of scanning with metre the name 'ti-tumming theory', because of the monotonous pattern the Modernists ascribe to metre based on their experience of public readings.[246] Steele notes:

> Pound's ti-tumming accounts for the metrical norm of the pentameter line and for the way a student might scan or read the line to bring out its metrical identity. But the ti-tumming does not account for the necessary and happily infinite varieties [...] that can exist within the norm of the conventional pentameter. [...]. It might also be observed that the ti-tumming method of reading continues to inform attitudes towards metrical composition. (*Missing Measures* 61-62)

The Modernists use the 'ti-tumming' and the 'unavoidable-feet' theories to prove two fundamentally incompatible concepts: they conceived of free verse *and* formal verse along the lines of the 'ti-tumming theory', drawing different conclusions from this. On the one hand, they use the theory to discredit metrical verse as artificial and monotonous, and at the same time they apply the concept to the analysis of free verse to prove, based on the 'unavoidable-feet theory', that it can indeed be scanned and is therefore a genuine form of verse. This type of reasoning is, of course, tautological. The argument that the worst verse can be scanned, does not make free verse metrical. The question has to be whether or not free verse can be scanned so as to produce a strict repetitive pattern that organises the entire formal structure of the poem in every line. This is not the case in free verse.

It comes as no surprise that Eliot's conclusion from the above arguments, namely that there is no division between traditional verse and free verse, does not hold up to scrutiny either. This is only true if one applies the 'ti-tumming' and 'unavoidable-feet' theories separately to free and formal verse. These theories, viewed separately, prove that free verse is verse and that free verse is different from formal verse. Both proofs cannot be unified, though, because they are mutually exclusive. Within one line of reasoning, Eliot succeeds in proving that free verse is indeed a genuine

---

[246] Cf. Pound, who remarks about the iambic pentameter that it is a "ti tum ti tum ti tum ti tum ti tum from which every departure is treated as an exception" ("Treatise" 203-204).

form of verse. In doing so, however, he contradicts and even disproves his other line of reasoning that constitutes free verse as different from, in Eliot's point of view, monotonous and artificial formal verse: Eliot proves that free verse is verse by stating that it follows the 'unavoidable-feet theory'; this, however, negates free verse and turns it into a loose form of traditional verse. Within the conceptual and theoretical framework established by Eliot (and the other Modernists), free verse can either be free or it can be verse. It cannot be both. As soon as one attempts to unify both lines of reasoning one is left with a paradox.[247]

The idea of the inevitability of metrical feet is obviously central to the Modernist free verse theory; however, this notion is inadequate to prove that free verse is genuine verse. Firstly, the 'unavoidable-feet theory' is closely related to and indeed based upon the 'ti-tumming theory' which is itself untenable. Secondly, the 'unavoidable-feet theory' represents an extension of the conflation of metre and scanning. In principle, the notion of 'unavoidable feet' is not wrong, but the conclusions drawn from it by the Modernists are. There is no doubt that every line of a text is metrical in the sense that every line can be subdivided into metrical feet of various kinds. This is true for free verse as well as prose. Ramsay rightly states that "any piece of prose can be scanned 'as' accentual-syllabic verse" (100). The fault in the Modernists theory is that scansion and metrical feet are specifically designed for, or better, have originated from the study and practice of poetry. It is downright stupid to try and scan a line of prose. One will find metrical feet in any such line, maybe even a pattern of the same, because, like verse, prose cannot but follow the rhythmical patterns of the natural flow of language. This does not change the fact, however, that prose is not *meant* to be scanned. Here is an example taken at random from Eliot's first Milton lecture:

```
    x   /   x   /   x   /   x  /      /  x    x    x   /   x   /   x   /    x
The most | impor | tant fact | about | Milton, for | my pur | pose, is | his blind | ness. (259)
```

Eliot's sentence, taken from a critical essay and therefore definitely meant to be prose, can be scanned as a relatively regular line of iambic verse. The fifth foot constitutes an

---

[247] Further examples can be found in Eliot, who notes that "the ghost of some simple metre should lurk behind the arras of even the 'freest' verse; to advance menacingly as we doze, to withdraw as we rouse. Or, freedom is only truly freedom when it appears against the background of an artificial limitation" ("Reflections" 34-35). At another instance, Eliot contends that "the lines [of free verse] are usually explicable in terms of prosody. Any line can be divided into feet and accents" (ibid. 32). This very paradox is also implicitly present in the following statement by Pound when he states that "[a]lexandrines and other grammarians have made cubby-holes for various groupings of syllables; they have put names upon them, and have given various names to 'metres' consisting of combinations of these different groups. Thus it would be hard to escape contact with some group or other; [...] The known categories would allow a fair liberty to the most conscientious traditionalist. The most fanatical vers-librist will escape them with difficulty" ("T.S. Eliot" 421).

irregularity, but this is well within the variations allowed for by traditional prosody.[248] The fifth foot can easily be construed as a dactylic substitution of the expected iamb, a not uncommon substitution. The final foot ("ness") is a feminine ending and as such extrametrical with regard to the scansion of the line. Since scansion is an abstraction only, it delineates the dominant metrical pattern of a line and it is the dominant pattern which is used to classify the line. The above example is thus a line of iambic octameter with a feminine ending. While this shows that every line can be scanned, it still remains a rather useless exercise, because there is no need and no purpose in establishing a metrical pattern for a line of prose. The same is true for a line of free verse. There is no need or purpose to scan a line of free verse. If the lines of the poem scan regularly, it is no longer free verse, but formal verse which rather disproves than proves the existence of *vers libre* as verse. If only one line scans, or a couple of lines scan according to different metres, this does not prove that the poem is written in some form of verse. It only proves that one can find metrical feet everywhere, and not surprisingly so, as they have originated from the features of the language they serve.

To sum up, the Modernist defence of free verse is based on two theories. The first is what Steele terms the 'ti-tumming theory' which denotes the conflation of scanning with metre, resulting in the belief that metre is monotone, boring, artificial and therefore to be discarded. The second is the 'unavoidable-feet theory' which turns free verse into a proper form of verse based on the concepts of the 'ti-tumming theory'. It is not hard to see that these theories are mutually exclusive. This notwithstanding, "together they constitute a highly efficacious defense of experimental poetry: while the 'ti-tumming theory' discredits conventional meter, the unavoidable-feet theory legitimises free verse as being metrical" (Steele, *Missing Measures* 64-65). The Modernists' defence of free verse is thus mostly polemical, based on misapprehensions and arguments that are only seemingly sound.

There is no doubt about the fact that free verse is indeed verse and that there can be genuine poetry without adherence to traditional metrics. Ramsay answers the pertinent question of what free verse indeed is with the by now familiar paradox, stating: "It is, by the previous definition of 'verse' [as regular] and the plain meaning of 'free', verse which is (1) measureably regular, (2) free from being measureably regular. More briefly, it is unmeasured measured discourse, a flat self-contradiction" (100). The paradox Ramsay rightly constitutes here is, of course, based on the Modernists' insistence that free verse conform simultaneously to the 'ti-tumming' and 'unavoidable-feet' theories. For want of a new prosody, free verse remains caught up in this definition and the paradox cannot be solved. Two things, however, are worth mentioning as they pertain to an understanding of free verse that is relevant for its application in

---

[248] I am aware that this line can be scanned differently, resulting in a less regular iambic metre (for example by putting stress on the 'my'). The fact remains, however, that this line of prose is scanned in order to artificially transform it into a line of verse. Eliot's prophesy that free verse "is perhaps the first appearance of the kinetic, or revolutionary theory of poetry" ("The Use of Poetry and the Use of Criticism" 85), was premature.

poetry therapy. The first notion is that, indeed, "there is *a* principle common to free verse and not to other kinds: namely, that the line is intuited as a unit" (Ramsay 106). Although the word 'intuited' suggests an unconscious principle, it is true that the line as it appears on printed paper serves as a structural unit in free verse. In formal verse, the metre determines line length. In free verse, the poet's intuition determines the line, the desire to emphasise words and phrases by means of line breaks, something which also serves the creation of rhythm. With regard to poetry therapy, this freedom can have positive influence as it supports clients in the expression of their individual feelings and can become expressive of their own harmonious or disharmonious life rhythms. The second point is that free verse understood as a non-prose medley of fragmented pieces of traditional verse mixed with prose "is perhaps the commonest sort of free verse. The poet has something to say, hears a rhythm or so, slides into differing rhythms or prose. This is the temptation the serious free-verse poet should be most aware of and should most attempt to avoid" (Ramsay 103). Ramsay addresses the problem of free verse's similarity to prose here, something Eliot, as was noted, was already concerned with glossing over. Free verse turning into prose, Ramsay notes, is "more prominent throughout the range of free verse than many of its practitioners understand or would care to admit" (101). This second point is not only something every serious poet writing in free verse should be careful to avoid. The same is true for clients in poetry therapy. The poems written in therapy should be true poetry and not simply prose that is made to look like poetry. In the latter case, the advantages of poetry for therapy that have been delineated in the previous chapters would be nullified and poetry therapy would turn into regular writing therapy. This is where a connection can be drawn to the first point, namely to be mindful of the fact that, while line breaks are one of the chief organising principles in free verse writing, there is more to producing poetry than a cunning breaking of lines.

  The freedom of the poet writing free verse is far greater than in formal verse. Although free verse does not follow any predetermined, strict metre and is therefore "deprived of pattern in one dimension, the metrical, [it] tends to compensate by employing another kind of pattern, conspicuous repetition of phrases or syntactical forms" (Fussel 79). How to practically fashion this underlying pattern is for the individual poet to decide free of any predetermined formal tradition. Consequently, every free verse poem displays a unique kind of pattern and can be seen as a more individual creation than a poem in formal verse. This greater creative freedom of free verse is certainly no bad thing as the bulk of fine 20th and 21st century poetry can bear witness to, but, with respect to poetry therapy, it can be a disadvantage. Since individuals writing within the confines of poetry therapy are more often than not amateur writers rather than professional poets, the freedom granted to them by free verse may prohibit their deeper immersion into the creative process. The very freedom of *vers libre* that expands poetic possibilities in the hands of a skilful poet can flatten the same when offered to an amateur. Since in free verse there are little to no boundaries with regard to the use of language, it is easy for the amateur to get lost in its linguistic vastness and his/her verses which, to be useful in the therapeutic context, should exhibit the condensed, symbolically charged language characteristic of poetry, will deteriorate into mere prose. Deterioration into prose results in a lessening of therapeutic effect as poetry encourages the use of symbols to a greater extent than prose does. Rodney Pybus, for instance, comments on the danger of free verse becoming prose, stating: "Problems arise when this free/metered verse relationship is forgotten/ignored/not realized: the result is too often free verse that is chopped up prose, expressing, usually, poorly focused emotion or personal responses of no value" (379). It becomes clear that when free verse deteriorates into prose it loses that part of its nature, namely "focused emotion," that is essential for poetry therapy. Therefore, it is indispensable that those texts used in poetry therapy are indeed poems rather than "chopped up prose." Traditional verse can be used to avoid this problem in the first place, which is the context in which I will continue to discuss formal verse in more detail.

7.2 Formal Verse: Misconceptions and Advantages for Poetry Therapy

The contemporary understanding of metre is shaped almost exclusively by the arguments brought forth by the Modernists. The break with the long tradition of metrics which the Modernist revolution constitutes has been an almost complete success and consequently the once common knowledge of metre and versification is often gravely misunderstood today. Even the Modernists themselves – many of who lived to see the days when creative writing workshops began to appear at universities and evening schools – voiced concerns about the decline of traditional verse and the success of *vers libre*.[249] William Carlos Williams laments that poetry "has always led the way to the other arts as to life. Being explicit, the only art which is explicit has lately been left to fall into decay. Without measure we are lost. But we have lost even the ability to count. [...] There are a few exceptions but there is no one among us who is consciously aware of what he's doing" ("On Measure" 340). Williams' statement dates from 1954, a time when the Modernist revolution had long been consolidated. What is interesting in Williams is first of all his admission that poets (and by implication readers) "have lost the ability to count." This is to say that the skill of writing metrical verse has, in a space of only thirty years, been lost.[250] Williams' vision of the state of poetry is even

---

[249] Cf., for instance, Eliot in a letter to Jane Adam Smith: "I was shocked when my grandniece presented me with some verses that she had written as school exercises to find that little girls in an American school were *encouraged* to write in vers libre" (qtd. in Steele *Missing Measures* 66).

[250] Williams' argument here is yet another instance of the conflation of metre and scansion as he constitutes the ability to count, i.e. to scan a line, with the ability to write metrically. Poets, as Steele rightly argues, "do not write in a foot by foot or metronomic manner. They compose in phrases and sentences which fit or can be adjusted to fit a metre or a portion of the same. When, for example, Shakespeare wrote 'His life was gentle, and

bleaker. Not only has the knowledge of traditional verse been lost, but "there is not one among [the poets] who is consciously aware of what he's doing." Williams implies that the practitioners of free verse write without a basis, using a form of verse that is without a recognised system of prosody or other fixed pattern.[251] Williams also links measure with life and culture on a larger level. It is here that a connection can be drawn to the importance and effectiveness of metre in poetry therapy. Williams states:

> Our lives also have lost all that in the past we had to measure them by, except outmoded standards that are meaningless to us. In the same way our verses, of which our poems are made, are left without any metrical construction of which you can speak, any recognizable, any new measure by which they can be pulled together. [...] The very grounds of our beliefs have altered. We do not live that way anymore; nothing in our lives, at bottom, is ordered, according to that measure; our social concepts, our schools, our very religious ideas, certainly our understanding of mathematics are greatly altered. ("On Measure" 337)

Williams clearly draws a connection between measure in poetry – which for him denotes some unspecified form of metrical arrangement – and measure in life. The connection is established implicitly on the basis of the regularity of traditional metre. Williams contends that "nothing in our lives, at bottom, is ordered." For Williams, life has fallen into chaos because the "social concepts" that give orientation to one's life have been "greatly altered" and no "measure," i.e. no pattern, has been found to reconceptualise this chaos into a (new) structural order. What Williams describes here is the

---

the elements | So mix'd in him that Nature might stand up | And say to all the world, 'This was a man!'" it is unlikely that he did so in a 'His life ...was gen ... tle and ... the el ... e ments' fashion. At points a poet may analyze the particular feet of a particular passage with a view to the modulations or perfecting the cadence, but this is quite a different thing from counting, syllable by syllable, through a poem." (*Missing Measures* 60-61).

[251] Cushman notes of Williams' concern with 'measure' that "Williams crusaded on behalf of his theory of measure for nearly fifty years. During that time, a period which extends from the infancy of modernism to the emergence of the contemporary poetic generation, his theory of measure grew beyond prosody into mythology" (1). Williams' term 'measure' is not synonymous with metre. At the same time, it does not denote 'rhythm' as understood by the Modernists. The term is somewhere in between the two and changes as Williams' theory develops. This notwithstanding, Williams wants the term to have strong connotations of the regular patterns of formal verse. 'Measure' for Williams is the signifier (which eventually remains empty) of the new prosody of free verse he was hoping to discover or create. Williams' dissatisfaction with the state of poetry and the in-betweenness of his own theory can be discerned from the following quotation: "We have no measure to guide ourselves except a purely intuitive one which we feel but do not name. I am not speaking of verse which has long been frozen into a rigid mold signifying its death, but of verse which shows that it has been touched with some dissatisfaction with its present state. It is all over the page at the mere whim of the man who has composed it. This will not do. Certainly an art which implies a discipline as the poem does, a rule, a measure, will not tolerate it. There is no measure to guide us, no recognizable measure" ("On Measure" 339-340).

fragmentation of the texture of society in the wake of the two world wars and associated dramatic changes in values and cultural practices, all of which induce in him a feeling that "nothing in [life], at bottom, is ordered." This is fundamentally the same situation the client is forced to face when the dominant life-story has been thrown into disarray by some (traumatic) event or identity conflict. The origin of psychopathologies are broken, or shattered structures; structures the client has previously depended upon, used as guidelines and taken for granted in his or her life and which have become shattered or have lost their truth-value – their verisimilitude – in the context of the life-story. Essentially, like Williams, clients in poetry therapy are seeking "any new measure by which [their lives] can be pulled together" again. Poetry can provide this not only metaphorically, but quite practically through the idiosyncratic rhythms that emerge in the client-created poems. Generally, it can be said that "[a]s an aspect of the total psychotherapeutic spectrum, poetry can help to create order where chaos existed, whether the chaos is in the patient himself or in his relationship with others, including the therapist" (Berger 76). Berger rightly contends that the power of poetry to produce a "new measure" which clients can use as orientation to bring order back into their life is universal and independent of the poetic form. This guarantees that all forms of poetry unfold that unique therapeutic effect which has been so far delineated. One has to be careful, however, not to confuse freedom with licence, or, as Eco states it, openness with chance:

> At this point, however, we must avoid a possible misunderstanding: life in its immediacy is not "openness", but chance. In order to turn this chance into a cluster of possibilities, it is first necessary to provide it with some organization. In other words, it is first necessary to choose the elements of a constellation among which we will then – and only then – draw a network of connections. (*The Open Work* 116)

The freedom that free verse allows – a freedom that can be beneficial to therapy – should not be confused with an 'anything-goes' approach. Free verse poetry for all its lack of proper theory still has to exhibit fundamental poetic qualities. The attentive client and therapist will know whether or not a poem is genuine despite the lack of a proper definition. As Beyers phrases it, people "regard free verse in the same way that many people regard pornography: they do not know how to define it, but they recognize it when they see it" (15). Unregulated freedom, however, can turn the poetic text into prose and thus negate approaches of poetry therapy. Using formal verse in poetry therapy helps guard against the strong tendency of free verse to deteriorate into prose. In addition to this, formal verse strengthens the effects of the creative phase of poetry therapy by allowing the versifying client to become more intimately involved in reflecting upon and playing with the structures and meta-structures of language. This aspect is a particularly crucial one, because it further emphasises the centrality of language in poetry therapy in general, and in the creative phase in particular. The chance events of life that have initially caused the client to develop psychopathologies and a poetic form that represents a realm of pure chance, of disorganisation, and chaos prove counterproductive to therapy. It is thus a misconception that free verse is naturally and necessarily the better mode of therapeutic writing. This misconception is based on the link that is perceived between free verse and free association.

Free verse is generally the preferred mode of poetic writing in poetry therapy not least because it is thought to be intimately connected to the concept of free association whereas formal verse is perceived as counterproductive to free association. Consequently, free verse is often even regarded as the only appropriate form of verse for therapy. Free verse can leave clients lost and keep them from tapping into their creative powers, however, because it is precisely *not* like free association. In free association, the basically chaotic thoughts that emerge are given order, are placed within some form of framework by the therapist. Without this, these thoughts would remain chaotic and without a discernable message to communicate. Although the thoughts that make up a free verse poem are also subjected to psychotherapeutical discourse, this is not done almost simultaneously, but is facilitated in the receptive phase, that is, after the creative phase. During the process of creation, clients are on their own in imposing some form of (linguistic) order on their thoughts, which might prove too challenging. In such cases, formal structures and, depending on the client and advancement in therapy, formal verse structures constitute a valid and may even be the preferred mode of poetic expression as it provides a more clearly defined framework within which to be creative.[252] Along similar lines, formal verse, I contend, is intrinsically connected to the rhythm of human life and the human body as such: "[t]he pleasure which universally results from foot tapping and musical time-beating does suggest that the pleasures of meter are essentially physical and as intimately connected with the rhythmic quality of our total experience as the similarly alternating and recurring phenomena of breathing, walking, or love-making" (Fussel 5). Leedy corroborates Fussel's argument. He states:

> With some patients, poems that are more regular in their rhythmic scheme have proved more helpful than poems with less conventional patterns. Poems with regular rhythms, those that most nearly approximate the beat of the human heart, affect many patients deeply. That is to say that some masterpieces of poetry may not be therapeutic, whereas mediocre poems, never included in anthologies, may be extremely helpful or right for a patient, and may be his bridge to reality. ("Principles of Poetry Therapy" 72)

The gist of Leedy's argument here is the following: for the purpose of therapy, the more simple and regular the metre, the more effective the poem for therapy.[253] At first glance, the conclusion drawn from Leedy and Fussel appears hard to believe.[254] One

---

[252] Of course, as everything within the circumference of poetry therapy, this depends on the individual client and the therapeutic situation as a whole.

[253] This is only partly the case. Too regular a metre has negative consequences for therapy, which is a point that will be dealt with in more detail shortly. The essential regularity of metre, however, is superior therapeutically to looser rhythms.

[254] Of course, Leedy, working from the ISO-principle, argues from the point of the client's reception of a poem. This is, however, irrelevant for the present discussion because (a) there is also a receptive phase in the poetry therapy model proposed in this thesis and

inevitably wonders, having internalised the Modernists' arguments against formal verse, whether the regular arrangement of formal verse, though tuned to central patterns of human life, is not in fact a straightjacket of the Symbolic. The question presents itself whether metre works to uphold and support old Symbolic and discursive structures and to which extent metre is the poetical representation of that life-story which has caused the client's mental imbalance in the first place; in short, whether metre is not an agent of Symbolic and discursive curtailment of the subject-in-language and in-discourse.

I contend that metre is not essentially a dividing practice, nor in a harmful way supporting Symbolic structures. To begin with, metre, in its repetitiveness, is in fact more flexible than commonly assumed. In contrast to what the Modernists believed and propagated, scanning is *not* metre and metre is *not* the true rhythm of a line of poetry. What scanning does is that it forgoes rhythm and clarifies metre, superimposing an artificial abstraction on a living and dynamic entity:

```
x   /   x   /     x   /   x    /    x   /
A mill | ion eyes, | a mill | ion boots | in line,
  x   /   x   /     x   /    x   /    x   /
Without| express | ion, wait | ing for | a sign.²⁵⁵
```

The example above shows two lines of iambic pentameter which are scanned to denote the iambic pattern. Scanning divides the line into regular units of rhythm, not units of sense and a reading according to this abstracting would be entirely against the natural cadence of English, occluding the flexible and dynamic qualities inherent in these lines. Timothy Steele proposes a more finely tuned scale of scanning in which the stress is measured at a strength between 1 (no stress) – 5 (very strong stress). One must keep in mind that this is still an abstraction from natural speech, but it shows that the nature of metre is not monotonous at all but rather inseparably connected with the natural rhythm and cadence of English. Applying Steele's scale to the example above, the lines might be seen as scanning like this:

```
2   5   1   3     2   4    1    3    2   3
A mill | ion eyes, | a mill | ion boots | in line,
  2   3    1   5    2     4   1    2   1   3
Without | express | ion, wait | ing for | a sign.
```

This representation of the iambic pentameter is much closer to the natural pronunciation of these lines by a contemporary speaker of English. Still, one can easily deduce from it the iambic pattern for it retains the organising principle of lesser stress followed by weightier stress that is characteristic of iambic metre. It becomes clear that

---

(b) it can be safely assumed, on the grounds brought forth in Chapters 3 to 5, that the effects described by Leedy with regard to the reception of poetry occur in an even more pronounced form during the creative process. Cf. also Bolton: "All the stages of writing help create order and understanding out of mental chaos. A poem is an ordered entity with a beginning, a middle and an end. If an even greater order is required, a poet will often choose to write in a strict form. […] or in meter or a strict rhyme form" (101).

²⁵⁵ Lines 14 and 15 from Auden's *The Shield of Achilles* in Auden, *Collected Poems*.

metre is everyday language following an ordering principle which is neither dogmatic nor constraining. Rather, metre is flexible, capable of accommodating countless varieties of pronunciation without sacrificing its metrical cohesion. "It is from this interplay between the unchanging metrical pattern and the many-shaded rhythms of natural speech – this interplay between the steady underlying pulse of the meter and the variable phrases, clauses, and sentences riding over it – that iambic verse draws its vitality and delight" (Steele, http://instructional1.calstatela.edu/tsteele/TSpage5/meter.html). Metre can thus express new variety of cadence and rhythm within a playing field of known regularity that acts as a safety net and supports clients as they venture into new territories. These territories are rhythmical and metrical and they exist in the Symbolic as a discernable structure. During the creation of metrical poetry, the client becomes conscious of these structures and begins to manipulate them. Clients consequently manipulate the Symbolic proper, gaining power over this otherwise oppressive structure, penetrating its fabric and going beyond it in reshaping it. Hence, metre produces two important effects: firstly, metre makes poetic language self-referential and increases the client's concern with language as such. As mentioned in the previous chapter, this in turn pushes conscious thoughts about the problems and conflicts to the periphery and makes way for the playful and relaxed state of creativity. The Symbolic is thus simultaneously used and subverted by metrical poetry. In the process of metrical composition, clients' behaviour in language becomes increasingly poetical, which is distinctly different from their usual prosaic behaviour. The known regularity of metre represents the inevitable and necessary cultural embeddedness of the client which poetry therapy seeks to infuse with new mobility and activity rather than to negate or supplant. The rhythmical varieties within metre constitute this new activity which emerges from within the structural field of (culturally (pre)determined) metre.

Secondly, metre facilitates juncture points, allowing for an increased influx of the Semiotic, because it has close ties to the unconscious. According to Lacan, the Symbolic is instituted to gloss over a perpetual lack and the infant's fears associated with this process (the loss of the Real). These fears re-emerge in the process of therapy and the structure of verse provides Symbolic safety while clients reorganise their relationship to these fears. "Poetic behavior, therefore, is that behavior which is evoked and maintained by the structure and process, by the cognition and imagery of a poem. It is, one might say, an esthetic organization which makes it possible for a person to feel his thoughts and imagery and to imagine and think his feelings" (Stainbrook 1). Formal verse secures the client's poetic behaviour in therapy, guaranteeing the facilitation of juncture points in the form of language charged with Semiotic energy, while maintaining the structure of the Symbolic. There is thus a connection between metre and the unconscious. This can also be traced in the following statement by Heninger:

> Poetry exposes unconscious forces to consciousness and organizes them into an understandable form. This is a therapeutic process. It makes arrangement out of derangement, harmony out of disharmony, and order out of chaos. [...] It allows these ideas and conflicts to circumvent the usual repressive barriers and come to the surface. At the same

time, it exposes them to the observing ego so that they can be examined and organized. (56)

In addition to poetry as a means of making conscious or understandable what would otherwise remain unconscious and oblique, Heninger emphasises the organising function of poetry, particularly its function of balancing conscious and unconscious and giving each its due. Formal verse, more so than free verse, holds the possibility of simultaneous expression both of the natural rhythms of life and of Symbolic structures. Eco observes that form in literature is "an effect partly of art and partly of nature. The result will be a curious mixture of spontaneity and artifice, in which artifice defines and chooses the spontaneity, and spontaneity determines the artifice both in its conception and its realization" (*The Open Work* 112). Metre adds an important dimension to poetry therapy – another layer to the palimpsest – in combining the necessary order with the freedom to explore new directions. "Like an effective leader, rhythm holds the tension and maintains the dynamic interplay among the participants. It does not divisively pit one aspect against another as verbal argument does. Flowing within a rhythmic meter, differences are welcomed: they create together and augment one another" (McNiff, *Art Heals* 233).

Apart from giving structure and allowing flexibility within it, metre supports the influx and manifestation of the Semiotic in yet another capacity. The regular and repetitive pattern of metre has close ties to the fundamental nature of the Semiotic as represented by the *chora*. It has already been shown that metrical patterns correspond to such bodily rhythms as breathing and the heartbeat. It is not surprising then that formal verse is also closely related to the psychical entity of the *chora*, which, let it be remembered, was based on the somatic on and off of drives.[256] Metre can be conceptualised as the manifestation of the *chora* within the Symbolic Order: "Just as rhythmic fragmentation characterizes psychosis, rhythmic synchrony characterizes health. The enduring power of the arts can be ascribed to their ability to heighten the essential rhythms of life, to bring them to a more complete level of awareness and community participation" (McNiff, *Art Heals* 235). What McNiff denotes as "rhythmic synchrony" is just another term for the regular pattern of metre. Consequently, metre is aligned to bodily rhythms that are associated with health. These metrical patterns have a positive effect psychotherapeutically because they are directly connected with the *chora* and therefore the Semiotic, i.e. the unconscious. Abraham and Rand corroborate this. Having previously discussed the pacifying effects of metre by means of trochees, they state:

> The meaning intended in this fundamental rhythm, the repetition of trochees, is to be found in the most primitive temporal structure man can experience, the connection of tension with the easing of tension, of an appetite with its satisfaction. There is no better

---

[256] Although the intervals of the on and off of drives are chaotic – based on somatic, intrapsychical and external (somatic) stimuli – their fundamental nature is that of difference between two states which makes it metrical. The unpredictable intervals displace this difference into *différance*.

illustration of the primordial structure of the creation of time than a cadence divided into strong and weak beats, a figure for sucking the breast, the child's first relational act. The organisation of time into parity and into multiples of the same parity is meant to deny symbolically the wish to be easily satisfied as once upon a time, in a first victory over post-natal reality. (9)

What is described here is exactly the function and nature of the *chora* according to Kristeva, namely as based on drives and the developmental state between the Real and the Symbolic. The *chora* as a precondition for the Symbolic is alluded to above in that the introduction of difference ("parity") is "meant to deny symbolically the wish" for satisfaction. It is precisely this which sets up the Symbolic over the primordial difference of the *chora*. It can be concluded thus that metre is a Symbolic structure which is inherently Semiotic. The key, as was already mentioned, lies in the variations within the general structure. Abraham and Rand note:

> All of this is meant to demonstrate that [...] a minute variation in the rhythm leads to implicit incompatibilities with repercussions for the unity of the entire work and that [...] the most subtle nuances are accessible to psychoanalytical interpretations. Needless to say, far from being limited to the study of rhythm, this type of analysis concerns all the expressive and material aspects of a poem and of a work of art in general. (11)

The variations in metre are Semiotic drive motilities. In the repetitive flow of metre, these rhythmical changes constitute units of Semiotic energy which are in flux and flow along with the metrical pattern, signifying juncture points and symbolic formations by means of their irregularities. These re-polarise the structure continuously and facilitate the centre as non-locus by means of constant change and supplementation. The *chora* (and the unconscious as a whole) is characterised by rhythmical fragmentation. Although she is by nature differential, there is no pattern to the *chora*'s outbursts of Semiotic energy. Metre has "the ability to heighten the[se] essential rhythms of life" within an organisational framework. In this sense, metre manifests the essentially dyadic nature of the *chora* in its alternating pattern while retaining its fundamental dynamism in the flexible rhythms, all this within the boundaries of the Symbolic which is at the same time subverted and asserted. Linking metre with the Semiotic in this manner turns metre into the channel or riverbed which holds and transports the currents of Semiotic energy. The flow of metre – in its repetitive pattern modulated by (rhythmic) variety – allows Semiotic energy to become fluid and serves as a conduit between Semiotic nodes – symbols and other figurative language – within the Symbolic structure thus producing a dynamic and active tissue of the Semiotic that the client-as-reader actualises in the therapeutic discourse. These actualisations are "accessible to psychoanalytical interpretations" and have to be related to "expressive and material aspects of [the] poem." In other words, they are to be related to the whole palimtext and by means of this empirical textual space to the entire textual tissue of the palimpsest which is poetry therapy.

Formal verse used in poetry therapy provides a structural framework and is a means of helping the client to focus. "Thanks to these conventions [of formal verse], the poet is no longer the victim of his enthusiasms and emotions: the rules of rhyme restrain him but at the same time liberate him" (Eco, *The Open Work* 137*)*. This twofold effect of metre[257] can provide an additional edge to poetry therapy. When creating metrical verse the client as much creates anew as he constructs from and within known patterns. These known patterns constitute linguistic representations of what clients consider safe ground in their life-stories.

> The creative process is most actively engaged when a configuration evokes a response yet leaves room for the individual imagination to complete the scene with its own unique expression. [...] Perhaps this is why work with simple art forms tends to evoke such penetrating emotions and engagements with archetypical themes. There has to be room for the person to freely interact with the situation and make a personal contribution to the process. (McNiff, *Art Heals* 142)

McNiff rightly notes that in simple art forms – 'simple' being his phrase for 'traditional' or non-experimental – clients can nonetheless "freely interact with the situation and make personal contributions" suggesting that formal frameworks do not limit individual contributions to the final product. Rather, he contends, such formal structures induce "penetrating emotions." For poetry therapy, this phrase can be taken literally, as verse indeed facilitates the penetration of the Symbolic and a breaking through of the Semiotic. From a safe place – which the patterns of formal verse represent – clients can venture towards a revaluation of their life-stories and identities and integrate conflicting parts of their identity as well as traumatic events into a newly structured and harmonised narrative that is free of repression. Metre offers a way to express previously unstoried or conflicting experiences in an organised form, to shape them within the Symbolic – a necessity for them to be communicated and thus consciously understood – while retaining as much of their Semiotic qualities as possible. Metre is a means of introjection (in the sense of Abraham and Torok).

Metre also strengthens the poem's usefulness as a device of externalisation. "Crafting the writing into a form seems to make it even more of an object, increasing its power to communicate back to the writer" (Bolton 98). This superior mode of objectification does not only benefit the second, receptive phase of poetry therapy (cf. Chapter 5), but by thus becoming, during the process of creation, "even more of an object," the poem also increasingly appeals to the fundamental human drive to play.

> The return of need is directed towards consumption placed at the service of appetite. Repetition demands the new. It is turned towards the ludic, which finds its dimension in this new. Whatever, in repetition, is varied, modulated, is merely alienation of its meaning. The adult, and even the more advanced child, demands something new in his activities, in his games. But this 'sliding-away' (*glissement)* conceals what is the true secret of the ludic, namely, the most radical diversity constituted by repetition in itself. It can be seen in the child in his first movement, at the moment when he is formed as a human being, manifesting himself as an insistence that the story should always be the same, that its recounted realization should be ritualized, that is to say, textually the same. (Lacan, *Four Lessons* 61; emphasis original)

---

[257] Eco speaks of the "rules of rhyme," his arguments are true for metre as well. In fact, I take Eco to speak (metonymically) of metre here in the first place.

Metre combines, as has been repeatedly argued, the known and the new, repetition and modulation, rigidity and flexibility. Lacan contends here that what is "modulated" in repetition is an "alienation from its meaning." This is precisely what is required of poetry therapy, for the modulations in the metrical structure are, or at least point at, the influxes of the Semiotic, which, fundamentally, cannot be known or experienced other than mediated through language. The nature of the Semiotic is thus indeed alien to the realm of the Symbolic and, at the same time, constitutive of it. It is this which Lacan names "the secret of the ludic." Freud's pleasure principle thus enters the creative phase of poetry therapy to a greater extent when metre is involved. For poetry therapy this intensifies the client's engagement with the shaping of the text during the process of writing. The pleasure derived from immersing themselves in the language and the possibilities of metre causes clients to relax; this increases the ludic possibilities even more and furthers a temporary displacement of the client's problems to the periphery of consciousness. Otto Rank derives "the problem of art from the play instinct" (98) and states that, in artistic creation, the artist "finds it possible to conquer creatively his fundamental human dualism and to derive pleasure therefrom" (109). Art and play are, for Rank, closely associated and he sees the artistic creation as an adult continuance of the child's play for the sake of experiencing pleasure. A feeling of pleasure is not absent from Kristeva's understanding of the creative process as well. She contends that the Symbolic

> function is [...] dissociated from all pleasure, made to oppose it, and is set up as the parental place, the place of the superego. According to this view, the only way to react against the consequences of repression imposed by the compulsion of the pleasure principle is to renounce pleasure through symbolization by setting up the sign through the absence of the object, which is expelled and lost forever. (*Revolution* 149)

Kristeva's Symbolic "is dissociated from all pleasure," which means that pleasure is renounced during symbolisation and the sign is set up in its stead. In the writing of poetry, as was noted before, a second symbolisation takes place, in which new drive charges – that is, pleasures – are attached to sign-functions. These sign-functions gravitate towards figurative language. The Semiotic is thus constituted as a realm or function that generates pleasure through creativity. Coming into contact with this realm induces a further letting go of mental control, making pervious the bar between signifier and signified, the Symbolic and the Semiotic, consciousness and the unconscious. "Play in therapy involves the capacity to relax intellectual controls, and to become non-goal oriented and open-ended, in experiencing and working with psychological space. In this space the images and symbols move into consciousness with their own logic and organization regarding space and time" (Robbins 62).[258] The ability to find means in therapy, especially art therapy, to tap into the resources of the ludic drives of the pleasure principle goes a long way towards securing therapeutic success.

---

[258] Note here that Robbins mentions "images" and "symbols" as the manifestations of unconscious content.

Wallace comments on this in the context of visual art, stating that "[b]y adulthood, we are so conditioned that we have to trick ourselves into being open. One trick is to play, and that means: play seriously and work playfully. We must step aside to allow the depth, the unconditioned, to speak" (100). This stepping back is made easier when metre is concerned and, what is more, it does not require any additional techniques but happens automatically during the process of poetic writing.

While it is not a necessity as such for poetry therapy to involve formal verse, because the concepts and theories delineated in the previous chapters apply to any form of poetry when used in therapy, adding the metrical dimension definitely increases its effectiveness throughout the spectrum of its application and helps avoid some fallacies of using free verse. To summarise, four main aspects can be isolated with regard to the usefulness and effectiveness of formal verse in poetry therapy.

Firstly, formal verse can enhance therapeutic effectiveness since it forces the versifying client to become more intimately involved in reflecting upon and playing with(in) the structures and meta-structures of language. This has a twofold effect. In the first place, it forces the client to inscribe his/her observations and thoughts into a predetermined metrical framework. This, in turn, demands a more flexible and creative handling of the linguistic material since a number of syntactic, lexical and grammatical options of expression have to be tested in the mind in order to make them compatible with meta-linguistic structures like metre, rhythm, rhyme, and stanzas.

> [T]he demands of structure sometimes force writers to consider phrasings that would not otherwise occur to them. At times, the process of weighing one word against another can reveal significant feelings. By the same token, certain forms are very compressed and thus stimulate the participant to sort out what is most important and meaningful. (McCarty Hynes/Hynes-Berry 181)

These meta-structures supersede 'The Law of the Father' and can partly replace it for the duration of writing. This can bring about more linguistic freedom and a weakening of the boundaries of the Symbolic against the incursions of the Semiotic.

Secondly, the formal restrictions dictated by metre invite the use of metaphors and symbols thus suggesting the composition of speech acts which are highly susceptible to unconscious influences. Eco describes this as a "curious mixture of spontaneity and artifice" (*The Open Work* 112). What Eco calls spontaneity is another word for what art therapy terms creativity. Artifice, in Eco's sense, is what formal verse might bring to poetry therapy. The reciprocal relation of metrical verse and creativity supports the production of the work for, to repeat once more, life in its immediacy is not "'openness', but chance. In order to turn this chance into a cluster of possibilities, it is first necessary to provide it with some organization. In other words, it is first necessary to choose the elements of a constellation among which we will then – and only then – draw a network of connections" (ibid.). In order to bring into some intelligible form the inherently chaotic influxes of the Semiotic during the phase of production, the organising principle of verse can serve as a filter, or better as a catalyst bringing symbols into the right focus to be more useful as unique outcomes during the second phase of reception. This function as a catalyst constitutes the second important advantage of formal verse over free verse in poetry therapy.

A third advantage is that the rhythmic patterns found in formal verse, which are without a doubt stronger than in free verse, play a role in the therapeutic effectiveness during the process of poetic production. The repetitive pattern of formal verse links with fundamental patterns of human life such as walking or the heartbeat, but also with the differential nature of the *chora*. The simultaneous existence in metre of regular and repetitive rhythms and variations and dynamic modulations of the same, turn metre into the ideal conduit between the Symbolic and the Semiotic.

A fourth aspect that is relevant for the therapeutic use of formal verse is the increased playfulness involved in composing it. Formal verse is a repetition of a certain pattern which is, as shown above, constantly infused by the new, by slight individual nuances of rhythmic diversity of what Steele calls the "many-shaded rhythms of natural speech" (http://instructional1.calstatela.edu/tsteele/TSpage5/meter.html). Formal verse can indeed be perceived as "diversity constituted by repetition in itself" (Lacan, *Four Lessons* 61) and as such it is "turned towards the ludic" (ibid.); it increases the pleasure of the activity by diminishing psychological tensions while at the same time unleashing the creative potential of the client. Hence, by being forced to construct and put to the test various linguistic possibilities that may fit the requirements of metre, the client's tensions are cast to the periphery of his consciousness and his creative potential is liberated. This essentially playful state of poetic production is strengthened by the use of formal verse and in turn strengthens the effect of verse as a catalyst. Metrical verse can introduce into the phase of production a self-perpetuating effect in which the ludic tendencies of versification allow images and symbols to appear which in turn become more focused through the medium of verse as they have to be included into the metrical pattern. This is again a form of play and may produce pleasure thus closing the circle.

The apparent potential of formal verse to stimulate the creative faculties of the mind most potently is significant in another way, namely in that it represents the approach of *art as therapy* in that it puts the application of art at its core and considers not only the completed piece of art, but the entire creative process as essential to therapeutic success. Formal verse thus congenially interfaces with the concept of the unconscious and its way of influencing the poetic text and strengthens the inherent potential of poetry to manifest the client's conflicts in symbols and images. It can therefore be considered a useful tool for the therapist as well as a valuable asset in the practice of poetry therapy.

Conclusion

As was shown at the beginning of this study, the field of poetry therapy is characterised by its diverse and wide-ranging practical horizon and application as well as its comparably narrow and vague theoretical foundations. Consequently, the poetic aspect of poetry therapy is misunderstood and generally underdeveloped in both theory and practice. The potential and possibilities of poetry therapy when it is understood as an interdisciplinary endeavour have remained unactualised and curtailed precisely because poetry as a (literary) discipline is not sufficiently recognised by poetry therapists. This study set out to investigate, chart and supply the interdisciplinary field of poetry therapy with a thorough theoretical foundation from the perspective of literary studies and theory. It has concentrated on exploring poetry in the therapeutic context, integrating the proposed methods and concepts into existing psychotherapeutic approaches wherever possible. Fundamental to this endeavour have been two realisations regarding the present situation of poetry therapy, namely that, firstly, poetry is used mainly reflectively in poetry therapy and, secondly, that poetry, its processes, mechanisms and textual nature, are not properly understood within poetry therapy. In order to constitute poetry therapy as an independent approach, the concept of 'poetry' was narrowed down to denote a "[c]omposition in verse or some comparable patterned arrangement of language in which the expression of feelings and ideas is given intensity by the use of distinctive style and rhythm" (*OED*). This, as we have seen, has led to a clear differentiation between poetry therapy and its sister therapies. Along the same lines, the purely receptive use of poetry therapy was dismissed on the ground that (a) it blurs the disciplinary boundaries with other literature-based therapies (mainly bibliotherapy) and (b) that it leaves untapped the therapeutic process of the creative act.

Following from this, poetry therapy has been re-defined as an artefactual expressive art therapy, a definition that accounts for the importance of the creative artefact (the poem) and the expression in the context of art and therapy. Based on the awareness that "[a]rt and healing include two universally recognized features of the artistic experience: the making of art as a therapeutic process and the contemplation of artworks in order to be influenced by their expressive qualities [...]" (McNiff, *Art Heals* 132), this study reconceptualised the function of the poem in therapy as a dynamic entity and a third node in the therapeutic dialogue. In doing so, the reciprocity of creation and interpretation has been accounted for. Interpretation is itself a creative act and not purely receptive. Along the same lines, the creative act is not purely unconscious, but includes conscious facets as well, and both processes are not static ones, but highly dynamic. Eco notes in this respect that the "reception of a work of art is both an *interpretation* and a *performance* of it, because in every reception the work takes on a fresh perspective for itself" (*The Open Work* 49; emphasis original). In the context of this study, this has suggested that poetry therapy is a uniquely active and dynamic semiotic field in which sign-functions of various origins and forms come together. By means of isolating these sign-functions and by mapping their interrelations, we have seen that the poetic text, its production and reception, are intricately interwoven with the traditional psychotherapeutic methods. The first step in defining and mapping the semiotic space of poetry therapy has been the delineation of the Symbolic and Semiotic in the context of meaning production. In addition to configuring the unconscious as 'structured like language', Kristeva's concepts of the pheno- and genotext were utilised to transfer the notions of the Symbolic and the Semiotic onto the textual matrix of the poetic text, thus enabling their application in an (empirical) textual space.

The discussions on figurative language in Chapter 4 reconceptualised the poem as inherently dynamic rather than static. The indeterminate nature of the literary symbol was shown to make the poetic text s/Semiotically extremely mobile. To account for this, the concept of Semiotic energy has been introduced. With this notion it is possible to fathom both the semiotic flexibility of figurative language and its Semiotic content. Semiotic energy helps to understand and keep in mind that the poem remains an active agent even in what I have termed the receptive phase following its creation. The varying interpretations of the client during the receptive phase represent different actualisations of s/Semiotic content with which symbols are charged. The notion of Semiotic energy is a useful means of mapping symbols of therapeutic value and of modelling their connections through the idea of the flow of Semiotic energy currents. By connecting poetic symbols, 'frozen' Semiotic energy is given new motility, connecting different symbolic nodes, thus facilitating the production of meaning that is useful for therapeutic purposes.

By taking over the notion of the life-story from narrative therapy, another semiotic system was introduced. This investigation into the contact areas between life-story and poetry therapy as an artefactual expressive art therapy led to the formulation of the following aim: one of the central therapeutic agendas of poetry therapy is specifically not to exchange a client's old and pathological life-story with a completely new one, but of re-writing the existing one through an integration of new plot possibilities surrounding unique outcomes. In this context, the problem of discursive normalisation (in Foucault's sense) was tackled by means of appropriating the dividing practices. By linking the notion of subjectivation to the therapist conceptualised as commentary, this study was able to suggest strategies enabling the insurrection of subjugated knowledges within a broader framework of culturally determined discursive formations. It has further been determined that symbols as nodes of Semiotic energy signify unique outcomes and as such also function as devices of externalisation, re-authoring and re-writing. Taking the client's life-story (a virtual textual space) and its rewriting as a central notion of poetry therapy made obvious the need for a closer investigation of the concept of re-writing itself. This was accomplished in Chapter 6 via Derrida and his notion of arche-writing; a notion that, in turn, paved the way for the reconceptualisation of poetry therapy along the lines of the metaphor of the palimpsest.

The metaphor of the palimpsest has established poetry therapy as a thoroughly semiotic process and constitutes an integrative concept. By conceptualising poetry therapy as a palimpsestuous process of writing, it becomes possible to encompass the heterogeneous practices and aspects that partake in poetry therapy within one theoretical framework. The palimpsest is a congenial concept in this respect, as it is inherently textual in both the traditional and a post-structural, semiotic sense. The central palimtext – the poem – can thus be interfaced (a) with the virtual texts of the client's lifestory and, via the life-story, with the client's identity, (b) with the semiotic texture of the therapeutic setting including the text of the therapist's commentary, and (c) with the psyche of the client, namely the unconscious, or Id, being structured like language, the Ego, the function of which has also been conceptualised as basically linguistic, and the Superego in the form of the Symbolic. It has further been shown that formal verse exhibits features that help facilitate and strengthen the links to the other writings of the palimpsest. By reconfiguring these participating entities as sign-functions and the therapeutic practice as a semiotic process of meaning production and interpretation, we have in essence returned poetry therapy to the Freudian basis as a *talking cure* while putting the poetry side on firm foundations in contemporary literary theory. The model of poetry therapy delineated in this study is thus able to harmonise the contradiction between the humanistic approach and the post-structuralist one by means of the concepts of authorship and of the palimpsest it introduces and appropriates.

The palimtext of the poem has been clearly shown to be the centre and the beginning of a poetry therapy that takes its poetic side seriously. The poem, understood in this sense, has been conceptualised as another fully self-sufficient entity that interacts freely and unpredictably with the other two principal (biological) entities of the client and the therapist:

> Any work of art functions like another person, having independent life of its own. An excessive wish to control it prevents the development of a passive watchfulness towards the work in progress that is needed for scanning half consciously its still scattered and fragmented structure. We have seen how 'accidents' that crop up during the work could well be the expression of parts of the artist's personality that have become split off and dissociated from the rest of the self. Fragmentation, to a certain extent, is an unavoidable [...] stage in shaping the work and mirrors the artist's own unavoidably fragmented personality. The artist must be capable of tolerating the fragmented state without undue persecutory anxiety. [...] His final integrated structure is then taken back (re-introjected) into the artist's ego and contributes to the better integration of the previously split-off parts of the self. (Ehrenzweig, *The Hidden Order of Art* 102)

The fragmented state of the subject is a fundamental fact, and it is here, as has been shown, that poetry therapy does its most fundamental work, but is also most important and effective. In the creative act of poetic writing, clients experience fragmentation first hand and actively manage to overcome it, if only ever temporarily. This suggests that poetic writing constitutes a quasi-return to the Real, a glimpse back at the primordial unity. This glimpse is therapeutic, but only for as long as the creative phase endures. Consequently, writing poetry simultaneously makes conscious the subject's fragmentation and heals it; in this way, it can show a way out of the pathological state of psychic repression that is constitutive of most symptoms dealt with in poetry therapy. The post-structuralist reading of poetry therapy's humanistic approach at the heart of this study suggests that, in accepting its fragmented state, the subject becomes whole. The text of the poem – the empirical marks on the page as well as the potential for meaning inherent in them – is the catalyst for this process. The creation and interpretation of the poem have been shown to be essential to poetry therapy, which negates all such approaches which do not give poetry and the creative process its due. The process of the interpretation of the palimtext of the poem constitutes the central writing of the palimpsest of poetry therapy in a very Derridean sense: it is central in the sense that it functions as the centre for the palimpsestuous structure of poetry therapy, but as a non-locus – it is that writing which supplements and is supplemented by the other texts, virtual as well as empirical:

> Through conversation with another reader we co-create a potentially modified response to the text, and by this means each of us will separately co-create a rather different virtual text next time we read the work. It is a three-way co-creation: author, reader and the second reader who discussed the work with the first reader. Each of our virtual texts will still be different from the other's virtual text, but less so than before, and different from our own future readings. Despite closer agreements and mutually modified perceptions, there can be no single correct and final virtual text. (Payne 93)

The palimpsest of poetry therapy is thus a collaborative work (synchronically between the client, the poem and the therapist, but also diachronically, between the author-client and the reader-client within the virtual text of the current, yet historically determined life-story) and it is a work in progress; like every text it is a limitless hoard of meanings that depend on actualisation. Consequently, there cannot be a single truth in poetry therapy, nor is there stable meaning. This study has shown that meaning which emerges in the discourse between the client, the poem and the therapist is episodical and is given specific functions that pertain to and affect clients in their lives. Meaning which emerges in this fashion and in this context provides an insight which can be applied to the problem-saturated life-story, the pathological existence the client is caught in, in order to inaugurate change. Such a desirable change – a change that originates from clients themselves and is perceived as a new, but evident truth – shifts the client's perspective and thus creates the outlook for a more positive future; it puts clients in a position to become active agents – creative authors – of their lives again; it re-instigates the feeling of control over their lives (imaginary as this feeling may be) and can secure a developmental process – a new subjectivation motility – that allows for personal growth and a move away from pathologising influences. This is what poetry therapy should achieve; it is what it can indeed achieve by following a serious interdisciplinary approach where the poetic side plays a more important role than in most previous approaches.

Works Cited

Abraham, Nicholas, and Nicholas Rand. "Psychoanalytic Esthetics: Time, Rhythm, and the Unconscious." *Diacritics* 16.3 (Autumn 1986): 3-14.

Abraham, Nicholas, and Maria Torok. "Mourning *or* Melancholia: Introjection *versus* Incorporation." Abraham and Torok, *The Shell and the Kernel*. 125-138.

---. "Introjection-Incorporation: *Mourning* or *Melancholia*." Lebovici and Widlöcher 3-16.

---. *The Shell and the Kernel*. Trans. Nicholas Rand. Chicago: University of Chicago Press, 1994.

---. *The Wolf Man's Magic Word: A Cryptonymy*. Trans. Nicholas Rand. Minneapolis: University of Minnesota Press, 1986.

Abrams, Allan S.. "Poetry Therapy in the Psychiatric Hospital." Lerner, *Poetry in the Therapeutic Experience* 63-71.

Ackroyd, Peter. *T.S. Eliot*. New York: Simon & Schuster, 1984.

Adams, Hazard, ed. *Critical Theory since Plato*. Revised Edition. Fort Worth [et al.]: Harcourt Brace Jovanovich, 1992.

Adams, Kathleen, and Stephen Rojcewics. "Mindfulness on the Journey ahead." Chavis and Weisberger 7-35.

Ahrens, Rüdiger, and Laurenz Volkmann, eds. *Why Literature Matters: Theories and Functions of Literature*. Heidelberg: C. Winter, 1996.

Allan, Mowbray. *T.S. Eliot's Impersonal Theory of Poetry*. Lewisburg: Bucknell UP, 1974.

Ansell, Charles. "Psychoanalysis and Poetry." Lerner, *Poetry in the Therapeutic Experience* 12-23.

Arieti, Silvano. *Creativity. The Magic Synthesis*. New York, NY: Basic Books, 1976.

Aristotle. *Poetics*. New York: Dover Publ., 1997.

---. *The Art of Rhetoric*. London: Penguin, 1991.

Arrivé, Michel. *Linguistics and Psychoanalysis*. Amsterdam [et al.]: Benjamins, 1992.

Assmann, Aleida, and Dietrich Harth, eds. *Kultur als Lebenswelt und Monument*. Frankfurt a. M.: Fischer, 1991.

Attridge, Derek, ed. *Acts of Literature*. London: Routledge, 1992.

Auden, W.H.. *Collected Poems*. Ed. Edward Mendelson. New York: Vintage, 1991.

---. *The Dyer's Hand and other Essays*. London: Faber, 1975.

Ayoob, Emily. "Black & Davidson on Metaphor." *Macalester Journal of Philosophy* 16.1 (Spring 2007): 57-64.

Bann, Stephen, and John E. Bowlt, eds. *Russian Formalism. A Collection of Articles and Texts in Translation.* Edinburgh: Scottish Academic Press, 1973.

Baron-Cohen, Simon, and John A. Harrison. *Synaesthesia: Classic and Contemporary Readings.* Oxford: Blackwell, 1996.

Barthes, Roland. "The Death of the Author." Adams, *Critical Theory* 1130-1133.

Bass, Alan. Translator's Introduction. Derrida, *Writing and Difference* ix-xx.

Baßler, Moritz. *Die kulturpoetische Funktion und das Archiv: Eine literaturwissenschaftliche Text-Kontext-Theorie.* Tübingen: Francke, 2005.

Bennington, Geoffrey, and Jacques Derrida. *Jacques Derrida.* Chicago, London: University of Chicago Press, 1993.

Berger, Milton M. "Poetry as Therapy – and Therapy as Poetry." Leedy, *Poetry Therapy* 75-89.

Berry, Eleanor. "The Free Verse Spectrum." *College English* 59:8 (Dec. 1997): 873-897.

Berry, Franklin M. "Approaching Poetry Therapy from a Scientific Orientation." Lerner, *Poetry in the Therapeutic Experience* 127-142.

Beyers, Chris. *A History of Free Verse.* Fayetteville: University of Arkansas Press, 2001.

Birtchnell, John. "Art Therapy as a Form of Psychotherapy." Dalley 30-44.

Bjorklund, Beth. "Form, Anti-Form, and Informality: Reinventing Free Verse." *Poetics Today* 16.3 (Autumn 1995): 547-567.

Bjorklund, Robert W. "Exploring Diagnostic Identity of Psychiatric Patients Through Poetry Therapy." *Journal of Poetry Therapy* 12.4 (1999): 211-217.

Black, Max. "How Metaphors Work: A Reply to Donald Davidson." *Critical Inquiry* 6.1 (Autumn, 1979): 131-143.

---. "Metaphor." *Proceedings of the Aristotelian Society* 55 (1955): 273-294.

---. *Models and Metaphors.* Ithaca, NY: Cornell UP, 1962.

---. "More about Metaphor." Ortony, *Metaphor and Thought* 19-41.

Blanck, Gertrude, and Rubin Blanck. *Ego Psychology: Theory and Practice.* New York: Columbia UP, 1974.

Blatner, Adam. Preface. *Poetry as Therapy.* Ed. Morris Morrison. 17-19.

Bloom, Harold [et al.]. *Deconstruction and Criticism.* New York, London: Continuum, 2004.

Bode, Christoph. "Why Theory Matters." Ahrens and Volkmann 87-100.

Bolton, Gillie. *The Therapeutic Potential of Creative Writing: Writing Myself.* London: Kingsely, 1999.

Brown, Catrina. "Situating Knowledge and Power in the Therapeutic Alliance." Brown and Augusta-Scott, *Narrative Therapy* 3-22.

---. "Dethroning the Suppressed Voice. Unpacking Experience as Story." Brown and Augusta-Scott, *Narrative Therapy* 177-195.

Brown, Catrina, and Tod Augusta-Scott. Introduction. Brown and Augusta-Scott, *Narrative Therapy* i-xliii.

---., eds. *Narrative Therapy: Making Meaning, Making Lives.* London [et al.]: Sage, 2006.

Brownjohn, Sandy. *What Rhymes with Secret?* London: Hodder & Stoughon, 1982.

Bruner, Jerome. "The Narrative Construction of Reality." *Critical Inquiry* 18.1 (Autumn 1991): 1-21.

Burgoyne, Bernard. *The Klein-Lacan Dialogue.* New York: Other Press, 1999.

Burke, Sean. *The Death and Return of the Author: Criticism and Subjectivity in Barthes, Foucault and Derrida.* 2nd Edition. Edinburgh: Edinburgh UP, 2004.

Burks, Arthur W., ed. *Reviews, Correspondence and Bibliography. Collected Papers of Charles Sanders Peirce.* Vol. VIII. Cambridge: Harvard UP, 1958.

Burns, Robert. *The Letters of Roberts Burns.* Vol. I. Ed. G. Ross Roy. 2nd Edition. Oxford: Oxford UP, 1985

---. "Letter to Dr. John More." Burns, *Letters* 133-146.

Butler, Judith. *Bodies That Matter.* London: Routledge, 1993.

Carrey, Normand. "Practicing Psychiatry Through a Narrative Lens: Working with Children, Youth, and Families." Brown and Augusta-Scott, *Narrative Therapy* 77-101.

Cartwright, T.. "Poetry, Therapy, Letter-writing and the lived Life. Comment on Maryhelen Snyder, Gonzalo Bacigalupe and Alfred Lange." *Journal of Family Therapy* 18.4 (1996): 389-395.

Chavis, Geri Giebel, and Lila Lizabeth Weisberger, eds. *The Healing Fountain.* St. Cloud, Minnesota: North Star Press of St. Cloud, 2003.

Crawford, Lawrence. "Viktor Shklovskij: *Différance* in Defamiliarisation." *Comparative Literature* 36:3 (Summer 1984): 209-219.

Crootof, Charles. "Poetry Therapy for Psychoneurotics in a Mental Health Center." Leedy, *Poetry Therapy* 38-51.

Cuddon, J.A., ed. *Dictionary of Literary Terms and Literary Theory.* 3rd Edition. London: Penguin, 1991.

Culler, Jonathan. *The Pursuit of Signs.* London: Routledge & Kegan Paul, 1981.

Cushman, Stephen. *William Carlos Williams and the Meanings of Measure.* New Haven, London: Yale UP, 1985.

Cytowic, Richard E.. *Synesthesia: A Union of the Senses*. 2nd Edition. Cambridge, Mass.: Bradford Books, 2002.

Dalley, Tessa, ed. *Art as Therapy: An Introduction to the Use of Art as a Therapeutic Technique.* London: Routledge, 1999.

Davidson, Donald. "What Metaphors Mean." *Critical Inquiry* 5.1 (Autumn 1978): 31-47.

Davidson, Michael. "Palimtexts: Postmodern Poetry and the Material Text." Perloff 75-95.

Davis, Cortney. "Touching Creation's Web: Key Images in Poetry." *Journal of Poetry Therapy* 11:4 (1998): 215-222.

de Berg, Henk. *Freud's Theory and Its Use in Literary and Cultural Studies. An Introduction.* Columbia, SC [et al.]: Camden House, 2004.

Derrida, Jacques. "Fors: The Anglish Words of Nicholas Abraham and Maria Torok." Abraham and Torok, *The Wolf Man's Magic Word* xi-xlviii.

---. "Freud and the Scene of Writing." Derrida, *Writing and Difference* 196-231.

---. "'Genesis and Structure' and Phenomenology." Derrida, *Writing and Difference* 154-168.

---. "Living On." Bloom, *Deconstruction and Criticism* 62-142.

---. *Of Grammatology*. Trans. Gayatri Chakravorty Spivak. Baltimore: Johns Hopkins UP, 1976.

---. *Positions*. Trans. Alan Brass. London: Continuum, 2004.

---. "'This strange Institution called Literature': An interview with Jacques Derrida." Attridge 33-75.

---. "Structure, Sign and Play in the Discourse of the Human Sciences." Derrida, *Writing and Difference* 278-293.

---. *Writing and Difference*. Trans. Alan Bass. Chicago: University of Chicago Press, 1978.

De Quincey, Thomas. *Confessions of an English Opium-Eater and Other Writings*. Ed. Grevel Lindop. Oxford: Oxford UP, 1998.

---. *Suspiria de Profundis*. DeQuincey, *Confessions* 87-181.

Dillon, Sarah. *Palimpsest: Literature, Criticism, Theory.* London: Continuum, 2007.

Dirven, René, ed. *Metaphor and Metonymy in Comparison and Contrast*. Berlin [et al.]: Mouton de Gruyter, 2003.

Eagleton, Terry. *How to Read a Poem*. Oxford: Blackwell, 2007.

Easthope, Anthony, *The Unconscious.* London, New York: Routedge, 1999.

Eco, Umberto. *Interpretation and Overinterpretation*. Ed. Stefan Collini. Cambridge [et al.]: Cambridge UP, 1996.

---. *The Open Work.* Trans. Anna Cancogni. Cambridge, Mass.: Harvard UP, 1989.

---. *The Role of the Reader.* Bloomington: Indiana UP, 1979.

---. "The Scandal of Metaphor: Metaphorology and Semiotics." *Poetics Today* 4.2 (1983): 217-257.

---. *A Theory of Semiotics.* Bloomington: Indiana UP, 1978.

Edgar, Kenneth F., and Richard Hazley. "A Curriculum Proposal for Training Poetry Therapists." Leedy, *Poetry Therapy* 260-268.

Edwards, Michael. "Jungian Analytic Art Therapy." Rubin, *Approaches to Art Therapy* 81-94.

Ehrenzweig, Anton. *The Hidden Order of Art: A Study in the Psychology of Artistic Imagination.* Berkeley [et al.]: University of California Press, 1992.

Eliot, T.S. "Milton I." Eliot, *Selected Prose* 258-264.

---. "The Music of Poetry." Eliot, *Selected Prose.* 107-114.

---. "Reflections on Vers Libre." Eliot, *Selected Prose* 31-36.

---. *Selected Prose of T.S. Eliot.* Ed. Frank Kermode. London [et. al.]: Harcourt, 1975.

---. "Tradition and the Individual Talent." Eliot, *Selected Prose* 37-44.

---. "The Use of Poetry and the Use of Criticism." Eliot, *Selected Prose* 79-96.

Ellmann, Maud. "Deconstruction and Psychoanalysis." Royle 211-237.

Epston, David and Michael White. *Experience, Contradiction, Narrative and Imagination. Selected Papers of David Epston and Michael White 1989-1991.* Adlaide: Dulwich Centre Publications, 1992.

Erll, Astrid et al., eds. *Literatur – Erinnerung – Identität. Theoriekonzeptionen und Fallstudien.* Trier: WVT, 2003.

Evans, Dylan. *An Introductory Dictionary of Lacanian Psychoanalysis.* New York: Brunner-Routledge, 2001.

Fauconnier, Giles. *Mappings of Thought and Language.* Cambridge: Cambridge UP, 1997.

Feirstein, Frederick, ed. *Expansive Poetry. Essays on the New Narrative and the New Formalism.* Santa Cruz, Cal.: Story Line Press, 1989.

Ford Maddox Ford. *The Critical Writings of Ford Maddox Ford.* Ed. Frank MacShane. Lincoln, NB: University of Nebraska Press, 1964.

Foucault, Michel. *The Archaeology of Knowledge & The Discourse on Language.* New York: Pantheon Books, 1972.

---. *Discipline & Punish: The Birth of the Prison.* New York: Random House (Vintage Edition), 1995.

---. *The Foucault Reader.* Ed. Paul Rabinow. New York: Pantheon Book, 1984.

---. "Interview conducted by Alessandro Fontana and Pasquale Pasquino." Rabinbow 51-75.

---. *Madness and Civilization*. New York: Random House (Vintage Edition), 1988.

---. *The Order of Things: An Archaeology of Human Sciences*. New York: Random House, 1994.

---. *"Society Must Be Defended:" Lectures at the Collège de France, 1975-1976*. Trans. David Macey. New York: Picador, 2003.

---. "What is an Author?" Rabinow 101-120.

Fox, John. *Poetic Medicine: The Healing Art of Poem-Making*. New York: Tarcher, 1997.

Freud, Sigmund. "Beyond the Pleasure Principle." Freud, *Complete Psychological Works*. Vol. 18. 7-64.

---. "Civilization and its Discontents." Freud, *Complete Psychological Works*. Vol. XXI. 57-145.

---. "The Claims of Psycho-Analysis to Scientific Interest." Freud, *Complete Psychological Works*. Vol. XIII. 163-190.

---. "Creative Writers and Daydreaming." Freud, *Complete Psychological Works*. Vol. IX. 141-153.

---. "The Dynamics of Transference." Freud, *Complete Psychological Works*. Vol. XII. 97-108.

---. "The Ego and the Id." Freud, *Complete Psychological Works*. Vol. XIX. 3-66.

---. "Formulations on the Two Principles of Mental Functioning." Freud, *Complete Psychological Works*. Vol. XII. 213-226.

---. "Instincts and their Vicissitudes." Freud, *Complete Psychological Works*. Vol. XIV. 109-140.

---. "The Interpretation of Dreams." Freud, *Complete Psychological Works*. Vols. IV + V.

---. "A Metapsychological Supplement to the Theory of Dreams." Freud, *Complete Psychological Works*. Vol. XIV. 217-235.

---. "Mourning and Melancholia." Freud, *Complete Psychological Works*. Vol. XIV. 237-258.

---. "A Note on the Mystic Writing Pad." Freud, *Complete Psychological Works*. Vol. XIX. 225-232.

---. "A Note on the Prehistory of the Technique of Analysis." Freud, *Complete Psychological Works*. Vol. XVIII. 261-265.

---. "An Outline of Psycho-Analysis." Freud, *Complete Psychological Works*. Vol. XXIII. 139-207.

---. "Repression." Freud, *Complete Psychological Works*. Vol. XIV. 141-158.

---. *The Standard Edition of the Complete Psychological Works*. Trans. and Ed. James Strachey [et. al.]. 23 Volumes. London : Hogarth, 1962.

---. "Studies on Hysteria." Freud, *Complete Psychological Works* Vol. II.

---. "The Unconscious." Freud, *Complete Psychological Works*. Vol. XIV. 159-215.

Friedmann, Susan Stanford, and Rachel Blau DuPlessis, eds. *Signets: Rending H.D.* Wisconsin: University of Wisconsin Press, 1990.

Friedmann, Susan Stanford. "Return of the repressed in H.D.'s Madrigal Cycle." Friedmann and DuPlessis 233-252.

Fussel, Paul. *Poetic Meter and Poetic Form*. Revised Edition. New York [et al.]: University of Pennsylvania Press, 1979.

Gallagher, Catherine, and Stephen Greenblatt. *Practicing New Historicism*. Chicago, London: University of Chicago Press, 2000.

Garai, Josef. "Humanistic Art Therapy." Rubin, *Approaches to Art Therapy* 149-162.

Gavin, Paul L., ed. *A Prague School Reader on Esthetics, Literary Structure and Style*. Georgetown: Georgetown UP, 1964.

Geertz, Clifford. *The Interpretation of Cultures: Selected Essays*. New York: Basic Books, 1973.

Gibbs, Raymond W., Jr. "When Is Metaphor? The Idea of Understanding in Theories of Metaphor." *Poetics Today* 13. 4 [Aspects of Metaphor Comprehension] (Winter 1992): 575-606.

Gioia, Dana. "Notes on the New Formalism." Feirstein 158-175.

Goethe, Johann Wolfgang. *Faust. Der Tragödie erster und zweiter Teil. Urfaust*. München: C.H. Beck, 1996.

Greenblatt, Stephen. "The Circulation of Social Energy." Greenblatt, *Shakespearean Negotiations* 1-20.

---. *Shakespearean Negotiations*. Berkley, Los Angeles: University of California Press, 1988.

---. "Towards a Poetics of Culture." Veeser, *The New Historicism Reader* 1-14.

Greifer, Eli. *Principles of Poetry Therapy*. New York: Poetry Therapy Center, 1963.

Guntrip, Harry. *Psychoanalytic Theory, Therapy, and the Self*. London: Maresfield Reprints, 1977.

Gymnich, Marion et al., eds. *Kulturelles Wissen und Intertextualität. Theoriekonzeptionen und Fallstudien zur Kontextualisierung von Literatur*. Trier: WVT, 2006.

Hall, Stuart, and Paul du Gay, eds. *Questions of Cultural Identity*. London: Sage Publishing, 2007.

Harrower, Molly. *The Therapy of Poetry*. Springfield: Charles C. Thomas, 1972.

Hartmann, Heinz. *Essays on Ego Psychology. Selected Problems in Psychoanalytic Theory.* New York: International Univ. Press, 1964.

Hausman, Carl R.. *Metaphor and Art: Interactionism and Reference in the Verbal and Nonverbal Arts.* Cambridge [et al]: Cambridge UP, 1989.

Heidegger, Martin. *Being and Time.* Malden, MA [et al.]: Blackwell, 2002.

Heninger, Owen E.."Poetry Therapy in Private Practice: An Odyssey into the Healing Powers of Poetry." Lerner, *Poetry in the Therapeutic Experience* 56-62.

Henzell, John. "Art, Psychotherapy and Symbol Systems." Dalley 15-29.

Hillman, James. *A Blue Fire.* New York: Harper Collins Pub., 1991.

Hinchman, Lewis P., and Sandra K. Hinchman, eds. *Memory, Identity, Community: Idea of Narrative in the Human Sciences.* New York: State University of New York Press, 1997.

Hirsch, E.D. "Objective Interpretation." Adams, *Critical Theory* 1100-1115.

Hughes, Ted. Foreword. Brownjohn, *What Rhymes with Secret?*

Huntington, Samuel P. *Who are We? The Challenges to America's National Identity.* New York. Simon & Schuster, 2004.

Iser, Wolfgang. *The Act of Reading: A Theory of Aesthetic Response.* Baltimore [et al.]: John Hopkins UP, 1997.

---. "The Current Situation of Literary Theory: Key Concepts and the Imaginary." *New Literary History* 11.1[Anniversary Issue II] (Autumn 1979): 1-20.

---. "The Interplay between Creation and Interpretation." *New Literary History* 15.2 (Winter 1984): 387-395.

Jakobson, Roman. *The Fundamentals of Language.* New York: Mounton de Gruyter, 2002.

---. "Linguistics and Poetics." Seboek 350-377.

---. "Two Aspects of Language and Two Types of Aphasic Disturbances." Jakobson, *Fundamentals of Language* 69-96.

Jannaris, Antonius N. *A Historical Greek Grammar Chiefly of the Attic Dialect. As Written and Spoken from Classical Antiquity down to the Present Time. Founded upon the Ancient Texts, Inscriptions, Papyri and Present Popular Greek.* Hildesheim: Georg Olms Verlagsbuchhandlung, 1968 [1897].

Jaskoski, Helen. "Notes on a Competency-Based Curriculum in Poetry Therapy." *The Arts in Psychotherapy* 11.2 (1984): 77-88.

KLUGE: Etymologisches Wörterbuch der deutschen Sprache. Ed. Elmar Seebold. 24th revised and amended Edition. Berlin, New York: de Gruyter, 2002.

Kramer, Edith. "Sublimation and Art Therapy." Rubin, *Approaches to Art Therapy* 28-39.

Kristeva, Julia. *Desire in Language. A Semiotic Approach to Literature and Art.* Ed. Leon S. Roudiez. New York: Columbia University Press, 1980.

---. *The Kristeva Reader.* Ed. Toril Moi Oxford: Basil Blackwell, 1986.

---. *Revolution in Poetic Language.* Trans. Margaret Waller. New York [et al.]: Columbia University Press, 1984.

---. "The System and the Speaking Subject." Kristeva, *The Kristeva Reader* 24-33.

---. "Word, Dialogue, and Novel." Kristeva, *Desire in Language* 64-91.

Lacan, Jacques. *Écrits: The First Complete Edition in English.* Trans. Bruce Fink. New York [et al.]: Norton, 2006.

---. "The Freudian Thing, or the Meaning of the Return to Freud in Psychoanalysis." Lacan, *Écrits* 334-363.

---. *The Four Fundamental Concepts of Psychoanalysis.* Trans. Alan Sheridan. Ed. Jacques-Alain Miller. London: Karnac Books, 2004.

---. "The Function and Field of Speech and Language in Psychoanalysis." Lacan, *Écrits* 197-268.

---. "The Instance of the Letter in the Unconscious, or Reason Since Freud." Lacan, *Écrits* 412-441.

---. "In Memory of Ernest Jones: On his Theory of Symbolism." Lacan, *Écrits* 585-601.

---. "The Mirror Stage as Formative of the *I* Function." Lacan, *Écrits* 75-81.

---. "Presentation on Psychical Causality." Lacan, *Écrits* 123-158.

---. "Presentation on Transference." Lacan, *Écrits* 176-188.

---. "Psychoanalysis and its Teaching." Lacan, *Écrits* 364-383.

---. *The Seminar of Jacques Lacan I: Freud's Papers on Technique. 1953-1954.* Trans. John Forrester. New York [et al.]: Norton, 1991.

---. *The Seminar of Jacques Lacan II: The Ego in Freud's Theory and in the Technique of Psychoanalysis. 1954-1955.* Trans. Sylvana Tomaselli. New York [et al.]: Norton, 1991.

---. *The Seminar of Jacques Lacan: Book 1.* Trans. John Forrester. Cambridge: Cambridge UP, 1988.

---. "Seminar on 'The Purloined Letter." Lacan, *Écrits* 6-48.

---. *Speech and Language in Psychoanalysis.* Trans. Anthony Wilden. Baltimore [et al.]: Johns Hopkins UP, 1991.

---. "The Signification of the Phallus." Lacan, *Écrits* 575-584.

---. "The Situation of Psychoanalysis and the Training of Psychoanalysts in 1956." Lacan, *Écrits* 364-411.

---. "The Subversion of the Subject and the Dialectic of Desire." Lacan, *Écrits* 671-702.

Laclau, E. *New Reflections on the Revolution of Our Time*. London: Verso, 1990.

Lakoff, George, and Mark Johnson. *Metaphors We Live By*. Chicago: University of Chicago Press, 1980.

---. *Philosophy in the Flesh: The Embodied Mind and Its Challenges in Western Thought*. New York: Basic Books, 1999.

Larkin, Philip. *Collected Poems*. London: Faber, 2003.

Lebovici, Serge, and Daniel Widlöcher, eds. *Psychoanalysis in France*. New York: International Universities Press, 1980. 3-16.

Leedy, Jack J. Introduction. Leedy, *Poetry Therapy* 11-13.

---., ed. *Poetry Therapy: The Use of Poetry in the Treatment of Emotional Disorders*. Philadelphia [et al.]: Lippincott, 1969.

---., ed. *Poetry as Healer: Mending the Troubled Mind*. New York: The Vanguard Press, 1985.

---. "The Principles of Poetry Therapy." Leedy, *Poetry Therapy* 67-74.

Lerner, Arthur. "Editorial. A Look at Poetry Therapy." *Art Psychotherapy* 3.1 (1976): i-iii.

---, ed. *Poetry in the Therapeutic Experience*. 2nd Edition. St.Louis: MMB Music, 1978.

---. "Poetry Therapy Corner." *Journal of Poetry Therapy* 11.2 (1997): 119-122.

---. "Poetry Therapy Corner." *Journal of Poetry Therapy* 11.3 (1998): 183-186.

Lippin, Richard A. "Poetry and Poetry Therapy: A Conversation with Arthur Lerner." *The Arts in Psychotherapy* 9.3 (Autumn 1982): 167-174.

Lorenz, Dahlia. "The 'Healing Process' of a Developmental Creative Poetry Therapy as Reflected by Written Poems (Product Analysis)." *Journal of Poetry Therapy* 12.2 (1998): 77-83.

Lotman, Yuri M.. *Universe of the Mind. A Semiotic Theory of Culture*. Trans. Ann Shukman. Bloomington-Indianapolis: Indiana University Press, 1990.

Madigan, Stephen. "Watching the Other Watch: A Social Location of Problems." Brown and Augusta-Scott, *Narrative Therapy* 133-150.

Malchiodi, Cathy A., ed. *Handbook of Art Therapy*. New York: The Guilfort Press, 2003.

---. "Humanistic Approaches." Malchiodi, *Handbook of Art Therapy* 58-71.

Mazza, Nicholas. *Poetry Therapy. Theory and Practice*. New York: Brunner-Routledge, 2003.

McCarty Hynes, Arleen, and Mary Hynes-Berry. *Biblio/Poetry Therapy – The Interactive Process: A Handbook*. St.Cloud: North Star Press of St Cloud, 1994.

McNiff, Shaun. *Art as Medicine: Creating a Therapy of the Imagination*. Boston [et al.]: Shambhala, 1993.

---. *Art Heals: How Creativity Cures the Soul*. Boston [et al.]: Shambhala, 2004.

Miller, J. Hillis. "Deconstruction and a Poem." Royle 171-186.

Moi, Toril. "Reading Kristeva: A Response to Calvin Bedient." *Critical Inquiry* 17.3 (Spring 1991): 639-643.

Moon, Bruce L. *Introduction to Art Therapy: Faith in the Product*. Illinois: Charles C. Thomas, 2008.

Morrison, Morris R., ed. *Poetry as Therapy*. New York: Human Sciences Press, 1987.

Mukarovsky, Jan. "Standard Language and Poetic Language." Gavin 17-30.

---. *Word and verbal Art*. New Haven [et al.]: Yale UP, 1977.

Nabokov, Vladimir. *The Annotated Lolita*. Revised and updated Edition. Ed. Alfred Appel, Jr. New York: Vintage Books, 1991.

Neumann, Birgit. "Kulturelles Wissen und Literatur." Gymnich et al. 29-51.

Neumann, Birgit, Ansgar Nünning, and Bo Petterson, eds. *Narrative and Identity: Theoretical Approaches and Critical Analyses*. Trier: WVT, 2008.

Neumann, Birgit, and Ansgar Nünning. "Ways of Self-Making in (Fictional) Narrative: Interdisciplinary Perspectives on Narrative and Identity." Birgit Neuman, Ansgar Nünning, and Bo Petterson 3-22.

Niles, John. *Homo Narrans: The Poetics and Anthropology of Oral Culture*. Philadelphia: University of Philadelphia Press, 1999.

Ochs, Elinor, and Lisa Capps. "Narrating the Self." *Annual Review of Anthropology* 25 (1995): 19-43.

Ortony, A., ed. *Metaphor and Thought*. 2nd Edition. Cambridge: Cambridge UP, 1993.

Osborn, Alex F. *Applied Imagination: Principles and Procedures of creative Problem-Solving*. New York: Scribner, 1953.

Parker, Robert S. "Poetry as a Therapeutic Art." Leedy, *Poetry Therapy* 156-170.

Payne, Martin. *Narrative Therapy*. 2nd Edition. London [et al.]: Sage, 2006.

Peacock, Thomas Love. *The Four Ages of Poetry*. Adams, *Critical Theory* 509-514.

Peirce, Chales Sanders. "To F.A. Woods on 'would be' (1913)." Burks 246-248.

Perloff, Marjorie G., ed. *Postmodern Genres*. Norman: University of Oklahoma Press, 1989.

Perrine, Laurence. "Four Forms of Metaphor." *College English* 33.2 (Nov. 1971): 125-138.

Petzold, Hilarion, ed. *Poesie und Therapie*. Paderborn: Junfermann, 1985.

Plato, *Phaedrus*. Trans. Christopher Rowe. London [et al.]: Penguin, 2005.